Lecture Notes in Computer Science 16327

The series Lecture Notes in Computer Science (LNCS), including its subseries Lecture Notes in Artificial Intelligence (LNAI) and Lecture Notes in Bioinformatics (LNBI), has established itself as a medium for the publication of new developments in computer science and information technology research, teaching, and education.

LNCS enjoys close cooperation with the computer science R & D community, the series counts many renowned academics among its volume editors and paper authors, and collaborates with prestigious societies. Its mission is to serve this international community by providing an invaluable service, mainly focused on the publication of conference and workshop proceedings and postproceedings. LNCS commenced publication in 1973.

Liming Zhai · Qing Guo · Jinquan Luo

Editors

Security and Privacy in Social Networks and Big Data

11th International Symposium, SocialSec 2025
Wuhan, China, December 5–7, 2025
Proceedings

 Springer

Editors
Liming Zhai [iD]
Central China Normal University
Wuhan, China

Qing Guo [iD]
Nankai University
Tianjin, China

Jinquan Luo
Central China Normal University
Wuhan, China

ISSN 0302-9743　　　　　　　　ISSN 1611-3349　(electronic)
Lecture Notes in Computer Science
ISBN 978-981-95-7026-3　　　　ISBN 978-981-95-7027-0　(eBook)
https://doi.org/10.1007/978-981-95-7027-0

This Springer imprint is published by the registered company Springer Nature Singapore Pte Ltd.
The registered company address is: 152 Beach Road, #21-01/04 Gateway East, Singapore 189721, Singapore

If disposing of this product, please recycle the paper.

Preface

Social networks and big data have become integral to our daily lives. These platforms have evolved from simple communication and news-sharing tools into essential resources for professional networking, social recommendations, marketing, and online content distribution. As social networks combine with various activities, they generate big data that surpasses the capacity of conventional computer software and hardware to capture, manage, and process in a reasonable timeframe. It is widely acknowledged that security and privacy pose significant challenges for social networks and big data applications due to their scale, complexity, and diversity.

The 11th edition of the International Symposium on Security and Privacy in Social Networks and Big Data (SocialSec 2025) was organized by Central China Normal University and Wuhan University on 5-7 December 2025 in Wuhan, China, co-organized with the 19th International Conference on Network and System Security (NSS 2025). It followed the success of SocialSec 2015 in Hangzhou, China; SocialSec 2016 in Fiji; SocialSec 2017 in Melbourne, Australia; SocialSec 2018 in Santa Clara, CA, USA; SocialSec 2019 in Copenhagen, Denmark; SocialSec 2020 in Tianjin, China; SocialSec 2021 in Fuzhou, China; SocialSec 2022 in Xi'an, China; SocialSec 2023 in Canterbury, UK; and SocialSec 2024 in Abu Dhabi, UAE. The SocialSec conference series aims to provide a leading-edge forum to foster interactions among researchers and developers within the security and privacy communities in social networks and big data.

The conference's technical program included 12 research papers selected by the Technical Program Committee (TPC) from 25 submissions received in response to the call for papers. The review process was organized and managed through EasyChair. All the papers were peer-reviewed by at least three reviewers among the TPC members. The submission process was anonymous, and author names were not visible to the reviewers. Received reviews were also anonymized to other TPC members, as well as to the paper's authors. The reviewers were asked to declare any conflicts of interest for all submissions at the beginning of the process, and the EasyChair system was configured to ensure TPC members (including TPC chairs) could see neither the reviewer assignments nor the reviews of the papers for which they had a conflict of interest. If one TPC Co-Chair had a conflict of interest, a discussion on each document was held, and the decision was made between the other two TPC Co-Chairs without a conflict of interest.

SocialSec 2025 and the co-located NSS 2025 shared three invited keynote talks for both conferences' participants, given by Willy Susilo from University of Wollongong in Australia, Jian Shen from Zhejiang Sci-Tech University in China, and Qianhong Wu from Beihang University in China.

The SocialSec 2025 TPC selected one paper for the Best Paper Award; the winner of the best paper award received a certificate issued by Central China Normal University and Wuhan University.

For the success of SocialSec 2025, we would like to first thank the authors of all submissions and all the PC members for their great efforts in selecting the papers. We also thank all the organizing committee members and local chairs. Finally, we thank everyone else, student helpers and session chairs, for their

December 2025   Liming Zhai
                                                                         Qing Guo
                                                                         Jinquan Luo

Organization

General Chairs

Qian Wang	Wuhan University, China
Jianqun Cui	Central China Normal University, China
Hongwei Liu	Central China Normal University, China
Weizhi Meng	Lancaster University, UK

Technical Program Chairs

Liming Zhai	Central China Normal University, China
Guo Qing	A*STAR, National University of Singapore, Singapore
Jinquan Luo	Central China Normal University, China

Publication Co-chairs

Pei Li	Central China Normal University, China
Weizhi Meng	Lancaster University, UK

Publicity Co-chairs

Na Ruan	Shanghai Jiao Tong University, China
Chunhua Su	University of Aizu, Japan
Je Sen	Teh Deakin University, Australia

Web Co-chair

Yahong Chen	Central China Normal University, China

Local Co-chairs

Hui Liu   Central China Normal University, China
Wenna Song   Central China Normal University, China

Registration Co-chair

Shixiong Yao   Central China Normal University, China

Program Committee

Nora Boulahia-Cuppens   Polytechnique Montréal, Canada
Aniello Castiglione   University of Salerno, Italy
Jiageng Chen   Central China Normal University, China
Yahong Chen   Central China Normal University, China
Koji Chida   Gunma University, Japan
Wenjun Fan   Xi'an Jiaotong-Liverpool University, China
Davide Ferraris   University of Málaga, Spain
Shoichi Hirose   University of Fukui, Japan
Donghui Hu   Hefei University of Technology, China
Ju Jia   Southeast University, China
Sokratis Katsikas   Norwegian University of Science and Technology,
                                   Norway
Hui Liu   Central China Normal University, China
Weizhi Meng   Lancaster University, UK
Daniela Pöhn   Universität der Bundeswehr München, Germany
Chen Qian   Shandong University, China
Fatemeh Rezaeibagha   Murdoch University, Australia
Jun Shao   Zhejiang Gongshang University, China
Mohammad Shojafar   University of Surrey, UK
Yangguang Tian   University of Surrey, UK
Ehsan Toreini   University of Surrey, UK
Ding Wang   Nankai University, China
Tian Wu   xx
Zhe Xia   Wuhan University of Technology, China
Jianhua Yang   Guangdong Polytechnic Normal University, China
Shixiong Yao   Central China Normal University
Kazuki Yoneyama   Ibaraki University, Japan
Liming Zhai   Central China Normal University, China
Mingwu Zhang   Hubei University of Technology, China

Contents

PMDID: A Privacy-Preserving and Migratable Decentralized Identity Using PUF and Blockchain

Yueyue He[1], Wenxuan Fan[1], Kaiming Chen[2], Atsuko Miyaji[2], and Koji Inoue[1]([✉])

[1] Graduate School of Information Science and Electrical Engineering,
Kyushu University, Fukuoka 8190385, Japan
`he.yueyue.922@m.kyushu-u.ac.jp, inoue@ait.kyushu-u.ac.jp`
[2] Department of Information and Communications Technology, The University
of Osaka, Osaka 5650871, Japan
`kaiming@cy2sec.comm.eng.osaka-u.ac.jp, miyaji@comm.eng.osaka-u.ac.jp`

Abstract. With the increasing reliance on digital identity, Decentralized Identity has become a promising paradigm to enhance user autonomy and privacy. However, existing decentralized identities face challenges such as secure key management, device migration, and unlinkability across contexts. To address these issues, we propose PMDID, a privacy-preserving and migratable decentralized identity system. First, PMDID introduces a two-layer identity mechanism in which a master ID derived from the ePassport (eID) enables Sybil resistance, while context-specific identities are registered via zero-knowledge proofs of master ID possession to ensure unlinkability across scenarios. Second, PMDID provides secure key management by combining Physical Unclonable Functions (PUFs) and biometric features with error correction and key derivation, guaranteeing key uniqueness, non-clonability, and recoverability. Third, PMDID designs a user registration protocol that supports secure identity migration, where a Merkle-structured issuance list maintained on the blockchain allows users to restore identity control on new devices without exposing sensitive information. We further implement a prototype and evaluate its performance, demonstrating that PMDID achieves strong guarantees of security, privacy, and scalability.

Keywords: Decentralized Identity · PUF · Blockchain · Privacy · Zero-knowledge proofs

1 Introduction

With the rapid development of the Internet, digital identity has become an indispensable part of modern life. Users rely on digital identities to access online services, manage personal data, and perform authentication in both virtual and physical environments. However, most existing digital identity systems remain centralized, which introduces inherent risks, including single points of failure, privacy leakage, and loss of user autonomy. To address these issues, Decentralized Identity has been proposed as a new paradigm that shifts control of personal data from centralized authorities to individuals themselves, empowering users to manage and protect their digital identities [1]. The World Wide Web Consortium (W3C) defined Decentralized Identifiers (DIDs) and Verifiable Credentials (VCs), which provide the foundation for decentralized identity representation and attribute verification [2]. A typical Decentralized Identity ecosystem consists of Issuers, Holders, Verifiers, and a decentralized registry, often implemented on blockchain. However, despite research and development efforts, existing Decentralized Identity systems still exhibit limitations in user authentication and identity management.

Regarding user authentication, the absence of strict identity generation constraints enables adversaries to create numerous pseudonymous identities, thereby facilitating large-scale Sybil attacks [3]. Furthermore, user interactions across distinct contexts can be correlated by malicious verifiers or external observers, compromising both identity and behavioral privacy. Additionally, current credential issuance and verification protocols often disclose superfluous information, posing a fundamental challenge of reconciling privacy preservation with system auditability [4,5]. Regarding identity management, decentralized systems fundamentally rely on key pair management. Existing approaches either store private keys locally, which risks irreversible loss upon device compromise, or rely on custodial wallets, reintroducing centralization [6,7]. While Physical Unclonable Functions (PUFs) have been employed to enhance key security, most designs neglect device migration [8]. SPDID [9] also adopted PUFs to secure private keys. However, once the device becomes unavailable, identities cannot be recovered or transferred, thereby undermining long-term usability.

To address these challenges, we propose PMDID, a privacy-preserving and migratable decentralized identity system that integrates PUFs with blockchain. The contributions of this paper are summarized as follows:

- We design a two-layer identity mechanism in which a unique ID_{mst} is obtained from the ePassport (eID), and a master anchor N_{mst} is derived from the ID_{mst} to provide Sybil resistance. Context-specific DIDs are registered via a zero-knowledge proof (ZKP) of ID_{mst} possession, ensuring unlinkability across contexts. All steps are executed locally without any trusted authority.
- We design a secure key generation module that combines intrinsic PUF responses with biometric information, eliminating long-term key storage and improving resilience against device compromise.
- We design registration protocols that support device migration. The user's ID_{mst} and device-binding information are inserted into a Merkle-structured issuance list, with only the Merkle root recorded on the blockchain for public verifiability. When the old device is unavailable, the user re-runs registration protocols on the new device with the same ID_{mst} to generate a fresh leaf and update the issuance list root, thereby restoring control of the identity. The

process relies on ZKPs to ensure membership and correct derivation, and does not require any trusted authority.
- We implement a prototype of PMDID and demonstrated its viability through formal security and performance analyses. Experimental results demonstrate that the system is both practical and efficient.

The rest of this paper is organized as follows. Related work is introduced in Sect. 2. Section 3 presents preliminaries that will be used in the scheme. The system overview is described in Sect. 4. Section 5 discusses the security definition. The details of system operations are introduced in Sect. 6. Section 7 and Sect. 8 provide security analysis and experimental performance of SPDID respectively. Finally, the conclusions are drawn in Sect. 9.

2 Related Work

Decentralized identity has emerged as a paradigm to overcome the limitations of centralized identity systems. According to the W3C, a DID is a verifiable identifier that resolves to a DID document containing public keys, authentication methods, and service endpoints, enabling users to manage their identities without relying on a single authority [2]. Decentralized identities have been applied in domains such as finance, healthcare, and IoT. Representative implementations include WeIdentity [4], Sovrin [10], and uPort [5], most of which rely on blockchain for decentralized registration and verification. However, existing decentralized identities still face challenges in preserving user privacy and ensuring secure key management.

To enhance privacy, anonymous credential schemes allow users to authenticate without revealing their credentials. Since Chaum's seminal work [11], many constructions have improved efficiency and applicability [12–14], and the concept has been incorporated into decentralized identity systems. However, most works do not explain how to achieve Sybil-resistant credential issuance. Can-DID [6], for example, separates identities into a master credential and multiple context-specific credentials, but requires multi-party computation for master credential registration, incurring high overhead. SmartDID [7] adopts a similar structure with a master identifier and pseudonymous identifiers, but relies on trusted authorities for registration. zk-creds [14] records credential issuance using Merkle structures, reducing reliance on issuers but facing update limitations. In contrast, PMDID avoids reliance on external trusted parties and achieves a more lightweight balance between privacy and auditability.

A further open issue is secure key management. Software wallets remain vulnerable to malware attacks [15], while hardware wallets mitigate some risks by keeping keys offline, but are still exposed to physical attacks and lack a binding between user attributes and cryptographic keys [16]. DOOR [17] strengthens security by binding authentication factors to hardware keys via Roots-of-Trust (RoT), but introduces new trusted parties such as DAA issuers. Meanwhile, PUFs [18] have been widely studied as lightweight and unclonable hardware primitives for device authentication and key generation, often combined with fuzzy extractors to improve reliability. Yet most PUF-based works remain limited to device-level authentication, overlooking user-centric identity management and the common requirement of cross-device migration [8,9]. PMDID addresses these limitations by employing PUFs for hardware-rooted key generation, supporting secure identity migration across devices, and integrating with privacy-preserving decentralized identity design to provide unlinkability in decentralized environments.

3   Preliminaries

For ease of reference, the main notations of this paper are listed in Table 1.

Table 1. The notations used in this paper.

Notations	Descriptions	Notations	Descriptions
PUF	Physical Unclonable Function	ID_{mst}	the master ID
(C, R)	Challenge-Response Pair	N_{mst}	the master anchor
HD	the helper data	DID_{ctx}	A context-specific DID
eID	Electronic identity document	N_{ctx}	context-specific anchor
ctx	a context	Cred	The verifiable credential

3.1   Physical Unclonable Functions

The PUF leverages intrinsic manufacturing variations of integrated circuits to generate unique and unclonable outputs [18]. Given an n-bit challenge C $\in \{0,1\}^n$, the PUF produces an m-bit response R $\in \{0,1\}^m$ as PUF(C) $\to$ R. Due to uncontrollable sub-microscopic variations, PUF responses are practically impossible to replicate, making them suitable for device identification and key generation.

3.2   Fuzzy Extractor

A Fuzzy Extractor (FE) is a cryptographic primitive that derives stable keys from noisy sources such as PUFs or biometrics [19]. Using public helper data HD, it supports two modes: enrollment, where an input w yields a key and helper data, $FE_{en}(w) \to (K, HD)$; and reconstruction, where a noisy input w' reproduces the same key, $FE_{rec}(w', HD) \to K$. This enables reliable key generation from inherently noisy physical sources.

3.3   Merkle Tree

A Merkle tree (MT) is a hash-based tree structure in which leaves store data hashes and internal nodes store hashes of their children, culminating in the root MTR [20]. MTs enable efficient integrity verification: a Merkle proof verifies membership of a value using only a subset of nodes rather than the entire structure. In PMDID, MTs are used for set membership with the following operations:

- MT.Insert(v) $\rightarrow$ (p, MT$'$): inserts value v and outputs the updated tree MT$'$ and an authentication path p.
- MT.Remove(v) $\rightarrow$ MT$'$: removes v (if present) and outputs the updated tree.
- MT.Ver(v, p, MTR) $\rightarrow$ (0/1): verifies inclusion of v by recomputing MTR from path p.

3.4   Non-interactive Zero-Knowledge Proofs

Non-Interactive Zero-Knowledge proofs (NIZKs) are cryptographic protocols that enable a prover to convince a verifier of a statement's validity without revealing information beyond its truthfulness [21]. Unlike interactive proofs, NIZKs require no back-and-forth communication; a single proof can be generated once and verified by anyone. For example, a prover who knows a committed value v can demonstrate that v satisfies certain conditions (e.g., range membership) without disclosing v. Such proofs π can be published on a blockchain for public verification, enabling privacy-preserving attestations. A general-purpose NIZK scheme for an NP language $\mathcal{L}$ consists of the following algorithms:

- NIZK.Setup($\mathcal{L}, 1^\lambda$) $\rightarrow crs$: generates a common reference string crs.
- NIZK.Prove(crs, stmt, w) $\rightarrow \pi$: produces a proof π for statement stmt and witness w such that (stmt, w) $\in \mathcal{L}$.
- NIZK.Ver(crs, stmt, π) $\rightarrow$ (0/1): verifies the validity of π for stmt.

3.5   Electronic Identity Documents

Electronic identity documents (eIDs) are standardized IDs embedded with a secure chip for storing and transmitting personal data. A common example is the biometric passport (ePassport) defined by ICAO Doc. 9303 [22], which specifies 16 data groups (DGs); for instance, DG1 contains basic attributes such as name, date of birth, and passport number. To guarantee authenticity, critical data are digitally signed by the issuing authority (e.g., U.S. ePassports include an RSA signature verified against the State Department's public key). In our work, eIDs serve as the foundation of user identities, and we denote the employed signature scheme by (Sign, Ver).

4   System Overview

4.1   System Model

The PMDID architecture consists of five roles: User, UserDevices, Issuer, Verifier, and Blockchain, which are defined as follows:

- User: The identity owner who provides biometric features (e.g., fingerprints), eID, or other auxiliary information for identity registration and credential acquisition.
- UserDevices (UD): The medium through which users manage and use their identities. Each UD is equipped with a PUF for key generation and supports biometric acquisition (e.g., fingerprint sensors on PCs). A digital wallet on the UD stores the user's DIDs, VCs, and auxiliary data.
- Issuer: The Issuer, such as the school or hospital, verifies the user's submitted information and issues VCs bound to the user's DID. Each Issuer maintains a Merkle tree–based Issuance List to record the credentials it has issued.
- Verifier: A service provider or third-party application that validates the authenticity and validity of the user's submitted credentials during interactions, and decides whether to grant access to services.
- Blockchain: Serves as an immutable public ledger in PMDID, supporting DID registration and management. It stores the Merkle root of the issuance list, which records the binding between ID_{mst} and user devices.

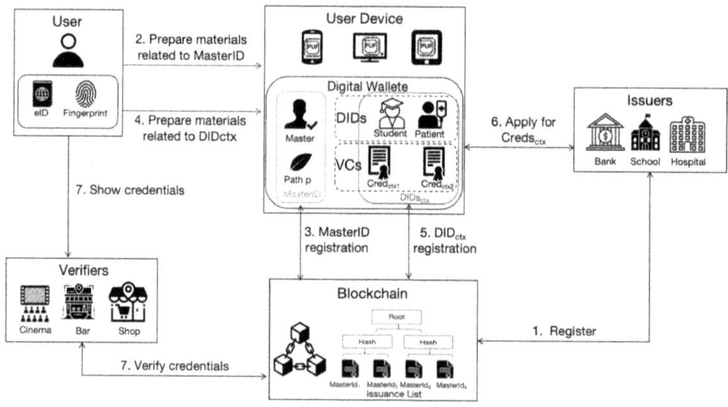

Fig. 1. Architecture and workflow of PMDID.

The workflow of PMDID is illustrated in Fig. 1. After system initialization, issuers register on the blockchain and obtain their DIDs. Each user possesses a master ID and multiple context-specific identities $DIDs_{ctx}$. The ID_{mst} is taken from a unique field of the eID, and a master anchor N_{mst} is derived from it. N_{mst}, combined with the device's information, is used to generate the registration materials. The user submits these materials, which, once verified, are recorded in the MT–based issuance list on the blockchain, and the corresponding path is returned to the user. The user then prepares the registration materials for DIDs_{ctx}, which requires generating a key pair on the device and proving possession of the registered ID_{mst}. After successfully obtaining DIDs_{ctx}, the user can request VCs from the relevant issuers. For service access, the user presents the selected DIDs_{ctx} and VCs to the verifier, who validates them and grants access. PMDID also supports device migration of identities, as detailed in Sect. 6.

4.2 Security Model

Adversarial Model: We assume the adversary may corrupt issuers, verifiers, and most users, with collusion among them. It can also compromise some user devices to extract PUF responses and private keys; yet, uncompromised devices remain secure. The blockchain provides immutability and consensus finality, secure as long as the adversary controls less than one-third of the stake. To preserve anonymity, the system requires at least two honest users with valid credentials to form a non-trivial anonymity set. Our security proof is conducted in the Random Oracle Model (ROM), where hash functions are modeled as ideal random functions.

The security properties of PMDID are summarized below and are formally defined and analyzed in Sect. 5 using game-based models.

- Sybil-Resistance (Def. 2): The adversary cannot create or utilize more valid identities than the number of entities it actually controls.
- Unlinkability (Def. 3): The adversary cannot link a user's identities or interactions across different contexts.
- Unforgeability (Def. 4): The adversary cannot forge the identities or actions of honest users.
- User Privacy (Def. 5): Credential issuance and verification do not reveal any information beyond what the user voluntarily discloses.
- Migration Security (Def. 6): Only holders of the ID_{mst} and PUF witnesses can perform identity migration across devices; any unauthorized migration succeeds with negligible probability.

4.3 System Operations

We define the PMDID operations, GlobalSetup, ZKSetup, KeyEnroll, KeyGen, mstIDReg, DIDReg, CredGen, and CredVer as follows.

- GlobalSetup(1^λ) $\to pp$: Generates the global public parameters of the system pp based on the security parameter λ.
- ZKSetup($pp, desc$) $\to crs$: Initializes the common reference string crs for ZKPs with respect to a given circuit description desc.

- KeyEnroll(PUF_U, C, B_U) $\rightarrow$ HDs_U: Initiated by the user U. U inputs the biometric B_U and the response of PUF_U under challenge C, and outputs the helper data $\text{HDs}_U = \{\text{HD}^U_{\text{PUF}}, \text{HD}^U_b\}$.
- KeyGen(PUF_U, C, B_U, HDs_U) $\rightarrow$ (pk, sk): Initiated by the user U. U provides biometric data B_U and applies the device's PUF_U with challenge C. Together with the helper data HDs_U, this process outputs the key pair.
- mstIDReg(crs_{mst}, eID_U, PUF_U, C)$\rightarrow p$: Registers the master ID by deriving ID^U_{mst} from eID_U and binding it to the user's device via PUF_U under challenge C, subject to $crs\text{mst}$, and returns the path p.
- DIDReg(crs_{ctx}, "ctx", pk^U_{ctx}, $\text{info}^U_{\text{PUF}}$, $\text{info}^U_{\text{mst}}$)$\rightarrow \text{DID}^U_{\text{ctx}}$: On input the context "ctx", a public key pk^U_{ctx}, user U's device information $\text{info}^U_{\text{PUF}} = \text{HD}^U_R, r, C$, and master ID information $\text{info}^U_{\text{mst}} = \text{ID}^U_{\text{mst}}, p$, it outputs a $\text{DID}^U_{\text{ctx}}$ satisfying the constraints of crs_{ctx}.
- CredGen (Ld_U, $\text{DID}^U_{\text{ctx}}$, sk_I) $\rightarrow \text{Cred}^U_{\text{ctx}}$: This operation is performed by the issuer I, taking as input the user U's Legacy document Ld_U, the identifier $\text{DID}^U_{\text{ctx}}$, and I's private key sk_I. The output is the issued credential $\text{Cred}^U_{\text{ctx}}$.
- CredVer(crs_{ver}, $\text{Cred}^U_{\text{ctx}}$, sk^U_{ctx}) $\rightarrow (1/0)$: user U input the private key sk^U_{ctx} to check whether the credential $\text{Cred}^U_{\text{ctx}}$ satisfies the condition crs_{ver}.

5   Security Definition

We define the security requirements of PMDID under the random oracle model (ROM). Security is captured via game-based definitions between a probabilistic polynomial-time (PPT) adversary $\mathcal{A}$ and a challenger $\mathcal{C}$, where $\mathcal{A}$ interacts with system oracles and protocol transcripts, while $\mathcal{C}$ enforces the game rules.

Secure PUF. PUFs serve as unclonable hardware anchors for device-specific keys, ensuring that no two devices derive the same secret state. A secure PUF must satisfy uniqueness, i.e., each PUF response is distinct due to inherent physical variations. Following [23], this property is captured by the Decisional Uniqueness Problem (DUP) assumption. Intuitively, for a challenge C and adversarial instance $\text{PUF}_\mathcal{A}$, $\mathcal{A}$'s behavior on a random $z \in \{0,1\}^n$ must be indistinguishable from its behavior on the genuine n-bit response $\text{PUF}_N(C)$.

Definition 1 *DUP Assumption. The problem of fabricating a honest PUF instance PUF_N using another instance $PUF_\mathcal{A}$ is hard. Formally, for any stateful PPT adversary $\mathcal{A}$, there exists a negligible function $\mathrm{negl}(\cdot)$ such that:*
$$|\Pr\left[\mathcal{A}\left(C, PUF_\mathcal{A}, z\right) = 1\right] - \Pr\left[\mathcal{A}\left(C, PUF_\mathcal{A}, PUF_N(C)\right) = 1\right]| \leq \mathrm{negl}(\lambda).$$

Sybil-resistance. The Sybil-resistance of PMDID ensures that an adversary $\mathcal{A}$ cannot generate more valid identities than the number of compromised devices it controls. The property is formalized through the game G_{Sybil}, where $\mathcal{O}=\{\text{mstIDReg}, \text{DIDReg}, \text{CredGen}, \text{CredVer}\}$ are system oracles accessible to $\mathcal{A}$, and $\mathcal{O}_{\text{eID}}=\{\text{Init}, \text{GeteID}\}$ simulate the eID provider:

- $\mathsf{Init}(L)$: initializes the provider with a list $L=(id,eID)$ of size n, where each eID is bound to a unique identifier id.
- $\mathsf{GeteID}(id)$: returns the authentic, provider-signed eID for $id \in L$.

In G_{Sybil}, $\mathcal{A}$ first initializes n corrupted devices, each bound to its own PUF instance. It may then query $\mathcal{O}_{\mathrm{eID}}$ to obtain valid eIDs and interact with $\mathcal{O}$ to register master identities, generate DIDs, and issue or verify credentials. If $\mathcal{A}$ eventually outputs more than n valid identities or credentials, it wins.

1. $\mathcal{C}$ runs $\mathsf{GlobalSetup}$ to obtain public parameters pp and gives them to $\mathcal{A}$.
2. $\mathcal{A}$ calls $\mathcal{O}_{\mathrm{eID}}.\mathsf{Init}(L)$ to initialize the eID provider's user list, where $|L| = n$.
3. At any time, $\mathcal{A}$ can call $\mathcal{O}_{\mathrm{eID}}.\mathsf{GeteID}$ to retrieve an authentic eID, and then interact with the system oracles $\mathcal{O}$ to perform user registration, credential issuance, and verification.
4. $\mathcal{A}$ outputs a set S of identities/credentials. The game returns 1 if the number of valid elements in S exceeds n; otherwise it returns 0.

Definition 2 *Sybil-resistance. PMDID provides Sybil-resistance if, for any stateful PPT adversary $\mathcal{A}$, there exists a negligible function* $\mathrm{negl}(\cdot)$ *such that:*
$\Pr\left[G_{Sybil}\left(\lambda, \mathcal{A}, \mathcal{O}, \mathcal{O}_{eID}\right) \to 1\right] \leq \mathrm{negl}(\lambda).$

Unlinkability. PMDID ensures that an adversary $\mathcal{A}$ cannot link a user's identities or interactions across contexts; even with multiple $\mathrm{DID}_{\mathrm{ctx}}$s, $\mathcal{A}$ cannot decide whether two $\mathrm{DID}_{\mathrm{ctx}}$s originate from the same $\mathrm{ID}_{\mathrm{mst}}$. We formalize this via the game G_{UL} with system oracles $\mathcal{O}=\{\mathsf{mstIDReg}, \mathsf{DIDReg}, \mathsf{CredGen}, \mathsf{CredVer}\}$ and eID provider oracles $\mathcal{O}_{\mathrm{eID}}=\{\mathsf{Init}, \mathsf{GeteID}\}$.

1. $\mathcal{C}$ runs $\mathsf{GlobalSetup}$ to get pp and $\mathsf{ZKSetup}$ to get crs; both are given to $\mathcal{A}$.
2. $\mathcal{A}$ calls $\mathcal{O}_{\mathrm{eID}}.\mathsf{Init}(L)$ to initialize the eID provider's user list, where $|L| = n$.
3. At any time, $\mathcal{A}$ may call $\mathcal{O}_{\mathrm{eID}}.\mathsf{GeteID}$, and interact with $\mathcal{O}$ to register $\mathrm{ID}_{\mathrm{mst}}$s, generate $\mathrm{DID}_{\mathrm{ctx}}$s, and issue/verify credentials.
4. Challenge: $\mathcal{A}$ selects two honest users U^0 and U^1 from the list and specifies a context ctx.
5. $\mathcal{C}$ flips a hidden bit $b \in \{0, 1\}$, generates $\mathrm{DID}_{ctx}^{U^b}$ and the corresponding credential, and returns the transcript to $\mathcal{A}$.
6. $\mathcal{A}$ outputs a guess b'. It wins if $b' = b$.

Definition 3 *Unlinkability. PMDID provides unlinkability if, for any stateful PPT adversary, for any stateful PPT adversary $\mathcal{A}$, there exists a negligible function* $\mathrm{negl}(\cdot)$ *such that:* $\left|\Pr\left[G_{\mathrm{UL}}\left(\lambda, \mathcal{A}, \mathcal{O}, \mathcal{O}_{eID}\right) \to 1\right] - \frac{1}{2}\right| \leq \mathrm{negl}(\lambda).$

Unforgeability. PMDID prevents $\mathcal{A}$ from impersonating honest users or producing valid credentials without authorization. Even with authentic eIDs, $\mathcal{A}$ cannot derive a valid $\mathrm{ID}_{\mathrm{mst}}$ or a signing key without the corresponding PUF. We formalize this via the game G_{UF} with system oracles $\mathcal{O}=\{\mathsf{KeyEnroll}, \mathsf{KeyGen}, \mathsf{mstIDReg}, \mathsf{DIDReg}, \mathsf{CredGen}, \mathsf{CredVer}\}$, eID provider oracles $\mathcal{O}_{\mathrm{eID}}=\{\mathsf{Init}, \mathsf{GeteID}\}$, and a signing oracle $\mathcal{O}_{\mathrm{sk}}$ that returns signatures under a user's public key but never reveals the sk.

1. $\mathcal{C}$ runs GlobalSetup to obtain public parameters pp and gives them to $\mathcal{A}$.
2. $\mathcal{A}$ calls $\mathcal{O}_{\mathrm{eID}}$.Init(L) to initialize the eID provider's user list, where $|L| = n$.
3. At any time, $\mathcal{A}$ may query $\mathcal{O}_{\mathrm{eID}}$.GeteID; query $\mathcal{O}$.KeyEnroll on a chosen device to obtain the associated HD, query $\mathcal{O}$.KeyGen with HD and the device's PUF to reconstruct a key pair, and further interact with other oracles to register identities, issue credentials, and verify them. In addition, $\mathcal{A}$ may query $\mathcal{O}_{\mathrm{sk}}$ with any chosen message and public key to obtain a valid signature.
4. Eventually, $\mathcal{A}$ outputs a tuple (m^*, σ^*), where m^* is a message and σ^* is a signature.
5. $\mathcal{A}$ outputs 1 if m^* was never queried to the signing interface but pass the verification; otherwise it returns 0

Definition 4 *Unforgeability. PMDID provides unforgeability if, for any stateful PPT adversary $\mathcal{A}$, there exists a negligible function* $\mathrm{negl}(\cdot)$ *such that:*
$$\Pr\left[G_{\mathrm{UF}}\left(\lambda, \mathcal{A}, \mathcal{O}, \mathcal{O}_{eID}, \mathcal{O}_{sk}\right) \to 1\right] \leq \mathrm{negl}(\lambda)$$

User Privacy. PMDID guarantees that credential issuance and verification reveal nothing beyond the attributes that disclosed by the user. We formalize this via the game G_{Priv} with system oracles $\mathcal{O}=\{$KeyEnroll, KeyGen, mstIDReg, DIDReg, CredGen, CredVer$\}$ and eID provider oracles $\mathcal{O}_{\mathrm{eID}}=\{$Init, GeteID$\}$.

1. $\mathcal{C}$ runs GlobalSetup to get pp and ZKSetup to get crs; both are given to $\mathcal{A}$.
2. $\mathcal{A}$ calls $\mathcal{O}_{\mathrm{eID}}$.Init(L) to initialize the eID provider's user list, where $|L| = n$.
3. At any time, $\mathcal{A}$ may query $\mathcal{O}_{\mathrm{eID}}$.GeteID to retrieve an authentic eID, query $\mathcal{O}$.KeyEnroll on a chosen device to obtain the associated HD, $\mathcal{O}$.KeyGen with HD and reconstruct a key pair, and further interact with the system oracles to register identities, issue credentials, and verify them.
4. Challenge: $\mathcal{A}$ selects two honest users U^0 and U^1 who share the same attribute values that satisfy a disclosure policy.
5. $\mathcal{C}$ flips a hidden bit $b \in \{0, 1\}$, runs the issuance or verification protocol for user U^b, and returns the transcript to $\mathcal{A}$.
6. $\mathcal{A}$ outputs a guess b'. It wins if b' = b.

Definition 5 *User Privacy. PMDID provides User Privacy if, for any efficient PPT adversary $\mathcal{A}$, there exists a negligible function* $\mathrm{negl}(\cdot)$ *such that:*
$$\left| \Pr\left[G_{Priv}\left(\lambda, \mathcal{A}, \mathcal{O}, \mathcal{O}_{eID}\right) \to 1\right] - \tfrac{1}{2}\right| < \mathrm{negl}(\lambda)$$

Migration Security. PMDID ensures that, even when the old device is unavailable, no adversary can rotate a DID's public key without the correct $\mathrm{ID}_{\mathrm{mst}}$ and device (PUF-derived) secrets. Migration is modeled as a rerun of DIDReg whose final on-chain action is a key rotation rather than a fresh registration. We formalize this via the game G_{Mig} with oracles $\mathcal{O}=\{$KeyEnroll, KeyGen, mstIDReg, DIDReg, CredGen, CredVer$\}$ and $\mathcal{O}_{\mathrm{eID}}=\{$Init, GeteID$\}$.

1. $\mathcal{C}$ runs GlobalSetup to get pp and ZKSetup to get crs; both are given to $\mathcal{A}$.
2. $\mathcal{A}$ calls $\mathcal{O}_{\mathrm{eID}}$.Init(L) to initialize the eID provider's user list, where $|L| = n$.

3. At any time, $\mathcal{A}$ may query $\mathcal{O}_{\text{eID}}$.GeteID to retrieve an authentic eID, query $\mathcal{O}$.KeyEnroll on a chosen device to obtain the associated HD,$\mathcal{O}$.KeyGen with HD and reconstruct a key pair, and further interact with the system oracles to register identities, issue credentials, and verify them.
4. Challenge: $\mathcal{A}$ outputs a tuple $(\text{N}_{\text{ctx}},\ \text{pk}'_{\text{ctx}},\ \pi_{\text{ctx}})$. If the system accepts π_{ctx}, it updates the DID document of N_{ctx} with new public key pk'_{ctx}.
5. The game returns 1 (win) if the rotation is accepted yet $\mathcal{A}$ does not possess the required witnesses to generate a valid π_{ctx}; otherwise, it returns 0.

Definition 6 *Migration Security. PMDID provides Migration Security if, for any stateful PPT adversary $\mathcal{A}$, there exists a negligible function* $\text{negl}(\cdot)$ *such that:* $\Pr\left[G_{Mig}\left(\lambda, \mathcal{A}, \mathcal{O}, \mathcal{O}_{eID}\right) \to 1\right] \le \text{negl}(\lambda)$

6 The PMDID Scheme

This section provides a detailed description of the PMDID scheme, which is divided into five phases: initialization, key generation, user registration, credential usage, and device migration. We will explain the operations executed in each of these phases.

6.1 Initialization Phase

First, given the security parameter λ, the system selects a bilinear pairing-friendly elliptic curve of prime order q, generating cyclic groups $\mathbb{G}_1, \mathbb{G}_2$ with generators $g_1 \in \mathbb{G}_1, g_2 \in \mathbb{G}_2$, and a bilinear map $e : \mathbb{G}_1 \times \mathbb{G}_2 \to \mathbb{G}_T$. A collision-resistant extendable-output hash $\text{H}_S : \{0,1\}^* \to \mathbb{F}_q$ is defined to derive private keys. The system also instantiates a SNARK-friendly hash $\text{H}_P : \mathbb{F}_q^t \to \mathbb{F}_q$, parameterized according to Poseidon. A commitment scheme is defined as $\text{Com}(m,r) = \text{H}_P(m\|r)$ for $m \in \mathbb{F}_q^k$ and random $r \in \mathbb{F}_q$, providing binding and hiding. Finally, a digital signature scheme (Sign, Ver) is selected. The public parameters are: $pp = \{q, \mathbb{G}_1, \mathbb{G}_2, \mathbb{G}_T, g_1, g_2, e, \text{H}_S, \text{H}_P,\ \text{Com},\ (\text{Sign, Ver})\ \}$. Next, issuers register their DIDs on the blockchain. The system then runs the ZKSetup operation: it first define a language $\mathcal{L}$ to describe the specific standards or constraints that users need to satisfy, and then execute $\text{NIZK.Setup}(\mathcal{L}, 1^\lambda)$ to generate the crs. We denote by $\mathcal{L}_{\text{mst}}$ and $\mathcal{L}_{\text{ctx}}$ the standards for master ID and context-specific DID registration requirements, respectively. Verifiers may also perform ZKSetup in later phases to update these standards as needed.

6.2   Key Generation Phase

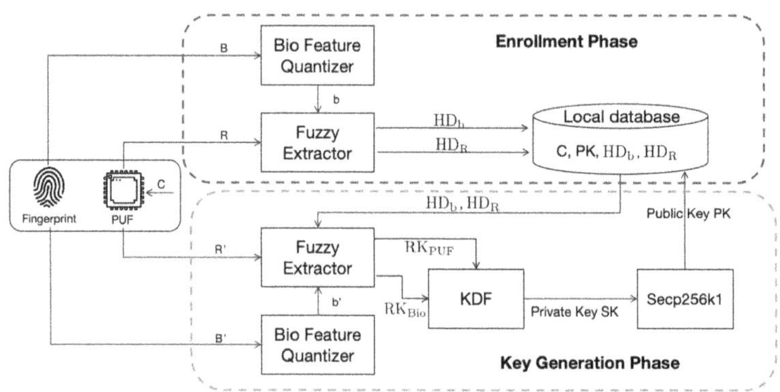

Fig. 2. PUF-based key generation.

In the key generation phase, the user executes two operations: KeyEnroll and KeyGen. A secure key is jointly derived from biometric traits and the device's embedded PUF, reconstructed on demand without persistent storage. As shown in Fig. 2, the first step (red dashed box) is KeyEnroll. The fingerprint image B is processed by the Bio Feature Quantizer to produce a stable 2048-bit feature string b, which is input to a fuzzy extractor: $\mathsf{FE}_{en}(b) \to (RK_{Bio}, HD_b)$. The Bio Feature Quantizer includes CNN-based feature embedding, random projection, binary quantization, and bit selection. In parallel, the PUF generates a response R under a fixed challenge C, which is also processed through a fuzzy extractor: $\mathsf{FE}_{en}(R) \to (RK_{PUF}, HD_R)$. Only helper data HD_b and HD_R are stored on the device; root keys RK_{Bio} and RK_{PUF} are never stored and are reconstructed on demand. When the user requires a key, KeyGen (blue dashed box) is executed: a fresh biometric sample B' and the PUF response R' (under the same challenge C) are collected. Using the stored helper data and FE_{rec}, the system reconstructs the root keys RK_{Bio} and RK_{PUF}. The root keys are concatenated and processed by the hash to derive the private key $sk = H_S(RK'_{Bio} \| RK'_{PUF})$ $RK_{Bio} = FE_{rec}(b', HD_b)$. Finally, the system is instantiated on the secp256k1 elliptic curve, where sk is used to compute the corresponding public key pk.

6.3   User Registration Phase

During user registration, two operations are executed—mstIDReg and DIDReg, both modeled as two-party protocols. The former anchors the eID as the unique ID_{mst}, while the latter generates unlinkable context-specific DIDs. The user conducts local data collection and computation, while the Operator serves as the communication channel to the blockchain, authorized to append entries to the smart contract. As shown in Fig. 3, during mstIDReg the user locally reads the

mstIDReg

User U:

on input $(eID_U, PUF_U, C, crs_{mst})$:

1.parse $(\{DG_i\}_{i=1}^{16}, h_{eID}, SOD) := eID$

2.$ID_{mst}^U := DG_1.att$

3.$N_{mst}^U := H_P("mstID", ID_{mst})$

4.$RK_{PUF}^U, HD_R^U := FE_{en}(PUF_U(C))$

5.$r \xleftarrow{\$} \{0,1\}^\lambda$

6.$cm := Com(RK_{PUF}^U, r)$

7.$Leaf := H_P("master", N_{mst}^U, cm)$

8.$stat := (h_{eID}, N_{mst}^U)$

9.$w := (DG_1, DG_2, \{H(DG_i)\}_{i=3}^{16}, ID_{mst}^U)$

10.$\pi_{mst} := NIZK.Prove(crs_{mst}, stat, w)$

11.send $(Leaf, N_{mst}^U, h_{eID}, SOD, \pi_{mst})$ to the Operator

Operator:

on receive $(Leaf, N_{mst}^U, h_{eID}, SOD, \pi_{mst})$ from U:

1.assert $PA_{Ver}(SOD) \wedge \neg seen[N_{mst}^U]$

2.assert $NIZK.Ver(crs_{mst}, (h_{eID}, N_{mst}^U), \pi_{mst})$

3.seen$[N_{mst}^U] := true$

4.$(p, MT') := MT.Insert(Leaf)$

5.send p to U

Relation $(stat, w) \in \mathcal{L}_{mst}$

1.parse $(h_{eID}, N_{mst}) := stat \wedge (DG_1, DG_2, \{H(DG_i)\}_{i=3}^{16}, ID_{mst}) := w$

2.assert $h_{eID} = H(H(DG_1), ...)$

3.assert $N_{mst} = H_P("mstID", ID_{mst})$

Fig. 3. mstIDReg Protocol.

eID and extracts the unique identifier ID_{mst} (e.g., the eID number). From this, the master anchor N_{mst} is derived as $N_{mst} = H_P("mstID", ID_{mst})$, which is then combined with the device PUF root key RK_{PUF} and a one-time random salt r to form the commitment. The user then assembles the issuance leaf and generates a ZKP π_{mst} that proves "the econtent hash value h_{eID} recorded in the eID matches and N_{mst} is correctly derived". Here, $H(\cdot)$ denotes the ICAO Doc. 9303–compliant hash function applied to eID data groups to obtain h_{eID}. Off-chain, the Operator executes $PA_{Ver}(SOD)$ to verify that the public input h_{eID} in π_{mst} matches the value contained in the SOD, and also validates π_{mst}. $PA_{Ver}(SOD)$ (Passive Authentication on the SOD) ensures that the chip's data-group hash list is signed by a valid Document Signer Certificate. Finally, the Operator submits the summary and proof on-chain and updates only the issuance MTR and the de-duplication flag seen$[N_{mst}]$, an on-chain mapping that records whether N_{mst} has already been registered.

When user U registers a context-specific DID, he first runs KeyEnroll and KeyGen via the device locally to obtain the key pairs. The user then executes DIDReg: using stored PUF helper data info$_{PUF}^U$ to reconstruct the commitment cm bound to the master ID ID_{eID}^U, locally recovering N_{mst}^U, and deriving N_{ctx}^U. With the on-chain issuance root MTR and the Merkle path p, the user generates a ZKP π_{ctx}^U attesting that the issuance leaf belongs to the current MTR; the user can open cm, and N_{ctx}^U is correctly derived (context binding). The tuple $(\pi_{ctx}^U, MTR, N_{ctx}^U, pk_{ctx}^U)$ is submitted on-chain via the Operator. The contract checks that N_{ctx}^U is unused (enforced by seenctx$[N_{ctx}^U]$), and upon successful verification, updates the DID_{ctx}^U document to bind pk_{ctx}^U, yielding the final DID_{ctx}^U. Protocol details are illustrated in Fig. 4.

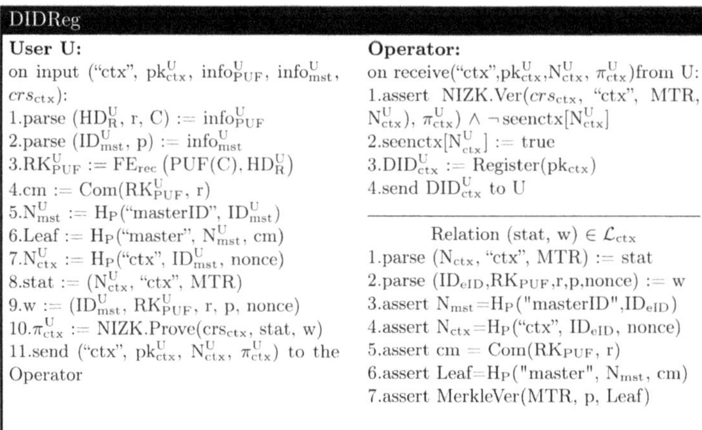

Fig. 4. DIDReg Protocol.

6.4   Credential Usage Phase

In this phase, the user performs two operations: CredGen (credential issuance) and CredVer (credential presentation and verification).

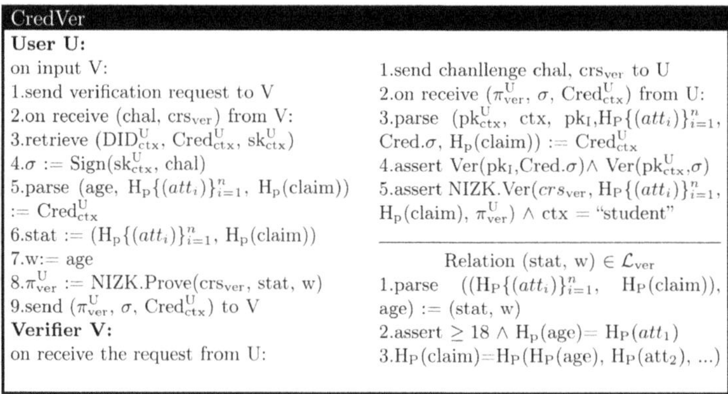

Fig. 5. Credential Verification.

In CredGen, the user U or issuer I provides a legacy document Ld containing the core information to be digitized. The issuer extracts the required fields, binds them with the user's DID_{ctx}^{U}, and structures them into a credential. A claim hash is computed as an integrity commitment and signed with the issuer's private key sk_I. The signature is embedded in the proof section, yielding the final $Cred_{ctx}^{U}$.

In CredVer, modeled as a two-party protocol between the user U and the Verifier V, the credential is presented when U requests service. V issues a random challenge, and U reconstructs the private key via KeyGen to sign it, proving possession of the credential. U then generates a ZKP according to V's policy, disclosing only the required attributes. For example, in a cinema scenario, U proves "student $=$ true $\wedge$ age ≥ 18" without revealing full infomation. The Verifier (cinema) checks the issuer and $\text{DID}_{\text{ctx}}^{\text{U}}$ bindings via public keys on-chain, verifies the issuer's signature, and validates the ZKP, granting access if conditions are satisfied. Figure 5 illustrates the process.

6.5   Device Migration

In this phase, the user performs device migration—rotating the verification key of a registered DID_{ctx} from the old device to a new one while preserving ownership continuity of the master ID without revealing the value. If the old device is available, the user runs KeyGen on it to reconstruct sk_{ctx} and sign a rotation message, while the new device runs KeyEnroll and KeyGen to generate pk_{ctx}'; the signed transaction is then submitted (directly or via the Operator) to rebind DID_{ctx} to pk_{ctx}'. If the old device is unavailable, the user re-issues the master ID on the new device via mstIDReg with the eID, after which the Operator updates the issuance root MTR and returns a new Merkle path p'. The new device then generates pk_{ctx}', and migration proceeds as a modified DIDReg, where the contract performs a rotate operation binding pk_{ctx}' to the existing DID_{ctx}. The ZKP created in this process attests to membership under the updated master ID, opening of the new master commitment, and correct derivation of DID_{ctx}.

In PMDID, both user and credential revocation are supported through Merkle-based structures. For user revocation, when a user deregisters their identity or a compromise of the eID/PUF root key is detected, the Operator removes or flags the corresponding leaf and updates the Merkle root, which is then re-anchored on-chain. This prevents any revoked Master ID from being reused and keeps the on-chain state consistent. For credential revocation, each issuer maintains an independent credential issuance tree. When a credential expires or is revoked, the issuer updates the root accordingly. During verification, the verifier checks the credential hash against the latest on-chain root using its Merkle path, if the path is valid and not marked as revoked, the credential is considered active.

7   Security Analysis

Theorem 1. *If the signatures on eID are existentially unforgeable under adaptive chosen-message attacks (EUF-CMA), and the underlying ZKPs are computationally sound in the ROM, then PMDID provides Sybil-resistance.*

Proof. In G_{Sybil}, $\mathcal{A}$ wins only by outputting more than n valid identities at Step 4. Assume this happens with non-negligible probability. Then either $\mathcal{A}$ forges a valid eID for some identifier id $\notin$ L, or it makes mstIDReg or DIDReg accept while the witness does not satisfy the registration relation. In our instantiation, Groth16 zkSNARKs (made non-interactive via Fiat–Shamir in the ROM) are knowledge- and computationally sound, and the registration circuit uses Poseidon-based hash commitments that are computationally binding from Poseidon's collision resistance over the base field. Hence acceptance without a valid witness occurs with negligible probability. And the eID employs the RSA PKCS#1 v1.5 signature with SHA256, which under the RSA assumption and in the ROM is considered EUF-CMA secure [24]. Therefore the probability that $\mathcal{A}$ wins G_{Sybil} is negligible, and PMDID provides Sybil-resistance in the ROM.

Theorem 2. *If the underlying ZKP system is zero-knowledge and computationally sound in the ROM, then PMDID provides Unlinkability.*

Proof. In G_{UL}, the goal of $\mathcal{A}$ is to output a guess b' in Step 6, winning if $b' = b$. Suppose $\mathcal{A}$ wins with non-negligible advantage. This would imply that the transcripts for U^0 and U^1 are distinguishable, which can only occur if the zero-knowledge proofs leak additional information or if invalid proofs are accepted. However, since the proof system is zero-knowledge in the ROM, the transcript of the protocol reveals nothing beyond the explicitly disclosed attributes, and by computational soundness, $\mathcal{A}$ cannot exploit malformed witnesses to bias the transcript. Therefore, $\mathcal{A}$'s distinguishing advantage is negligible, and PMDID provides Unlinkability.

Theorem 3. *If Def. 1 holds and the underlying signature scheme is EUF-CMA unforgeable in the ROM, then PMDID provides Unforgeability.*

Proof. In G_{UF}, at Step 4 the adversary outputs (m^*, σ^*); it wins at Step 5 if $\mathrm{Ver}(pk^*, m^*, \sigma^*) = 1$ and m^* was never queried to $\mathcal{O}_{sk}$ under pk^*. Assume, towards contradiction, that $\mathcal{A}$ wins with non-negligible probability. If pk^* is an honest user's public key (i.e., a key reconstructed via KeyEnroll and KeyGen for an honest device, to which $\mathcal{A}$ only had signing-oracle access), then producing σ^* on a fresh m^* is an EUF–CMA forgery. A standard reduction $\mathcal{B}$ simulates Steps 1–3 for $\mathcal{A}$, answers signing queries via its own EUF–CMA oracle, and outputs (pk^*, m^*, σ^*) when $\mathcal{A}$ wins, thereby breaking unforgeability with the same non-negligible advantage. Otherwise, $\mathcal{A}$ must either reconstruct a valid secret key sk^* bound to an honest device's PUF without oracle access, or register a key pair that the system accepts as bound to a target honest identity. Both contradict Def. 1: the former amounts to cloning/predicting the honest device's PUF response, and the latter breaks the binding enforced by KeyEnroll and KeyGen between identities and device-rooted keys, since Step 3 reveals neither PUF secrets nor sk only oracle evaluations tied to the actual device instance. Hence $\Pr[G_{\mathrm{UF}} = 1]$ is negligible and PMDID provides Unforgeability.

Theorem 4. *If the commitment scheme used in PMDID is computationally hiding, the underlying ZKP system is computationally zero-knowledge in the ROM, and the signature scheme is EUF-CMA unforgeable, then PMDID provides User Privacy.*

Proof. We argue via hybrids that the challenge transcript in Steps 5-6 of G_{Priv} reveals no information about b beyond the disclosed attributes. Game G_0 is the real G_{Priv}, where the adversary $\mathcal{A}$ receives the full issuance/verification transcript for U^b, including attribute commitments, NIZK proofs, and the protocol signature. Game G_1 is identical to G_0 except that in the challenge transcript we replace each commitment by a fresh commitment to an independently sampled random message using fresh randomness. By computational hiding, these are indistinguishable from the originals and reveal nothing about their openings. Game G_2 is identical to G_1 except that the challenge NIZKs are replaced by simulated proofs: we invoke the simulator with a simulated *crs* (or program the random oracle per Fiat–Shamir) and produce proofs depending only on public statements consistent with the disclosed attributes. By computational zero knowledge in the ROM, simulated and real proofs are indistinguishable. Game G_3 is identical to G_2 except that any signatures in the challenge transcript are recomputed on canonically randomized messages derived solely from public data and the simulated proof commitments. Since $\mathcal{A}$ lacks openings to hidden commitments and cannot obtain a signature on the exact challenge message in the challenge phase, any distinguishing advantage yields an EUF–CMA forger. Therefore, the adversary's distinguishing advantage in Step 6 is negligible, and PMDID achieves User Privacy in the ROM.

Theorem 5. *If the DUP assumption holds for PUFs, the underlying commitment scheme is binding, and the ZKP system is knowledge-sound in the ROM, then PMDID provides Migration Security.*

Proof. In G_{Mig}, $\mathcal{A}$ outputs $(N_{ctx}, pk'ctx, \pi_{mig})$ in Step 4, and wins at Step 5 if the DID document is updated to bind pk'_{ctx} even though $\mathcal{A}$ does not possess the correct masterID or PUF secrets. Suppose $\mathcal{A}$ wins with non-negligible probability. Then either π_{mig} is accepted without a valid witness, which contradicts the knowledge-soundness of the Groth16 proof system in the ROM; the new master identity commitment cm$'$ can be opened to inconsistent values, which contradicts the binding of the Poseidon-based commitment scheme; a fake Merkle path p' can be accepted, which contradicts the collision resistance of the underlying hash function; or $\mathcal{A}$ reconstructs the $\mathrm{ID_{mst}}$ and device key without access to the correct PUF secrets, contradicting the DUP assumption. In all cases, success would imply breaking a standard assumption. Therefore, the probability that $\mathcal{A}$ wins the migration security game is negligible, and PMDID provides Migration Security in the random oracle model.

8   Implementation and Performance

8.1   Implementation and System Setup

We employ SRAM PUF for key generation, as most CPU-based devices include small SRAM memory, incurring no additional cost or complexity. To ensure stability against noisy responses, we use a BCH-based fuzzy extractor to correct errors and reliably reconstruct keys. In our prototype, the SRAM on Arduino Mega 2560 boards emulates different mobile devices and provides distinct PUF modules. For NIZK proofs, we adopt Groth16 [25], a zkSNARK scheme with trusted setup that yields succinct proofs under the q-DLOG and linear independence assumptions. Poseidon [26] is used as the hash function for Sparse Merkle trees and commitments due to its efficiency in ZK circuits. For digital signatures, we adopt RSA, ensuring compatibility with legacy identity infrastructures. We implement the bulletin board as a smart contract on an Ethereum blockchain [27], leveraging the EVM ecosystem for decentralization, robust tooling, and mature documentation. All experiments were conducted on a desktop with a 3.60 GHz Intel(R) Core(TM) i7-12700K CPU(8 physical cores) and 32 GB RAM. Smart contracts were implemented in Solidity and deployed on an Ethereum-compatible blockchain. We train a Siamese CNN fingerprint encoder on FVC2002 dataset. Grayscale images are preprocessed by CLAHE, center square cropping, resizing to 256×256, and per-channel normalization. The encoder yields is optimized with contrastive loss on 50/50 genuine–impostor pairs. At inference, a cosine-similarity threshold chosen at the validation EER gates processing: only pairs with sim $\geq \tau$ proceed to quantization and error correction; otherwise they are rejected. SRAM PUFs were emulated by sampling 2048-bit responses from the on-chip SRAM of Arduino Mega 2560 boards. Unless otherwise stated, each experiment was repeated 50 times and we report averaged results.

8.2   Performance

Table 2. Comparison with existing schemes

Scheme	Properties							
	Sybil Resistance	Unlink -ability	Unforge -ability	migr -ability	User Privacy	Compat -ibility	Revoc -ability	Public Auditability
WeIdentity	✓	✗	✗	✓	✗	✗	✓	✗
CanDID	✓	✓	✗	✓	✓	✓	✓	✗
SmartDID	✓	✓	✗	✓	✓	✗	✓	✗
PMDID	✓	✓	✓	✓	✓	✓	✓	✓

We first compare the properties of PMDID with WeIdentity [4], CanDID [6] and SmartDID [7]. As shown in Table 2, all schemes support Sybil resistance and credential revocation. However, WeIdentity lacks unlinkability, as its reliance on centralized entities for identity verification increases the risk of correlation. CanDID, SmartDID, and PMDID all achieve unlinkability while preserving Sybil resistance, but through different approaches: CanDID relies on multi-party computation (MPC), incurring significant computational overhead; SmartDID requires interaction with trusted entities; whereas PMDID leverages the user's eID as a root anchor and combines it with zero-knowledge proofs to provide unlinkability in a lightweight, non-interactive manner. Although all schemes allow identity migration, most overlook key protection and therefore cannot guarantee unforgeability. In contrast, PMDID employs PUFs to derive unclonable keys, thereby resisting physical key-extraction attacks and ensuring unforgeability. Furthermore, PMDID ensures public auditability by recording the user registration list on the blockchain, preventing undetectable registrations. We also compare the performance of PMDID with SmartDID, and WeIdentity. The evaluation considers three metrics with five credential attributes: Cred generation (CredGen), user-side proof generation (Prove), and Cred verification (CredVer). PMDID, SmartDID, and WeIdentity were tested under the same environment. As shown in Fig. 6a, PMDID achieves the lowest latency across all tasks. These results highlight that PMDID attains both strong security and practical efficiency.

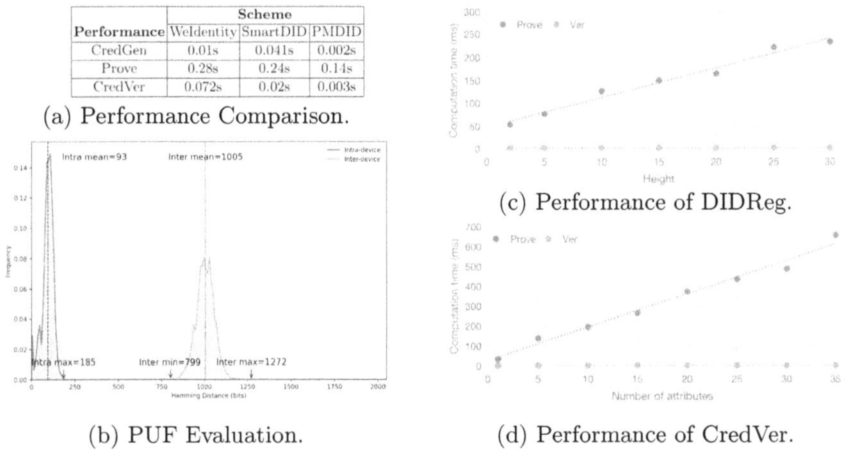

Performance	Scheme		
	WeIdentity	SmartDID	PMDID
CredGen	0.01s	0.041s	0.002s
Prove	0.28s	0.24s	0.14s
CredVer	0.072s	0.02s	0.003s

(a) Performance Comparison.

(b) PUF Evaluation.

(c) Performance of DIDReg.

(d) Performance of CredVer.

Fig. 6. Performance of PMDID.

We evaluated the performance of the main operations of PMDID, which are divided into three phases: key generation, user registration, and credential usage.

Key Generation. In PMDID, PUFs are combined with biometric features to build the key generation module. PUF quality can be assessed using Hamming distance (HD) [28]. The intra-HD (same PUF, repeated measurements) reflects robustness, while the inter-HD (different PUFs) reflects uniqueness. Ideally, intra-HD should approach zero, and inter-HD should be 50%. As shown in Fig. 6b, the maximum intra-HD was 185 (error rate 9.0%), which can be fully corrected using BCH(511,48). The inter-HD distribution had a mean of 1005 (49.1%), showing strong uniqueness. In terms of performance, KeyEnroll completes in 15.5 ms and KeyGen, including key reconstruction, in 13.8 ms.

User Registration. In mstIDReg, the user reads the eID, computes a Poseidon hash and commitment, and generates a ZKP π_{mst}. The user-side latency is about

100 ms. On the blockchain side, the operator verifies π_{mst} and updates a Merkle tree of height 27 within 6 ms, then uploads the new MTR and deduplication tag at a gas cost of 54k. The total latency is 136 ms. In DIDReg, the user reconstructs the device key RK, computes a Poseidon hash and commitment, and generates π_{ctx}. The circuit primarily involves hash verification and Merkle path validation, with the proving time increasing linearly with the tree height, as shown in Fig. 6c. At a height of 25, the tree can accommodate 2^{25} identities, with user-side latency approximately 232 ms. The operator verifies π_{ctx} in 3 ms, checks seenctx$[N_{\mathrm{ctx}}]$ is unused, and binds the document. On-chain execution is millisecond-level, with delay dominated by block confirmation.

Credential Usage. In CredGen, a credential consists of the attribute set, the attribute hash set, and the issuer's digital signature on the credential hash. With 100 attributes, generation latency remains 5 ms. In CredVer, the user generates π_{ver} to prove that selected attributes satisfy the Verifier's policy while ensuring correctness. Proving time grows linearly with the number of verified attributes, while verification cost remains constant, as shown in Fig. 6d.

9 Conclusion

This paper presents PMDID, a privacy-preserving and migratable decentralized identity system. PMDID combines PUFs and biometric features with fuzzy extractors to construct a key generation module that yields unique, stable, and unclonable keys for secure identity management. It adopts a two-layer identity structure: a master ID derived from eID ensures Sybil-resistance, while multiple context-specific DIDs provide unlinkability across applications. PMDID further introduces registration protocols that support cross-device identity migration while preserving ownership continuity. To guarantee privacy in credential issuance and verification, the system employs zero-knowledge proofs and commitment schemes. Finally, we formalize its security properties, provide game-based proofs, and implement a prototype with performance evaluations demonstrating practicality and efficiency.

Acknowledgement. This work was supported in part by JSPS KAKENHI under Grants JP22H05000 and JP21H03443, by the JSPS ASPIRE under Grant JPM-JAP2411, and by the SECOM Science and Technology Foundation.

References

1. Dib, O., Rababah, B.: Decentralized identity systems: architecture, challenges, solutions and future directions. Ann. Emerg. Technol. Comput. (AETiC) **4**(5), 19–40 (2020)
2. Reed, D., et al.: Decentralized identifiers (dids) v1. 0. Draft Community Group Report (2020)
3. Aggarwal, S., Kumar, N.: Attacks on blockchain. Adv. Comput. **121**, 399–410 (2021)

4. Weidentity documentation (2024). https://weidentity.readthedocs.io/en/latest/
5. Lundkvist, C., Heck, R., Torstensson, J., Mitton, Z., Sena, M.: Uport: A platform for self-sovereign identity, vol. 128, p. 214 (2017). https://whitepaper.uport.me/uPort_whitepaper_DRAFT20170221.pdf
6. Maram, D., et al.: Candid: Can-do decentralized identity with legacy compatibility, sybil-resistance, and accountability. In: IEEE symposium on security and privacy (SP), pp. 1348–1366 (2021)
7. Yin, J., et al.: SmartDID: a novel privacy-preserving identity based on blockchain for IoT. IEEE Internet Things J. **10**(8), 6718–6732 (2022)
8. Wang, Y.: A novel blockchain's private key generation mechanism based on facial biometrics and physical unclonable function. J. Inf. Secur. Appl. **78**, 103610 (2023)
9. He, Y., Fan, W., Inoue, K.: SPDID: a secure and privacy-preserving decentralized identity utilizing blockchain and PUF. In: 2024 IEEE 23rd International Conference on Trust, Security and Privacy in Computing and Communications (TrustCom). IEEE, pp. 1622–1631 (2024)
10. Windley, P.J.: Sovrin: an identity metasystem for self-sovereign identity. Front. Blockchain **4**, 626726 (2021)
11. Chaum, D.: Security without identification: transaction systems to make big brother obsolete. Commun. ACM **28**, 1030–1044 (1985)
12. Camenisch, J., Lysyanskaya, A.: An efficient system for non-transferable anonymous credentials with optional anonymity revocation, pp. 93–118. Springer (2001)
13. Garman, C., Green, M., Miers, I.: Decentralized anonymous credentials. Cryptology ePrint Archive (2013)
14. Rosenberg, M., White, J., Garman, C., Miers, I.: zk-creds: Flexible anonymous credentials from zksnarks and existing identity infrastructure. In: IEEE Symposium on Security and Privacy (SP), pp. 790–808. IEEE (2023)
15. Li, C., et al.: Android-based cryptocurrency wallets: attacks and countermeasures. In: 2020 IEEE International Conference on Blockchain (Blockchain). IEEE (2020)
16. Rezaeighaleh, H., Zou, C.C.: New secure approach to backup cryptocurrency wallets. In: IEEE Global Communications Conference (GLOBECOM), pp. 1–6. IEEE (2019)
17. Larsen, B., et al.: Achieving higher level of assurance in privacy preserving identity wallets. In: 2023 IEEE 22nd International Conference on Trust, Security and Privacy in Computing and Communications (TrustCom), pp. 1049–1059. IEEE (2023)
18. Holcomb, D.E., Burleson, W.P., Fu, K.: Power-up SRAM state as an identifying fingerprint and source of true random numbers. IEEE Trans. Comput. **58**(9), 1198–1210 (2008)
19. Ebrahimi, S., Bayat-Sarmadi, S.: Lightweight fuzzy extractor based on LPN for device and biometric authentication in IoT. IEEE Internet Things J. **8**(13), 10 706–10 713 (2021)
20. Szydlo, M.: Merkle tree traversal in log space and time, pp. 541–554. Springer (2004)
21. Fiege, U., et al.: Zero knowledge proofs of identity. In: Proceedings of the Nineteenth Annual ACM Symposium on Theory of computing, pp. 210–217 (1987)
22. Machine Readable Travel Documents (2021). https://www.icao.int/publications/pages/publication.aspx?docnum=9303
23. Chatterjee, U., Chakraborty, R.S., Mukhopadhyay, D.: A PUF-Based secure communication protocol for IoT. ACM Trans. Embed. Comput. Syst. **16**(3) (2017)

24. Jager, T., Kakvi, S.A., May, A.: On the security of the pkcs# 1 v1. 5 signature scheme. In: Proceedings of the 2018 ACM SIGSAC Conference on Computer and Communications Security, pp. 1195–1208 (2018)
25. Groth, J.: On the Size of Pairing-Based Non-interactive Arguments. In: Fischlin, M., Coron, J.-S. (eds.) EUROCRYPT 2016. LNCS, vol. 9666, pp. 305–326. Springer, Heidelberg (2016). https://doi.org/10.1007/978-3-662-49896-5_11
26. Grassi, L., Khovratovich, D., Rechberger, C., Roy, A., Schofnegger, M.: Poseidon: a new hash function for {Zero-Knowledge} proof systems. In: 30th USENIX Security Symposium (USENIX Security 21), pp. 519–535 (2021)
27. Buterin, V., et al.: Ethereum white paper. GitHub Repository 1(22–23), 5–7 (2013)
28. Prada-Delgado, M.Á., Baturone, I., Dittmann, G., Jelitto, J., Kind, A.: PUF-derived IoT identities in a zero-knowledge protocol for blockchain. Internet of Things 9, 100057 (2020)

Lightweight Mutual Authentication for End-to-End Communication in Satellite Internet

Yuanjing Hou[1,2] and Shixiong Yao[1,2]

[1] School of Computer Science, Central China Normal University,
Wuhan, Hubei, China
`{yj0,yaosx}@ccnu.edu.cn`
[2] Zhongyuan University of Technology, Zhengzhou, Henan, China

Abstract. In recent years, satellite terrestrial integrated networks (STIN) have become crucial global communication infrastructure, playing irreplaceable roles in emergency response. However, their open architecture and dynamic nature expose them to security threats like identity spoofing and data eavesdropping. While current solutions have flaws, including single-factor authentication vulnerabilities and centralized architecture risks. In this paper, we propose a lightweight authentication protocol featuring security and dynamic key management. It integrates Physical Unclonable Functions (PUF), biometrics, and lightweight cryptography with hash-chain-based key updates. Formal verification under the Random Oracle Model (ROM) confirms the protocol resists ephemeral secret leakage and machine learning attacks while balancing anonymity and traceability. Compared to existing schemes, it maintains strong security while significantly reducing computational overhead, offering an efficient solution for STIN authentication.

Keywords: Satelite internet · Authentication protocal · Physical unclonable functions

1 Introduction

With the rapid development of global informatization, satellite Internet has become an important pillar of global connectivity. Compared with traditional terrestrial networks, it has wide coverage and is particularly suitable for high-speed communication in remote areas; compared with traditional cellular networks, STIN features high openness, high dynamic topology, resource constraints, and a multi-layered heterogeneous architecture, which generate diverse communication requirements and pose challenges to security mechanism design. Therefore, it is necessary to balance security, real-time performance, and resource adaptability through three-layer security, hash chain key updates, and differentiated distribution:

L. Zhai et al. (Eds.): SocialSec 2025, LNCS 16327, pp. 23–42, 2026.
https://doi.org/10.1007/978-981-95-7027-0_2

- For the problem of multi-dimensional attack protection, a three-layer authentication mechanism combining PUF and biometric lightweight encryption algorithms is proposed to eliminate computationally intensive public key operations while ensuring system security.
- To address the one-size-fits-all issue in key management for heterogeneous devices, a differentiated key distribution method is proposed. It adopts different key generation and distribution strategies according to the computational capabilities of devices, reducing exposure of sensitive parameters and central dependency while lowering key generation overhead.
- A differentiated key distribution mechanism is proposed to address the differences in resource heterogeneity and computing power, adopting different distribution mechanisms for Low Earth Orbit (LEO) and terminal devices.
- To address the high computational overhead in key agreement, a dynamic key update method based on hash chains is proposed. It uses lightweight hash operations to generate and update keys, eliminating the computational burden of public keys. Moreover, the private key is encrypted before local storage, preventing long - term key attacks.
- Regarding the problem of protocol security verification, a formal security proof method is proposed. The protocol is proven secure under the ROM and informal security analysis, confirming its compliance with STIN security requirements.

The structure of this paper is organized as follows. Section 2 reviews related research. Section 3 elaborates on the system model, security requirements, design objectives and threat model. Section 4 focuses on the proposed lightweight authentication protocol. Subsequently, Sects. 5 and 6 conduct in-depth analyses of the protocol's security and performance, respectively. Finally, Sect. 7 summarizes the paper and provides future research directions.

2   Related Work

Over the past few years, many scholars have conducted research on ECC-based anonymous authentication for STIN, and below I will analyze and study it from the perspectives of security and computational overhead.

Existing ECC-based protocols are not only complex in process, but also perform poorly in preventing anonymous attacks, long-term key attacks, privileged internal attacks, impersonation attacks, and so on. Xue et al. [1] proposes an ECC ElGamal protocol that reduces bottlenecks by removing Network Control Center (NCC) but ignores semi-honest relay satellite risks. He et al. [2] modifies it, yet Li et al. [3] note that [2] has a desynchronization vulnerability, and Wu et al. [4] point out the added risks of imitation, password guessing, and sensor node capture. Li et al. [5] puts forward a Telecare Medical Information System (TMIS) cloud-assisted strategy claiming to resist all known attacks, but Kumar et al. [6] indicates flaws in impersonation and patient anonymity contradiction. Sureshkumar et al. [7] proposed protocol, within the realm of the medical Internet of Things (IoT), faces a desynchronization risk and is prone to traceability attacks. The scheme proposed by Yang et al. [8] fails to ensure anonymity and remains traceable even in scenarios where untraceability is required. Servati et al. [9] show that Aghili et al.'s scheme [10] remains vulnerable to desynchronization, integrity contradiction, and traceability attacks.

Moreover, existing schemes struggle against device loss attacks: Yu et al. [11] points out that the context-aware authentication protocol for home automation in Xiang et al. [12] is susceptible to risks such as device theft, impersonation, and session key leakage. Hajian et al. [13] pointed out that both the ECC-based smart home authentication protocol by Shuai et al. [14] and the wearable sensor protocol by Gupta et al. [15] are vulnerable to insider attacks, compromised device attacks, and desynchronization attacks. Alzahrani et al. [16] highlighted that while the scheme proposed by Xu et al. [17] mitigates device loss attacks, it remains susceptible to key leakage, replay attacks, and impersonation. Meanwhile, the ECC-based AKA scheme introduced by Nikooghadam et al. [18], despite its energy efficiency, fails to safeguard anonymity and resist device loss/insider attacks.

To further prevent single-dimensional attacks, existing multi-factor authentication schemes still have limited factors (only biometrics and passwords) and simplistic integration: The ECC two-factor AKA scheme in Chen et al. [19], with password protection and session key security, lacks formal proof of forward secrecy and is vulnerable to temporary key leakage. The three-factor scheme in Challa et al. [20] cannot resist replay, DoS, or forgery attacks. The lightweight method (smart cards + biometrics + hash functions) in Mohammad et al. [21] works well, but the IoT ECC protocol in Gabsi et al. [22], per Arslan et al. [23], risks traceability and forward-backward secrecy contradictions.

For STIN's heterogeneous resources and low computing power, existing solutions should be lightweight in computing and storage but mostly underperform: The ECC protocol (password + biometric keys) in Guo et al. [24] fails against untraceable attacks and is costly. The three-party ECC protocol in Guo et al. [25] supports multi-users but lacks batch authentication and has high computing overhead. Mahmood et al. [26] develops ECC-based smart grid protocols with high overhead. The approach in Guo et al. [29] improves batch processing via SM2 proxy signatures but still has excessive overhead.

To further prevent single-dimensional attacks, this paper uses multi-factor authentication with PUF as a key factor. However, existing PUF-based schemes, mostly limited to IoT, IoV, etc., perform poorly in dynamic node management: The PUF protocol in Zhang et al. [27] achieves basic functions but has limited anonymity and relies on centralized node management. The PUF+ECC protocol in Li et al. [28] has strong anonymity but high computational costs and no dynamic node management. The hybrid weak or strong PUF scheme for IoT in Modarres et al. [30] ignores dynamic node management and PUF noise, unsuitable for STIN.

Finally, STIN authentication also encompasses protocols based on bilinear pairing, blockchain, and lattice—all of which are ill-suited to the STIN scenario addressed in this paper due to their high communication overhead. These include the bilinear pairing-based protocol by Subramani et al. [31], blockchain-based ones in [32–38], and the lattice-based protocol by Cao et al. [39].

Existing research on multi-factor fusion authentication and hash chain dynamic key management has limitations. Current hash chain key management studies are mainly limited to specific scenarios like blockchain data retrieval and wireless sensor networks. Differentiated key distribution is a novel concept in this paper. Decentralized authentication architectures are complex, leading to high deployment and maintenance costs. Overall, existing STIN authentication protocols cannot optimally balance security, efficiency, adaptability, and privacy. Thus, a multi-factor lightweight authentication protocol is urgently needed to enable secure, efficient decentralized communication.

3 System Models

This section outlines the system model, threat model, security requirements, and design objectives.

Network Model. As shown in Fig. 1, our system model includes four entities: network control center, LEO satellite, terminal devices, users, and malicious attackers in STIN who aim to disrupt authentication and compromise service reliability/security. The main functions of each entity during user access are as follows: Network Control Center (NCC). In STIN's terrestrial segment, has superior computing, storage, bandwidth and security capabilities. As the system's administrative core, it stores public parameters and distributes configuration information during initialization. In our scheme, master private keys are generated differently based on node computing power, ensuring overall security even if one node is compromised. The NCC can also trace anonymous malicious users.

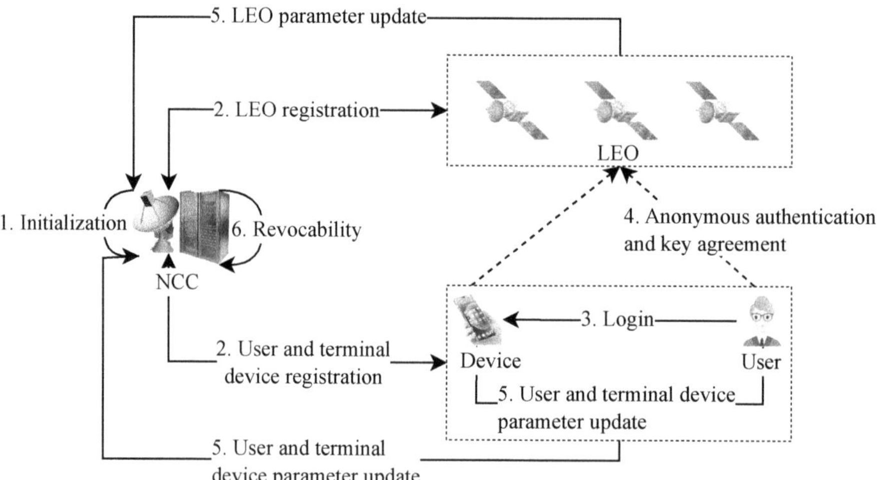

Fig. 1. Satellite-terrestrial integrated network system model.

Low Earth Orbit (LEO). LEO satellites have limited computing and storage resources but can assist in key recovery for terminal devices to avoid service loss from device failure.

Terminal Device (TD). Users register and log in to the TD, which then sends service requests to LEO satellites, ensuring identity security and data integrity.

User. As the ultimate consumer of STIN, users access it via satellite-capable terminal devices (TD_s) for all-weather communication and services, and control devices by transmitting data.

Threat Model. In STIN, malicious attacker node $\mathcal{A}$ has enhanced capabilities beyond classic Canetti-Krawczyk [40] and Dolev-Yao [41] models, adapted to STIN specifics: physical attacks to extract keys from captured devices/satellites; passive eavesdropping on data; active forgeries/replays for impersonation, Man-in-the-Middle (MITM) or Denial of Service (DoS); session key exploitation to derive past/future keys; and tracking via long-term monitoring to breach anonymity.

Security Requirements and Design Goals. To meet STIN's security needs, the authentication scheme must have these key features to fend off known attacks and ensure robustness:

- Mutual authentication: Terminal devices and LEO satellites mutually verify legitimacy to block unauthorized/disguised nodes from stealing resources.
- Forward/backward secrecy: Compromised current session key $Key_{s,l}$ won't let attackers derive past/future keys, ensuring long-term security.
- Dynamic key agreement and update: Post-authentication, LEO satellites and terminal devices negotiate secure session keys. A hash-chain-based mechanism reduces public-key overhead and resists MITM attacks.
- Device-user identity decoupling: User identity is separate from devices; lost compromised devices allow secure service recovery without exposing biometrics/PUF keys.
- Revocability: Leaked device/user keys trigger quick access revocation and info propagation to prevent misuse.
- Decentralized authentication: Minimize reliance on NCC to avoid single points of failure and boost STIN's dynamic adaptability.
- Conditional anonymity and traceability: Users stay anonymous unless authorized; NCC can reveal identities for accountability in malicious cases (e.g., forgery) without storing sensitive data.
- Resistance to multiple attacks: Fend off eavesdropping, replay, tampering, spoofing, MITM, lost device, insider, and long-term key compromise attacks.

The goal is a lightweight, privacy-preserving scheme balancing security and efficiency for resource constrained STIN nodes.

4   Proposed Protocol

Based on the system model, threat model, and security requirements, this section details the proposed decentralized lightweight authentication protocol (Table 1).

Table 1. Symbol list

Notation	Description
NCC	the management server in STIN
LEO_l	The identity of service node LEO_l
TD_s	The identity of terminal device TD_s
ID_u	The identity of user ID_u
pk_{ncc}	The system master public NCC
sk_{ncc}	The system master private NCC
X_l	The public key of LEO_l
x_l	The private key of LEO_l
$< (Y_1, y_1), (Y_2, y_2) >$	The public/private key pair of TD_s
$\overline{py_1}, \overline{py_2}, py_1, py_2$	The template public/private key pair of TD_s
$PUF_s(\cdot)$	The PUF of TD_s
$PUF_l(\cdot)$	The PUF of LEO_l
$Gen(\cdot), Rep(\cdot)$	the generation and reproduction functions of fuzzy extractor
c	The challenge of PUF
r	The response of PUF
p	the help data generated by fuzzy extractor
n, a, b	Random values
$Key_{s,l}, Key_{l,s}$	The session key shared between TD_s and LEO_l
ts_i	Timestamps
$H_i(\cdot)\ (i = 1, 2, 3, 4, 5)$	One-way hash functions

4.1 System Initialization

System Initialization. NCC generates master private key sk_{ncc}, public key pk_{ncc}, and system parameters.

(1) The NCC selects a secure elliptic curve $E_{a,b}$ from the finite field F_p, defined as: $y^2 = x^3 + ax + b \mod q$. Subsequently, the NCC randomly selects a private key $sk_{ncc} \in Z_p^*$ and computes the public key $pk_{ncc} = sk_{ncc} \cdot P$.

(2) The NCC selects PUF. PUF_s denotes the PUF function of the terminal device, which takes a challenge c and generates a unique response r: $r = PUF_s(c)$. Therefore, a fuzzy extractor is employed to stabilize key generation. The generation process is: $(K_{puf}, p_{puf}) = Gen_s(r)$; Reconstruction: $K_{puf} = Rep(r', p_{puf})$. Only if the distance between r and r^* is within a certain threshold can the same key K_{puf} be recovered.

(3) To support identity authentication and key agreement, the NCC also selects five secure one-way hash functions: $H_1 : \{0,1\}^* \rightarrow Z_p^*$, $H_2 : \{0,1\}^* \times G \rightarrow Z_p^*$, $H_3 : \{0,1\}^* \times G \times G \rightarrow Z_p^*$, $H_4 : \{0,1\}^* \times G \times G \times G \rightarrow Z_p^*$, and $H_5 : \{0,1\}^* \times G \times G \times G \times G \rightarrow Z_p^*$.

(4) Finally, the NCC publishes the system parameters $E_{a,b}, P, PK_{ncc}, PUF_s,$ $Gen_s, Gen_{bio}, Rep, H_1, H_2, H_3, H_4, H_5$, while securely storing the private key sk_{ncc} without disclosing it externally.

4.2   Registration and Login

Registration Phase (satellite and user registration). NCC assists LEO_l and $User_u$ in generating keys x_l, py_1, and py_2 for secure communication.

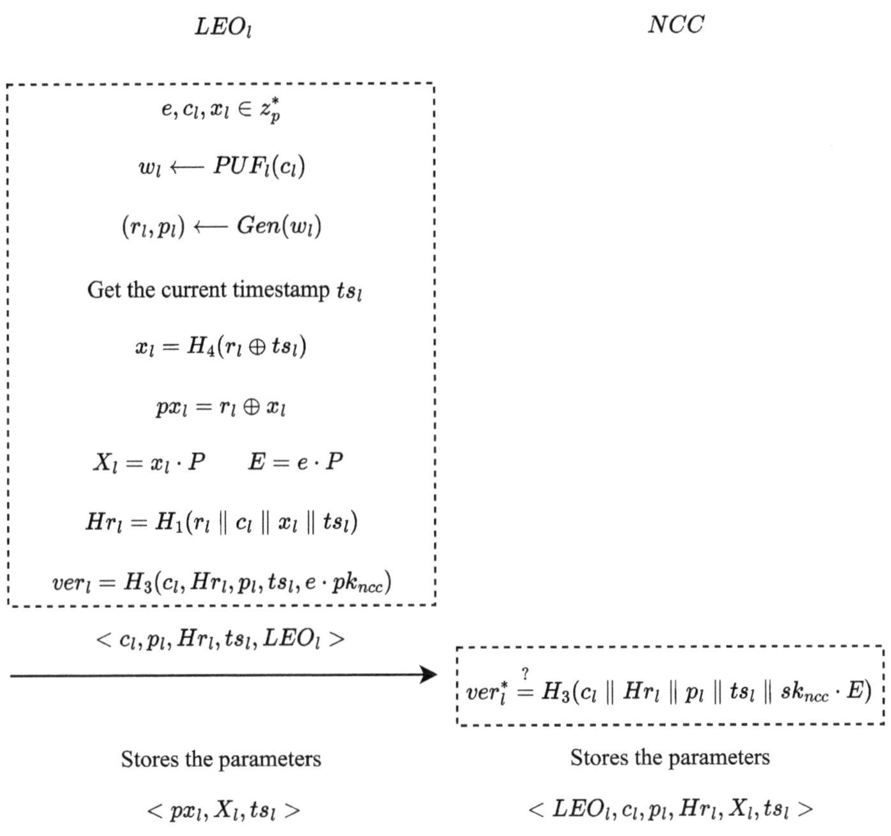

Fig. 2. LEO registration.

LEO Registration. As shown in Fig. 2 the LEO satellite node LEO_l registers with the Network Control Center (NCC) to become an authorized network entity: LEO satellite selects $e, c_l, x_l \in \mathbb{Z}_p^*$, computes $w_l \leftarrow \mathrm{PUF}_l(c_l)$, generates (r_l, p_l) via fuzzy extractor, derives $x_l = H_4(r_l \oplus ts_l)$, encrypts as $px_l = r_l \oplus x_l$, and computes $X_l = x_l \cdot P$. To mitigate risks, it sends request $\langle c_l, p_l, Hr_l, ts_l, LEO_l \rangle$ with $E = e \cdot P$, $Hr_l = H_1(r_l \parallel c_l \parallel x_l \parallel ts_l)$, and $ver_l = H_3(c_l, Hr_l, p_l, ts_l, e \cdot pk_{ncc})$ to NCC. The NCC verifies via $ver_l^* \stackrel{?}{=} H_3(c_l \parallel Hr_l \parallel p_l \parallel ts_l \parallel sk_{ncc} \cdot E)$, terminating on failure.

User and Terminal Device Registration. User $User_u$ and terminal device TD_s register with the NCC: User $User_s$ inputs ID_u, PW_u, BIO_u, generates biometric pair (δ_u, v_u) via $Gen(BIO_u)$, computes $RPW_u = H_2(ID_u, PW_u, \delta_u, v_u)$, and sends $< ID_u, RPW_u >$ to TD_s. TD_s uses PUF with c_s to get $w_s \leftarrow PUF_s(c_s)$, generates (r_s, p_s) via $Gen(w_s)$, calculates $h_{bio_s} = H(RPW_u \parallel r_s)$, and sends $< ID_u, ID_s, h_{bio_s}, c_s, p_s, LEO_l >$ to NCC. NCC generates $n_1, n_2 \in \mathbb{Z}_p^*$, computes $Y_1 = n_1 \cdot P$, $Y_2 = n_2 \cdot P$, derives $y_1 = sk_{ncc} + n_1 \cdot h_{bio_s} + X_l$, $y_2 = sk_{ncc} + n_2 \cdot h_{bio_s} + X_l$ via sk_{ncc}, and returns $(y_1, Y_1), (y_2, Y_2), X_l, c_l, ts_s$ (with ts_s against replay). TD_s stores $py_1 = r_s \oplus y_1$, $py_2 = r_s \oplus y_2$ (not original keys), keeping r_s in PUF volatile memory to reduce leakage.

Login Phase. $User_u$ logs in by inputting ID_u, BIO_u^*, PW_u^*. Device verifies via $dis(BIO_u^*, BIO_u) \leq T$, recovers r_s^* from PUF ($w_s^* \leftarrow PUF_s(c_s), r_s^* \leftarrow Rep(w_s^*, p_s)$), computes $\delta_u^* = Rep(BIO_u^*, v_u)$, $RPW_u^* = H_2(ID_u, PW_u^*, \delta_u^*, v_u)$, $h_{bio_s}^* = H(RPW_u^* \parallel r_s^*)$, recovers y_1^*, y_2^* using r_s^*, verifies Y_1^*, Y_2^* integrity, checks $ver_u \overset{?}{=} H_3(ID_u, h_{bio_s}^*, Y_1^*, Y_2^*)$. Login succeeds if it is valid; otherwise, the session terminates.

4.3   Anonymous Authentication and Key Agreement Phase

As shown in Fig. 3, after successful user login, the terminal device TD_s requests services from the LEO_l and authenticates by sending $< A, DT_s, DH_s, ver_1, ts_1, p_s >$ (where $A = a \cdot P$, $DH_s = H_3(ts_1 \parallel h_{bio_s})$, $ver_1 = H_3(ts_1 \parallel DH_s \parallel A)$, $DT_s = ts_1 \oplus LEO_l \oplus RPW_u^*$); LEO_l verifies timestamps, recovers keys, and proceeds if valid, then negotiates with $< B, DT_l, DH_l, ver_2, ts_3 >$ (where $B = b \cdot P$, $DH_l = H_3(ts_3 \parallel Hr_l)$, $ver_2 = H_3(ts_3 \parallel DH_l \parallel B)$, $DT_l = ts_3 \oplus px_l^*$); TD_s checks timestamps, recovers keys, and computes session key $Key_{s,l} = H_2(a \cdot B \parallel ts_1 \parallel ts_3)$ if verified, as shown in formula 1; TS_s and LEO_l establish a shared session key for secure communication, and delete all anonymous authentication parameters post-communication.

$$
\begin{aligned}
Key_{s,l} = H_2(a \cdot B \parallel ts_1 \parallel ts_3) &= Key_{s,l} = H_2(a \cdot b \cdot P \parallel ts_1 \parallel ts_3) \\
&= Key_{s,l} = H_2(b \cdot A \parallel ts_1 \parallel ts_3) = Key_{s,l} = H_2(k_l \parallel ts_1 \parallel ts_3) \quad (1) \\
&= Key_{l,s}.
\end{aligned}
$$

4.4   Parameter Update

In STIN, frequent device/communication path changes require periodic updates of parameters stored in LEO satellites and terminal devices to adapt to dynamics and prevent long-term key leakage and replay attacks.

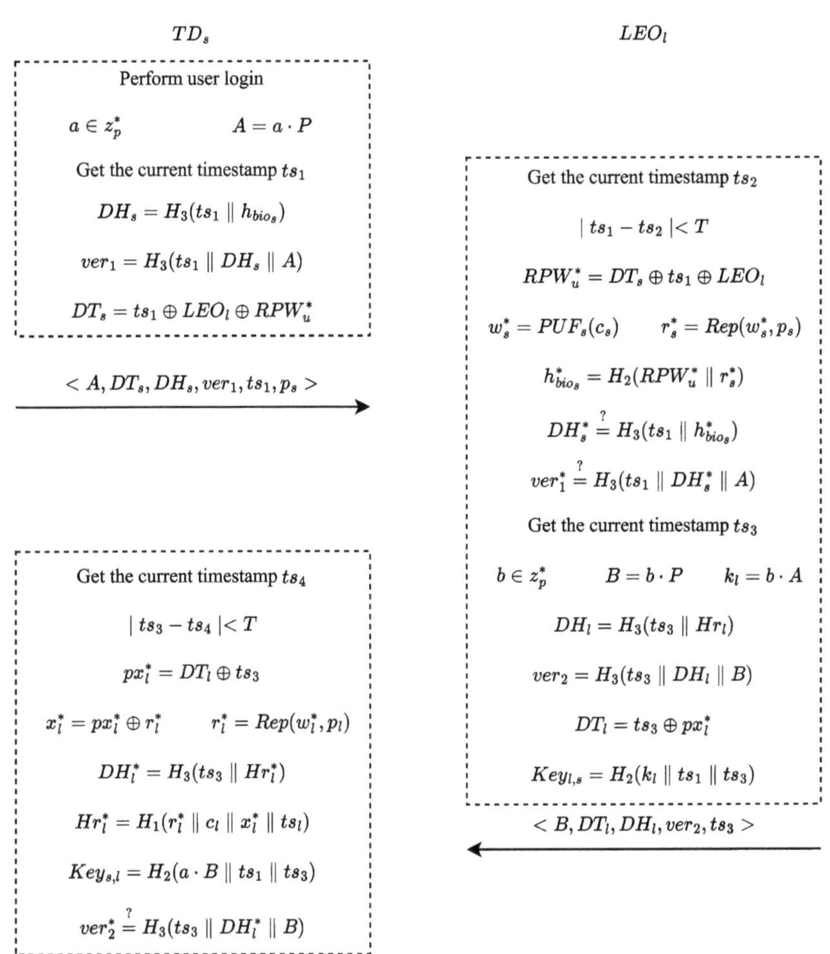

Fig. 3. Authentication and key agreement.

LEO Parameter Update. NCC Distribution: Sends $< c_l, p_l, KN, Hr_l, ts_l >$ to LEO_l ($k_n \in \mathbb{Z}_p^*$, $KN = k_n \cdot P$); Verification: LEO_l checks $|ts_1 - ts_2| < T$, recovers $\overline{r_l}$ via PUF, verifies $Hr_l = H_1(\overline{r_l} \parallel c_l \parallel \overline{x_l} \parallel ts_l)$; New Parameter Generation: LEO_l computes $x_l^{new} = H_4(r_l^{new} \oplus ts_l^{new})$, $X_l^{new} = x_l^{new} \cdot P$, sends $< c_l^{new}, p_l^{new}, Hr_l^{new}, ts_l^{new}, ver_l >$; NCC Confirmation: Checks $|ts_l^{new} - ts_3| < T$ and $ver_l^* = H_3()$; Cleanup: Both delete old params; LEO_l stores $< px_l, X_l^{new}, ts_l^{new} >$, NCC stores $< LEO_l, c_l^{new}, p_l^{new}, Hr_l^{new}, X_l^{new}, ts_l^{new} >$.

User and Terminal Device Parameter Update. User-Terminal Update Phase (Fig. 4): Login and Initial Verification: User logs in with ID_u, PW_u^*, BIO_u^*; regenerates δ_u^*, computes RPW_u^*. TD_i verifies via PUF (r_s^*, $h_{bio_s}^* = H(RPW_u^* \parallel r_s^*)$); New Credentials: User provides PW_u^{new}, BIO_u^{new}; TD_i computes RPW_u^{new}, creates (c_s^{new}, r_s^{new}), updates $h_{bio_s}^{new}$; NCC Interaction: TD_i sends

$< LEO_l, ver_s, KS, h_{bio_s}, ts_l >$ (with $ver_s = y_1 \oplus H_3()$). NCC checks timestamps, verifies y_1, generates $y_1^{new}, y_2^{new}, Y_1^{new}, Y_2^{new}$, sends $< Y_1^{new}, Y_2^{new}, ts_3, ver_{ncc} >$; Finalization: TD_i checks timestamps, reconstructs keys, stores $py_1^{new} = r_s^{new} \oplus y_1^{new}$, $py_2^{new} = r_s^{new} \oplus y_2^{new}$; Both delete old params; TD_i updates PUF, NCC stores $< ID_u, h_{bio_s}^{new}, Y_1^{new}, Y_2^{new}, ts_3 >$.

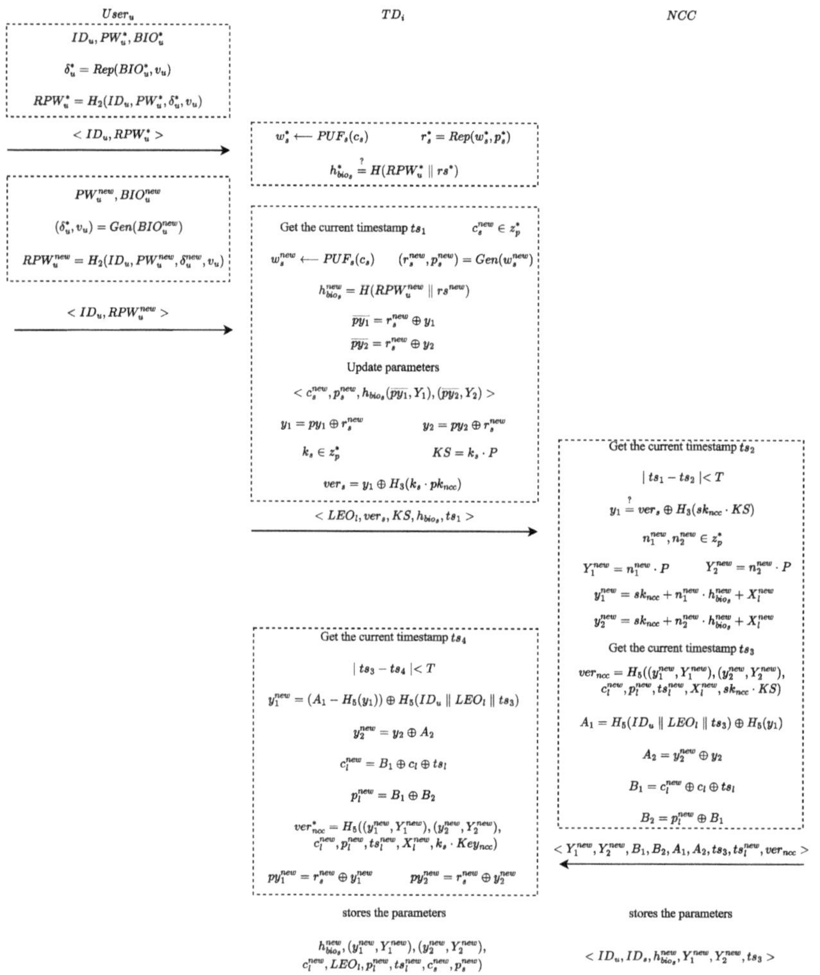

Fig. 4. Terminal device parameter update.

5 Security Analysis

This section formally and informally analyzes the proposed anonymous authentication protocol, proving its security under the random oracle model and satisfying STIN's required security properties.

5.1   Formal Security Analysis

Formal security analysis under the ROM: System entities ($User_u$, TD_s, LEO_l, NCC) interact via protocol instances (oracles), with participant P_i's instance i denoted $\Pi_{P_i}^i$.

Oracle Queries. The adversary $\mathcal{A}$ can simulate various active and passive attacks by initiating different types of queries:

(1) Execute query ($\pi_{TD_s}^i$, $\pi_{LEO_l}^i$, π_{NCC}^i). Adversary $\mathcal{A}$ passively attacks P_c, forcing honest returns of public messages, obtaining $< A, DT_1, DH_1, ver_s, ts_1, ps >$ and $< B, DT_l, DH_l, ver_2, ts_3 >$.

(2) Send query ($\pi_{P_i}^i$, message). Adversary $\mathcal{A}$ forwards message to $\pi_{P_i}^i$, which returns computed messages per protocol.

(3) Hash query. Maintains $List_{Hash_i}$ to simulate $Hash_i$, storing ($HashIn_i$, $HashOut_i$). Returns $HashOut_i'$ for existing $HashIn_i'$; else adds random $HashOut_i^{new}$ with $HashIn_i'$.

(3) Reveal query ($\pi_{P_i}^i$). $\mathcal{A}$ gets session keys ($Key_{l,s}$, $Key_{s,l}$) from $\pi_{P_i}^i$ only if the instance has computed keys, completed mutual authentication, and is in accept state; else null.

(4) Attack query ($Attack(P_i)$). $\mathcal{A}$ extracts parameters: TD_s's h_{bio_s}, (py_1, Y_1), (py_2, Y_2), $c_l, p_l, ts_s, c_s, p_s, LEO_l, ver_u$; LEO_l's $< px_l, X_l, ts_l >$.

(5) Test query ($\pi_{P_i}^i$). Verifies session key semantic security. Returns key if exists with peer, else null. $\mathcal{A}$ makes one query; $\pi_{P_i}^i$ flips a coin, $\mathcal{A}$ guesses $Coin'$ — wins if $Coin' = Coin$.

Theorem 1. *Define $ADV_{\mathcal{A}}^{P_i}(t)$ as $\mathcal{A}$'s advantage in breaking the scheme. With one-way hash functions as random oracles, $\mathcal{A}$ makes Q_{hash}, $Q_{execute}$, Q_{send} queries in time t to break P_c, with advantage:*

$$
\begin{aligned}
ADV_{\mathcal{A}} =\,& 2 \cdot Q_{Hash}\left(ADV_{\mathcal{A}}^{List_{Hash}} + \frac{Q_{Hash}}{2^{l-2}} \right) + \frac{2 \cdot Q_{send}}{p^2} \\
& + \frac{1}{2} \cdot (Q_{execute} + Q_{send})^2 \cdot \left(\frac{1}{2^{p-2}} + \frac{1}{p^2} \right) \\
& + 2 \cdot T_{PUF} + 4 \cdot T_{ECDLP} + 2 \cdot T_{ECCDHP}.
\end{aligned}
\tag{2}
$$

Here, T_i is the advantage in breaking problem i; Q_{Hash} is that in compromising the one-way hash function.

Proof. Assume adversary $\mathcal{A}$ compromises π's privacy/security, with challenger $\rfloor$ breaching $H(\cdot)$ in polynomial time. Define $Game_i (0 \leq i \leq 6)$, where $Game_0$ is a real attack on π. $E_j (0 \leq j \leq 6)$ is $\mathcal{A}$'s success in compromising π. An independent event E (detectable by $\rfloor$) may occur; before E, $Game_i$ and $Game_{i+1}$ are indistinguishable, so $\mid P_c[E_{j+1}] - P_c[E_j] \mid \leq P_c[j]$. Below explain $Game_0$ to $Game_6$ with E:

- $Game_0$: This game simulates the one-way hash function as a random oracle and executes actual attack operations. Starting from $Game_0$, we derive:

$$\text{ADV}_{\mathcal{A}} = \left| P_c[E_0] - \frac{1}{2} \right|. \tag{3}$$

- $Game_1$: In this game, unlike $Game_0$, PUF output is replaced with a random value of the same length. A list $List_{PUF}$ stores $(PrintIn_{PUF}, PrintOut_{PUF})$ pairs to simulate PUF_s: for query $PrintIn'_{PUF}$, if in $List_{PUF}$, return $PrintOut'_{PUF}$; else, generate and store a random $PrintOut_{PUF}^{new}$. If $\mathcal{A}$ can distinguish $Game_0$ from $Game_1$, it implies the ability to differentiate true PUF output from random values. Due to PUF unpredictability, $\mathcal{A}$'s advantage satisfies:

$$|P_c[E_1] - P_c[E_0]| \le T_{PUF}. \tag{4}$$

- $Game_2$: $Game_2$ differs from $Game_1$ only in two collision events:
  - E_{c_1}: Hash query collisions during simulation, with probability $P_c[E_{c_1}] \le \frac{Q_{Hash}^2}{2^l}$ by the birthday paradox.
  - E_{c_2}: Entity interaction record collisions, with probabilities $\frac{(Q_{execute}+Q_{send})^2}{(2p)^2}$ and $\frac{(Q_{execute}+Q_{send})^2}{2p}$.

Without collisions, $Game_2$ and $Game_1$ are indistinguishable:

$$|P_c[E_2] - P_c[E_1]| \le \frac{Q_{Hash}^2}{2^l} + \frac{(Q_{execute} + Q_{send})^2}{2^p} + \frac{(Q_{execute} + Q_{send})^2}{(2p)^2}. \tag{5}$$

- $Game_3$: This game modifies $Game_2$ by:
  (1) TD_s randomly selecting a, ts_1, computing $DH_s = H_3(ts_1 \parallel h_{bio_s})$ and $DT_s = ts_1 \oplus LEO_l \oplus RPW_u$, then storing $\{DH_s, DT_s\}$ in $List_{Hash}$.
  (2) LEO_l randomly selecting b, ts_3, computing $DH_l = H_3(ts_3 \parallel Hr_l)$ and $DT_l = ts_3 \oplus px_l$, then storing $\{DH_l, DT_l\}$ in $List_{Hash}$.

The distinction from $Game_2$ is whether $\mathcal{A}$ can identify hash oracle queries (probability $\frac{1}{Q_{Hash}}$), with $Game_3$ and $Game_2$ indistinguishable otherwise:

$$|P_c[E_3] - P_c[E_2]| \le Q_{Hash} \cdot \text{ADV}_A^{List_{Hash}}. \tag{6}$$

- $Game_4$: This game prevents $\mathcal{A}$ from obtaining a, b to compute session key $Key_{l,s} = Key_{s,l} = H_2(a \cdot b \cdot P \parallel ts_1 \parallel ts_3)$. $\mathcal{A}$ may try to extract a, b via:
  (1) public params $P, A = a \cdot P, B = b \cdot P$ (probability $\le T_{ECDLP}$ by ECDLP).
  (2) directly getting $a \cdot b \cdot P$ (probability $\le T_{ECCDHP}$ by ECCDHP).
  (3) guessing a, b (probability $\le \frac{Q_{send}}{p^2}$). Thus:

Thus, the difference between $Game_4$ and $Game_3$ is bounded by:

$$|P_c[E_4] - P_c[E_3]| \le 2 \cdot T_{ECDLP} + T_{ECCDHP} + \frac{Q_{send}}{p^2}. \tag{7}$$

- $Game_5$: This game ensures $\mathcal{A}$ cannot compute the current session key $Key_{l,s}$ using previous or subsequent keys $Key_{l,s}^{pre}, Key_{l,s}^{later}$, as $Key_{l,s}$ is independent of prior/future keys.

$$P_c[E_5] = P_c[E_4]. \tag{8}$$

– $Game_6$: By this stage, all advantages for $\mathcal{A}$ to compute the session key are eliminated. Thus, $\mathcal{A}$ can only win by unbiased guessing, with $P_c[E_6] = \frac{1}{2}$. Applying the triangle inequality:

$$|P_c[E_m] - P_c[E_n]| \leq |P_c[E_m] - P_c[E_o]| + |P_c[E_o] - P_c[E_n]|, \tag{9}$$

We conclude that $\mathcal{A}$ does not have an advantage in breaking the protocol proposed in formula 2.

5.2   Informal Security Analysis

Besides formal analysis, this paper uses informal methods to demonstrate the protocol's security.

Mutual Authentication. Per protocol, LEO verifies TD_s via $ver_1^* = H_3(ts_1 \parallel DH_s^* \parallel A)$: with $A = a \cdot P$, $DH_s^* = H_3(ts_1 \parallel h_{bio_s}^*)$, $h_{bio_s} = H(RPW_u \parallel r_s)$, only legitimate TD_s (with a, r_s, RPW_u) computes valid h_{bio_s}. TD_s verifies LEO via $ver_2^* = ver_2$, relying on ECDLP/ECCDHP hardness. The check requires TD_s's unique challenge-response and LEO's $DT_l = ts_3 \oplus px_l^*$ (where $px_l = r_l \oplus x_l$); illegitimate parties lacking x_l, r_l cannot compute valid ver_2^*. Thus, the protocol satisfies mutual authentication.

$$\begin{aligned}
ver_2^* &= H_3(ts_3 \parallel DH_l^* \parallel B) \\
&= H_3(ts_3 \parallel H_3(ts_3 \parallel H_1(r_l^* \parallel c_l \parallel x_l^* \parallel ts_l)) \parallel B) \\
&= H_3(ts_3 \parallel H_3(ts_3 \parallel H_1(Rep(w_l*, p_l) \parallel c_l \parallel (px_l^* \oplus r_l^*) \parallel ts_l)) \parallel B) \\
&= H_3(ts_3 \parallel H_3(ts_3 \parallel H_1(Rep(w_l*, p_l) \parallel c_l \parallel (DT_l \oplus ts_3 \oplus r_l^*) \parallel ts_l)) \parallel B).
\end{aligned} \tag{10}$$

Secure Session Key Negotiation. In this protocol, TD_s computes session key $Key_{s,l} = H_2(a \cdot B \parallel ts_1 \parallel ts_3)$, LEO_l calculates $Key_{l,s} = H_2(k_l \parallel ts_1 \parallel ts_3)$. As formula 1 shows, keys are consistent, so the protocol meets session key agreement requirements.

Forward and Backward Secrecy. The session key between TD_s and LEO_l is $Key_{l,s} = Key_{s,l} = H_2(a \cdot b \cdot P \parallel ts_1 \parallel ts_3)$ with a, b as Z_p^* random numbers. Each session's random, ephemeral a, b ensure current key leakage doesn't affect prior/subsequent session keys, so the protocol meets forward/backward secrecy.

Conditional Anonymity. LEO_l registers with NCC by sending PUF data $< c_l, p_l, Hr_l, ts_l, LEO_l >$; after ver verification, NCC stores $< LEO_l, c_l, p_l, Hr_l, X_l, ts_l >$, LEO_l retains $< px_l, X_l, ts_l >$, with x_l, raw c_l, p_l not directly stored for privacy and conditional anonymity. NCC recovers LEO_l's key via $w_l^* = PUF_l(c_l)$, $r_l^* = Rep_l(w_l^*, p_l)$, then $H_4(r_l \oplus ts_l)$ for accountability. $User_u$ and

TD_s register via hashed RPW_u (no full identity exposure); TD_s generates PUF pairs, combines with user features into h_{bio_s}; after $ver = H_3(ID_u, h_{bio_s}, Y_1, Y_2)$ validation, NCC stores $< py_1, py_2 >$ (hiding y_1, y_2). Lost TD_s regenerates keys via r_s, c_s ($y_1 = r_s \oplus py_1$, $y_2 = r_s \oplus py_2$), ensuring anonymity and traceability.

Revocability. Registration: Users hash identity info (ID_u, PW_u, BIO_u) to generate $RPW_u = H_2(ID_u, PW_u, \delta_u, v_u)$ for terminal device interaction. On key leakage, NCC traces the user/device, revokes access by flagging ID_u (users) or Y_1, Y_2 (devices) to fail validation, and broadcasts revocation messages. For LEO nodes, NCC stores parameters, revokes permissions on key leakage/illegal activity, invalidates access by marking Hr_l during authentication (checking $ver_l = H_3(c_l \parallel Hr_l \parallel p_l \parallel ts_l \parallel e \cdot pk_{ncc})$), and propagates notices with LEO_l identifiers, meeting revocability.

Resistance to Replay Attacks. An attacker trying to impersonate users/devices via replaying historical messages ($A, DT_1, DH_1, ver_s, ts_1, ps$) is thwarted by LEO_l. it checks ts_1 validity, computes $DH_s^* = H_3(ts_1 \parallel h_{bio}^*)$, and verifies $ver_1 = H_3(ts_1 \parallel DH_s^* \parallel A)$. Thus, the protocol resists replay attacks.

Resistance to Modeling Attacks. In the protocol, LEO_l stores hashed PUF parameters (e.g., $Hr_l = H_1(r_l \parallel c_l \parallel x_l \parallel ts_l)$). For users and TD_s, $h_{bio_s} = H(RPW_u \parallel r_s)$ and $RPW_u = H_2(ID_u, PW_u, \delta_u, v_u)$; no original PUF CRP is stored. With no CRP exposure, the scheme resists PUF modeling attacks.

Resistance to Privileged Insider Attacks. Adversary $\mathcal{A}$ intercepts registration parameters ($< ID_u, RPW_u >$, $< ID_u, ID_s, h_{bio_s}, c_s, p_s, LEO_l >$, NCC-stored X_l, Y_1, Y_2) for privileged insider attacks. But session key $Key_{s,l} = H_2(a \cdot b \cdot P \parallel ts_1 \parallel ts_3)$ uses secret a, b not in intercepted data, so $\mathcal{A}$ cannot compute it. The protocol resists such attacks.

6   Performance Analysis

This section compares the registration, access authentication, and key update phases of protocols [27–29] in terms of security properties, rounds, communication overhead, and computational overhead.

Comparison of Security Attribute. Table 2 compares the proposed protocol's security properties with [27–29] for STIN (Sect. 4.3). The proposed protocol satisfies more properties, making it more suitable for high-security STIN.

Table 2. Comparison of security attribute

Security attribute	[1]	[2]	[3]	Ours
Strong anonymity and untraceability	-	✓	×	✓
Conditional anonymity	×	✓	✓	✓
Revocability	×	×	×	✓
Resistance to replay attacks	×	✓	✓	✓
Resistance to modeling attacks	✓	✓	×	✓
Resistance to device loss attacks	✓	−	-	✓
Resistance to privileged insider attacks	×	✓	✓	✓
Resistance to long-term authentication key leakage attacks	×	✓	✓	✓
Resistance to temporary secret leakage attacks	−	✓	✓	✓
PUF resistance to machine learning attacks	−	✓	×	✓

6.1   Simulation Environment and Comparison of Cost

Simulation Environment and Experimental Procedure. Due to limited hardware, conventional CPUs/GPUs (e.g., AMD Radeon) lack specialized modules, so we simulate PUF operations via software for equivalent effects. Testing environment: AMD CPU with Radeon 780M, STM32H743ZI Nucleo board (ARM Cortex-M7, 480 MHz, 1 MB Flash) as master; C++ simulates PUF response generation. Steps:

(1) Experimental procedure: Generate a 256-bit random challenge c via random number, randomly generate original response r_{raw} based on c, output stable response r after BCH error correction.

(2) Compare stable response r with pre-stored registration phase response r_{reg}. If Hamming distance $d = H(r, r_{reg}) \leq 3$, authentication passes. Terminal devices communicate with servers via WiFi (802.11n) at 150 Mbps; authentication messages (challenge-response) are encrypted via AES-256-GCM for channel security.

Comparison of Signaling Overhead. Signaling Overhead is the number of authentication message transmissions in access authentication. Table 3 shows protocols [27–29] and ours have 5, 3, 2, 2 rounds respectively in authentication and key agreement. Though ours and [29] both need 2 rounds, ours has lower computational cost (next subsection). Compared schemes are from the past two years (strong relevance, credible results), so ours meets Section 1.2 lightweight requirements with lower communication and computational overhead.

Comparison of Computation Cost. Computational overhead – key for satellite Internet authentication/key agreement, involving crypto operation time and message delay – has been tested on device 1 and device 2 respectively, as shown in Table 4. Results show consistent protocol overhead rankings, verifying evaluation stability. Password operation overhead under different configurations is

Table 3. Comparison of signaling overhead

Signal Direction	[27]	[28]	[29]	Ours
Terminal → LEO	1	2	1	1
LEO → Terminal	2	1	1	1
LEO → NCC	1	-	-	-
NCC → LEO	1	-	-	-
Total	5	3	2	2

in Table 5; XOR overhead is negligible. Satellite-ground (T_{l-t}) and satellite-trusted center (T_{l-n}) transmission times, with authentication/key negotiation overhead comparisons in Table 6, show ours reduces overhead by $T_{l-t} + 2T_{l-n}$, $1.63ms + T_{l-t}$, $1.80ms$ vs [27–29], better meeting STIN low-latency needs.

Table 4. Device hardware and development environment parameters

Attribute	Device 1	Device 2
OS	Windows 11	Windows 11
Processor	Intel Core i5-9300H	Intel Core i7-8845H
RAM	8 GB	32 GB
Clock Rate	2.40 GHz	3.80 GHz
Integrated Development Environment (IDE)	C++	C++

Table 5. Execution time of cryptographic operations

Symbol	Description	Execution Time (ms)	
		Device 1	Device 2
T_h	Hash function	0.0031	0.0023
T_{puf}	PUF operations	0.0568	0.0196
T_{rep}	Fuzzy extractor	0.0689	0.0116
T_{exp}	Modular exponentiation	0.0003	0.0001
T_{xor}	XOR operations	0.0004	0.0001
$T_{enc/dec}$	Symmetric encryption	0.0672	0.0073
T_{ea}	Point addition	0.0150	0.0096
T_{em}	Point multiplication	0.1915	0.0905
T_{bp}	Pairing operations	24.7126	19.7825

Comparison of Communication Overhead. This section compares the communication overhead of [27–29] and our protocol in authentication and key negotiation. For total overhead calculation: timestamp/XOR (32 bits), user/device

ID, password, F_p elements (160 bits), hash digest (128 bits), PUF (256 bits), $E_p(a, b)$ points (320 bits). Table 7 shows our protocol has 416, 224, 896 bits lower communication overhead than [27–29], reducing overhead in authentication and key negotiation to meet STIN's lightweight needs.

Table 6. Comparison of computation cost

Computation Cost	[27]	[28]	[29]	Ours
Initiator	$2T_{puf} + 6T_h + 5T_{xor}$	$T_{puf}+T_{rep}+3T_h+T_{ea}+6T_{em}+2T_{xor}$	$5T_h + 3T_{ea} + 7T_{em} + 4T_{exp} + T_{xor}$	$6T_h + 3T_{xor} + T_{rep} + 2T_{em}$
LEO	$7T_h + 9T_{xor}$	$T_{puf}+T_{rep}+4T_h+3T_{ea}+6T_{em}+T_{xor}$	$4T_h + 3T_{ea} + 7T_{em} + 4T_{exp}$	$T_{puf} + 6T_h + 3T_{xor} + T_{rep} + 2T_{em}$
NCC	$6T_h + 3T_{xor}$	0	0	0
Computational overhead	$2T_{puf}+19T_h+17T_{xor}$	$2T_{puf} + 2T_{rep} + 7T_h + 4T_{ea} + 12T_{em} + 3T_{xor}$	$9T_h + T_{xor} + 8T_{exp} + 6T_{ea} + 14T_{em}$	$T_{puf} + 12T_h + 6T_{xor} + 2T_{rep} + 4T_{em}$
Transmission delay	$3T_{l-t} + 2T_{l-n}$	$3T_{l-t}$	$2T_{l-t}$	$2T_{l-t}$
Total(bit)	$0.1793 + 3T_{l-t} + 2T_{l-n}$	$2.6323 + 3T_{l-t}$	$2.8017 + 2T_{l-t}$	$1.0002 + 2T_{l-t}$

Table 7. Comparison of communication overhead

Communication Cost	[27]	[28]	[29]	Ours
Initiator	$C_{xor} + 2C_{hash}$	$C_{time} + 2C_i + 2C_{puf} + 2C_{E_p}$	$C_{xor} + C_{time} + C_{hash} + 2C_{F_p} + 2C_{E_p}$	$2C_{xor} + C_{time} + 2C_{hash} + C_{puf} + C_{E_p}$
LEO	$5C_{xor} + 5C_{time} + 3C_{hash} + C_i + C_{puf}$	$C_{hash} + C_{E_p}$	$C_{time} + 2C_{F_p} + 3C_{E_p}$	$C_{xor} + C_{time} + 2C_{hash} + C_{E_p}$
NCC	$C_{xor} + C_{time} + 4C_{hash}$	0	0	0
Total	$7C_{xor} + 6C_{time} + 9C_{hash} + C_i + C_{puf}$	$C_{time} + C_{hash} + C_i + 2C_{puf} + 3C_{E_p}$	$C_{xor} + 2C_{time} + C_{hash} + 4C_{F_p} + 5C_{E_p}$	$3C_{xor} + 2C_{time} + 4C_{hash} + C_{puf} + 2C_{E_p}$
Total(bit)	1984	1792	2464	1568

7   Conclusion

With the rapid development of satellite Internet, ensuring secure and efficient user access to STIN services via terminal devices is vital. Addressing existing authentication protocols' issues (single security protection, high computational overhead, central node dependence), this paper proposes a new STIN access authentication protocol. Formal/informal security and performance analyses show it meets STIN's security and lightweight requirements.

Acknowledgments. This work has been partly supported by the Natural Science Foundation of Hubei Province of China [grant number 2023AFB394], the Fundamental Research Funds for the Central Universities [Grant Number: CCNU24AI010, No. CCNU24JC004], and the National Natural Science Foundation of China [No. 62377019].

References

1. Xue, K., Meng, W., Li, S., Wei, D.S.L., Zhou, H., Yu, N.: A secure and efficient access and handover authentication protocol for internet of things in space information networks. IEEE Internet Things J. **6**(6), 5485–5499 (2019)
2. He, D., Kumar, N., Chen, J., Lee, C.C., Chilamkurti, N., Yeo, S.S.: Robust anonymous authentication protocol for health-care applications using wireless medical sensor networks. Multimed. Syst. **21**(1), 49–60 (2015)
3. Li, X., Niu, J., Kumari, S., Liao, J., Liang, W., Khan, M.K.: A new authentication protocol for healthcare applications using wireless medical sensor networks with user anonymity. Secur. Commun. Netw. **9**(15), 2643–2655 (2016)
4. Wu, F., Xu, L., Kumari, S., Li, X.: An improved and anonymous two-factor authentication protocol for health-care applications with wireless medical sensor networks. Multimed. Syst. **23**(2), 195–205 (2017)
5. Li, C.T., Shih, D.H., Wang, C.C.: Cloud-assisted mutual authentication and privacy preservation protocol for telecare medical information systems. Comput. Methods Programs Biomed. **157**, 191–203 (2018)
6. Kumar, V., Ahmad, M., Kumari, A.: A secure elliptic curve cryptography based mutual authentication protocol for cloud-assisted TMIS. Telemat. Inform. **38**, 100–117 (2019)
7. Sureshkumar, V., Amin, R., Vijaykumar, V., Sekar, S.R.: Robust secure communication protocol for smart healthcare system with FPGA implementation. Future Gener. Comput. Syst. **100**, 938–951 (2019)
8. Yang, X., Yi, X., Nepal, S., Khalil, I., Huang, X., Shen, J.: Efficient and anonymous authentication for healthcare service with cloud based WBANs. IEEE Trans. Serv. Comput. **15**(5), 2728–2741 (2022)
9. Servati, M.R., Safkhani, M.: ECCbAS: an ECC based authentication scheme for healthcare IoT systems. Pervasive Mob. Comput. 101753 (2023)
10. Aghili, S.F., Mala, H., Shojafar, M., Peris-Lopez, P.: LACO: lightweight three-factor authentication, access control and ownership transfer scheme for e-health systems in IoT, future generation computer systems. Future Gener. Comput. Syst. **96**, 410–424 (2019)
11. Oh, J., Yu, S., Lee, J., Son, S., Kim, M., Park, Y.: A secure and lightweight authentication protocol for IoT-based smart homes. Sensors **21**(4), 1488 (2021)
12. Xiang, A., Zheng, J.: A situation-aware scheme for efficient device authentication in smart grid-enabled home area networks. Electronics **9**(6), 989 (2020)
13. Hajian, R., ZakeriKia, S., Erfani, S.H., Mirabi, M.: SHAPARAK: scalable healthcare authentication protocol with attack-resilience and anonymous key-agreement. Comput. Netw. **183**, 107567 (2020)
14. Shuai, M., Yu, N., Wang, H., Xiong, L.: Anonymous authentication scheme for smart home environment with provable security. Comput. Secur. **86**, 132–146 (2019)

15. Gupta, A., Tripathi, M., Shaikh, T.J., Sharma, A.: A lightweight anonymous user authentication and key establishment scheme for wearable devices. Comput. Netw. **149**, 29–42 (2019)
16. Alzahrani, B.A., Irshad, A., Albeshri, A., Alsubhi, K.: A provably secure and lightweight patient-healthcare authentication protocol in wireless body area networks. Wirel. Pers. Commun. **117**(1), 47–69 (2021)
17. Xu, Z., Xu, C., Chen, H., Yang, F.: A lightweight anonymous mutual authentication and key agreement scheme for WBAN. Concurr. Comput. Pract. Exp. **31**(14), e5295 (2019)
18. Nikooghadam, M., Amintoosi, H., Islam, S.H., et al.: A provably secure and lightweight authentication scheme for Internet of Drones for smart city surveillance. J. Syst. Archit. EUROMICRO J. **115**, 101955 (2021)
19. Qi, M., Chen, J.: An enhanced authentication with key agreement scheme for satellite communication systems. Int. J. Satell. Commun. Network. **36**(3), 296–304 (2018)
20. Challa, S., et al.: An efficient ECC-based provably secure three-factor user authentication and key agreement protocol for wireless healthcare sensor networks. Comput. Electr. Eng. **69**, 534–554 (2018)
21. Mohammad, W., Das, A.K., Bhat, V., Vasilakos, A.V.V.: LAM-CIOT: lightweight authentication mechanism in cloud-based IoT environment. J. Netw. Comput. Appl. **150**, 102496 (2020)
22. Gabsi, S., Kortli, Y., Beroulle, V., Kieffer, Y., Alasiry, A., Hamdi, B.: Novel ECC-based RFID mutual authentication protocol for emerging IoT applications. IEEE Access **9**, 130895–130913 (2021)
23. Arslan, A., Bingöl, M.A.: Security and privacy analysis of recently proposed ECC-based RFID authentication schemes. Cryptology ePrint Archive (2022)
24. Guo, J., Ye, D., Zhang, Y., et al.: A provably secure ECC-based access and handover authentication protocol for space information networks. J. Netw. Comput. Appl. **193**, 103183 (2021)
25. Guo, J., Du, Y., Zhang, Y., Li, M.: A provably secure ECC-based access and handover authentication protocol for space information networks. J. Netw. Comput. Appl. **188**, 103183 (2021)
26. Mahmood, K., Chaudhry, S.A., Naqvi, H., Kumari, S., Li, X., Sangaiah, A.K.: An elliptic curve cryptography based lightweight authentication scheme for smart grid communication. Future Gener. Comput. Syst. **81**, 557–565 (2018)
27. Zhang, Z., et al.: PRLAP-IoD: a PUF-based robust and lightweight authentication protocol for internet of drones. Comput. Netw. **242**, 110118 (2024)
28. Li, S., Huang, Y., Yu, B.: A practical and flexible PUF-based end-to-end anonymous authentication protocol for IoT. Comput. Netw. **247**, 110426 (2024)
29. Guo, J., Chang, L., Song, Y., et al.: AHA-BV: access and handover authentication protocol with batch verification for satellite-terrestrial integrated networks. Comput. Standards Interfaces **91**, 103870 (2025)
30. Modarres, A.M.A., Sarbishaei, G.: A lightweight authentication protocol for IoT-based applications using reconfigurable noisy PUFs. IEEE Trans. Industr. Inf. **20**(1), 1–9 (2024)
31. Subramani, J., Maria, A., Rajasekaran, A.S., Al-Turjman, F.: Lightweight privacy and confidentiality preserving anonymous authentication scheme for WBANs. IEEE Trans. Industr. Inf. **18**(5), 3484–3491 (2022)
32. He, D., Zeadally, S., Xu, B., Huang, X.: An efficient identity-based conditional privacy-preserving authentication scheme for vehicular ad hoc networks. IEEE Trans. Inf. Forensics Secur. **10**(12), 2681–2691 (2015)

33. Qian, K., Liu, Y., He, X., Du, M., Zhang, S., Wang, K.: Hpcchain: a consortium blockchain system based on CPU-FPGA hybrid PUF for industrial internet of things. IEEE Trans. Industr. Inf. **19**(11), 1–11 (2023)
34. Shan, X., Yu, H., Chen, Y., Yang, Z.: Physical unclonable function based lightweight and verifiable data stream transmission for industrial IoT. IEEE Trans. Industr. Inf. **19**(10), 1–11 (2023)
35. Li, D., Liu, D., Qi, Y., Liu, F., Guan, Z., Liu, J.: PUF-based lightweight authentication framework for large-scale IoT devices in distributed cloud. IEEE Netw. Mag. Glob. Internetworking **37**(1), 56–62 (2023)
36. Fatima, S., Akram, M.A., Mian, A.N., Chen, S.K.: On the security of a blockchain and PUF-based lightweight authentication protocol for wireless medical sensor networks. Wirel. Pers. Commun. **135**(2), 1079–1106 (2024)
37. Guo, Y., Zhang, Z., Guo, Y., Xiong, P.: BSRA: blockchain-based secure remote authentication scheme for fog-enabled internet of things. IEEE Internet Things J. **11**(7), 3348–3361 (2024)
38. Awais, S.M., et al.: PUF-based privacy-preserving simultaneous authentication among multiple vehicles in VANET. IEEE Trans. Veh. Technol. **73**(5), 6727–6739 (2024)
39. Ma, R., Cao, J., Feng, D., Li, H.: LAA: lattice-based access authentication scheme for IoT in space information networks. IEEE Internet Things J. **7**(4), 2791–2805 (2020)
40. Hanzlik, L., Kutyłowski, M.: Restricted identification secure in the extended Canetti-Krawczyk model. J. Univ. Comput. Sci. **21**(3), 419–439 (2015)
41. Ponikwar, C., Hof, H.-J., Gopinath, S., et al.: Beyond the Dolev-Yao model: realistic application-specific attacker models for applications using vehicular communication (2016)

Parallel Implementation of Activation Functions and Arithmetic Operations Based on TFHE

Miaomiao Li, Pei Li$^{(\boxtimes)}$, and Jiageng Chen

Central China Normal University, Wuhan 430079, China
peili@ccnu.edu.cn

Abstract. Cloud platforms have become a primary environment for training machine learning models. However, the security of sensitive data could be compromised due to storage and computation in the cloud provided by the third party. Fully Homomorphic Encryption over the Torus (TFHE) offers a promising solution to this issue. However, integrating the wildly used Artificial Neural Networks (ANNs) with TFHE still faces significant challenges, particularly in the efficient implementation of activation functions and arithmetic operations. In this work, we present a parallel implementation of activation functions and arithmetic operations based on TFHE. By leveraging the parallel computing capabilities of multi-core CPUs and GPUs, our approach significantly improves computational performance. Experimental results demonstrate that our method achieves competitive accuracy while delivering a 12x speedup for 32-bit multiplication on GPUs and up to 30x acceleration for ReLU computations across various bit widths.

Keywords: Data security · TFHE · Activation functions · Arithmetic operations

1 Introduction

Modern cloud platforms are widely used to train machine learning models [14]. By submitting computational tasks to the cloud, users can leverage powerful computational resources and elastic scalability to efficiently process large-scale data. However, the lack of transparency in cloud operations and the absence of effective regulatory mechanisms pose serious challenges to data privacy and computational security [17–19]. In recent years, multiple incidents of data leakage and tampering caused by cloud service providers or third-party attacks have been reported, further highlighting the severity of data security risks in cloud environments.

Homomorphic encryption is a key technique for solving these problems, as it enables computation on encrypted data in untrusted environments. The concept was first introduced by Rivest et al. in 1978 [15], though early schemes

L. Zhai et al. (Eds.): SocialSec 2025, LNCS 16327, pp. 43–59, 2026.
https://doi.org/10.1007/978-981-95-7027-0_3

supported only limited operations or specific computation types. In 2009, Gentry proposed the first fully homomorphic encryption (FHE) scheme capable of evaluating arbitrary computations [8], introducing the bootstrapping technique to manage noise growth.

Artificial neural networks are widely adopted machine learning models, in which activation functions and arithmetic operations are core components. Activation functions provide nonlinearity to the model, enhancing its feature extraction and expressive capabilities. Arithmetic operations facilitate information flow during forward and backward propagation and support model training through weight updates. Together, they enable neural networks to effectively handle high-dimensional data and complex tasks. In this work, we utilize the TFHE homomorphic encryption library [2] to implement homomorphic computation of common arithmetic operations and activation functions (Sigmoid and ReLU) based on the TFHE encryption scheme [16]. Additionally, The TFHE scheme is constructed upon the Learning With Errors (LWE) problem [4,11], in which plaintexts are encrypted using polynomial-based techniques and represented as vectors. This vectorized representation enables efficient parallel computation. Exploiting this characteristic, we further optimize the implementation for both CPU and GPU platforms to enhance computational performance.

The paper is organized as follows: Sect. 2 reviews related work. Section 3 introduces some key concepts. Sections 4 and 5 present the design and parallelization of operations in TFHE, respectively. Section 6 presents experimental results. Finally, Sect. 7 concludes the paper.

2   Related Work

In earlier research, several studies attempted to design homomorphic activation functions for neural networks. In 2016, CryptoNets [9] introduced a specialized approach to hand activation functions by representing them as low-degree polynomials, enabling computation within the framework of homomorphic encryption. Subsequent studies further refined this approach by approximating activation functions with polynomials within a specific error range while constraining the polynomial coefficients to powers of two [3], thereby minimizing approximation errors. Different from other polynomial-based approximation methods, Hesamifard et al. proposed a novel representation of the ReLU function [10], where instead of directly approximating the function's values, they employed an approach that approximates its derivative.

In 2018, Bourse et al. proposed a novel approach to secure neural network computations [1]. They quantized the data values into the range $\{-1, 1\}$ and employed the sign function as the activation function to achieve scale invariance. This method leveraged the properties of the TFHE fully homomorphic encryption scheme, enabling efficient computation of the nonlinear sign function within the bootstrapping process. Although this approach simplified data representation in neural networks and improved computational efficiency, its applicability remained limited, making it challenging to extend to more complex network architectures and task scenarios.

In this work, we propose an optimized design scheme for activation functions and arithmetic computations in fully homomorphic encryption environments based on TFHE. Unlike traditional polynomial approximations of the sigmoid function, we employ a lookup table technique that precomputes and stores function values to avoid expensive numerical calculations, significantly reducing computational overhead. For the ReLU function, we efficiently compute outputs by directly determining the sign bit of the input, eliminating complex arithmetic operations. Additionally, we introduce two parallel computing strategies to reduce ciphertext operations in neural network arithmetic, and leverage the parallelism of multi-core CPUs and GPUs to further improve overall computational efficiency.

3   Preliminary

3.1   Homomorphic Encryption Algorithm and TFHE

Homomorphic Encryption (HE) is characterized by its ability to perform specified mathematical or logical operations on ciphertexts, producing ciphertexts that decrypt to the same result as if the operations had been performed on the plaintexts. However, homomorphic encryption schemes typically support only specific types of operations or allow a limited number of operations, as each homomorphic computation introduces noise. When accumulated beyond a certain threshold, this noise can affect decryption correctness. These schemes are known as Partially Homomorphic Encryption (PHE) or Somewhat Homomorphic Encryption (SHE) [13].To overcome these limitations, Fully Homomorphic Encryption (FHE) introduces the bootstrapping technique, which refreshes the noise in ciphertexts, thereby enabling an arbitrary number and type of computations on encrypted data.

TFHE is a fully homomorphic encryption scheme featuring fast bootstrapping. By combining LWE and GSW ciphertext structures [7], TFHE replaces the inner product computation in the bootstrapping process with an outer product. The bootstrapping procedure involves a Fast Fourier Transform (FFT) with complexity $O(nlogn)$. In the TFHE library implementation, this FFT is executed using the FFTW library [6] and accelerated by leveraging Intel's AVX instructions [12] for parallel vector computations. This optimization reduces the bootstrapping time to 0.1 s, resulting in performance approximately 50 times faster than FHEW [5] on a single core. TFHE performs fast bootstrapping after each homomorphic logic gate operation and supports flexible gate counts and structural configurations, making it suitable for both manually designed and automatically generated circuits.

3.2   Artificial Neural Networks

Artificial Neural Networks are computational models inspired by biological neural networks. They consist of a large number of interconnected nodes, each node is typically referred to as a neuron. Each neuron (except those in the input layer) performs two primary operations on the vector formed by the inputs it receives from the preceding layer:

Compute the weighted sum $y = \langle x, \omega \rangle + \beta$, where w represents the weights and β represents the bias.

Compute the activation function, with the output given by $c = f(y)$, where $f(.)$ is the activation function. The Fig. 1 illustrates how a neuron processes its inputs and produces the final output. The activation function introduces nonlinearity into the neuron, enabling the neural network to approximate any nonlinear function arbitrarily.

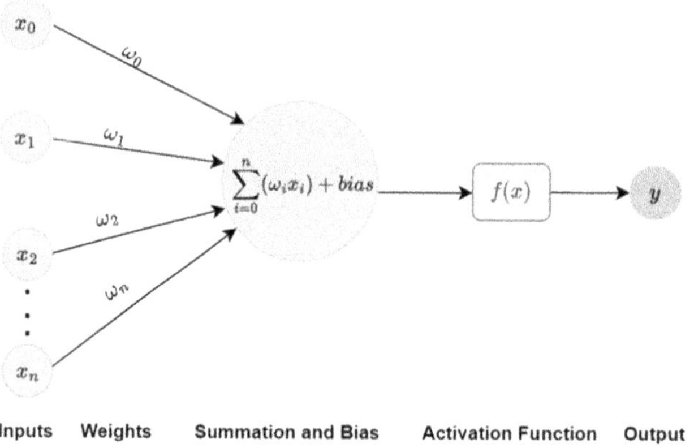

Fig. 1. Neuron Operations.

3.3 Activation Function

Sigmoid Activation Function. The sigmoid function is a differentiable, non-decreasing function and is one of the most common activation functions. It is mathematically defined as Eq. (1), in which $x \in (-\infty, \infty)$, $f(x) \in (0, 1)$.

$$sigmoid(x) = \frac{1}{1 + e^{-x}} \tag{1}$$

The graphic depiction of the sigmoid function and its derivative are shown in the Fig. 2. From the graph, it can be observed that the sigmoid function forms a smooth S-shaped curve, with the graph being symmetric about the point $(0, 0.5)$. Additionally, two key characteristics of the sigmoid function can be derived from the graph.

Property 1:

$$sigmoid(x) + sigmoid(-x) = 1 \tag{2}$$

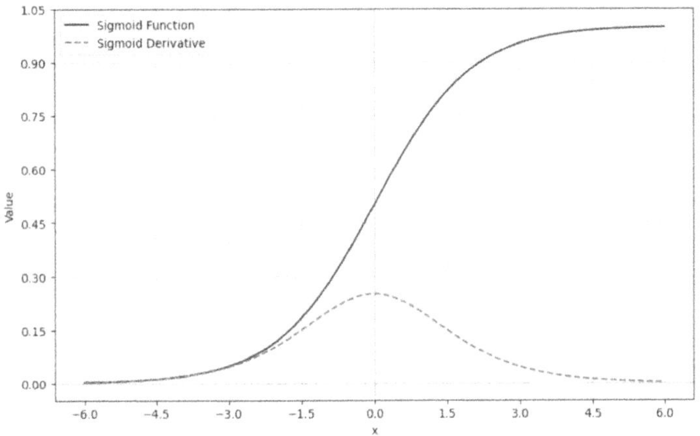

Fig. 2. The graphic depiction of sigmoid function and its derivative.

Property 2:

$$\lim_{x \to -\infty} sigmoid(x) = 0;\ \lim_{x \to \infty} sigmoid(x) = 1 \tag{3}$$

ReLU Activation Function. The ReLU function is the most commonly used activation function in current neural networks. It is mathematically defined as Eq. (4).

$$ReLU(x) = max(0, x) \tag{4}$$

As shown in Fig. 3, the ReLU graph has a kink point at the origin $(0, 0)$. For $x < 0$, the graph is a horizontal line, for $x \geq 0$, the graph is a straight line with a slope of 1, where $ReLU(x) = x$.

Property

$$x < 0, ReLU(x) = 0; x \geq 0, ReLU(x) = x \tag{5}$$

4 Design of Activation Functions with TFHE

4.1 Design of Sigmoid Function

Sigmoid's LUT Design. The sigmoid function is difficult to implement in TFHE due to its exponential form, while polynomial approximation requires numerous operations, resulting in high complexity. To address this, we adopt a lookup table (LUT)-based approach. Unlike conventional one-to-one mappings, multiple inputs are allowed to share the same stored value as long as the deviation remains within an acceptable range. Each LUT entry corresponds to a subinterval and stores the average of its boundary values. By exploiting the properties of the sigmoid function, the LUT size is significantly reduced, thereby improving computational efficiency. The design is summarized as follows:

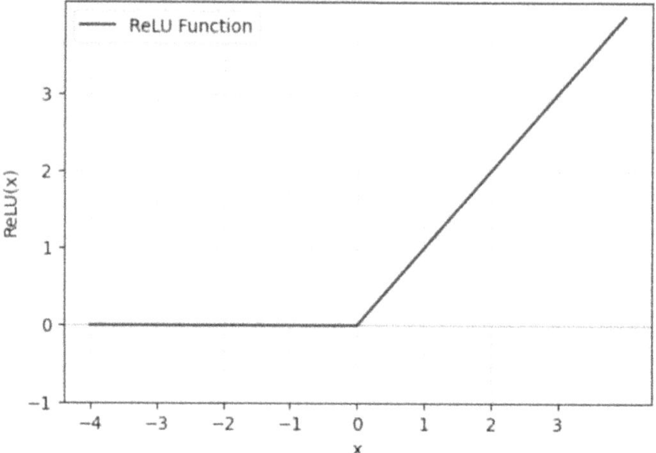

Fig. 3. The graphic depiction of ReLU function.

(1) Since the sigmoid function is symmetric about the point $(0, 0.5)$, only the right half of the curve needs to be stored (Fig. 4). For $x < 0$, the value can be obtained through ciphertext subtraction.

(2) The primary variation of $sigmoid(x)$ occurs within the interval $[-5, 5]$, while changes beyond this range are negligible. Hence, all values with $x \geq 4.595076$ are stored as 1.

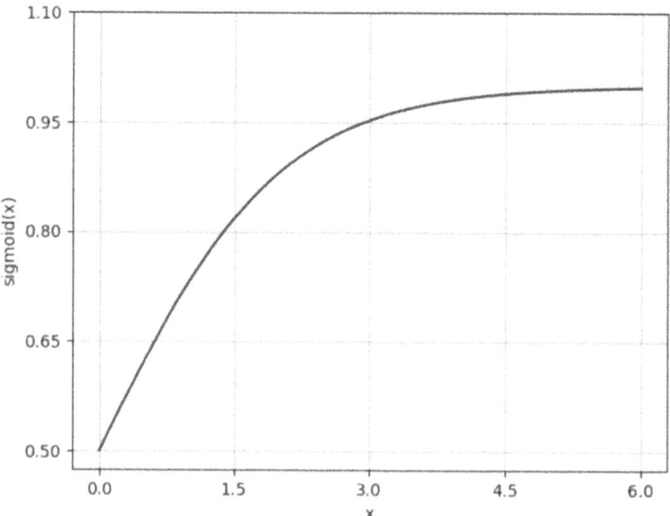

Fig. 4. Right half of the Sigmoid function.

(3) As the rate of change is non-uniform, different x values may correspond to the same LUT entry, further reducing storage requirements.

The final LUT design, shown in Table 1, requires only 26 precomputed encrypted values to ensure a maximum deviation of 0.01, enabling efficient computation of the sigmoid function.

Table 1. LUT of sigmoid function

LUT location	Limits of Positive Sub-domain		Store	Max
	X1	X2	value	deviation
1	0	0.040006	0.5	0.01
2	0.040006	0.120145	0.52	0.01
3	0.120145	0.200672	0.54	0.01
4	0.200672	0.281852	0.56	0.01
5	0.281852	0.363966	0.58	0.01
6	0.363966	0.447313	0.60	0.01
7	0.447313	0.532216	0.62	0.01
8	0.532216	0.619039	0.64	0.01
9	0.619039	0.708186	0.66	0.01
10	0.708186	0.800119	0.68	0.01
11	0.800119	0.895385	0.70	0.01
12	0.895385	0.994623	0.72	0.01
13	0.994623	1.098618	0.74	0.01
14	1.098618	1.208316	0.76	0.01
15	1.208316	1.324928	0.78	0.01
16	1.324928	1.45012	0.80	0.01
17	1.45012	1.585628	0.82	0.01
18	1.585628	1.734604	0.84	0.01
19	1.734604	1.900960	0.86	0.01
20	1.900960	2.090746	0.88	0.01
21	2.090746	2.313638	0.90	0.01
22	2.313638	2.568686	0.92	0.01
23	2.568686	2.944435	0.94	0.01
24	2.944435	3.476087	0.96	0.01
25	3.476087	4.595076	0.98	0.01
26	4.595076	/	1	0.01

Structure of Sigmoid Function. Based on the design principles and optimization recommendations for the LUT of the sigmoid function, we have designed the computation process for the sigmoid function. As illustrated in the Fig. 5, it demonstrates the computation process of the function for a 16-bit input.

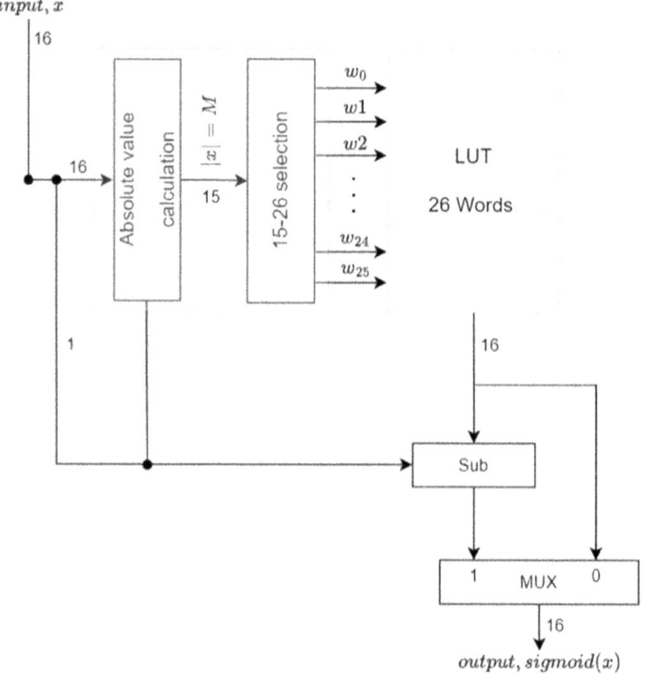

Fig. 5. The structure of sigmoid function.

First, we transform x into M, where M represents the 15-bit absolute value of x. This transformation is implemented using logic gates. Subsequently, we compute 26 selection indicators, where each $w_i = 1$ corresponds to computing the output of the sigmoid function for a specific range of M. The logical expressions for (from Eq. 6 to Eq. 10) are derived by simplifying bitwise comparison formulas.

$$w_0 = t_0, \quad w_1 = t_1 \cdot \overline{t_0}, \quad w_i = t_i \cdot \overline{t_{i-1}} \quad \text{for } 2 \leq i \leq 25 \tag{6}$$

$$t_0 = (((m_1 \cdot m_2 + m_3 + m_4 + m_5 + m_6) \cdot m_7 \cdot m_8 \\ + m_9 + m_{10}) \cdot m_{11} + m_{12} + m_{13}) \cdot m_{14} \tag{7}$$

$$t_1 = ((m_0 \cdot m_1 \cdot m_2 \cdot m_3 \cdot m_4 + m_5 + m_6) \cdot m_7 \cdot m_8 \\ \cdot m_9 \cdot m_{10} + m_{11}) \cdot m_{12} \cdot m_{13} + m_{14} \tag{8}$$

$$\vdots$$

$$t_{24} = ((m_2 + m_3 + m_4) \cdot m_5 + m_6) \cdot m_7 + m_8 + m_9 \\ + m_{10} + m_{11} + m_{12} + m_{13} + m_{14} \tag{9}$$

$$t_{25} = m_0 + m_1 + m_2 + m_3 + m_4 + m_5 + m_6 + m_7$$
$$+ m_8 + m_9 + m_{10} + m_{11} + m_{12} + m_{13} + m_{14} \qquad (10)$$

For instance, from these expressions, we observe that when $w_0 = t_0 = 1$, it indicates that $M > 4.595076$, resulting in an output value of $sigmoid(M) = 1$. Similarly, when $t_0 = 0$ and $t_1 = 1$, it represents $3.476087 < M < 4.595076$, leading to $w_1 = 1$ and an output of $sigmoid(M) = 0.98$. This pattern continues accordingly. Here, the two numbers being compared are non-negative, and the bitwise comparison expression can be simplified to Algorithm 1. The comparison process starts from the least significant bit and proceeds bit by bit, with the result of each comparison serving as input for the next higher bit. This operation is repeated until the most significant bit is reached. During this process, the bootsXNOR and bootsMUX operations are used to implement the exclusive NOR and multiplexer functions, respectively. When x is positive, the sigmoid function's output is directly $sigmoid(M)$. However, when x is negative, leveraging the symmetry property of the sigmoid function (Property 1), we can compute $sigmoid(x)$ indirectly using the transformation $1 - sigmoid(M)$.

Algorithm 1 Bitwise Encryption Comparison Algorithm

1: **function** FHE_COMPARE(C_a, C_b, bk)
2:     $tmps \leftarrow 0'$
3:     **for** $i \leftarrow 0$ to $n - 1$ **do**
4:         $tmps1 \leftarrow$ bootsXNOR(C_a^i, C_b^i, bk)
5:         $tmps \leftarrow$ bootsMUX($tmps1, tmps, C_b^i, bk$)
6:     **end for**
7:     **return** $tmps$
8: **end function**

4.2 Design of ReLU Function

Unlike the sigmoid function, which requires complex exponential computations, the output of ReLU depends solely on the sign bit of the input, thereby eliminating the need for lookup tables or additional sign-selection mechanisms. Leveraging the bit-level encryption property of TFHE, the sign bit can be directly extracted from encrypted data without decryption or auxiliary transformations. In the concrete implementation, TFHE sequentially traverses the two's complement representation of the input M, and the output is determined by the sign bit: when $M_{sign} = 1$ (negative input), all output bits are set to 0; conversely, when $M_{sign} = 0$ (non-negative input), each output bit is directly propagated from the input. It is worth emphasizing that although the algorithmic description follows a sequential bit-wise traversal, the computation of each bit is inherently independent. This independence makes ReLU highly amenable to parallel execution within homomorphic encryption frameworks, where parallel hardware such as CPUs and GPUs can map bit-wise operations to concurrent execution across multiple processing units, thereby avoiding the need for strict sequential traversal, as illustrated in Algorithm 2.

Algorithm 2 ReLU Function with Bit-level Parallelism

1: **function** FHE_RELU(M)
2:    **if** $M_{sign} = 0$ **then**   ▷ Input is non-negative
3:       **for all** bit $m_i \in M$ **in parallel do**
4:          $output_i \leftarrow m_i$
5:       **end for**
6:    **else**   ▷ Input is negative
7:       **for all** bit $m_i \in M$ **in parallel do**
8:          $output_i \leftarrow 0$
9:       **end for**
10:   **end if**
11: **end function**

---

5   Acceleration Strategies in CPU and GPU

In this section, we propose two parallel computing techniques: bit coalescing and composite gates.

5.1   Bit Coalescing

We use binary bit vectors to represent data and employ TFHE to encrypt the data. A LWE sample vector can represent a single encrypted bit, so an n-bit data set becomes n-LWE samples after encryption. In the CPU, the storage format of the encrypted data is shown in the Fig. 6.

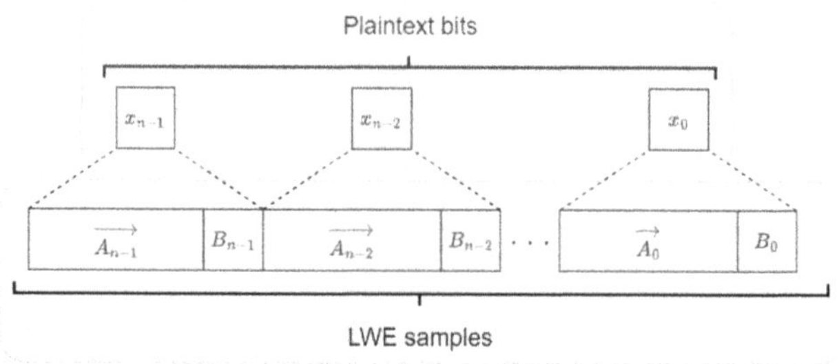

Fig. 6. n-LWE samples for n-bit.

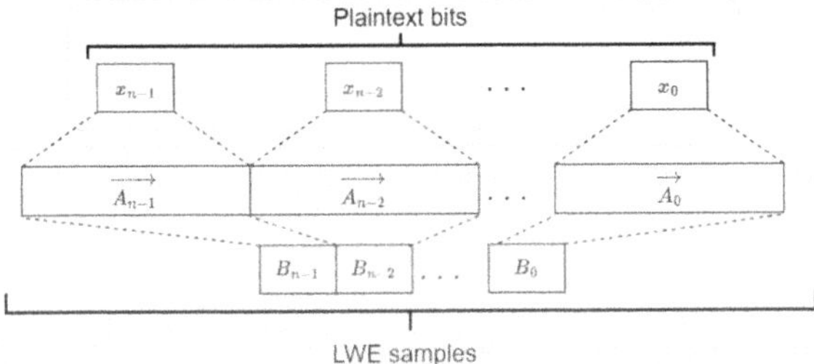

Fig. 7. Coalescing n-LWE samples for n-bit.

Each LWE sample consists of two parts, $\overrightarrow{A}$ and B, where $\overrightarrow{A}$ is defined as a vector. We have designed a storage technique, as shown in the figure, where instead of handling each encrypted bit vector separately, we represent an n-LWE sample by increasing the continuous storage length of the vector, as shown in Fig. 7. This storage method is well-suited for the GPU computation model.

5.2   Compound Gate

Addition is a fundamental and indispensable operation in most arithmetic computations. It is not only directly employed for numerical summation but also serves as a critical building block for more complex operations such as subtraction, multiplication, division, and exponentiation. Consequently, adders constitute essential components in arithmetic circuits.

For the addition operation $R = A + B$, we typically use the following two formulas to calculate the sum r_i and carry c_i for each bit:

Sum:
$$r_i = a_i \oplus b_i \oplus c_{i-1} \tag{11}$$

Carry:
$$c_i = (a_i \wedge b_i) \vee (b_i \oplus c_{i-1}) \vee (a_i \wedge c_{i-1}) \tag{12}$$

In these two Eqs. (11) and (12), a_i, b_i and r_i represent the i-th bits of A, B, and R, respectively, while c_i and c_{i-1} represent the carry of the current bit and the previous bit, respectively. $\wedge$ represents the AND operation, and $\oplus$ represents the XOR operation.

From the formula, it can be observed that the XOR and AND operations act on the same input bits and are independent of each other, which enables them to be executed in parallel. Based on this property, we propose a composite gate structure that integrates the two logic gates, allowing the circuit to simultaneously output r_i and c_i. This design not only improves parallel computation efficiency but also provides flexible extensibility for different arithmetic operations.

5.3 Arithmetic Operations

Addition. From Eq. (11) and Eq. (12), it is evident that in addition operations, each result bit r_i and carry bit c_i depend on the carry bit from the previous position c_{i-1}. This dependency inherently limits the parallelism of addition operations in CPUs, as each bit's computation must wait for the result of the preceding bit. However, on GPUs, techniques inspired by bitwise coalescing can be utilized to perform parallel computations across n data, thereby significantly enhancing performance.

For the addition operation $R = A + B$, the following steps can be employed to achieve more efficient parallel computation:

(1) Initialization: Initialize R to A, $R = A$.
(2) Carry Calculation: Compute the carry using $Carry = R \wedge B$.
(3) Sum Update: Update the sum using $R = R \oplus B$.
(4) Carry Propagation: Shift the carry one position to the left, $B = Carry \ll 1$, and use the updated B for the next iteration.

By repeating steps (2) to (4) n times, the addition for n-bit data can be completed. In steps (2) and (3), the AND and XOR operations are performed on the same operands. Therefore, the previously mentioned compound gate can be employed to merge these two steps, further improving computational efficiency.

Subtraction. Addition and subtraction are closely related, and in computers, subtraction is typically implemented indirectly through addition. Specifically, for the computation $R = A - B$, it can be transformed into $R = A + (-B)$, The result can then be obtained by performing the addition operation.

Multiplication. In the TFHE library, multiplication is typically implemented via the bootsAND function, which performs logical AND operations on ciphertexts to simulate multiplication. However, each Boolean operation involves an expensive bootstrapping procedure. In neural network training, weights are often represented as binary plaintexts, enabling the design of mixed operations between plaintext and ciphertext to reduce unnecessary bootstrapping. Based on the bootsAND function, we propose an optimized Boolean operation, termed the H-AND operation, specifically tailored for multiplication between ciphertext and plaintext.

$$H - AND(C, P) = \begin{cases} C & P = 1 \\ (0,0) & P = 0 \end{cases} \tag{13}$$

The ciphertext output is determined by checking whether the plaintext bit P is 1. In the equation above, inputs to the homomorphic gate are P and C, where C is the ciphertext input, and P represents the plaintext binary number. For an n-bit ciphertext A and an m-bit plaintext B, we perform the H-AND operation between each bit of A and the corresponding bit b_i in B, resulting in n encrypted data values. These encrypted data values are then left-shifted by i positions, and finally, the shifted encrypted data values are accumulated using addition.

Multiplication thus involves H-AND, left shifts, and accumulation. Since H-AND and left shifts are bitwise independent, they are parallelizable. On the CPU, OpenMP multi-threading is used. For accumulation, a custom OpenMP reduction with shared memory handles intermediate results. On the GPU, tree-based addition optimizes accumulation by recursively dividing the task via divide-and-conquer. For example, an n-LWE vector is split into two $n/2$-LWE vectors added in parallel, iteratively halving until the final sum is obtained.

6 Experimental Analysis

All experiments were carried out under the Ubuntu 22.04.4 operating system. The hardware configuration comprised an Intel Xeon Gold 6133 CPU operating at 2.5 GHz, 8 GB of system memory, and an NVIDIA GeForce RTX 4090 GPU. The implementations were developed in C/C++ and compiled with g++ 11.4.0. Input floating-point data were converted to signed two's complement binary representations of varying bit lengths and encrypted using TFHE. We analyzed the best arithmetic and activation function results on encrypted data in terms of computation time and deviation. Here, deviation was defined by designating the plaintext computation results as the reference baseline; multiple experimental repetitions were then conducted, and the results obtained under encryption were systematically compared against this baseline to quantify the precision loss introduced by homomorphic computation.

6.1 Addition

The Table 2 shows the computation time and corresponding error results for encrypted data addition in 16-bit, 24-bit, and 32-bit under sequential, CPU parallel, and GPU parallel execution modes. According to the data in the table, GPU parallel computing demonstrates a significant performance improvement compared to the sequential framework. Specifically, in 16-bit data addition, GPU provides a 6.13x speedup; in 24-bit data addition, the speedup ratio is 4.3x; and in 32-bit data addition, the GPU speedup ratio is 4.11x. This indicates that as the bit length increases, the acceleration effect of the GPU relative to sequential computation weakens, but it still significantly outperforms CPU parallel computation. Moreover, as the bit length increases, the deviation decreases.

Table 2. Runtime (sec) of n-bit addition

	16-bit	24-bit	32-bit
Sequence	3.66725	5.34827	6.92473
CPU Parallel	3.40982	5.10242	7.06476
GPU Parallel	1.25044	2.07041	2.78826
Deviation	0.000017	0	0

6.2 Subtraction

Subtraction operations, implemented via addition frameworks, show similar performance characteristics. CPU parallel execution time is comparable to sequential, while GPU parallel mode significantly outperforms both (Table 3). However, subtraction requires an extra step converting encrypted data to two's complement, where bitwise dependencies limit parallel efficiency across platforms. Thus, two's complement conversion does not benefit as much from parallel acceleration as addition. Similar to addition, deviation decreases as bit length increases.

Table 3. Runtime (sec) of n-bit substraction

	16-bit	24-bit	32-bit
Sequence	2.89669	3.83278	4.89501
CPU Parallel	2.41976	3.63841	4.99729
GPU Parallel	0.47291	0.89709	1.19232
Deviation	0.00031	0.00001	0

6.3 Mulplication

In sequential and CPU parallel modes, encrypted data multiplication is performed via sequential accumulation. In contrast, GPU parallel mode employs a tree-based addition algorithm. As shown in Table 4, both CPU and GPU parallel modes significantly accelerate computation compared to sequential execution, with GPU achieving the greatest speedups: 6.95× for 16-bit, 10.9× for 24-bit, and 12.56× for 32-bit multiplications. This demonstrates that the tree-based algorithm better exploits GPU parallelism, especially for larger bit widths and complex vector operations.

Table 4. Runtime (sec) of n-bit multiplication

	16-bit	24-bit	32-bit
Sequence	67.21596	159.58363	310.07035
CPU Parallel	26.01644	54.71292	92.90394
GPU Parallel	9.67703	14.72426	24.70621
Deviation	0.00013	0.00001	0

6.4 Sigmoid Function

From the Table 5, it can be observed that both CPU and GPU exhibit good acceleration performance when implementing this computational task. However, unlike arithmetic operations, the time difference between the CPU and GPU is not significant. This is mainly due to the computational bottleneck caused by the inability to parallelize the process of selecting the sign on the GPU platform. Nevertheless, the GPU still outperforms the CPU in terms of overall performance.

Table 5. Runtime (sec) of n-bit sigmoid operation

	16-bit	24-bit	32-bit
Sequence	46.96616	61.44928	82.93224
CPU Parallel	14.03765	19.13628	25.53334
GPU Parallel	12.43875	17.52377	23.43653

Figure 8 shows the computation deviation of the sigmoid function for input x, which remains below 0.01, indicating that the LUT size sufficiently meets precision requirements. Increasing the LUT could slightly reduce the deviation but would also increase computation time. It is worth noting that the typical applications of the sigmoid function in neural networks are not significantly affected by this level of deviation. This is because neural networks exhibit strong robustness to minor numerical perturbations; moreover, when the sigmoid function is employed in the output layer, such a deviation is insufficient to alter the predicted class decision, while in hidden layers, these minor deviations are further smoothed through subsequent nonlinear transformations and parameter updates. Consequently, the overall performance remains unaffected.

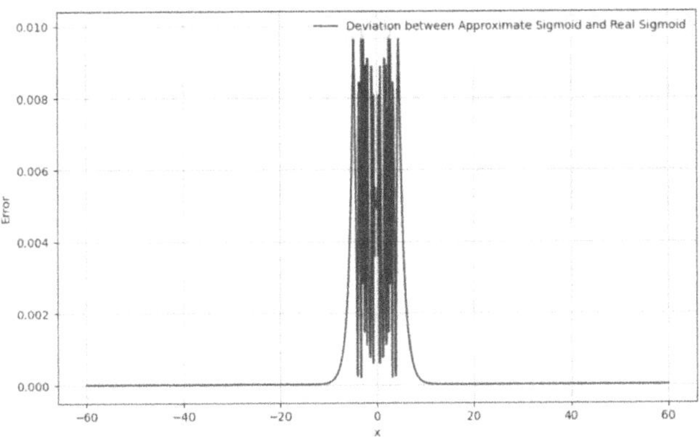

Fig. 8. Deviation of sigmoid function.

6.5 ReLU Function

As mentioned in the relevant section, the implementation of the ReLU function relies on the sign bit determination to choose the output value. As shown in Table 6, in GPU parallel mode, the computation time for the ReLU function is roughly equivalent to the time for a Boolean gate operation, and this time is largely independent of the increase in bit length, showing strong time stability.

Table 6. Runtime (sec) of n-bit Relu operation

	16-bit	24-bit	32-bit
Sequence	0.95413	1.33715	1.85709
CPU Parallel	0.07721	0.12341	0.19086
GPU Parallel	0.02789	0.03652	0.03719
Deviation	0	0	0

7 Conclusion

This paper focuses on the challenges of implementing activation functions and improving the computational efficiency of arithmetic operations in artificial neural networks under fully homomorphic encryption (FHE). An efficient implementation method and parallel acceleration strategies are proposed. Based on TFHE, we successfully design and implement the Sigmoid and ReLU activation functions using lookup table construction and sign-bit evaluation mechanisms, respectively. Moreover, compared to sequential implementations, this paper proposes two parallel acceleration strategies based on computational characteristics, which are specifically optimized for the implementation of activation functions and arithmetic operations on CPU and GPU platforms. Experimental results demonstrate that these parallel strategies achieve significant performance improvements across different hardware environments.

References

1. Bourse, F., Minelli, M., Minihold, M., Paillier, P.: Fast homomorphic evaluation of deep discretized neural networks. In: Shacham, H., Boldyreva, A. (eds.) CRYPTO 2018. LNCS, vol. 10993, pp. 483–512. Springer, Cham (2018). https://doi.org/10.1007/978-3-319-96878-0_17
2. Chillotti, I., Gama, N., Georgieva, M., Izabachène, M.: TFHE: fast fully homomorphic encryption library (2016). https://tfhe.github.io/tfhe/
3. Chou, E., Beal, J., Levy, D., Yeung, S., Haque, A., Fei-Fei, L.: Faster cryptonets: leveraging sparsity for real-world encrypted inference. arXiv preprint arXiv:1811.09953 (2018)

4. De Clercq, R., Roy, S.S., Vercauteren, F., Verbauwhede, I.: Efficient software implementation of ring-LWE encryption. In: 2015 Design, Automation & Test in Europe Conference & Exhibition (DATE), pp. 339–344. IEEE (2015)

5. Ducas, L., Micciancio, D.: Fhew: bootstrapping homomorphic encryption in less than a second. In: Annual International Conference on the Theory and Applications of Cryptographic Techniques, pp. 617–640. Springer (2015)

6. Frigo, M., Johnson, S.G.: Fftw: fastest fourier transform in the west. Astrophysics Source Code Library, pp. ascl–1201 (2012)

7. Garg, S., Gentry, C., Halevi, S.: Candidate multilinear maps from ideal lattices. In: Johansson, T., Nguyen, P.Q. (eds.) EUROCRYPT 2013. LNCS, vol. 7881, pp. 1–17. Springer, Heidelberg (2013). https://doi.org/10.1007/978-3-642-38348-9_1

8. Gentry, C.: Fully homomorphic encryption using ideal lattices. In: Proceedings of the Forty-First Annual ACM Symposium on Theory of Computing, pp. 169–178. No. 10 in STOC 2009. Association for Computing Machinery (2009)

9. Gilad-Bachrach, R., Dowlin, N., Laine, K., Lauter, K., Naehrig, M., Wernsing, J.: Cryptonets: applying neural networks to encrypted data with high throughput and accuracy. In: International Conference on Machine Learning, pp. 201–210. PMLR (2016)

10. Hesamifard, E., Takabi, H., Ghasemi, M.: Cryptodl: deep neural networks over encrypted data (2017)

11. Liu, Z., Seo, H., Roy, S.S., Großschädl, J., Kim, H., Verbauwhede, I.: Efficient ring-LWE encryption on 8-bit AVR processors. Cryptology ePrint Archive, Paper 2015/410 (2015)

12. Lomont, C.: Introduction to intel advanced vector extensions. Intel White Paper **23**, 1–21 (2011)

13. Lou, Q., Jiang, L.: She: a fast and accurate deep neural network for encrypted data. Adv. Neural Inf. Process. Syst. **32** (2019)

14. Mahesh, B., et al.: Machine learning algorithms-a review. Int. J. Sci. Res. (IJSR) **9**(1), 381–386 (2020)

15. Rivest, R.L., Adleman, L., Dertouzos, M.L.: On data banks and privacy homomorphisms found. Secure Comput. **4**(11), 169 (1978)

16. Rivest, R.L., Adleman, L., Dertouzos, M.L., et al.: On data banks and privacy homomorphisms. Found. Secure Comput. **4**(11), 169–180 (1978)

17. Shan, Z., Ren, K., Blanton, M., Wang, C.: Practical secure computation outsourcing: a survey. ACM Comput. Surv. (CSUR) **51**(2), 1–40 (2018)

18. Tang, J., Cui, Y., Li, Q., Ren, K., Liu, J., Buyya, R.: Ensuring security and privacy preservation for cloud data services. ACM Comput. Surv. (CSUR) **49**(1), 1–39 (2016)

19. Yang, Y., et al.: A comprehensive survey on secure outsourced computation and its applications. IEEE Access **7**, 159426–159465 (2019)

Enabling Secure and Efficient Authenticated Edge Inference for the Internet of Things

Wenjie Li and Jiageng Chen(✉)

School of Computer Science, Central China Normal University, 430079 Wuhan,
People's Republic of China
liwenjie595hey@gmail.com

Abstract. The Internet of Things (IoT) is fundamentally reshaping various industries by enabling efficient data collection and sharing. However, the prevalence of centralized cloud architectures introduces significant latency and high computational burdens, which are often incompatible with the real-time demands of resource-constrained edge devices. While edge computing provides a viable alternative, critical issues of data privacy and integrity remain, as a single data breach can lead to severe consequences. To address this dual challenge of security and efficiency, we introduce a novel edge-based computing framework. Our approach leverages secret-sharing-based Secure Multi-Party Computation alongside a terminal data source auditing mechanism to achieve secure model inference. We developed highly optimized protocols for Neural Network inference layers, significantly reducing communication overhead by integrating both arithmetic and boolean secret sharing. An innovative secure comparison protocol further minimizes server interactions, thereby boosting the efficiency of nonlinear computations. In addition, our framework incorporates a signature scheme to verify data legitimacy. Experimental evaluations on public datasets confirm that our method surpasses existing solutions in overall performance and security, validating its practical feasibility in modern IoT environments.

Keywords: Edge computing · Data source auditing · Secret sharing

1 Introduction

The widespread adoption of the Internet of Things (IoT) is driving a profound transformation across various industries. By interconnecting a diverse range of devices and application systems, IoT enables the efficient collection, transmission, and sharing of massive volumes of data [1]. This capability facilitates the optimization of resource allocation and addresses challenges in traditional centralized systems. Particularly in scenarios demanding real-time data processing, the integration of IoT technology allows for accurate, low-latency monitoring of key indicators, which significantly reduces operational burdens and enhances

© The Author(s), under exclusive license to Springer Nature Singapore Pte Ltd. 2026
L. Zhai et al. (Eds.): SocialSec 2025, LNCS 16327, pp. 60–77, 2026.
https://doi.org/10.1007/978-981-95-7027-0_4

overall system efficiency. IoT-based systems heavily rely on a variety of complex data processing algorithms, including models like Decision Trees(DT), Support Vector Machines (SVM), and various deep learning architectures [5]. However, most existing systems that adopt this approach utilize a centralized cloud architecture. This model introduces significant network transmission latency, which can compromise the timeliness and reliability of real-time applications. Moreover, such centralized systems are inherently susceptible to single points of failure, meaning a disruption to the central server could cripple the entire service. To address these challenges, fog and edge computing technologies have been integrated into distributed IoT systems. By performing data preprocessing, analysis, and storage closer to the data source, edge computing effectively shortens data transmission paths and reduces network latency. Concurrently, through dynamic task scheduling and load balancing mechanisms, edge nodes can more efficiently manage and process massive volumes of IoT data, meeting the stringent demands for low latency, high mobility, and real-time performance.

The rapid growth of distributed IoT environments has also exposed significant challenges in data privacy and security. Throughout the entire process—from data collection and transmission to cloud-based computation and service feedback—data leakage at any stage can lead to severe consequences. To tackle this issue, researchers have employed various privacy-preserving computation methods, including homomorphic encryption(HE) [11,14,19], secure multi-party computation(MPC) [9,13,17], and differential privacy(DP) [16,18], aiming to securely process sensitive data while safeguarding privacy. However, several issues still persist. On one hand, efficiency is a key factor for the applicability of a scheme in a given scenario, and low-overhead solutions can provide a strong case for their practicality. On the other hand, system providers must also ensure the authenticity and trustworthiness of the data they receive. Only by establishing robust data provenance and authentication mechanisms can the system perform accurate analyses and subsequent services based on legitimate and reliable information.

1.1   Related Work

Privacy-Preserving Machine Learning. A range of cryptographic and privacy-enhancing techniques have been developed to address the challenge of privacy preservation in collaborative data analysis. Homomorphic Encryption, for instance, allows computations to be performed directly on encrypted data, protecting confidentiality throughout the entire process. Zhang et al.'s scheme [19], based on Fully Homomorphic Encryption (FHE), secures data from third-party breaches, while the LPME scheme [14] focuses on reducing computational and communication overhead in edge computing. The PVSSVM scheme [11] further enables public verification of prediction results while maintaining data and model secrecy. However, HE's main limitation is its high computational overhead, which can be a barrier for real-time applications. Another approach, Differential Privacy, provides strong privacy guarantees by introducing statistical noise. The TFL scheme [18] uses a two-stage DP framework to balance privacy, accuracy, and convergence, while Ryu et al.'s work [16] shows DP can effectively counter reconstruction attacks. Nevertheless, DP often sacrifices model accuracy, as the added noise can degrade performance. In contrast, MPC allows multiple parties to jointly compute a function on private data without revealing their inputs, effectively solving the data silo problem. The LPCNN [9] and Sonic [13] schemes have demonstrated lightweight MPC services for secure neural network inference, and the PCNN scheme [17] accelerates offline pre-computation to achieve low latency and high throughput. Beyond these methods, other cryptographic primitives like Pseudorandom Functions (PRF) and Pseudorandom Permutations (PRP) have been used to build verifiable and secure systems tailored for specific needs, for example, the research achievements of Liang et al. [12] and Lei et al. [11].

Authenticated Secret-Sharing. The problem of ensuring input authenticity and data integrity is a critical security concern in collaborative computation. Early research on this topic often focused on specific scenarios. For instance, several works, including those by Baum et al. [4] and Zhang et al. [20], explored the use of garbled circuit (GC)-based techniques to enforce input validation in two-party settings. Expanding on this, Blanton and Jeong [6] developed MPC protocols that support authenticated inputs, though their methods were tailored to specific, non-generic MPC frameworks. More recently, the focus has shifted towards more general and efficient solutions. Aranha et al. [3] proposed an innovative method for input certification using linear secret sharing isomorphisms, demonstrating its superior performance over existing techniques. Building on this, Dutta et al. [8] introduced a generic and efficient compiler. This compiler can systematically transform any linear secret sharing-based MPC protocol into one with robust input authentication capabilities, offering a flexible and broadly applicable solution to the problem.

Table 1. Comparison of representative certification systems

Scheme	Techniques	F1	F2	F3	F4
PVSSVM[11]	SVM, HE	●	○	●	○
LPME[14]	DT, HE	●	●	○	○
LPCNN[9]	NN, SS	○	●	○	◐
SONIC[13]	NN, SS	●	○	○	◐
PCNN[17]	NN, SS	●	●	○	●
Ours	**NN, SS**	●	●	●	●

Note: F1: Model Privacy; F2: Edge Computing;
F3: Input Authentication;
F4: Low Computing and Communication Cost;
In F4: ●: Low; ◐: Medium; ○: High;

1.2   Our Contributions

In this paper, we propose a secure and efficient multi-party edge neural network inference scheme. By integrating secret sharing with threshold signature technology, our framework achieves both highly efficient computation protocols and robust authentication for MPC input data. As shown in Table 1, our specific contributions are as follows:

- We designed a secure comparison protocol using secret sharing, which enables an efficient neural network edge inference algorithm.
- The threshold signature scheme provides a mechanism for verifying the legitimacy of MPC input data before inference, thereby enhancing the overall security of the system.
- Both theoretical analysis and experimental results demonstrate that our scheme incurs the lowest computation and communication overhead compared to other state-of-the-art solutions, thus validating its practicality.

The remainder of this paper is structured as follows: Sect. 2 introduces the technical background of the proposed scheme. Section 3 outlines the scheme's architecture, security model, and design objectives. Section 4 describes the key protocols in detail. Section 5 presents a comprehensive overview of the scheme's overall workflow and algorithms. Section 6 provides a security analysis. Section 7 details the theoretical and experimental evaluations. Finally, Sect. 8 concludes the paper.

2   Preliminaries

Notations. In this paper, we define a finite ring $\mathbb{Z}_q = \{0, 1, 2, \ldots, q-1\}$, where q is a large integer (typically a prime number). We use capital letters and bold capital letters to denote vector spaces and matrices, respectively. Specifically, in this paper, the letter e denotes a bilinear pairing, λ is the security parameter, the symbol $\mathbb{F}$ denotes a finite field, and the symbol $\mathbb{G}$ denotes a group.

2.1   Additive Secret Sharing

Additive Secret Sharing(ASS) is a fundamental primitive in cryptography and MPC. Its core function is to split a secret into multiple shares and distribute them to different participants.

Sharing. The scheme operates over a finite field $\mathbb{F}_q$ or the ring $\mathbb{Z}_q$ with parties $P_1, \ldots, P_n$. To share a secret $s \in \mathbb{Z}_q$, we randomly select $n - 1$ shares, $s_1, \ldots, s_{n-1} \in \mathbb{Z}_q$. The final share s_n is then computed deterministically as:

$$s_n = s - \sum_{i=1}^{n-1} s_i \pmod{q}$$

Each share s_i is subsequently distributed to the corresponding party P_i.

Reconstruction. For secret reconstruction, all n parties reveal their respective shares s_i and sum them. The sum of these shares will precisely reconstruct the original secret:

$$s = \sum_{i=1}^{n} s_i \pmod{q}$$

Addition and Multiplication. If two secrets x, y are shared as $\{x_i\}_{i=1}^{n}$ and $\{y_i\}_{i=1}^{n}$, then each party's local computation of $x_i + y_i$ results in a share of $x + y$, denoted as $\{z_i\}_{i=1}^{n}$. For any public constant c, each party's local computation of $c \cdot x_i$ results in a share of cx. Multiplication is a non-linear operation that typically requires a Beaver triple to facilitate pre-processing and online separation. In the offline phase, a set of random shared triples (u, v, w) satisfying $w = u \cdot v$ are pre-generated. In the online phase, each party locally computes open values $e = x - u$ and $f = y - v$. These values are then used to reconstruct the product using the following equation:

$$xy = w + e \cdot v + f \cdot u + e \cdot f$$

2.2   Threshold Signature

A Threshold Signature is a cryptographic primitive that distributes the generation, storage, and usage rights of a private key among a group of participants, thereby enabling decentralized control over the signing process. The core property of such a scheme is that a valid signature on a message m can only be produced when a predefined threshold of at least t participants (where $1 < t \leq n$, and n is the total number of participants) cooperate. Within the MPC paradigm, the signing process can be broken down into three key phases [3]:

Distributed Key Generation. This is a protocol that allows n participants $\{P_1, \ldots, P_n\}$ to jointly generate a public key pk and for each participant P_i to receive a unique private key share sk_i. This process can be defined as $pk = f(sk_1, \ldots, sk_n)$, where f is a mapping function, and the complete private key sk is never held by any single participant.

Distributed Signing Protocol. When a signature on a specific message m is required, at least t participants (e.g., a subset $\mathcal{S} \subseteq \{P_1, \ldots, P_n\}$ with $|\mathcal{S}| \geq t$) use their respective private key shares $\{sk_i\}_{i \in \mathcal{S}}$ as input to an MPC protocol. This protocol is designed to collaboratively produce a single, valid digital signature σ without reconstructing the full private key. This process can be abstracted as:

$$\sigma = \text{Sign}(m, \{sk_i\}_{i \in \mathcal{S}})$$

Standard Signature Verification. The final signature σ is externally indistinguishable from a standard signature and can be verified by any entity holding the corresponding public key pk. The verification process is expressed as:

$$\text{Verify}(m, \sigma, pk) \rightarrow \{\text{True}, \text{False}\}$$

2.3 Neural Network Structure

A Convolutional Neural Network (CNN) is a deep learning architecture specifically designed for processing image data. It excels at computer vision tasks like image classification and object detection by using a series of ordered layers to progressively extract features, from low-level details like edges to high-level semantic information. A typical CNN is composed of convolutional, activation, pooling, and fully connected layers.

Convolutional Layer. The convolutional layer applies a locally linear filter with a learnable convolutional kernel $W \in \mathbb{R}^{C_{out} \times C_{in} \times K_h \times K_w}$ to the input tensor $X \in \mathbb{R}^{C_{in} \times H \times W}$. The output for the k-th channel at spatial location (i, j) is:

$$Y_{k,i,j} = \sum_{c=1}^{C_{in}} \sum_{u=1}^{K_h} \sum_{v=1}^{K_w} W_{k,c,u,v} X_{c,i+u-1,j+v-1} + b_k,$$

It can be combined with operations such as stride, padding, and batch normalization to control the output dimensions and numerical distribution.

Activation Layer. The activation layer applies a non-linear function $\phi : \mathbb{R} \to \mathbb{R}$ to the elements of the linear mapping's output, thereby enhancing the network's representational capacity. Common activation functions include Rectified Linear Unit (ReLU), hyperbolic tangent (tanh), and Sigmoid. These operations are applied element-wise to the input tensor.

Pooling Layer. The pooling layer performs down-sampling on the input with a predefined window R and stride s. Common operators are max pooling and average pooling. The output for channel c at location (i, j) is:

$$Y_{c,i,j} = \max_{(u,v) \in R} X_{c,s_i+u,s_j+v} \quad \text{or} \quad Y_{c,i,j} = \frac{1}{|R|} \sum_{(u,v) \in R} X_{c,s_i+u,s_j+v}.$$

Fully-Connected Layer. The fully-connected layer flattens the input into a vector $x \in \mathbb{R}^d$ and produces an output vector $y \in \mathbb{R}^m$ through an affine transformation:

$$y = Wx + b, \quad W \in \mathbb{R}^{m \times d}, \quad b \in \mathbb{R}^m.$$

3 Secure Inference Framework

3.1 Framework Overview

As illustrated in Fig. 1, we consider a typical Internet of Things (IoT) scenario. A service provider P holds a pre-trained model to offer an external service. The provider outsources this model (step ①) to n edge servers, $S_1, \ldots, S_n$, which

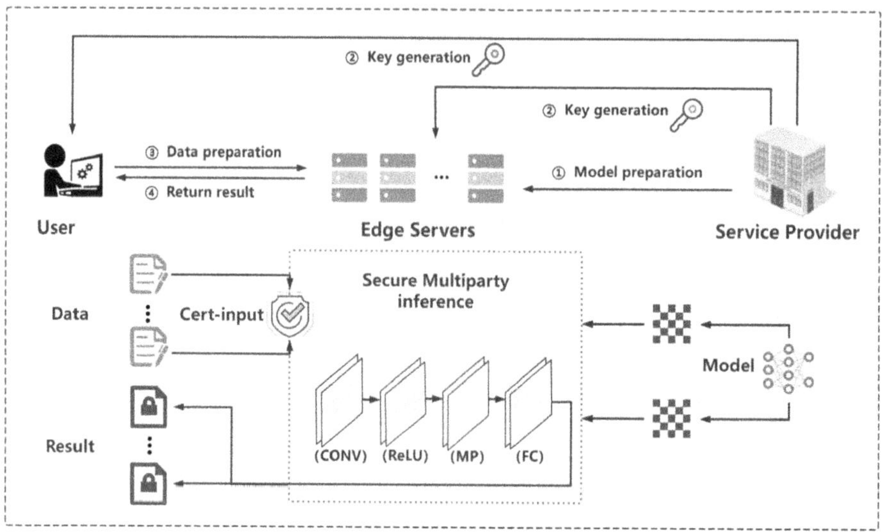

Fig. 1. The proposed secure edge inference scheme workflow.

are located in close proximity to the end users. As the primary computational resources, each server S_i receives a share of the model for local inference. Concurrently, the service provider generates a public-private key pair for signatures and sends the private key to the user (step ②). The user U transmits their data shares (step ③) to the edge servers. To ensure the authenticity of the user's input, a corresponding signature share is attached to each data share for input authentication. Upon successful signature verification, the user can access the desired service.

To ensure privacy throughout the entire inference process, both the model parameters and the user's data are fragmented using secret sharing and distributed among each S_i. All servers then collaboratively execute a secure inference protocol, where each layer of the neural network (NN) has a corresponding secure computation sub-protocol. After the inference is complete, the final local computation results from each S_i are returned to the user (step ④), who then reconstructs them to obtain the final, complete result.

3.2 Threat Model

In this protocol, the various entities possess the following capabilities and are subject to the following security assumptions:

- **Service Provider**(P): The service provider acts as the holder of the model and the signing key. As a trusted entity, P not only outsources the computation to the edge servers S, but also provides the necessary random numbers and Beaver triples for the secure computation protocols during the online phase.

- **Edge Servers(S)**: The edge servers are assumed to be honest-but-curious entities, typically provided by a third-party corporation. Throughout the entire service process, they are not expected to gain any information beyond their own computed results and publicly available parameters. This includes sensitive information such as the model, the signing private key, and user data.
- **User(U)**: The user is also considered an honest-but-curious entity. To prove they are a legitimate user and obtain the service, U must submit their data along with a corresponding signature, which is distributed to the servers for verification.
- **External Attacker(A)**: We assume the existence of an external attacker A. This attacker may attempt to obtain partial information to infer sensitive data, such as the model, user data, and the final results. The attacker may also try to forge signatures or otherwise compromise the integrity of the protocol.

3.3 Security Goals

Based on the potential threats identified, the proposed scheme is designed to achieve the following security objectives:

- **Privacy:** The confidentiality of all sensitive data, including model parameters, user inputs, and the final inference results, must be preserved against unauthorized disclosure.
- **Multi-party Input Validity:** The scheme must ensure that only legitimate, key-holding users can generate a signature for data verification, thus preventing unauthorized users from using the model.
- **Efficiency:** The overall protocol should exhibit low computational and communication overhead to demonstrate its practical viability and scalability.

4 Building Blocks

4.1 Certificated Inputs

In many real-world applications, the authenticity of data sources is a critical concern. For instance, in finance or healthcare, malicious inputs can disrupt service quality, an issue not addressed by traditional MPC security definitions. Our Source Authentication Protocol (Π_{SAuth}) draws upon the ideas of multi-party PS signatures [3, 15] and is designed to verify the authenticity of user input data(See Fig. 2).

Let's assume a user dataset M. Before a user U provides M to a model, they must attach a corresponding signature to prove the data's authenticity. Assuming the dataset M is secret-shared into shares $m_1, \ldots, m_n$, as shown in the figure, the protocol is divided into three phases: key generation, signing, and verification. Keys are distributed by the service provider P, who is responsible for selecting the secret-shared private key sk and computing the public key pk

via a mapping function. P then publishes the public key and securely distributes the private key to the users. In the signing phase, U uses their shares of sk and their data shares $[m_i]$ to generate a corresponding secret-shared signature Σ. The verification process is jointly completed by n edge servers S, who use the public key and bilinear pairing operations to compute both $[\alpha]_{\mathbb{G}_T}$ and $[\beta]_{\mathbb{G}_T}$, and then jointly check if they are equal. If they are equal, the signature is valid and the input data is authenticated as genuine; otherwise, the data is considered invalid.

Key Generation(Π_{KeyGen}):

- Input: $(p, \mathbb{G}_1, \mathbb{G}_2, \mathbb{G}_T, e)$, n.
- Output: pk, sk.
- Compute:
  - P invokes the $\mathcal{F}_{Coin}(\mathbb{G}_2)$ protocol to obtain R, and invokes the $\mathcal{F}_{Rand}(\mathbb{F})$ protocol a total of $n+1$ times to obtain $[s], [v_1], \ldots, [v_n]$.
  - Let $\phi_2 : \mathbb{F} \to \mathbb{G}_2$ be a mapping function defined by $\phi_2 : s \mapsto sR$.
  - P uses ϕ_2 to compute $S = \phi_2(s) = sR$ and $V_i = \phi_2(v_i) = v_i R$ for $i = 1, \ldots, n$.
  - P publishes the public key $pk = (R, V_1, \ldots, V_n, S)$ to all parties.
  - P securely distributes the secret key $sk = ([s], [v_1], \ldots, [v_n])$ to U.

Signing Phase(Π_{Sign}):

- Input: $sk = ([s], [v_1], \ldots, [v_n])$, $m = ([m_1], \ldots, [m_n])$.
- Output: $[\Sigma]$.
- Compute:
  - U Randomly generate $\sigma_1 \in \mathbb{G}_1$ such that $\sigma_1 \neq 0$.
  - $[y] \leftarrow \mathcal{F}_{Dot}(([v_i]_{i=1}^n)^T, ([m_i]_{i=1}^n)^T)$.
  - $[t] \leftarrow [s] + [y]$.
  - $[\sigma_2] \leftarrow \mathcal{F}_{Mul}([t], \sigma_1)$.
  - Let $[\Sigma] = (\sigma_1, [\sigma_2])$.(where $\mathcal{F}_{Dot}$ computes the dot product, and $\mathcal{F}_{Mul}$ computes the multiplication of a secret-shared scalar with a point on the elliptic curve.)

Verification(Π_{Verify}):

- Input: $[\Sigma] = (\sigma_1, [\sigma_2])$, pk, $m = ([m_1], \ldots, [m_n])$
- Output: $result$
- Compute:
  - $[\alpha]_{\mathbb{G}_T} \leftarrow e([\sigma_2], S)$.
  - $[\beta]_{\mathbb{G}_T} \leftarrow e(\sigma_1, R + \sum_{i=1}^n [m_i] V_i)$.
  - Check if $[\alpha]_{\mathbb{G}_T}$ and $[\beta]_{\mathbb{G}_T}$ are equal. If they are equal, then $result = 1$; otherwise, $result = 0$.

Fig. 2. Sub-protocols for the Source Authentication Protocol Π_{SAuth}.

4.2 Secure Computation Functions

Secure Comparison Protocol. In MPC, the computational and communication overhead from non-linear operations is a major bottleneck. Non-linear computations, such as activation functions and pooling functions in neural networks, exacerbate this issue. For instance, using a ReLU activation function or a max-pooling algorithm requires pairwise comparisons of elements, while the exponential calculations for a sigmoid activation function introduce immense overhead. To address these challenges, we first propose a novel n-party secure comparison protocol.

As shown in Fig. 3, the core idea of the secure comparison protocol (Π_{Comp}) is to transform the comparison of two secret-shared values, $[x]$ and $[y]$, into a sign determination of an intermediate variable c. The protocol first computes $c = 2([x] - [y]) + 1$. By this definition, c is positive when $[x] \geq [y]$ and negative when $[x] < [y]$. To perform this sign determination without revealing the original data, the protocol employs a random masking technique. Specifically, each party uses a secret share of a random non-zero mask r and its most significant bit (MSB) to blind the computation of c. Finally, through local XOR operations, the parties securely obtain a masked share of the MSB of c, denoted as $[[c_{MSB}]]_i$. This share directly reflects the sign of c and, consequently, determines the size relationship between $[x]$ and $[y]$ while preserving privacy.

Offline Phase:

- P randomly generates $r \in \mathbb{Z}_{2^{l_x}}$ ($r \neq 0$), and calculates r_{MSB}.
- P calculates $[r]_i \leftarrow Share_A(r)$, $[[r_{MSB}]]_i \leftarrow Share_B(r_{MSB})$, and sends $[r]_i, [r_{MSB}]_i$ to S_i.

Online Phase:

- S_i holds $[x]_i, [y]_i \in \mathbb{Z}_{2^l}$, and calculates $[c]_i \leftarrow 2([x]_i - [y]_i) + 1$.
- S_i calculates $[h]_i \leftarrow \Pi_{Mul}([c]_i, [r]_i)$.
- S_i sends $[h]_i$ to S_{i+1} to construct h.
- S_i calculates $[[h_{MSB}]]_i \leftarrow Share_B(h_{MSB})$.
- S_i calculates $[[c_{MSB}]]_i \leftarrow [[h_{MSB}]]_i \oplus [[r_{MSB}]]_i$.
- S_i gets $[z]_i \leftarrow \Pi_{B2A}([[c_{MSB}]]_i)$.

Fig. 3. Secure Comparison Protocol Π_{Comp}.

5 Secure NN Inference Scheme

The process of a user performing inference with an outsourced model on a service provider's platform commences with the authentication of input data. Following this, the authenticated data is directed to the neural network model residing on the edge server to undergo inference. Throughout the entire computation, the inputs and outputs of the MPC are processed over the ring $\mathbb{Z}_{2^L}$. The data propagates through the model's layers in sequence: convolutional, activation, pooling, and fully connected. Ultimately, the final inference result is derived by reconstructing the shares of the computed output.

5.1 Input Authentication Before Inference

We leverage the input authentication protocol introduced in Sect. 4 to complete the authentication process, as depicted in the figure. First, P generates a key pair, a public key pk and a secret key sk, for signing. P then transmits sk to the U and publishes pk. Subsequently, U executes the signing algorithm to obtain the signature shares $[\Sigma]$ corresponding to the data shares, which are then sent to the respective servers S_i. Each S_i executes a verification algorithm to determine the validity of the signature shares. Upon completion of the input authentication process, the data shares are then directed into the inference model.

5.2 Linear Computation

In the inference phase of a neural network, linear computations are primarily concentrated in the convolutional and fully connected layers, with multiplication-accumulation operations as the core computation. For example, in a convolutional layer, a filter performs element-wise multiplication with the input data, and the results are then summed to produce a single output value. Similarly, in a fully connected layer, each element of the input vector is multiplied by the corresponding column of the weight matrix, and all products are summed to get the output. Therefore, the main computations for both layers are a combination of multiplication and addition.

- **Convolutional Layer:** The output feature map $[y_i]$ of a convolutional operation is obtained by performing a series of secure multiplication and summation operations on the secret-shared input feature map $[x_i]$ and the secret-shared convolutional kernel $[P_i]$. This process can be formally summarized as:

$$[y_i] \leftarrow \sum_i \mathrm{Mult}([x_i], [P_i])$$

  At the protocol level, this formula represents an aggregation of multiple secure multiplication and addition protocols, ensuring that the entire computation is performed without ever revealing the underlying data.
- **Fully Connected Layer:** The computation of a fully connected layer involves the secure matrix multiplication of the secret-shared input vector $[x]$ and the secret-shared weight matrix $[W]$. When executed on secret-shared data, this matrix multiplication decomposes into a series of more fundamental operations. Specifically, each component $[y_j]$ of the output vector is obtained by a secure inner product, or a series of multiplications and summations,

between the input vector $[x]$ and the corresponding row of the weight matrix $[W]$. This can be expressed as:

$$[y_j] \leftarrow \sum_i \text{Mult}([W_{ji}], [x_i])$$

Input Authentication:

- For original data D, U calculates $[D_i] \leftarrow Share_{Add}(D)$.
- $\Sigma_i \leftarrow \Pi_{Sign}([D_i], sk)$.
- U sends $([D_i], \Sigma_i)$ to the S_i.
- S_i runs $\Pi_{Verify}([D_i], [\Sigma_i])$ to verify if $[D_i]$ is valid.

Convolutional Layer:

- **Online Phase:**
    - S_i calculates $[y_i] \leftarrow [x_i] \times [P_i] + [b_i]$.

Activate Layer:

- **Offline Phase:**
    - P generates $[h_i] \leftarrow Share_{Add}(0)$ and sends to S_i.
- **Online Phase:**
    - S_i calculates $[f_i] \leftarrow \Pi_{Comp}([x_i], [h_i])$.
    - S_i calculates $[y_i] \leftarrow [h_i] + ([x_i] - [h_i]) \cdot (1 - [f_i])$.

Pooling Layer:

- **Online Phase:**
    - For each feature share $X_{v \times v}$, S_i inputs $[x_i]_j^k$ $(k \in [1, d], j \in [0, v^2 - 1])$.
    - S_i lets $[c_i] = [x_i]_0^k$.
    - **for** $j = 1, \ldots, v^2 - 1$
    - S_i calculates $[f_i] \leftarrow \Pi_{Comp}([x_i]_j^k, [c_i])$.
    - S_i calculates $[n_i] \leftarrow [x_i]_j^k + ([c_i] - [x_i]_j^k) \cdot (1 - [f_i])$.
    - **end for**
    - S_i outputs $[y_i]^k = [n_i]$.

Fully Connected Layer:

- **Online Phase:**
    - For input vector $[x_i']$, S_i calculates $[y_i] \leftarrow [W] \cdot [x_i'] + b_i'$.

Fig. 4. Overall Flowchart of the Secure Neural Network Inference Algorithm($SNIA$).

5.3   Non-linear Computation

The activation function layer and pooling layer account for the main portion of nonlinear computations. Here, we focus on the Rectified Linear Unit (ReLU) and Max Pooling functions, as they are commonly used in neural networks.

- **ReLU Function**: The computation formula for the ReLU function is:

$$f(x) = \max(0, x)$$

  The core idea is to compare two numbers and output a non-negative result. This simple, piecewise linear function allows neural networks to effectively avoid the vanishing gradient problem during training, thereby accelerating convergence. The primary operations in the ReLU function are comparison and output selection. Output selection can be implemented using the concept of a multiplexer, i.e., $y = I_0 \cdot t + I_1 \cdot (1 - t)$, to compute and output the correct result. As shown in the figure, server S_i receives inputs $[x_i]$ and $[h_i]$ (which is the secret share of 0) for comparison. When $[x_i] > [h_i]$ (i.e., $x > 0$), the Π_{Comp} protocol computes the comparison result $[f_i]$ whose plaintext value is 0. According to the formula $[y_i] \leftarrow [h_i] + ([x_i] - [h_i]) \cdot (1 - [f_i])$, it ultimately selects and outputs $[x_i]$. When $[x_i] \leq [h_i]$ (i.e., $x \leq 0$), the plaintext value of $[f_i]$ is 1, ultimately selecting and outputting $[h_i]$.
- **Max Pooling Function**: Max Pooling is a down-sampling operation used to compress the spatial dimensions of a feature map. Within a predefined sliding window, it selects the maximum value as the output, which not only reduces the data volume but also retains the most important features. Assuming the sliding window size is $k \times k$, the input feature map size is $v \times v$, and the stride is d. Max Pooling selects the maximum value within the sliding window, then slides by a stride of d, continuing the maximum value selection until the entire feature map has been traversed. Therefore, its core computation is still a comparison algorithm. Similarly, within each new sliding window, edge servers collaboratively execute a secure cyclic comparison algorithm, performing pairwise comparisons on the elements within the window and outputting the maximum value of the window. The specific protocol is shown in the Fig. 4.

6   Security Analysis

This section formally proves the security of our proposed scheme under the Universal Composability (UC) framework [7]. The UC model defines security by comparing a protocol's real-world execution against an abstract ideal functionality. A protocol is secure if a computationally bounded adversary can't distinguish between these two worlds. A protocol Π is UC-secure if a probabilistic polynomial-time (PPT) adversary $\mathcal{A}$ cannot computationally distinguish interaction with the real protocol from interaction with a simulator $\mathcal{S}$ in an ideal world. We establish the security of our scheme by proving the security of its constituent protocols and components:

- **Lemma 1:** If all sub-protocols of a protocol are perfectly simulatable, then the protocol itself is perfectly simulatable.
- **Lemma 2:** If a random element r is uniformly distributed on $\mathbb{Z}_{2^l}$ and independent from $x \in \mathbb{Z}_{2^l}$, then $x \pm r$ and $x \cdot r$ are also random and independent from x.
- **Lemma 3:** The protocols for addition (Π_{Add}), multiplication (Π_{Mul}), and bit-to-arithmetic conversion (Π_{B2A}) are secure [10].
- **Lemma 4:** The input authentication protocol (Π_{SAuth}) in [3] is secure.

Theorem 1. *In the honest-but-curious model, Π_{Comp} is secure.*

Proof. We construct a simulator $\mathcal{S}$ for an adversary $\mathcal{A}$ corrupting a party ES_i. The adversary's view consists of various shares. Based on Lemma 2, all shared values (e.g., $[u]_i$, $[s]_i$, $[z]_i$) are computationally indistinguishable from random values. Since the simulator can generate random shares that match the real view, the adversary cannot distinguish the two.

Theorem 2. *In the honest-but-curious model, the Secure Neural Network Inference Algorithm (SNIA) is secure.*

Proof. This algorithm is composed of secure sub-protocols (proven by Theorem 1 and Lemma 3) and local, non-interactive computations. Since all sensitive data is processed either locally or through these secure sub-protocols, and the composition method introduces no new vulnerabilities, the overall algorithm is secure by Lemma 1.

Theorem 3. *The entire scheme is secure.*

Proof. The overall security is proven by constructing a PPT simulator $\mathcal{S}$ for the ideal functionality.

- Input Phase: A user's raw data is split into random shares. The simulator generates simulated, indistinguishable shares for the adversary. The adversary cannot reconstruct the original data, and the data source is authenticated via the protocol (Π_{SAuth}) from Lemma 4.
- Computation Phase: The collaborative inference process, which includes layers like Convolution, ReLU, and Max pooling, is executed using secure sub-protocols (from Theorem 2). Since the adversary cannot compromise enough parties to exceed the security threshold for secret reconstruction, they cannot infer any information from the intermediate data.
- Output Phase: The final output shares are also computationally indistinguishable from the simulated shares, preventing the adversary from learning the result.

Since the scheme is built on cryptographically secure primitives and its composition method is sound, the simulator can successfully replicate all views observed by the adversary. This substantiates the scheme's security, protecting data privacy and source authenticity against a PPT adversary.

7   Theoretical Analysis and Experiment

To evaluate the overall effectiveness of the proposed secure inference scheme, we conducted a series of experiments for demonstration, including both theoretical and empirical analyses.

7.1   Theoretical Analysis

In order to conduct a fair and focused theoretical analysis, we compare our proposed scheme with three technically similar schemes. Our primary focus is on the number of interaction rounds and the communication complexity of their core modules. To ensure a fair comparison, all analyses are performed in a two-party secure computation setting. The communication cost is measured by the data length l transmitted in each round. Specifically, for the pooling layer, the communication cost is also related to the number of elements h in the pooling window.

Table 2. Comparison of different schemes' complexity

Scheme	ReLU		Max pooling	
	Rounds	Comm.	Rounds	Comm.
SONIC [13]	$2 + log_2 l$	$8l + 4log_2 l$	$(2 + log_2 l)h + 2$	$(8l + 4log_2 l)h + 8l$
LPCNN [9]	l	$10l - 4$	$l \cdot log_2 h$	$(10l - 4)h$
PCNN [17]	4	$13l$	$4log_2 h$	$13l \cdot h$
Ours	4	$6l$	$4log_2 h$	$6l \cdot h$

During the secure inference process, the efficiency of non-linear layers, such as activation and pooling functions, is critical to overall performance and is therefore the main focus of our analysis. Our proposed secure comparison protocol requires a total of four interaction rounds with a corresponding communication cost of $6l$, which primarily comes from the reconstruction of intermediate results. Both the ReLU and Max pooling functions are built upon this secure comparison protocol. The detailed complexities of these two core modules are listed in Table 2. The results show that our ReLU and Max-Pooling functions achieve a constant number of communication rounds and the lowest communication cost compared to the other three schemes. In contrast to other schemes where the number of communication rounds is positively correlated with l, our non-linear functions are theoretically more efficient. In a multi-party setting, the benefits of our constant number of communication rounds become even more pronounced as the number of participants increases.

7.2   Experimental Results and Analysis

We conducted a series of programming experiments to demonstrate the practicality of our proposed scheme in IoT scenarios. The experimental environment was set up on a personal computer with the following hardware specifications: an Intel(R) Core(TM) i5-8265U CPU @ 1.60GHz, 8.00 GB of RAM, and running the Ubuntu-20.04 operating system. For framework validation, we implemented an end-to-end secret-shared CNN inference system that includes input authentication. The implementation utilized the CrypTen library and the RELIC cryptography toolkit [2]. To effectively simulate an edge computing communication environment, we deployed multiple virtual edge server nodes on a single machine. The computational parameters for our secure multi-party computation were configured with a large ring size $L = 64$ for fixed-point arithmetic, a data element bit length of $l_x = 32$, and a fixed-point conversion factor of $l_d = 16$. Our input authentication mechanism, which provides a 128-bit security level, is based on a threshold signature scheme using the BLS12-381 curve.

Table 3. Performance Evaluation of Different Stages

Stages	Comp. Cost	Comm. Cost
Signature	0.0048(s)	0.04(KB)
Verification	0.0021(s)	0.03(KB)
Inference	1.0527(s)	8.2547(MB)

We evaluated our scheme with two parties on a LeNet-5 Convolutional Neural Network, which comprises two convolutional layers and one fully connected layer, with an input image size of $28{\times}28$ pixels. Table 3 shows the experimental results, covering the entire process from input authentication to final inference. As demonstrated, the computation cost for inferring a single sample is only 1.0527 s, with a communication cost of just 8.2547MB. Within this total, the overhead for signature generation and verification is negligible, almost insignificant compared to the overall cost. Furthermore, our model maintains the same accuracy as its plaintext counterpart while achieving high efficiency. These experimental results validate our preceding theoretical analysis. Therefore, our proposed secure neural network inference framework with input authentication not only provides excellent efficiency but also enhances overall security.

8   Conclusion

This paper presents a novel secure neural network inference scheme tailored for existing outsourced inference frameworks in the Internet of Things (IoT). Our scheme leverages multi-party secure computation based on secret sharing to enable secure inference among multiple parties. To enhance efficiency, we propose a more efficient secure comparison protocol. Furthermore, to ensure the authenticity of the input data, we integrate a threshold signature scheme to provide an authentication function. Both theoretical and experimental results demonstrate the superiority and practicality of our proposed scheme. In future work, we will further optimize the security models and privacy-preserving computation techniques, and explore the integration of other privacy-enhancing technologies.

Disclosure of Interests. The authors declare that they have no known competing financial interests or personal relationships that could have appeared to influence the work reported in this paper.

References

1. Allioui, H., Mourdi, Y.: Exploring the full potentials of IOT for better financial growth and stability: a comprehensive survey. Sensors **23**(19), 8015 (2023)
2. Aranha, D.F.: Relic is an efficient library for cryptography. http://code.google.com/p/relic-toolkit/ (2020)
3. Aranha, D.F., Dalskov, A., Escudero, D., Orlandi, C.: Improved Threshold Signatures, Proactive Secret Sharing, and Input Certification from LSS Isomorphisms. In: Longa, P., Ràfols, C. (eds.) LATINCRYPT 2021. LNCS, vol. 12912, pp. 382–404. Springer, Cham (2021). https://doi.org/10.1007/978-3-030-88238-9_19
4. Baum, C.: On garbling schemes with and without privacy. In: International Conference on Security and Cryptography for Networks, pp. 468–485. Springer (2016)
5. Bian, J., et al.: Machine learning in real-time internet of things (IOT) systems: a survey. IEEE Internet Things J. **9**(11), 8364–8386 (2022)
6. Blanton, M., Jeong, M.: Improved signature schemes for secure multi-party computation with certified inputs. In: European Symposium on Research in Computer Security, pp. 438–460. Springer (2018)
7. Canetti, R.: Universally composable security: a new paradigm for cryptographic protocols. In: Proceedings 42nd IEEE Symposium on Foundations of Computer Science, pp. 136–145. IEEE (2001)
8. Dutta, M., Ganesh, C., Patranabis, S., Singh, N.: Compute, but verify: efficient multiparty computation over authenticated inputs. In: International Conference on the Theory and Application of Cryptology and Information Security, pp. 133–166. Springer (2024)
9. Huang, K., Liu, X., Fu, S., Guo, D., Xu, M.: A lightweight privacy-preserving CNN feature extraction framework for mobile sensing. IEEE Trans. Dependable Secure Comput. **18**(3), 1441–1455 (2019)
10. Knott, B., et al.: Crypten: secure multi-party computation meets machine learning. Adv. Neural. Inf. Process. Syst. **34**, 4961–4973 (2021)
11. Lei, D., et al.: Publicly verifiable and secure SVM classification for cloud-based health monitoring services. IEEE Internet Things J. **11**(6), 9829–9842 (2023)
12. Liang, J., Qin, Z., Xue, L., Lin, X., Shen, X.: Verifiable and secure SVM classification for cloud-based health monitoring services. IEEE Internet Things J. **8**(23), 17029–17042 (2021)
13. Liu, X., Zheng, Y., Yuan, X., Yi, X.: Securely outsourcing neural network inference to the cloud with lightweight techniques. IEEE Trans. Dependable Secure Comput. **20**(1), 620–636 (2022)

14. Ma, Z., et al.: Lightweight privacy-preserving medical diagnosis in edge computing. IEEE Trans. Serv. Comput. **15**(3), 1606–1618 (2020)
15. Pointcheval, D., Sanders, O.: Short Randomizable Signatures. In: Sako, K. (ed.) CT-RSA 2016. LNCS, vol. 9610, pp. 111–126. Springer, Cham (2016). https://doi.org/10.1007/978-3-319-29485-8_7
16. Ryu, J., et al.: Can differential privacy practically protect collaborative deep learning inference for IOT? Wireless Netw. **30**(6), 4713–4733 (2024)
17. Wang, J., et al.: PCNN CEC: efficient and privacy-preserving convolutional neural network inference based on cloud-edge-client collaboration. IEEE Trans. Netw. Sci. Eng. **10**(5), 2906–2923 (2022)
18. Zhang, L.: A two-stage differential privacy scheme for federated learning based on edge intelligence. IEEE J. Biomed. Health Inform. **28**(6), 3349–3360 (2023)
19. Zhang, L., et al.: An efficient FHE-enabled secure cloud-edge computing architecture for IOMT data protection with its application to pandemic modeling. IEEE Internet Things J. **11**(9), 15272–15284 (2023)
20. Zhang, Y., Blanton, M., Bayatbabolghani, F.: Enforcing input correctness via certification in garbled circuit evaluation. In: European Symposium on Research in Computer Security, pp. 552–569. Springer (2017)

New Insights into Effects of Fluctuations on Dynamical Degradation of Digital Chaos

Kai Lin[1,2], Xiangguang Sun[3] ⓘ, Jun Zheng[3(✉)] ⓘ, and Hanping Hu[1,3,4] ⓘ

[1] School of Artificial Intelligence and Automation, Huazhong University of Science and Technology, Wuhan, China
[2] Xiangyang Daan Automobile Test Center Corporation Limited, Xiangyang, China
[3] School of Cyberspace Security, Huazhong University of Science and Technology, Wuhan, China
zhengj@hust.edu.cn
[4] Wuhan Institute of Cyberspace Security Strategy, Wuhan, China

Abstract. To realize a chaotic system in digital world always leads a dynamical degradation of chaotic characteristics. Digital chaotic systems are increasingly utilized in modern cloud computing security architectures and big data analytics frameworks where precision degradation in large-scale, distributed, and heterogeneous environments can severely affect reliability. This paper focuses on the effects of fluctuations on digital chaotic systems and dynamical degradation related issues of those systems. A scheme based on hybrid structure is proposed for the solution to chaos degradation, in which the continuous chaotic system provides intrinsic random fluctuation. Further, the relationship between scaling of intrinsic randomness and chaos with different structure is studied. Symbolic dynamics is applied to rigorously prove that a class of digital systems is chaotic in the presence of fluctuations and to show that scaling behavior of fluctuations determines topological structure of chaos. Specifically, there are two critical fluctuation amplitudes at which topological structure of chaos essentially changes. Moreover, simulation studies are conducted to verify the theoretical results and further compare the effects of different random fluctuations on chaos degradation. These findings contribute to chaos-preserving mechanism designs applicable to precision-sensitive large-scale computing scenarios.

Keywords: Digital Chaotic System · Dynamical Degradation · Fluctuations · Scaling Behavior · Symbolic Dynamics

1 Introduction

Opening with Lorenz's studies of the weather prediction in meteorology, chaos theory took shape. Since then, chaos has aroused widespread continuing interest in mathematics [1], physics [2], information science [3] and so on. This is so because chaotic system has well properties like sensitivity to initial condition, inner randomness, infinite period and long-term unpredictability. However, the precision-limited effect is the toughest hurdle for practical applications of chaos [4–6]. Under such influence, the inner randomness is gone, hence chaotic system degenerates and becomes useless.

L. Zhai et al. (Eds.): SocialSec 2025, LNCS 16327, pp. 78–95, 2026.
https://doi.org/10.1007/978-981-95-7027-0_5

To address this problem, researchers have proposed different approaches to counteract the dynamical degradation of digital chaotic system based on different considerations. In general, they can be divided into the following three categories. (1) Using higher computing precision [7, 8], which is an eclectic remedy and cannot solve the underlying problem. (2) Cascading [9, 10] or switching [11, 12] multiple chaotic systems is an alternative research perspective under which new chaotic systems which are less affected by the precision-limited effect at best are constructed. (3) (Pseudo-)Randomly perturbing chaotic systems [13–15], which face up to dynamical degradation problem, have been verified to be more useful than the previous two methods. To be added, the second approach can be thought of as a perturbation method under extreme conditions. In a prior study [16], we indicate that all the solutions aim at extending the state space, which provides some explanations at a holistic level. Deep connection between the nature of chaos degradation and these methods is however ambiguous to us.

Actually, the main characteristic of chaos degradation is the loss of randomness. It is spontaneous to discuss the effects of random fluctuations on chaos. As mentioned in [17], there are three types of fluctuations. Firstly, observational noise, namely, instrumentation error, is due to the finite resolution of physical measurements. The observational noise describes random errors which is ineluctable and unknown to us. Second best, a higher precision is used to be a substitution of this fluctuation. Although the length of the cycles caused by chaos degradation increases exponentially with the level of precision adopted [7], all the orbits are still periodic and implementation costs increase as well. The second type of fluctuation adds a stochastic force or noise to the dynamical systems and corresponds to the random perturbation scheme, which can be modeled by stochastic equations. As we know, noise can induce many interesting phenomena including noise-induce chaos [18–20]. Crutchfield suggested that the effect of noise is to average the structure of deterministic attractors over some range of nearby parameters [21]. Although the resulting random problem can be solved with statistical assumptions and techniques, it is still unsolvable for communication. At last, the deterministic randomness chaotic systems exhibit is the third type of fluctuation, which is called intrinsic noise. Besides chaotic systems itself have internal randomness. This type of fluctuation seems promising to counteract chaos degradation. It can explain the pseudo-random perturbation scheme. All these random fluctuations aim at restoring the loss of randomness caused by finite precision, which appeals to common sense.

In recent years, the rapid proliferation of big data applications and cloud computing infrastructures has introduced new opportunities and challenges for the utilization of chaos-based algorithms in practice. Massive-scale data collections and distributed computing environments often demand highly parallelizable and precision-sensitive algorithms [22]. In cloud-based security platforms [23, 24], digital chaotic systems are increasingly explored for secure communication, authentication, and pseudo-random number generation, yet precision degradation can be amplified in virtualized and heterogeneous computing environments. Similarly, in big data analytics pipelines [25, 26], chaotic models are utilized for anomaly detection and complex pattern modeling, where dynamical degradation directly impacts accuracy and reliability. These contexts underscore the practical significance of designing chaos-preserving mechanisms that function robustly under large-scale, distributed, and resource-constrained computation.

In this paper, we study the role of fluctuations on the solution to the dynamical degradation of digital chaotic system. A continuous chaotic system is used to generate intrinsic noise to perturb the digital chaotic system and counteract its dynamical degradation. In the scheme, a class of perturbed digital system is proved to be chaotic in the sense of Devaney by symbolic dynamics. Moreover, scaling of the intrinsic noise is studied to show when chaos may survive and be indistinguishable from the original counterpart. We show that there are two critical noise amplitudes for the topological structure of chaotic system to change. The performance comparison with the other two fluctuations further shows three fluctuations have some of the same properties in the "microcosmic" level when dealing with the degradation of digital chaos. All the results imply the effectiveness of our scheme in counteracting the dynamical degradation. What's more, the relationship between fluctuations and chaos is revealed.

The rest of this paper is organized as follows. The description of our model and preliminaries are given in Sect. 2. Section 3 provides a concrete scheme to show the effects of intrinsic noise on the onset of chaos. Using symbolic dynamics, we prove the effectiveness of the scheme and analyze the scaling of intrinsic noise. The experimental results are presented in Sect. 4 to show the availability of the model and the relationship between fluctuations and chaos. Finally, conclusions follow in Sect. 5.

2 Preliminaries

In this section, we provide a picture of the dynamical degradation of digital chaotic systems and the effects of fluctuations. Some preliminary results of symbolic dynamics are also prepared for theoretical analysis.

2.1 Problem Statement and Modeling

Consider a discrete-time chaotic system:

$$x^i = F\left(x^{i-1}\right) \tag{1}$$

where x^i is the state vector and X_N is the finite version of real subset $X \in R^m$. $F : X \rightarrow X$ is a continuous chaotic map which is also suitable for X_N. When chaos is implemented on finite automata, a digital chaotic map is the composition of a quantization function and F as following:

$$x^i = F_N(x^{i-1}) = B_N(F(x^{i-1})) \tag{2}$$

where $B_N : X \rightarrow X_N$ is the quantization function. It is easy to see that $B_N(x^i) = x^i_{p-1}x^i_{p-2}\cdots x^i_0.x^i_{-1}\cdots x^i_{-Q} \in X_N, N = P + Q$, where P is the integer width and Q is the decimal width.

Aiming at the dynamical degradation of digital chaotic systems, a number of remedies have been proposed as possible methods: Using higher precisions; Cascading multiple chaotic systems; Perturbing the chaotic systems; We introduced the perturbation-based schemes in detail [16]. From the perspective of space expansion we also indicated that

only the scheme, in which perturbation source has its own dynamic behavior, can extend
state space to infinity.

We will model the effects of external fluctuations with following perturbed digital
chaotic map:

$$x^i = F_N\left(x^{i-1}\right) + B_N\left(P^{i-1}\right) \tag{3}$$

where P^{i-1} is the perturbation variable. Different fluctuations as the perturbation
variables and their scaling will be discussed in later sections.

The most popular definition of chaos is due to Devaney [27]. Consider a metric space
(X, d) with metric d and a continuous function $f : X \to X$.

Definition 1. f Is called chaos in the sense of Devaney if the following conditions are
satisfied:

1) f is topologically transitive, that is, for any two non-empty open subsets $U, V \subset X$
   in the topology of (X, d), there exists k $\geq$ 0 such that $f^k(U) \cap V \neq \phi$;
2) The periodic points are dense in X;
3) The property of sensitive dependence on initial conditions.

Shortly thereafter this definition was discussed in detail. Noticeably, Banks et al.
proved that the first two conditions can derive the third condition in a metric space [28].

2.2 Symbolic Dynamics and Topological Property

Let (S, d) be a separable metric space, and $card(S) \geq 2$, where $d(a, b) \equiv$
$|a - b|, \forall a, b \in S$, and $card(\cdot)$ denotes cardinal number of set. Let

$$\sum(S) = \prod_{i=0}^{+\infty} S_i, S_i = S, i = 0, 1, \ldots \tag{4}$$

and define the metric on $\Sigma(S)$ from many possible choices as follows:

$$\rho(s, \bar{s}) = \sum_{i=0}^{+\infty} \frac{1}{2^i} \frac{d(s_i, \bar{s}_i)}{1 + d(s_i, \bar{s}_i)}, s = (s_0, s_1, \cdots), \bar{s} = (\bar{s}_0, \bar{s}_1, \cdots) \in \sum(S) \tag{5}$$

Next denote by σ the shift map of $\Sigma(S)$ into itself,

$$\sigma((s_0, s_1, \cdots)) = (s_1, s_2, \cdots) \in \Sigma(S) \tag{6}$$

then $(\Sigma(S), \sigma)$ is a one-side symbolic dynamics.

However, in this case not all of the orbits may occur in the dynamics. That is,
symbol sequences must satisfy the admissibility condition. Let $\sum_*(S)$ be the set of
allowed symbol sequences. Now that the infinite sequence space $\sum_*(S)$ is established,
next denote by σ_* the shift map of $\sum_*(S)$ into itself:

$$\sigma_*((s_0, s_1, \cdots)) = (s_1, s_2, \cdots) \in \sum_*(S) \tag{7}$$

Theorem 1. [29] The shift map σ is chaotic in the sense of Devaney and Li-Yorke, if S is a metric space with $card\,(S) \geq 2$ and S is separable.

Definition 2. f And g are said to be topological conjugate (denoted by $(X,f) \simeq (Y,g)$) if there exists a homeomorphism $h : X \to X$ such that $h \circ f = g \circ h$, namely

$$
\begin{array}{ccc}
X & \overset{h}{\to} & Y \\
f \uparrow & & \uparrow g \\
X & \overset{h}{\to} & Y
\end{array}
\tag{8}
$$

If all the conditions hold except that h is not injective, then f and g are said to be topological semi-conjugate which we denote by $(X,f) \simeq (Y,g)$.

3 Theoretical Analysis Based on Symbolic Dynamics

Chaotic dynamics degradation occurs on a micro level due to finite precision. It naturally makes sense to explore the microscopic dynamics of chaos degradation. Heuristically, an understanding of the relationship between randomness and chaos degradation will determine the relevance of chaotic dynamics to fluctuations. In Sect. 1, three different types of fluctuations for counteracting dynamical degradation of digital chaotic systems have been introduced. In this section, a concrete scheme based on hybrid structure is proposed for the solution to chaos degradation. Furthermore, the relationship between scaling of intrinsic randomness and chaos with different structure is studied.

3.1 A Scheme Based on Hybrid Structure for Chaos Degradation

The continuous chaotic system generating intrinsic randomness is described as:

$$
\begin{aligned}
y'(t) &= G(y(t)) \\
y(0) &= y_0
\end{aligned}
\tag{9}
$$

where $y(t) \in R^n$ is a n-dimensional state vector, $G : R^n \to R^n$ is a function with both linear and nonlinear part. Let y^i be the state of continuous chaotic system at $t = t_i$, which is taken as a type of perturbation variable. Then consider the controlled system:

$$
x^i = \left(F_N\left(x^{i-1} + B_N\left(\mu y^{i-1}\right)\right)\right) mod \ \alpha
\tag{10}
$$

where the gain matrix μ controls the scaling of intrinsic randomness. α is a constant that depends on the domain of attraction of the system.

3.2   Chaos in the Presence of Intrinsic Randomness

However, it is not comfortable to prove the chaoticity of the system directly. Symbolic dynamical system as a generalization of real system may work more easily. Next, we rigorously prove that the controlled system is chaotic in the sense of Devaney via symbolic dynamics. Notably, the controlled systems are proven to be chaotic. But they are not topologically conjugate with each other under different scaling. We will study the scaling of intrinsic randomness in Sects. 3.3 and 4.2.

First we must make the transformation of state space clear in order to establish symbolic dynamics. As mentioned above, X and X_N are the state space of discrete-time chaotic system and the finite version under finite precision. Let Y be the state space of continuous chaotic system. Then in our control scheme, the extended state space of controlled system is $\overline{X_N} = X_N \times Y$. For the sake of narrative, defining the function:

$$\begin{aligned} F_G : \overline{X_N} &\to X_N \\ \left(x^i, y^i\right) &\mapsto F_N(x^i) + B_N(\mu y^i))\mathrm{mod}\ \alpha \end{aligned} \tag{11}$$

and

$$\begin{aligned} f_{F_G} : \overline{X_N} &\to \overline{X_N} \\ \left(x^i, y^i\right) &\mapsto \left(F_G\left(x^i, y^i\right), y^{i+1}\right) \end{aligned} \tag{12}$$

A new distance between two points $A = (x, y), \tilde{A} = (\tilde{x}, \tilde{y}) \in \overline{X_N}$ is defined by

$$\overline{d}\left(A, \tilde{A}\right) = d_x(x, \tilde{x}) + d_y(y, \tilde{y}) = \sum_{k=1}^{N} \delta\left(x_{P-k}, \widetilde{x_{P-k}}\right) + |y - \tilde{y}| \tag{13}$$

where P denotes the integer width of computing precision N.

Definition 3. For $x \in X$, let $C(x) = s \in \sum_* S$, where $s = (s_0 s_1 \ldots)$, such that $f^i(x) \in X_{s_i}. \forall i \in N^*,$ Meanwhile $X_{s_0 s_1 s_2 \cdots} = \left\{x \mid x \in X_{s_0}\right\} \cap \left\{x \mid x \in X_{s_1}\right\} \cap \left\{x \mid x \in X_{s_2}\right\} \cap \cdots \cap \cdots,$ where X_S is a partition consisting of identical hypercubic cells of side η.

Remark. For the given unit of least precision ε, $\eta > \varepsilon$ holds. Since there must be states in a cell, or symbolic dynamics makes no sense.

Definition 4. For $P \in \overline{X_N}$, let $\overline{C}(P) = s \in \sum_* S$, where $s = (s_0 s_1 \ldots)$, such that $F_G\left(f_{F_G}^i(P)\right) \in X_{s_i}, \forall i \in N^*. \overline{X_{s_0 s_1 s_2 \cdots}} = \left\{P \mid F_G(P) \in X_{s_0}\right\} \cap \left\{P \mid F_G(f_{F_G}(P)) \in X_{s_1}\right\} \cap \left\{P \mid F_G\left(f_{F_G}^2(P)\right) \in X_{s_2}\right\} \cap \cdots \cap \cdots$. Again, there exists a one-one mapping between points in $\overline{X_N}$ and symbolic sequences in $\sum_* S$. Then it is convenient to establish a conjugacy from $(\overline{X_N}, f_{F_G})$ to $(\sum_* S, \sigma_*)$ by theorem 1 in [16].

$$\begin{array}{ccc} \overline{X_N} & \xrightarrow{C} & \sum_* S \\ f_{F_G} \uparrow & & \uparrow \sigma_* \\ \overline{X_N} & \xrightarrow{C} & \sum_* S \end{array} \tag{14}$$

Next, we prove that the model satisfies Devaney chaos.

Lemma 1 (see Lemma 2.2.1 in [30]). For $s', s'' \in \sum_* S_N$, 1) if $d(s', s'') < 1/(2^{M+1})$, then $s'_i = s''_i$ for all $|i| \leq M$; 2) if $s'_i = s''_i$ for all $|i| \leq M$, then $d(s', s'') < 1/(2^{M-1})$.

Theorem 2. In commuting diagram (2), if the function f is continuous, then σ_* the shift map of $\sum_* S$ is continuous.

Proof. To prove the continuity of σ_* we must show that, for any given $\varepsilon > 0$, there exists a $\delta(\varepsilon) > 0$ such that $d(s', s'') < \delta$ implies $d(\sigma_*(s'), \sigma_*(s'')) < \varepsilon$ for $s', s'' \in \sum_* S_N$. Because f is continuous, obviously, f^n (e.g. f^2 means $f \circ f$ is also continuous on X. Then for any $n \in N^*$ and given $\varepsilon_1 > 0$, and $x', x'' \in X$, there exists a $\delta_1(\varepsilon_1) > 0$ where $|x' - x''| < \delta_1$, such that $|f^n(x'), f^n(x'')| < \varepsilon_1$. That is to say, when ε_1 is sufficiently small, $f^n(x'), f^n(x'')$ are in the same set of the partition, therefore $s'_i = s''_i$ for all $|i| \leq n$. According to Lemma 1, $d(s', s'') < 1/(2^{n-1})$ holds. So $d(\sigma_*(s'), \sigma_*(s'')) < 1/(2^{n-2})$. Therefore, for any $\varepsilon = \min\{\varepsilon_1, 1/(2^{n-2})\}$, there exists a $\delta(\varepsilon) = 1/(2^{n-1})$ such that $d(s', s'') < \delta$ implies $d(\sigma_*(s'), \sigma_*(s'')) < \varepsilon$. Namely, σ_* is continuous.

Theorem 3. f_{F_G} Is a continuous function.

Proof. We use the definition of continuity in topological space. Let $2^{X_N} = \{S | S \subseteq X_N\}$ be the power set of X_N, $U = \{(x, y) | x \in S, y \in (a, b) \subseteq Y\}$ be an arbitrary subset. For a point $P' = (x', y') \in U$, an a sufficiently small value $\varepsilon_1 > 0$, the spherical neighborhood of P' denotes by $B(P', \varepsilon_1) = \{P \in \overline{X_N} | d(P, P') < \varepsilon_1\}$. In fact, $d_x(x, \hat{x})$ is an integer, so in the spherical neighborhood, $d_x(x, \hat{x}) = 0$ holds. Let $\varepsilon = \min\{y - a, b - y, \varepsilon_1\}$, such that $B(P', \varepsilon) \subset U$, therefore, U is an open set, all the open sets construct a topology. We will prove that $f_{F_G}^{-1}(U)$ is an open set in U. Let us recall the function F_G, then $f_{F_G}^{-1}(U) = \{(x, y) | F_N^{-1}(x - B_N(\mu y)) \in S, y \in G^{-1}(a, b) \subseteq Y\}$. Considering that G is continuous and modular function makes topological space bounded, then $f_{F_G}^{-1}(U)$ is still an open set with any μ. To sum up, f_{F_G} is consequently continuous.

Theorem 4. The retentivity of Devaney chaos under topological semi-conjugate: suppose that $(X, f) \cong (Y, g)$, h is a continuous surjective map, and f is Devaney chaos, then g is Devaney chaos.

Proof: In [31], a proof that Devaney chaos are all preserved under topological is given. Inspired by this, we establish this theorem.

1) g is topologically transive.

    Let U, V be any nonempty open sets in Y. Since h is continuous and surjective, $h^{-1}(U)$ and $h^{-1}(V)$ are two empty open sets in X. And because f is topologically transive, there exists an integer $k > 0$ such that $f^k(h^{-1}(U)) \cap h^{-1}(V) = \varnothing$. This implies that

$$g^k(U) \cap V = g^k\left(h\left(h^{-1}(U)\right)\right) \cap h\left(h^{-1}(V)\right) = h\left(f^k\left(h^{-1}(U)\right)\right) \cap h\left(h^{-1}(V)\right)$$

$$\supset h\left(f^k\left(h^{-1}(U)\right) \cap h^{-1}(V)\right) = \varnothing \tag{15}$$

So g is topologically transive;

2) The periodic points of g are dense in Y.

Similarly, let U be any nonempty open set in Y. $h^{-1}(U)$ is an empty open set in X. Since the periodic points of f are dense in X, there exists a periodic point $x \in h^{-1}(U) \subset X$. Let $f^n(x) = x$, n is a period. Obiviously $g^n(h(x)) = h(f^n(x)) = h(x)$, so $h(x)$ is a periodic point of Y and $h(x) \in U$. This implies the periodic points of g are dense in Y.

In conclusion, g is Devaney chaos.

Theorem 5. f_{F_G} Is a chaotic map on $(\overline{X_N}, \overline{d})$ in the sense of Devaney.

Proof: It is not difficult to check that $\left(\sum S, \sigma\right) \cong \left(\sum_* S, \sigma_*\right)$ by Theorem 2 and Theorem 3. Next according to Theorem 1 and Theorem 4, $\left(\sum_* S, \sigma_*\right)$ is a chaotic system in the sense of devaney. Therefore, we conclude that f_{F_G} is chaotic with any μ on $\overline{X_N}$ in the sense of Devaney as the following diagram commutes:

$$\begin{array}{ccc} \overline{X_N} & \xrightarrow{\mathcal{C}} & \sum_* S \\ f_{F_G} \uparrow & & \uparrow \sigma_* \\ \overline{X_N} & \xrightarrow{\mathcal{C}} & \sum_* S \end{array} \tag{16}$$

3.3 Scaling of Intrinsic Randomness

Although the controlled system is proven to be chaotic in the sense of Devaney, it may have different topological structure when μ varies. Surprisingly, symbolic dynamics is powerful enough to help us understand this phenomenon. We illustrate the Eq. (3) in Fig. 1. As shown in Fig. 1a, $\|B_N(P^i)\| < \delta$, where P^i is the vector of intrinsic random noise added to the digital chaotic map at the iteration i, and δ is its maximum amplitude. Figure 1b shows that at a certain amplitude of noise, the symbol of a state changes depending on the position of point in hypercubic cell. Actually, it is desirable that the corresponding symbol for any state does not change. To achieve this, δ must be no larger than unit of least precision, which is obvious while seems hard to accomplish. By the way, our previous work provided an efficient solution [16]. However, symbolic dynamics is robust. In other word, the symbolic dynamics is not destroyed if the perturbation is small. Even so, the perturbation is still much larger than unit of least precision.

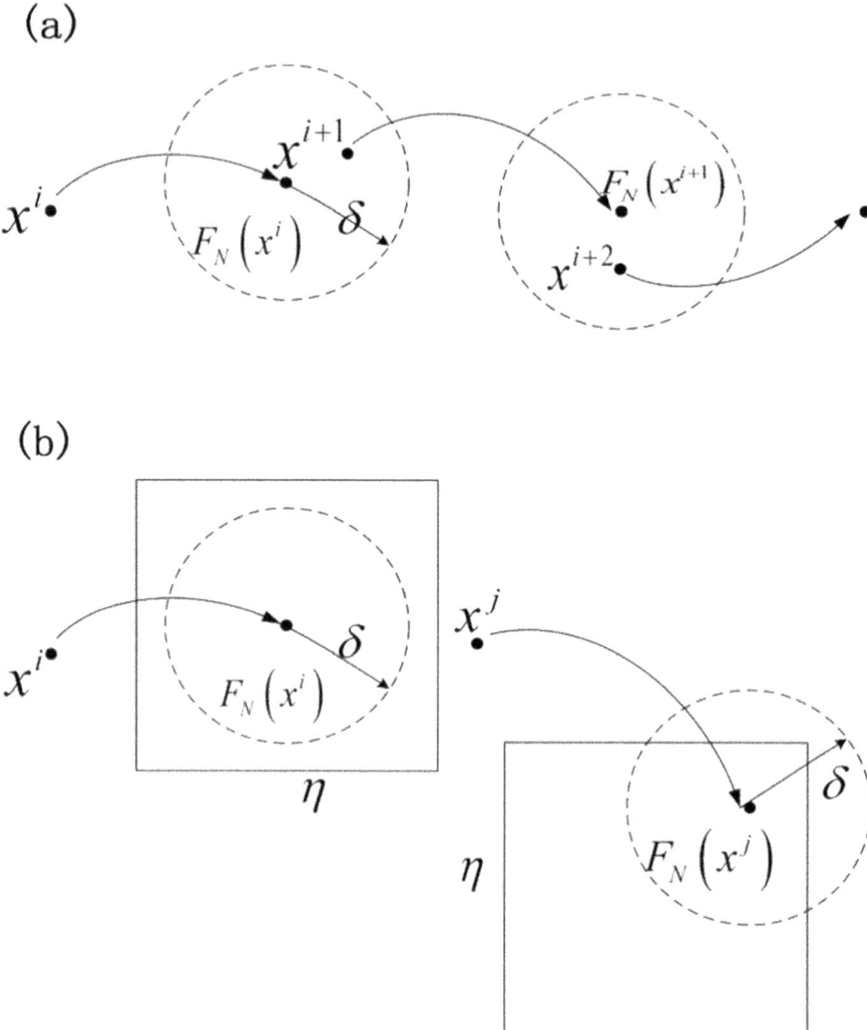

Fig. 1. (a) illustration of the perturbed dynamics with amplitude of intrinsic noise $||B_N\left(P^i\right)|| < \delta$. (b) hypercubic cells of side η in the partition (square). We illustrate that the points near the center of cell would not be pushed outside the square, that is, the symbol of state is unaltered. On the other hand, the points near the boundary are easily pushed out leading to the change of symbol.

We suppose that the dynamics of system may not be affected when the symbolic sequences of a small part of orbits change. We thus define two certain critical amplitudes δ_C and ρ_C. When $\delta < \delta_C$, only a few symbols of states change. In this case there is no fundamental change in the topology of system. As δ increases, the topology of system gradually changes and becomes completely different when $\delta < \rho_C$. In order to check this prediction, we numerically study the scaling of intrinsic randomness in next section.

4   Example and Experimental Simulations

In this section, a digital chaotic system is given to show the validity of proposed method, study the effects of scaling on topological structure of chaos and compare three fluctuations for chaos degradation. In addition, the statistical randomness of the generated chaotic sequences is evaluated using the NIST SP800-22 test suite.

Consider the classic Lorenz system as the continuous chaotic system, which is written as follows:

$$\begin{cases} \dot{x} = \sigma(y - x) \\ \dot{y} = \rho x - y - xz \\ \dot{z} = xy - \beta z \end{cases} \tag{17}$$

where $Y = (x, y, z)^T$ is the continuous system state vector, $\sigma = 10$, $\rho = 30$, $\beta = 8/3$ is chosen as the parameter of Lorenz system. Next, Logistic chaotic map is chosen as the digital chaotic map as follows:

$$x^i = B_N\left(ax^{i-1}\left(1 - x^{i-1}\right)\right) \tag{18}$$

When the control parameter $a = 4$, the Logistic map exhibits robust chaos.B_N keeps N significant and the unit of least precision $\varepsilon = \frac{1}{10^Q}$.The Lorenz chaotic system is applied to control the digital linear map. The control gain matrix is $\mu = diag(\gamma, 0, 0)$. Then the controlled digital linear map can be represented as follows:

$$x^{i+1} = \left(B_N\left(ax^i\left(1 - x^i\right)\right) + B_N(\gamma x(t))\right) mod \ \alpha \tag{19}$$

where $a = 4$, $\alpha = 1$, and the initial values $x^0 = 1$. The largest precision is set at 10^{-6}. The quantization function is chosen as $B_{N(\cdot)} = round(\cdot)$.

4.1   Chaos Characteristic Analysis

First, we analyze the chaos characteristic of the controlled system by studying several indicators, including orbits, correlation, phase space and complexity. We compare the digital Logistic map and the controlled digital map. The gain parameter is simply set at $\gamma = 1$. Simulation results are revealed in Fig. 2 and Fig. 3.

As shown in Fig. 2a, Logistic chaotic map degenerates into a periodic orbit. We can conclude that the digital Logistic map can only traverse part of the whole domain [0, 1] and its distribution is broken and jagged from Fig. 2b and 2c. Figure 2d shows strong correlation of neighbor points, which lacks of good randomness. On the contrary, what Fig. 3 shows perfectly verifies correctness of the theoretical analysis in Sect 3.2. The digital Logistic map has no cycles and its orbit can achieve ergodicity after control as shown in Fig. 2a and 2b respectively. Better yet, the hyperbolic attractor structure is destroyed, instead, the state space is filled which makes the generated sequence appear random. It is clear that the frequency distribution of outputs of the controlled system is better than before from Fig. 2c. Figure 2d also depicts the correlation of outputs is weak.

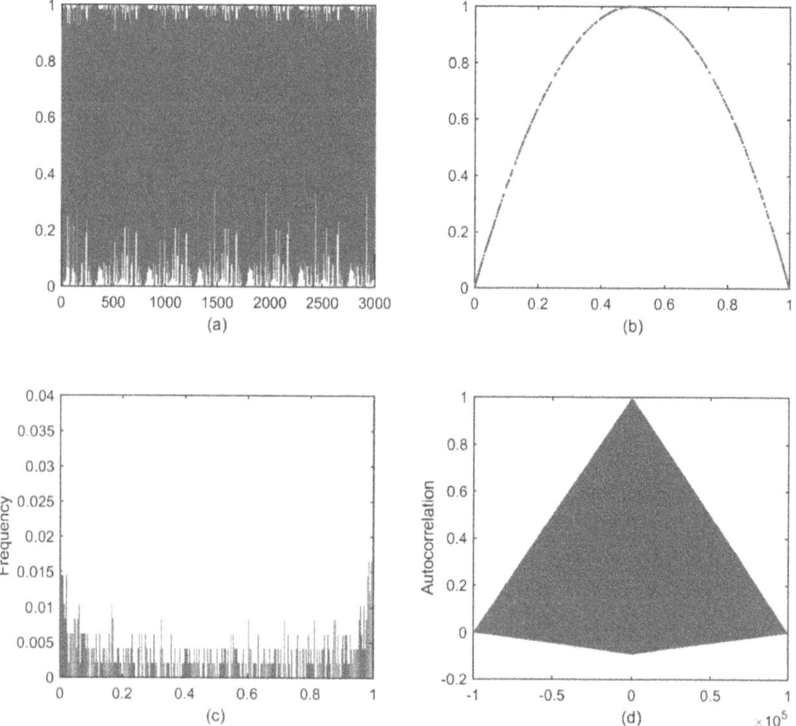

Fig. 2. Performance indicators of the digital Logistic map with precision $N = 6$ and initial value $x^0 = 0.1$. (a) the orbit of system. (b) phase diagram. (c) frequency distribution. (d) autocorrelation function.

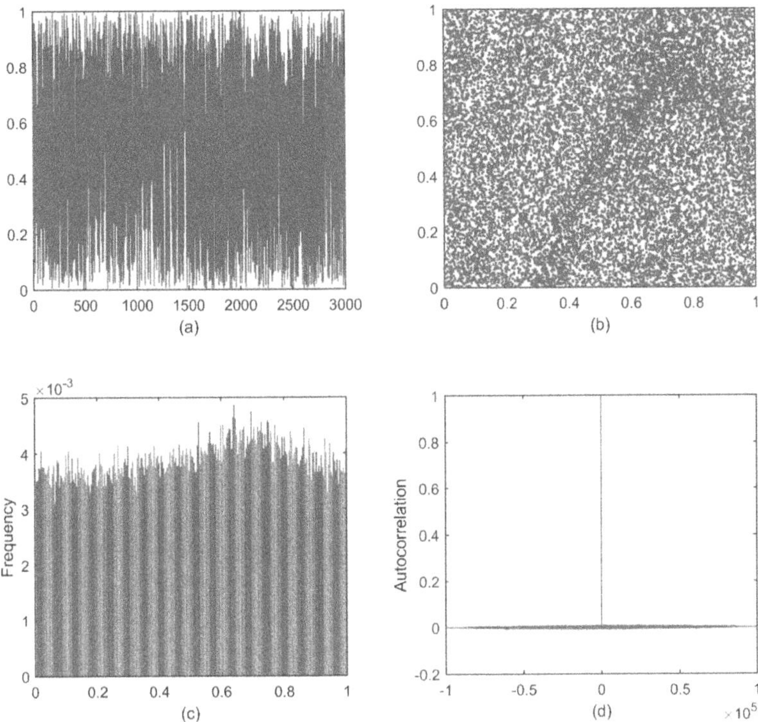

Fig. 3. Performance indicators of the controlled digital Logistic map with the same precision and initial value. (a) the orbit of system. (b) phase diagram. (c) frequency distribution. (d) autocorrelation function.

4.2 The Effects of Scaling on Chaos

After verifying chaos characteristic of the controlled system as a whole, the effects of scaling of gain parameter are probed further in the "microcosmic" level. Approximate entropy is often used to quantify the unpredictability and complexity of fluctuations [32]. To be more quantitative, we compute the approximate entropy values of the controlled system with different gain parameter γ. The results are shown in Fig. 4. The subplots reflect the change of topological structure of controlled map via several representative parameters. We refer to γ as the amplitude of perturbation variable δ. When $\delta < \delta_C \approx$ 0.001, approximate entropy of the controlled system is nearly invariable. By comparing the attractors of system with $\gamma = 10^{-6}$ and $\gamma = 10^{-3}$, we find that the hyperbola becomes blurred while the attractor's structure is largely intact. As δ increases, the approximate entropy has a sharp rise in the interval $[\delta_C, \rho_C]$, $\rho_C \approx 0.6$. Attractor of the controlled system at $\gamma = 0.03$ indicates that topological structure of chaos changes, but it still retains some topological structure of the Logistic chaos. However, when $\delta > \rho_C$, the curve flattens out and converges to a constant which relates to the continuous chaotic system. The phase spaces of system with $\gamma = 0.6$ and $\gamma = 7$ show that the topological structure of chaos is different entirely.

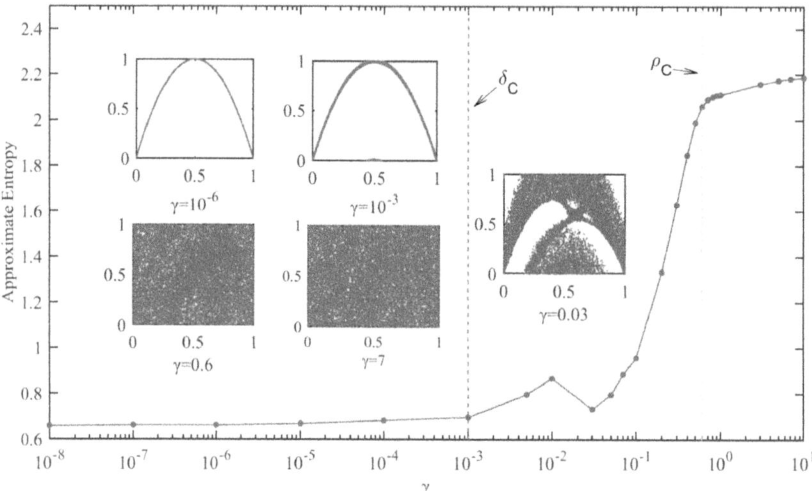

Fig. 4. Approximate entropy values of the controlled digital Logistic map with different gain parameter γ and the same initial value $x^0 = 0.1$. The subplots depict some phase space of the controlled map under several representative parameters. The red and green vertical dotted line show the critical amplitudes of perturbation $\delta_C \approx 0.001$ and $\rho_C \approx 0.6$.

4.3 Three Fluctuations Applied to Chaos Degradation

Finally back to where we start, that is, the relationship between randomness and chaos. Let us review three random fluctuations: observational noise, intrinsic noise (deterministic randomness) generated by chaotic systems, random noise. In order to solve the problem of chaos degradation, we have delved deeply into the intrinsic noise and its scaling. In fact, observational noise is a kind of random noise. However, it cannot be modeled, instead we use higher precisions to mimic this fluctuation. Chua indicated that chaotic behavior can be recovered when the wordlength exceeds a certain value [8]. In this subsection, the effect of random noise on digital chaotic system is analyzed. A simple but intuitive comparison of three fluctuations is also given.

The interplay between chaos and random noise has been an interesting topic in nonlinear dynamics. Many significant phenomena are revealed with statistical physics, including conclusions on the quantitative relationship between noise amplitude and induced chaos [21]. We do equally important work here in order to reflect the connections and differences with our solution. We here refer to standard deviation of Gaussian random variable σ as the amplitude of perturbation variable δ. Figure 5 shows that, as δ increases, the approximate entropy holds almost constant, then increases rapidly. However the curve flattens out in the final stage. Obviously, the effect of random noise on digital chaotic system is similar as intrinsic randomness. There also exist two critical values about 0.01 and 0.4.

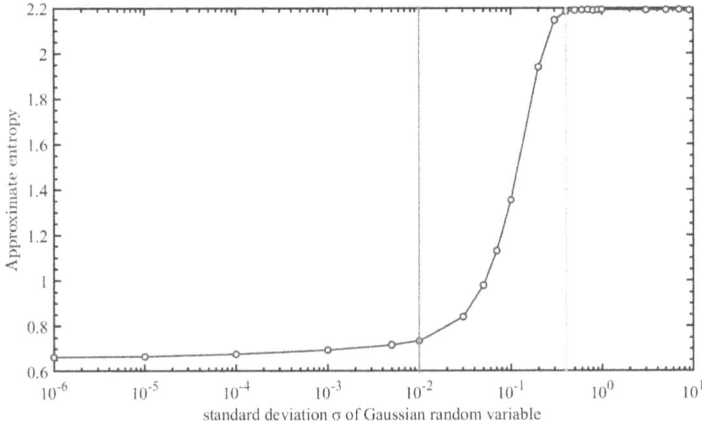

Fig. 5. Approximate entropy values of the controlled digital Logistic map with different gain parameter σ and the same initial value $x^0 = 0.1$. The red and green vertical dotted line show the critical amplitudes of perturbation $\delta_C \approx 0.01$ and $\rho_C \approx 0.4$.

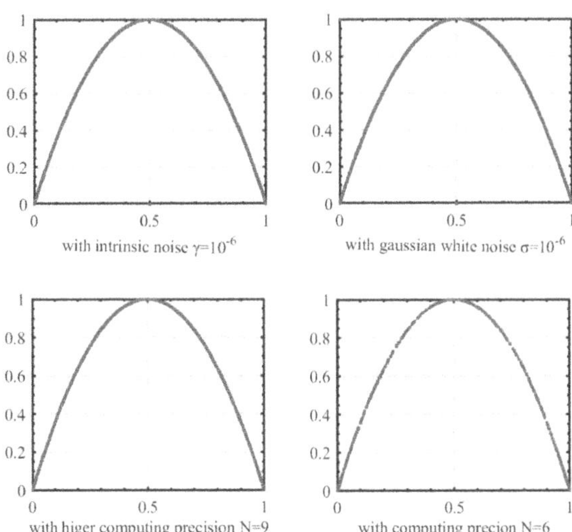

Fig. 6. Phase diagrams of digital Logistic map before (bottom right corner) and after being perturbed by three fluctuations with the same initial value $x^0 = 0.1$.

Figure 6 compares the digital Logistic map before and after being perturbed by three different fluctuations. All candidates seem to restore the chaotic attractors of the digital Logistic map. It worries us that the visual error may be caused by computing precision. Furthermore, we can see from Fig. 7 that the scheme of using higher computing precision does not overcome the chaos degradation, which only improve the chaos characteristic.

We attribute to the essential difference between observational noise and using higher computing precision. Anyhow, on the basis of these studies, we can conclude boldly that for counteracting the degradation of digital chaos there is something in common among the three fluctuations in the "microcosmic" level. It is too important to emphasize two points again. One is that observational noise can not be observed, the substitution of using higher computing precision does not solve the problem essentially. The other is that random noise can counteract the chaos degradation as effectively as intrinsic noise, but it cannot be used for communication.

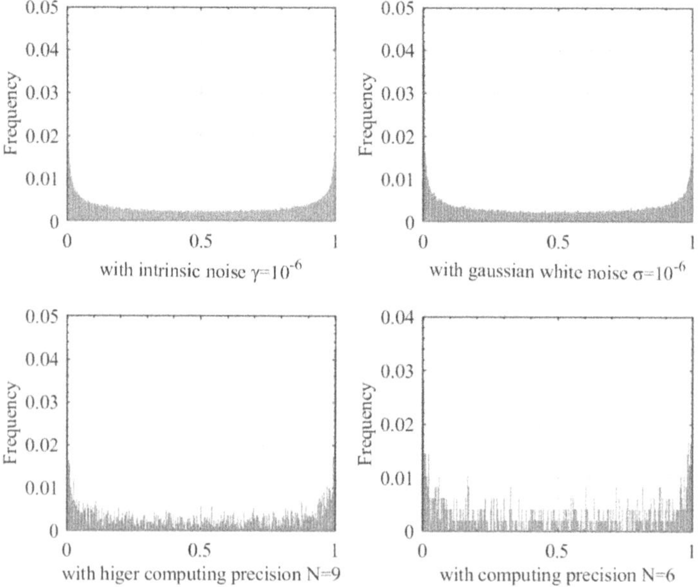

Fig. 7. Frequency distributions of digital Logistic map before (bottom right corner) and after being perturbed by three fluctuations with the same initial value $x^0 = 0.1$.

4.4 NIST SP800-22 Analysis

A total of 100 binary sequences, each with a length of 10^6 bits, were generated for evaluation. The tests were conducted under a fixed arithmetic precision of six decimal digits. As summarized in Table 1, the binary data obtained from the chaotic sequences produced by the proposed intrinsic-noise scheme, after a well-defined post-processing stage, successfully passed all 15 statistical subtests in the NIST SP800-22 suite. In contrast, unperturbed logistic map operating at the same precision failed all subtests, demonstrating complete degradation of statistical randomness in low-precision conditions and highlighting the robustness advantage of our scheme.

Table 1. NIST SP800–22 test results (proposed scheme vs. logistic map).

		Logistic map		Proposed scheme		
No	Sub-test	PROP	Result	P-value	PROP	Result
1	Frequency	0/100	Fail	0.0037	96/100	Pass
2	Block Frequency	0/100	Fail	0.0428	100/100	Pass
3	Cumulative Sums (F)	0/100	Fail	0.1626	98/100	Pass
	Cumulative Sums (R)	0/100	Fail	0.0288	98/100	Pass
4	Runs	0/100	Fail	0.0109	100/100	Pass
5	Longest Run	0/100	Fail	0.9878	99/100	Pass
6	Rank	0/100	Fail	0.2492	98/100	Pass
7	FFT	0/100	Fail	0.5544	99/100	Pass
8	Non-Overlapping Template	0/100	Fail	0.7791	100/100	Pass
9	Overlapping Template	0/100	Fail	0.1718	98/100	Pass
10	Universal	0/100	Fail	0.4011	98/100	Pass
11	Approximate Entropy	0/100	Fail	0.5749	99/100	Pass
12	Random Excursions	0/100	Fail	0.4011	53/53	Pass
13	Random Excursion Variant	0/100	Fail	0.7197	53/53	Pass
14	Serial(1)	0/100	Fail	0.6993	100/100	Pass
	Serial(2)	0/100	Fail	0.4749	100/100	Pass
15	Linear Complexity	0/100	Fail	0.6786	99/100	Pass

In the post-processing step, each chaotic value was multiplied by 10^5 and then taken modulo 256, mapping it to an 8-bit integer. This scaling-modulo operation is a widely adopted quantization method in chaos-based sequence generation, ensuring consistent byte-level mapping. This operation does not introduce measurable statistical bias. Moreover, the high randomness sequences generated by our scheme can be directly applied to cloud security scenarios such as cryptographic key generation. Cloud environments require anti-degradation chaotic systems to guarantee key randomness, and our approach, having passed all NIST subtests, meets the demand for high reliability random sources in cloud security applications.

5   Conclusions

In this paper, we would like to emphasize the interplay between fluctuations and chaos degradation. Based on this idea, we introduce a continuous chaotic system to generate intrinsic random fluctuation, which is a specific fluctuation. Next a hybrid method is proposed to solve the dynamical degradation of digital chaotic systems. We use symbolic dynamics to rigorously prove that digital chaotic systems can be perturbed to be chaotic in the sense of Devaney. The reason the topological structure of chaos changes is also studied with coarse-grained analysis. We show that there are two critical fluctuation amplitudes resulting in topological structure changes of chaos. The numerical experiments are consistent with the theoretical analysis and further shed some light on the similarities and differences among three types of fluctuations. This study reveals the deep connection between fluctuations and chaos degradation, providing guidance for understanding and solving the dynamical degradation problem of digital chaotic systems, as well as offering insights for both fundamental theory and future applications.

Acknowledgements. This work was supported by the National Key R&D Program of China [grant number 2017YFB0802000]; and the Cryptography Theoretical Research of National Cryptography Development Fund [grant number MMJJ20170109].

Conflict of Interest.. The authors declare that they have no conflict of interest concerning the publication of this manuscript.

References

1. Kennedy, J., Yorke, J.: Topological horseshoes. Trans. Am. Math. Soc. **353** (2001)
2. Leonov, G.A., Kuznetsov, N.V., Vagaitsev, V.I.: Localization of hidden Chua's attractors. Phys. Lett. A **375**(23), 2230–2233 (2011)
3. Mirzaei, O., Yaghoobi, M., Irani, H.: A new image encryption method: parallel sub-image encryption with hyper chaos. Nonlinear Dyn. **67**(1), 557–566 (2012)
4. Li, S., Chen, G., Mou, X.: On the dynamical degradation of digital piecewise linear chaotic maps. Int. J. Bifurcation Chaos **15**(10), 3119–3151 (2005)
5. Kwok, H.S., Tang, W.K.S.: A fast image encryption system based on chaotic maps with finite precision representation. Chaos Solitons Fractals **32**(4), 1518–1529 (2007)
6. Li, S., Mou, X., Cai, Y., Ji, Z., Zhang, J.: On the security of a chaotic encryption scheme: problems with computerized chaos in finite computing precision. Comput. Phys. Commun. **153**(1), 52–58 (2003)
7. Wheeler, D.D., Matthews, R.A.J.: Supercomputer investigations of a chaotic encryption algorithm. Cryptologia **15**(2), 140–152 (1991)
8. Lin, T., Chua, L.O.: On chaos of digital filters in the real world. IEEE Trans. Circ. Syst. **38**(5), 557–558 (1991)
9. Heidari-Bateni, G., Mcgillem, C.D.: Chaotic direct-sequence spread-spectrum communication system. IEEE Trans. Commun. **42**(234), 1524–1527 (1994)
10. Shu-Bo, L., Jing, S., Zheng-Quan, X., Jin-Shuo, L.: Digital chaotic sequence generator based on coupled chaotic systems. Chin. Phys. B **18**(12), 5219 (2009)
11. Tong, X.J.: The novel bilateral – diffusion image encryption algorithm with dynamical compound chaos. J. Syst. Softw. **85**(4), 850–858 (2012)
12. Nagaraj, N., Shastry, M.C., Vaidya, P.G.: Increasing average period lengths by switching of robust chaos maps in finite precision. Eur. Phys. J. Spec. Top. **165**(1), 73–83 (2008)
13. Liu, L., Lin, J., Miao, S., Liu, B.: A double perturbation method for reducing dynamical degradation of the digital baker map. Int. J. Bifurcation Chaos **27**(07), 295 (2017)
14. Liu, L.F., Hu, H.P., Deng, Y.S.: An analogue-digital mixed method for solving the dynamical degradation of digital chaotic systems. IMA J. Math. Control Inf. **32**(4) (2014)
15. Li, C.Y., Chen, Y.H., Chang, T.Y., Deng, L.Y., To, K.: Period extension and randomness enhancement using high-throughput reseeding-mixing PRNG. IEEE Trans. Very Large Scale Integr. (VLSI) Syst. **20**(2), 385–389 (2012)

16. Zheng, J., Hu, H., Xia, X.: Applications of symbolic dynamics in counteracting the dynamical degradation of digital chaos. Nonlinear Dyn. **94**(2), 1535–1546 (2018)
17. Crutchfield, J.P., Farmer, J.D., Huberman, B.A.: Fluctuations and simple chaotic dynamics. Phys. Rep. **92**(2), 45–82 (1982)
18. Cencini, M., Falcioni, M., Olbrich, E., Kantz, H., Vulpiani, A.: Chaos or noise: difficulties of a distinction. Phys. Rev. E **62**(1), 427–437 (2000)
19. Liu, Z., Ma, W.: Noise induced destruction of zero Lyapunov exponent in coupled chaotic systems. Phys. Lett. A **343**(4), 300–305 (2005)
20. Lei, Y., Hua, M., Du, L.: Onset of colored-noise-induced chaos in the generalized Duffing system. Nonlinear Dyn. **89**(2), 1371–1383 (2017)
21. Gao, J., Hwang, S., Liu, J.: When can noise induce chaos? Phys. Rev. Lett. **82**(82), 1132–1135 (1999)
22. Mehmood, M.S., Shahid, M.R., Jamil, A., Ashraf, R., Mahmood, T., Mehmood, A.: A comprehensive literature review of data encryption techniques in cloud computing and IoT environment. In: 2019 8th International Conference on Information and Communication Technologies (ICICT), Karachi, Pakistan, pp. 54–59 (2019)
23. Li, H., Yu, C., Wang, X.: A novel 1D chaotic system for image encryption, authentication and compression in cloud. Multimed. Tools Appl. **80**, 8721–8758 (2021)
24. Bhattacharjee, S., Sharma, H., Choudhury, T., et al.: Leveraging chaos for enhancing encryption and compression in large cloud data transfers. J. Supercomput. **80**, 11923–11957 (2024)
25. Eyupoglu, C., Aydin, M.A., Zaim, A.H., Sertbas, A.: An efficient big data anonymization algorithm based on chaos and perturbation techniques. Entropy **20**, 373 (2018)
26. Shafique, A., Sayeed, M., Tsakalis, K.: Nonlinear dynamical systems with chaos and big data: a case study of epileptic seizure prediction and control. In: Srinivasan, S. (eds.) Guide to Big Data Applications. Studies in Big Data, vol. 26. Springer, Cham (2018)
27. Chillingworth, D.R.J.: An Introduction to Chaotic Dynamical Systems by Robert L. Devaney. Benjamin/Cummings (1986)
28. Kolesov, A.Y., Rozov, N.K.: On the definition of 'chaos.' Russ. Math. Surv. **64**(4), 701–744 (2009). https://doi.org/10.1070/RM2009v064n04ABEH004631
29. Xin-Chu, F., Huan-Wen, C.: Chaotic behaviour of the general symbolic dynamics. Appl. Math. Mech. **13**(2), 117–123 (1992)
30. Wiggings, S.: Global Bifurcations and Chaos: Analytical Methods. Springer, Cham (1988)
31. Lu, T., Zhu, P., Wu, X.: The retentivity of chaos under topological conjugation. Math. Probl. Eng. **2013** (2013)
32. Pincus, S.M.: Approximate entropy as a measure of system complexity. **88**(6), 2297–2301 (1991)

Game-Theoretic Defense Against Encrypted Data Poisoning in Federated Learning for Social Networks

Zhe Sun[1], Wenxin Gao[1], Peijie Yin[2], Weiping Li[1], Ming Zhang[3](✉), Yahong Chen[4](✉), and Jiangang Shu[1]

[1] Cyberspace Institute of Advanced Technology, Guangzhou University, Guangzhou 510006, China
{sunzhe,shujg}@gzhu.edu.cn, {gaowenxin,liweiping}@e.gzhu.edu.cn
[2] Xi'an Electronic Engineering Research Institute, Xi'an 710199, China
[3] School of Cyber Science and Engineering, Nanjing University of Science and Technology, Nanjing 210094, China
zhangming2025@njust.edu.cn
[4] School of Computer Science, Central China Normal University, Wuhan 430079, China
chenyahong123@ccnu.edu.cn

Abstract. Federated learning (FL) enables social networks to utilize distributed user data without direct exposure. However, when FL updates are encrypted to prevent gradient inversion and privacy leakage, observability is significantly reduced and traditional anomaly detection is weakened. This creates opportunities for ciphertext poisoning while cryptographic audits incur prohibitive costs at scale. The key challenge is to design defenses that balance privacy protection, detection capability, and resource constraints. In this paper, we address this challenge by proposing an evolutionary game theoretic defense framework for encrypted FL in social networks. The framework models detection intensity of the server and poisoning propensity of clients as co-evolving strategies. It explicitly incorporates false positive penalties, external incentives for attackers, and practical constraints such as bandwidth and energy budgets. Through equilibrium analysis, we show how detection policies adapt to varying costs and incentives, and we identify stable strategy profiles under different deployment conditions. The framework yields actionable guidance for tuning server-side defenses, offering adaptive and cost-aware protection against ciphertext poisoning in large-scale social networks.

Keywords: Ciphertext poisoning attack detection · Defense strategy optimization · Evolutionary game

1 Introduction

Social networks have emerged as data intensive platforms that continuously generate vast volumes of user behavior, interaction, and relationship data. These data support essential applications such as recommendation, sentiment analysis, and misinformation detection. However, their sensitivity and the decentralized nature of data generation introduce significant privacy and security concerns. Federated Learning (FL) [16] has been widely adopted in this context: a central server coordinates model training while individual clients compute local gradients or parameter updates on private data and share only the updates for aggregation. Although FL reduces the direct exposure of raw data, it does not eliminate leakage risks. Recent studies have demonstrated that gradient inversion attacks [3] can reconstruct client training examples from the shared updates, thereby compromising privacy even when raw records never leave local devices.

A prevalent response in social FL is to protect client updates with cryptographic mechanisms, such as homomorphic encryption [5], secure multiparty computation [7], and secure aggregation [19], which conceal individual contributions from the server or intermediaries. While these techniques reinforce confidentiality, they also weaken observability: detection methods that rely on client-level statistics, gradient similarity, or coordinate consistency become infeasible, and auditing is limited by the requirement to decrypt only after aggregation. Cryptographic verification [15] and zero-knowledge techniques [13] can partially restore checking capability, but their computational and communication burden grows sharply with social network scale. This reduction in visibility lays the groundwork for ciphertext poisoning, where malicious updates remain hidden behind encryption.

In such encrypted settings, the challenge is not merely loss of plaintext information but the operational limits of defense. The server typically observes only aggregates or ciphertext, making it difficult to attribute anomalies to specific clients or apply outlier screening reliably. Introducing cryptographic proofs or secure audits adds heavy computational and traffic overhead, which competes with the real-time and resource-sensitive nature of social FL [14]. Furthermore, the system must operate within bandwidth budgets, latency targets, and compliance policies, while clients are mobile, asynchronous, and statistically heterogeneous. False positives also impose cost, since overzealous filtering can exclude benign updates and harm model quality. A static high-intensity policy [24] deters attacks but is unsustainable, whereas a static low-intensity policy [25] reduces cost but invites exploitation. What is required is a dynamic adjustment of defense intensity, balancing risk level with resource constraints while preserving privacy and service quality. This motivates the use of game-theoretic formulations, which offer a structured framework to capture the interplay between server defense, attacker incentives, and operational budgets.

Game theoretic studies of security address attacker and defender interaction in several strands. Foundational work models inspection and deterrence under limited detection budgets using leader follower games [17], bargaining game [9], and repeated or evolutionary formulations [11], and it analyzes how error costs shape equilibrium behavior. In federated learning, game theoretic models have been applied to participation incentives, reputation and sanction mechanisms, and Byzantine behavior [8], and some studies employ evolutionary dynamics [10] to capture time varying attack and defense intensities. Despite these advances, most models assume access to plain text updates [16] or consider non encrypted settings [9], and they pay limited attention to the loss of observability caused by encrypted aggregation. Joint treatment of false positive cost, external incentives, and deployment budgets is also uncommon, and practical guidance for tuning defense parameters remains sparse. These gaps motivate a framework that is tailored to encrypted social FL and that integrates error costs and operational constraints into the analysis, with the goal of producing actionable defense recommendations.

To address these limitations, we propose an evolutionary game theoretic defense framework for encrypted update settings in social FL. The framework models server detection intensity and client poisoning propensity as strategy populations that evolve over time, and it explicitly accounts for the operational cost of false positives on benign clients as well as external incentives that may motivate poisoning. We analyze the stability of strategy profiles and the location of equilibria, and we show how detection intensity, false positive cost, external incentives, and resource expenditure shift these equilibria. Based on these results, we derive deployment oriented guidance for defense tuning, including conditions for switching between detection regimes and rules for setting sampling frequency and budget allocation.

The main contributions of this paper are as follow:

- We formalize the ciphertext poisoning defense problem in social FL and clarify the tension between privacy protection and observability in encrypted update settings.
- We develop a two role evolutionary game that incorporates false positive penalties and external incentives, and we provide analytical and simulation based evidence on strategy dynamics and equilibria.
- We present practical server side recommendations for cost aware tuning, covering detection intensity, audit scheduling, and coordination with bandwidth and energy budgets.

2   Related Work

2.1   Privacy Protection and Cryptographic Methods for Social Networks

In social networks, which are data-intensive platforms containing highly sensitive information such as user behaviors, friend relationships, and interaction histories, protecting client updates is essential in federated learning. Representative approaches include secure aggregation, homomorphic encryption, and secure multiparty computation. Secure aggregation, first introduced by Bonawitz et al. [2], ensures that the server only receives aggregated results while individual client updates remain hidden. Homomorphic encryption enables arithmetic operations on ciphertexts [4], supporting model aggregation without decryption.

Secure multiparty computation (MPC) allows multiple parties to jointly compute a function without revealing their inputs [20], which is particularly useful in large-scale and heterogeneous social network environments.

Despite these strengths, cryptographic protections introduce limitations. For social network servers, encrypted updates reduce observability of individual behaviors, making anomaly detection and robust aggregation techniques that depend on plaintext statistics inapplicable. Although zero-knowledge proofs and verifiable computation [13] can partially restore auditability, they impose heavy computation and communication overhead, which is unsustainable in platforms involving millions of users. Thus, while cryptography improves confidentiality, it simultaneously increases the difficulty of detecting and defending against poisoning attacks in social network federated learning.

2.2   Ciphertext Poisoning Attacks and Detection

In encrypted federated learning for social networks, poisoning attacks manifest differently from plaintext settings. Because client updates are protected through secure aggregation, homomorphic encryption, or multiparty computation, the server typically observes only ciphertext or aggregates and cannot directly access individual updates. As a result, traditional robust aggregation rules such as Krum [1] or Trimmed Mean [22], which rely on cross-client consistency, become ineffective, creating favorable conditions for ciphertext poisoning.

Several approaches have been proposed to mitigate poisoning under encryption. Xu et al. [18] introduced DDFed, which combines fully homomorphic encryption with a two-stage similarity-based detection mechanism to enhance privacy while countering poisoning. Ma et al. [12] proposed a Shieldfl framework, which combines two-trapdoor homomorphic encryption with a dual-server architecture to identify and mitigate model poisoning without exposing plaintext updates. Yazdinejad et al. [21] employ additive homomorphic encryption to protect gradients and perform computations in the ciphertext domain, combined with an internal auditor to achieve Byzantine-resilient aggregation.

These studies demonstrate initial progress toward defending against poisoning in ciphertext settings. However, they rely heavily on additional cryptographic operations, leading to significant computational and communication overhead. Moreover, they seldom address strategic trade-offs among detection intensity, false positive penalties, external incentives, and resource constraints. Thus, ciphertext poisoning remains a challenging open problem and motivates the need for analytical frameworks that explicitly capture such trade-offs.

2.3   Game Theory in Security and Federated Learning

Game theory provides a structured tool for modeling strategic interactions between attackers and defenders, and has been widely used in security to analyze resource allocation, inspection and evasion strategies, and long-term behavioral dynamics. In federated learning, game theoretic models have also been applied to participation incentives, reputation enforcement, and Byzantine robustness.

Representative studies include bargaining game, which model the negotiated distribution of constrained inspection resources [9]; Stackelberg formulations, which capture asymmetric information between servers and clients [6]; and various repeated and evolutionary games, which explain how clients sustain cooperation under long-term interactions through punishment and reward mechanisms [11,23]. These studies highlight the potential of game theoretic reasoning to analyze adaptation and equilibrium in federated learning security.

Nevertheless, most existing approaches assume plaintext observability of client updates, an assumption that does not hold in encrypted settings. Moreover, they rarely consider the joint impact of detection intensity, false positive penalties, external incentives, and resource budgets. To address these limitations, this paper introduces an evolutionary game theoretic defense framework specifically designed for ciphertext poisoning in social FL, thereby filling a critical gap in this real-world scenario.

3   Model Design

As shown in Fig. 1, we propose a two-role evolutionary game model for federated learning in social networks, where the server balances privacy protection and poisoning detection, while the client decides whether to engage in poisoning to manipulate updates for maximum success and minimal detection. The model incorporates external incentives like third-party rewards for successful poisoning and penalties for clients involved in poisoning, with compliant can appeal the penalties. Given the large number of participants and asynchronous, non-rational behavior, the framework simulates the dynamic interaction between the server and attacker, with both adjusting their strategies over time to reach equilibrium and maximize their payoffs.

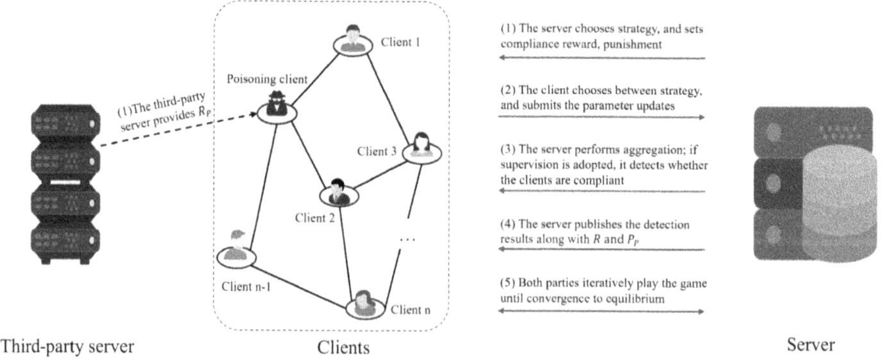

Fig. 1. Evolutionary Games in Social Federated Learning.

3.1   Model Assumptions

We design a two-player evolutionary game model, where the two roles are the server (data user) and the client (data holder). We assume that there are a variable number of clients participating in the federated learning task released by the server. Clients represent individual or group users in a social network, and their data is highly heterogeneous (such as user behavior, interests, and social relationships). At the same time, in social networks, the number of clients is large, and client participation is asynchronous, meaning not all clients participate at the same time, and participation may be intermittent or incomplete. The server chooses either a supervised or unsupervised strategy, and the probability of each strategy corresponds to the likelihood of the server choosing that strategy. Similarly, the clients decide whether to participate compliantly or maliciously (poisoning participation), and the probability of each strategy represents the proportion of clients choosing the corresponding strategy.

For poisoning behavior, we assume that clients participating in poisoning are incentivized by an external third party outside the federated learning environment, such as competitors of the server. Therefore, if the poisoning participation is successful, the client will receive additional rewards from the external third party.

The server will pay a reward to compliant clients. For clients identified as participating in poisoning through the server's attack detection methods, the server will impose penalties, including but not limited to financial penalties, restrictions on participation, or reputation downgrade. Compliant clients can appeal the penalties, while poisoning clients cannot use this appeal mechanism, resulting in different losses for compliant and poisoning clients.

3.2   Role Definitions

This paper designs a two-role evolutionary game model with the server and client as the two roles. In the federated learning scenario for social networks, the client represents a wide user base in the social network, and the clients not only hold data but may also participate in malicious activities such as poisoning attacks. The following are the definitions of the roles of the server and the client:

Server: As the task publisher of federated learning, the server is responsible for model aggregation and global security maintenance. Its core objective is to efficiently resist malicious attacks while ensuring model performance. The server's strategy space includes "supervised" and "unsupervised". When choosing the supervised strategy, the server activates attack detection methods, whereas the unsupervised strategy fully trusts the client's selections. The server's strategy choice needs to balance attack detection and overall effectiveness in federated learning, considering practical deployment constraints such as network bandwidth and energy limits.

Client: As the data holder in federated learning, the client trains a local model using its private data and uploads these models to the server for aggregation.

Clients in social networks represent a wide user base, with highly heterogeneous data and varying interests, behaviors, and privacy needs. The client's strategy space includes "compliant participation" and "poisoning participation". Compliant participation involves training and uploading a local model as per the normal federated learning workflow and receiving a reward from the server. Poisoning participation involves uploading a poisoned model and receiving additional rewards from an external third party.

In summary, the strategy spaces for the server and the client are defined as follows:

- Server strategy space $S_S = \{\text{supervised}, \text{unsupervised}\}$
- Client strategy space $S_C = \{\text{compliant participation}, \text{poisoning participation}\}$

3.3 Payoff Matrix

We model the participants' behaviors and decision-making in a federated learning system deployed in a social network. Clients in social networks exhibit significant heterogeneity, influenced not only by individual objectives but also by external incentives. The payoff matrices represent the rewards and penalties each participant (server or client) receives based on their strategy in the federated learning environment.

The following symbol definitions are used throughout the matrices, as shown in Table 1. The parameters reflect the local behavior of the participants. This framework allows us to investigate the dynamic interactions between participants and provides a formal foundation for interpreting the payoff matrices.

Table 1. Symbol Definitions and Their Meaning

Parameter Symbol	Parameter Meaning
R	Reward given by the server to compliant clients
C_S	Cost of using the supervised strategy by the server
θ_N	False positive rate for compliant clients under the supervised strategy
θ_P	Success rate for poisoning clients under the supervised strategy
L_N	Loss caused by false positive for compliant clients under the supervised strategy
P_P	Penalty for poisoning clients successfully detected under the supervised strategy
R_N	Reward from a compliant client to the server
L_P	Loss caused by poisoning clients to the server
C_N	Cost of choosing the compliant participation strategy by the client
C_P	Cost of choosing the poisoning participation strategy by the client
R_P	Additional reward received by the client for poisoning from an external third party
$x, 1-x$	Probability of the server choosing supervised or unsupervised strategy
$y, 1-y$	Probability of the client choosing compliant participation or poisoning participation

The payoff matrices for the server and the client represent their respective rewards and penalties, considering both their local decisions and the social network context. The server aims to balance the cost of supervision and the rewards for compliant and poisoning participants. Clients choose between compliant and poisoning participation, influenced not only by the rewards and penalties set by the server but also by external incentives.

Server's Payoff Matrix: As shown in Table 2, the server's payoff depends on the participation of clients, either compliant or poisoning. When the server chooses a supervised strategy, it incurs a cost C_S, and rewards compliant clients based on their contributions. The payoff for poisoning clients is reduced by the success rate θ_P. In unsupervised settings, the server does not enforce supervision, and rewards are based on the clients' chosen strategies.

Table 2. Server's Payoff Matrix

Strategy	Supervised (x)	Unsupervised $(1 - x)$
Compliant Participation (y)	$-C_S + (1 - \theta_N)(R_N - R)$	$R_N - R$
Poisoning Participation $(1 - y)$	$-C_S + (1 - \theta_P)(-L_P - R)$	$-L_P - R$

Client's Payoff Matrix: As shown in Table 3, the client's payoff depends on whether they participate in the federated learning task in a compliant or malicious (poisoning) manner. The client pays a cost for participating in either strategy. For compliant participation, they receive a reward from the server, but if they are penalized due to a false positive, the client suffers a loss. For poisoning participation, the client receives an additional reward from an external third party (R_P), but may face penalties if their malicious behavior is detected.

Table 3. Client's Payoff Matrix

Strategy	Supervised (x)	Unsupervised $(1 - x)$
Compliant Participation (y)	$-C_N + (1 - \theta_N)(R) - \theta_N L_N$	$-C_N + R$
Poisoning Participation $(1 - y)$	$-C_P + (1 - \theta_P)(R + R_P) - \theta_P P_P$	$-C_P + R + R_P$

From the payoff matrices, we observe the following difference in client payoff under the supervised strategy. The payoff difference between compliant participation and poisoning participation is given by:

$$\beta = [(-C_N + C_P - R_P) + (-\theta_N)(R + L_N) + (\theta_P)(R + R_P + P_P)] \quad (1)$$

When the server adopts the unsupervised strategy, the payoff difference between compliant and poisoning participation for the client is:

$$\delta = (-C_N + C_P - R_P) \quad (2)$$

For a compliant client, the payoff difference between the server's supervised and unsupervised strategies is:

$$\alpha = [-C_S + (-\theta_N)(R_N - R)] \tag{3}$$

For a poisoning client, the payoff difference between the server's supervised and unsupervised strategies is:

$$\gamma = [-C_S + (-\theta_P)(-L_P - R)] \tag{4}$$

The equations show the payoff differences for each participant (server and client) under different strategies.

4   Model Analysis

In this section, we derive the replication dynamics equations for the server and client based on the previously presented payoff matrices, forming a two-dimensional evolutionary system and solving for the equilibrium points (including four corner points and potential internal points). We then provide criteria for when the equilibrium points become evolutionarily stable strategies under different conditions. Finally, from the perspective of parameter sensitivity, we systematically analyze the impact of key parameters on strategy boundaries and the evolution speed/direction, extracting common patterns of change. In the context of social network federated learning, the behavior of clients is influenced only by their own objectives.

4.1   Replicator Dynamics and Equilibrium Point Analysis

This subsection calculates the replicator dynamics equations for the server and client and determines the strategy equilibrium points of the model. In social networks, clients' behavior is influenced by external incentives, and poisoning behavior can propagate through social relationship chains, impacting other clients' decisions. Therefore, the replicator dynamics equations in a federated learning system with social network characteristics need to account for these social factors.

First, we compute the expected payoff for the server and client. According to the payoff matrix, the expected payoff for the server under the supervised strategy is:

$$E_x = -C_S - R - L_P + \theta_P(L_P + R) + y\left[R_N + L_P + \theta_N(R - R_N) - \theta_P(L_P + R)\right] \tag{5}$$

If the server adopts the unsupervised strategy, the expected payoff formula is:

$$E_{(-x)} = -R - L_P + y(R_N + L_P) \tag{6}$$

Thus, the average payoff of the server is:

$$(E_x)' = xE_x + (1-x)E_{(-x)} \tag{7}$$

The replicator dynamics equation for the server is:

$$F(x) = \frac{dx}{dt} = x\left(E_x - (E_x)'\right) = x(1-x)\left(E_x - E_{(-x)}\right) \tag{8}$$

Similarly, if the client chooses the compliant participation strategy, the expected payoff is:

$$E_y = -C_N + R + x\left(-\theta_N(R + L_N)\right) \tag{9}$$

If the client chooses the poisoning participation strategy, the expected payoff is:

$$E_{(-y)} = -C_P + R + R_P + x\left(-\theta_P(R + R_P + P_P)\right) \tag{10}$$

Thus, the average payoff of the client is:

$$(E_y)' = yE_y + (1-y)E_{(-y)} \tag{11}$$

The replicator dynamics equation for the client is:

$$F(y) = \frac{dy}{dt} = y\left(E_y - (E_y)'\right) = y(1-y)\left(E_y - E_{(-y)}\right) \tag{12}$$

Equations (8) and (12) form the two-dimensional replicator dynamic system for federated learning with social network characteristics. Next, we calculate the equilibrium points of this system by solving the following system:

$$\begin{cases} F(x) = 0 \\ F(y) = 0 \end{cases} \tag{13}$$

We can obtain the fixed points as $(0,0)$, $(0,1)$, $(1,0)$, $(1,1)$, and for $x^* \in (0,1)$, $y^* \in (0,1)$, there is a non-fixed point (x^*, y^*), which are the equilibrium points of the two-dimensional system. The equilibrium lines are formed by $x^* = 0$, $x^* = 1$, $y^* = 0$, and $y^* = 1$.

Where the equilibrium points x^* and y^* are expressed as:

$$x^* = \frac{-(-C_N + C_P - R_P)}{(-\theta_N)(R + L_N) + (\theta_P)(R + R_P + P_P)} = \frac{-\delta}{\beta - \delta} \tag{14}$$

$$y^* = \frac{C_S - (-\theta_P)(-L_P - R)}{(-\theta_N)(R_N - R) - (-\theta_P)(-L_P - R)} = \frac{-\gamma}{\alpha - \gamma} \tag{15}$$

4.2 Stability Analysis of the Equilibrium Points

We now analyze the stability of the five equilibrium points.

For the equilibrium point $(1,1)$, when $\alpha > 0$ and $\beta > 0$, that is, when the server adopts the supervised strategy and rewards compliant participation more than poisoning participation, and when the server's supervised strategy rewards compliant participation more than poisoning participation, $(1,1)$ is an evolutionarily stable strategy.

For the equilibrium point $(1,0)$, when $\gamma > 0$ and $\beta < 0$, that is, when the server adopts the supervised strategy and rewards compliant participation more than poisoning participation, but the server's supervised strategy rewards poisoning participation more than compliant participation, $(1,0)$ is an evolutionarily stable strategy.

For the equilibrium point $(0,1)$, when $\alpha < 0$ and $\delta > 0$, that is, when the server adopts the unsupervised strategy and rewards compliant participation more than poisoning participation, but when the unsupervised strategy rewards compliant participation more than poisoning participation, $(0,1)$ is an evolutionarily stable strategy.

For the equilibrium point $(0,0)$, when $\gamma < 0$ and $\delta < 0$, that is, when the server adopts the unsupervised strategy and rewards compliant participation less than poisoning participation, $(0,0)$ is an evolutionarily stable strategy.

For the equilibrium point (x^*, y^*), the determinant of the Jacobian matrix is always zero. Therefore, this point is a saddle point and cannot be an evolutionarily stable strategy. Thus, we do not further discuss this point.

4.3 Evolutionarily Stable Strategy Analysis

In this section, we analyze the conditions for the existence of evolutionarily stable strategies (ESS) based on the parameters α, β, γ, and δ. As shown in Table 4, we find that the model can exhibit seven distinct evolutionarily stable states, with two of them being impossible due to contradictions with $\alpha < 0$. The analysis is summarized as follows:

Table 4. Evolutionarily Stable State Analysis

Evolutionarily Stable State	Conditions on $\alpha, \beta, \gamma, \delta$	Possible?
(1,1)	$\alpha > 0, \beta > 0$ and $\gamma < 0$ and $\delta < 0$ not simultaneously satisfied	×
(1,0)	$\beta < 0, \gamma > 0$ and $\alpha < 0$ and $\delta > 0$ not simultaneously satisfied	✓
(0,1)	$\alpha < 0, \delta > 0$ and $\beta < 0$ and $\gamma > 0$ not simultaneously satisfied	✓
(0,0)	$\gamma < 0, \delta < 0$ and $\alpha > 0$ and $\beta > 0$ not simultaneously satisfied	✓
(1,1) and (0,0)	$\alpha > 0, \beta > 0, \gamma < 0, \delta < 0$	×
(1,0) and (0,1)	$\alpha < 0, \beta < 0, \gamma > 0, \delta > 0$	✓
No Nash Equilibrium	Does not satisfy other ESS conditions on $\alpha, \beta, \gamma, \delta$	✓

4.4 Parameter Influence Analysis

As shown in Table 5, the evolutionarily stable strategy analysis is influenced by several model parameters. In this section, we analyze how different parameters affect the key values α, β, γ, and δ. Since the design of evolutionary game models involves multiple parameters, the dynamic behavior of these parameters plays a crucial role in the evolution of strategies. Below is the table summarizing the impact of each parameter on α, β, γ, and δ.

5 Experimental Evaluation

In this section, we conduct simulation experiments to analyze the evolution of strategies under various scenarios in social network federated learning (FL). The main goal is to examine how the initial strategy choices of participants, as well as the adjustments of different parameters, affect the evolutionarily stable strategies in a federated learning setup that also takes social network into account.

Table 5. Parameter Impact Analysis

Parameter	Impact on α	Impact on β	Impact on γ	Impact on δ	Full Local Rationality
R	θ_N	$\theta_N + \theta_P$	θ_P	\	$R \leq R_N, C_N \leq R, C_P \leq R + R_P$
C_S	-1	\	-1	\	\
θ_N	$R - R_N$	$R + L_N$	\	\	\
θ_P	\	$R + R_P + P_P$	$L_P + R$	\	\
L_N	\	$-\theta_N$	\	\	\
P_P	\	θ_P	\	\	\
R_N	$-\theta_N$	\	\	$R \leq R_N$	\
L_P	\	\	θ_P	\	\
C_N	\	-1	\	-1	$C_N \leq R$
C_P	\	+1	\	+1	$C_P \leq R + R_P$
R_P	\	$-1 + \theta_P$	\	-1	$C_P \leq R + R_P$

5.1 Mixed Strategy Nash Equilibrium

For the mixed strategy Nash equilibria at $(0, 1)$ and $(1, 0)$, the experimental parameters are set as $R = 2$, $C_S = 1$, $\theta_N = 0.3$, $\theta_P = 0.5$, $L_N = 10$, $P_P = 1$, $R_N = 3$, $L_P = 3$, $C_N = 1$, $C_P = 3$, and $R_P = 1$. These parameters are selected to reflect the trade-offs that typically arise in encrypted federated learning over social networks, where defense and attack behaviors are shaped by both cryptographic constraints and social influence.

Specifically, R and R_N represent the incentive alignment between the server and clients under privacy-preserving aggregation. C_S captures the computational and communication overhead of monitoring encrypted updates, which increases with network scale. The parameters θ_N and θ_P denote the detection accuracy of encrypted anomaly filters, where high false positives (θ_N) reduce user trust, while low detection success (θ_P) enables persistent poisoning. L_N and L_P quantify the impact of misclassification and successful poisoning on global model performance. P_P and R_P capture the external dynamics of the social network: malicious clients may gain reputation or competitive advantage (R_P) from coordinated attacks, but risk being penalized (P_P) if detected by encrypted audit mechanisms. C_N and C_P represent the participation costs under limited bandwidth and privacy budgets, which vary among heterogeneous social clients.

These parameters collectively model the multi-dimensional tension between privacy, security, and participation in social network federated learning. Under such settings, we simulate the evolutionary process to examine how encrypted poisoning incentives and adaptive defense strategies coevolve within a large-scale, socially connected environment.

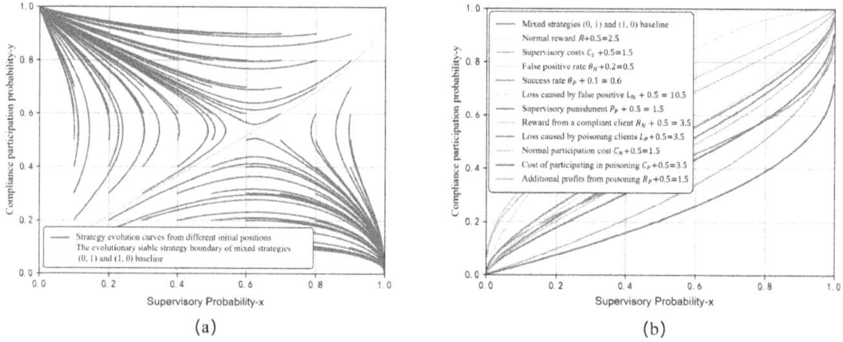

Fig. 2. The boundary between the evolutionarily stable strategies under the mixed strategy Nash equilibrium.

Mixed Strategy Boundary Analysis. Figure 2 illustrates the boundary between the evolutionarily stable strategies under the mixed strategy Nash equilibrium. Figure 2(a) shows the strategy evolution curves for different initial positions and the boundary between the two evolutionarily stable strategies, while Fig. 2(b) shows the boundary shifts after adjusting various parameters.

We first analyze the boundary changes after adjusting the following four parameters: normal service provider's reward R_N, false positive penalty L_N, supervision penalty P_P, and poisoning penalty L_P. These four parameters uniquely affect one of α, β, γ, and δ.

Normal Service Provider's Reward R_N: Increasing R_N reduces α, which increases the evolution towards $(0, 1)$ along the strongest momentum line, which is near $y = 1$. In social networks, higher rewards for normal behavior also influence other clients indirectly, making the evolution towards a cooperative strategy more likely.

False Positive Penalty L_N: Increasing L_N reduces β, which increases the evolution towards $(1, 0)$, with the strongest momentum line near $x = 1$. In the context of social networks, this penalty reinforces the deterrence effect, reducing the impact of malicious strategies.

Supervision Penalty P_P: Increasing P_P increases β, which strengthens the evolution towards $(0, 1)$, with the strongest momentum line at $x = 1$. This corresponds to a more strict supervision mechanism in the federated learning system, where the server applies higher penalties for malicious actions.

Poisoning Loss L_P: Increasing L_P increases γ, which strengthens the evolution towards $(1, 0)$, with the strongest momentum line at $y = 0$. In social networks, this represents the additional costs associated with poisoning actions, which are incentivized by external actors.

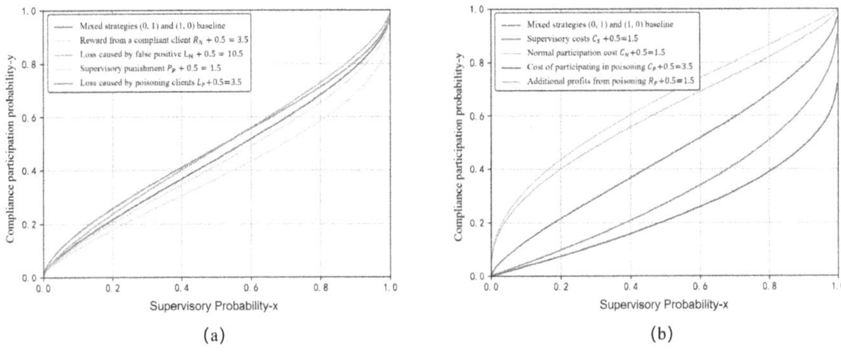

Fig. 3. The boundary lines adjusted for R_N, L_N, P_P, L_P and the boundary lines adjusted for C_S, C_N, C_P, R_P.

Boundary After Parameter Adjustments. As shown in Fig. 3(a), increasing the reward R_N from a compliant client causes the boundary to extend towards $(0, 1)$, and away from $(1, 0)$, with a greater extension near $y = 1$. Similarly, increasing the false positive penalty L_N causes the boundary to extend towards $(1, 0)$ and away from $(0, 1)$, with a greater extension near $x = 1$.

Increasing the supervision penalty P_P extends the boundary towards $(0, 1)$ and away from $(1, 0)$, with the greatest extension near $x = 1$, similar to the effect of R_N. Finally, increasing the poisoning loss L_P causes the boundary to extend towards $(1, 0)$ and away from $(0, 1)$, with the greatest extension near $y = 0$.

Thus, the four parameters – normal service provider's reward R_N, false positive penalty L_N, supervision penalty P_P, and poisoning loss L_P – show a common pattern: the boundary line extends towards the opposite direction, with the region closer to the strongest momentum line having a greater extension.

Analysis of Additional Parameters. Next, we analyze the impact of the following four parameters: supervision cost C_S, normal participation cost C_N, poisoning participation cost C_P, and additional poisoning reward R_P. These parameters have a common property in that they affect two of α, β, γ, and δ simultaneously, and the direction of influence is consistent across the two parameters.

Supervision Cost C_S: Increasing C_S decreases both α and γ, which strengthens the evolution towards $(0, 1)$, with the strategy ultimately evolving to $(0, 1)$.

Normal Participation st C_N: Increasing C_N decreases both β and δ, which strengthens the evolution towards $(1, 0)$, with the strategy ultimately evolving to $(1, 0)$.

Poisoning Participation Cost C_P: Increasing C_P increases both β and δ, which strengthens the evolution towards $(0, 1)$, with the strategy ultimately evolving to $(0, 1)$.

Poisoning Additional Reward R_P: Increasing R_P decreases both β and δ, which strengthens the evolution towards $(1, 0)$, with the strategy ultimately evolving to $(1, 0)$, but with a greater impact on δ compared to β.

Boundary after C_S, C_N, C_P, and R_P Adjustments As shown in Fig. 3(b), the supervision cost C_S increases, causing the boundary to extend towards $(0, 1)$ and away from $(1, 0)$, with the most extension concentrated in the middle, and decreasing as it moves towards the upper and lower sides. Similarly, the normal participation cost C_N increases, which causes the boundary to extend towards $(1, 0)$ and away from $(0, 1)$, with the most extension concentrated in the middle, and decreasing towards the left and right sides.

Increasing the poisoning participation cost C_P has a similar effect on the boundary, with the extension towards $(0, 1)$ being stronger in the middle. Increasing the additional poisoning reward R_P also shifts the boundary towards $(1, 0)$, with the most extension in the middle and decreasing towards the left and right sides.

Thus, the changes in C_S, C_N, C_P, and R_P share a common pattern: the boundary extends towards the opposite direction, with the most significant extension in the middle and a decrease in the extension as it moves towards the sides.

Boundary after Adjustments to θ_P, θ_N, and R. Finally, we analyze the effects of the accuracy rate θ_P, false positive rate θ_N, and compliance reward R on the boundary. The changes in the boundary are shown in Fig. 4.

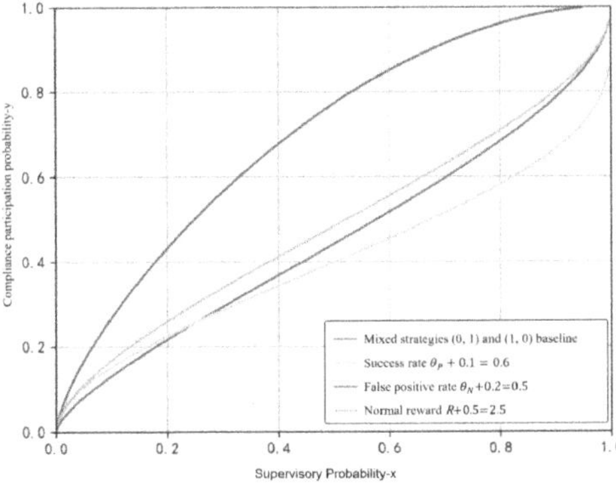

Fig. 4. Boundary after Adjustments to θ_P, θ_N, and R.

Increasing θ_P will increase both β and γ, strengthening the evolution towards $(0, 1)$ and $(1, 0)$ at $x = 1$ and $y = 0$. This influence manifests as a distortion of the boundary line, extending more towards $(1, 0)$ in the top-right corner and increasing the area of $(0, 1)$ strategy, while compressing $(1, 0)$.

Increasing θ_N will decrease both α and β, with a stronger effect on β. As α and β decrease, the boundary shifts towards $(0, 1)$.

The compliance reward R influences α, β, and γ, and increases both α and γ, which enhances the evolution towards $(0, 1)$, while β increases, enhancing the evolution towards $(1, 0)$.

When the evolutionarily stable state of the evolutionary game model is a mixed strategy Nash equilibrium, the initial strategy position can influence the final evolutionarily stable strategy. By adjusting the initial strategy positions, the model can ensure the final evolutionarily stable strategy. In adjusting the parameters to modify the boundary lines, it is essential to consider how different parameters affect the boundary at different positions and the strength of their impact. From the experimental results, particular attention should be paid to the accuracy parameter θ_P, as compared to other parameters, it changes the boundary unidirectionally and shifts the initial position of one evolutionarily stable strategy towards another.

5.2   No Nash Equilibrium

In this section, we examine the characteristics of the evolutionary strategy changes under non-Nash equilibrium conditions. Specifically, we analyze how parameter variations and different initial strategy positions influence the evolutionarily stable strategies (ESS) in the context of federated learning with social network dynamics.

The Equilibrium at (x^*, y^*). A set of model parameters is chosen such that (x^*, y^*) satisfies the equilibrium condition, i.e., the evolutionary stable state of the model is a non-Nash equilibrium. The parameters are set as follows: $R = 2$,

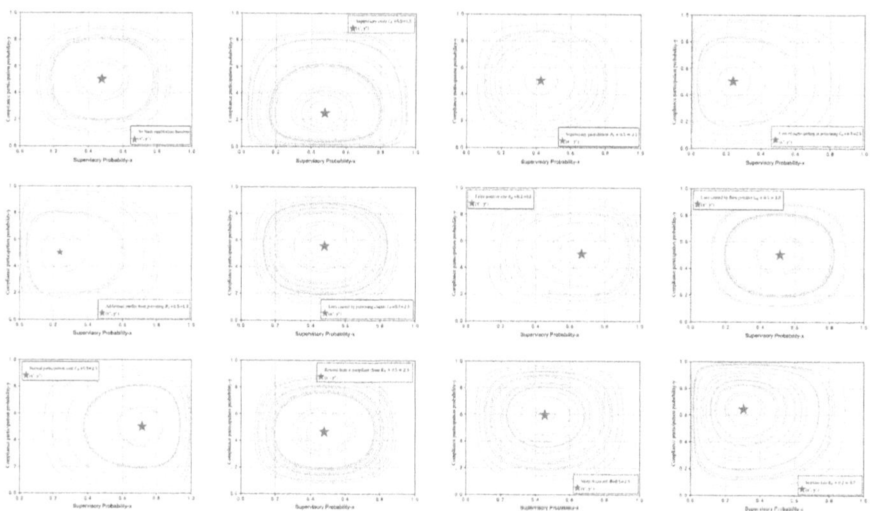

Fig. 5. The stable points (x^*, y^*) and the strategy evolution curves for different initial positions.

$C_S = 1$, $\theta_N = 0.3$, $\theta_P = 0.5$, $L_N = 1$, $P_P = 3$, $R_N = 2$, $L_P = 2$, $C_N = 2$, $C_P = 2$, and $R_P = 1$.

First, we observe the effect of parameter adjustments on the evolution of strategy curves from different initial positions under the non-Nash equilibrium condition. As shown in Fig. 5, the blue lines represent the strategy evolution curves for different initial positions, and the red star represents the corresponding equilibrium point (x^*, y^*). It can be observed that the strategy evolution curves from different initial positions revolve around the point (x^*, y^*) and are constrained by the boundaries. This behavior is consistent with the fact that in social network federated learning, clients' behavior is influenced by external incentives, which drive the strategies towards non-Nash equilibria.

In Fig. 6, the baseline equilibrium and the parameter-adjusted equilibrium points are shown. It is evident that only when both the accuracy rate θ_P and the compliance reward R shift simultaneously in both the horizontal and vertical directions do we observe substantial changes in the equilibrium point. Other parameters lead to more simple horizontal or vertical movements of the boundary.

The Boundary Line as the Equilibrium Line. Next, we set a group of parameters that satisfy $x^* = 0$, meaning that the equilibrium line is at $x^* = 0$. This section analyzes the situation where the equilibrium point is along a boundary line under a non-Nash equilibrium. The parameters are set as follows:$R = 3$, $C_S = 2$, $\theta_N = 0.3$, $\theta_P = 0.5$, $L_N = 2$, $P_P = 3$, $R_N = 4$, $L_P = 3$, $C_N = 2$, $C_P = 4$, and $R_P = 2$.

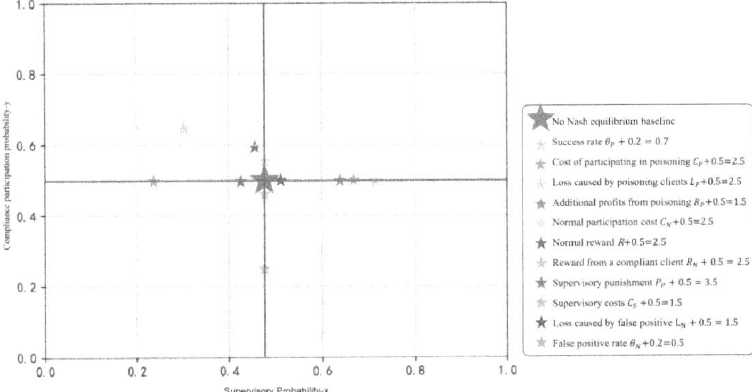

Fig. 6. (x^*, y^*) position summary map.

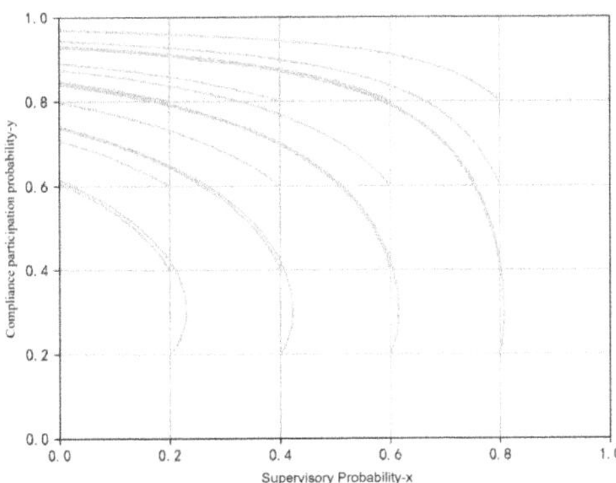

Fig. 7. The evolution strategy change curve at different initial positions when $(x^*)=0$.

As shown in Fig. 7, we observe the evolution of strategy curves starting from different initial positions. It is evident that the initial strategy position affects the equilibrium position in the absence of external interference. However, this influence is not always monotonic. For example, along the line where $x = 0.2$, the equilibrium point at $y = 0.2$ is higher than that at $y = 0.4$, but as y increases to 0.4, 0.6, and 0.8, the corresponding equilibrium points follow a consistent increase in y.

In contrast, along the line where $y = 0.2$, the impact of initial strategy positions on the equilibrium is linear: as x increases, the equilibrium y value increases.

Under non-Nash equilibrium conditions, it is important to differentiate the types of equilibrium points. For non-Nash equilibrium states where (x^*, y^*) is the equilibrium point, the evolution of strategy curves can be controlled around this point, ensuring that the strategies evolve within a specific region. For non-Nash equilibrium states with equilibrium lines, controlling the initial strategy positions ensures that the evolution of strategies converges to the desired equilibrium position. Social network dynamics, including external incentives, significantly impact how equilibrium points shift and evolve, making this analysis particularly relevant for federated learning in social network environments.

6   Conclusion and Future Work

In this paper, we proposed an evolutionary game-theoretic framework for defending against ciphertext poisoning attacks in federated learning, specifically within social network environments. Our analysis highlighted the key factors that influence the evolution of strategies, including the server's supervision strategy and the clients' compliance or poisoning behaviors. We demonstrated how parameters such as rewards, penalties, and costs impact the stability of evolutionary strategies and guide the server in adapting its defense mechanisms. The results showed that social network dynamics, such as external incentives, play a crucial role in shaping the equilibrium points and the evolution of strategies. By understanding these dynamics, we provided insights into how federated learning systems can be optimized for robustness and privacy preservation.

In the future work, we will focus on extending the model to incorporate scenarios with incomplete rationality, where clients may not always make optimal decisions due to limited information or computational resources. This extension will further enhance the realism of the model and broaden its applicability in real-world federated learning systems.

Acknowledgment. This research was supported in part by the Guangdong Basic and Applied Basic Research Foundation (No. 2024A1515011492), in part by the Tertiary Education Scientific Research Project of Guangzhou Municipal Education Bureau (No. 2024312190), in part by the National Natural Science Foundation of China (No. 62402195, 62002077), in part by the Talent Program of Guangdong Province (No. 2021QN02X898), in part by the Guangdong Provincial Key Research Project for Regular Universities in Priority Areas (No. 2025ZDZX3019).

References

1. Blanchard, P., El Mhamdi, E.M., Guerraoui, R., Stainer, J.: Machine learning with adversaries: byzantine tolerant gradient descent. In: Advances in Neural Information Processing Systems, vol. 30 (2017)
2. Bonawitz, K., et al.: Practical secure aggregation for privacy-preserving machine learning. In: proceedings of the 2017 ACM SIGSAC Conference on Computer and Communications Security, pp. 1175–1191 (2017)
3. Carletti, V., Foggia, P., Mazzocca, C., Parrella, G., Vento, M.: SoK: gradient inversion attacks in federated learning. In: 34th USENIX Security Symposium (USENIX Security 2025), pp. 6439–6459 (2025)
4. Gentry, C.: Fully homomorphic encryption using ideal lattices. In: Proceedings of the Forty-First Annual ACM Symposium on Theory of Computing, pp. 169–178 (2009)

5. Hu, C., Li, B.: Maskcrypt: federated learning with selective homomorphic encryption. IEEE Trans. Dependable Secure Comput. **22**(1), 221–233 (2024)
6. Huang, G., Wu, Q., Sun, P., Ma, Q., Chen, X.: Collaboration in federated learning with differential privacy: a stackelberg game analysis. IEEE Trans. Parallel Distrib. Syst. **35**(3), 455–469 (2024)
7. Huang, S., Li, G., Zhou, W.: Fedroad: secure and efficient road network queries over traffic data federation. In: 2025 IEEE 41st International Conference on Data Engineering (ICDE), pp. 2240–2252. IEEE Computer Society (2025)
8. Jiang, S., et al.: Towards compute-efficient byzantine-robust federated learning with fully homomorphic encryption. Nat. Mach. Intell. 1–12 (2025)
9. Li, Y., Li, F., Yang, S., Zhang, C., Zhu, L., Wang, Y.: A cooperative analysis to incentivize communication-efficient federated learning. IEEE Trans. Mob. Comput. **23**(10), 10175–10190 (2024)
10. Lin, Y., Gao, Z., Du, H., Niyato, D., Kang, J., Liu, X.: Incentive and dynamic client selection for federated unlearning. In: Proceedings of the ACM Web Conference 2024, pp. 2936–2944 (2024)
11. Lu, J., Zhang, Y., Jia, R., Cao, S., Liu, J., Fu, H.: Fedcross: intertemporal federated learning under evolutionary games. In: Proceedings of the AAAI Conference on Artificial Intelligence, vol. 39, pp. 19115–19123 (2025)
12. Ma, Z., Ma, J., Miao, Y., Li, Y., Deng, R.H.: Shieldfl: mitigating model poisoning attacks in privacy-preserving federated learning. IEEE Trans. Inf. Forensics Secur. **17**, 1639–1654 (2022)
13. Sun, H., Bai, T., Li, J., Zhang, H.: ZKDL: efficient zero-knowledge proofs of deep learning training. IEEE Tran. Inf. Forensics Secur. (2024)
14. Sun, Z., Wan, J., Wang, B., Cao, Z., Li, R., He, Y.: An ownership verification mechanism against encrypted forwarding attacks in data-driven social computing. Front. Phys. **9**, 739259 (2021)
15. Wang, S., Zheng, Y., Jia, X., Yi, X.: Pegraph: a system for privacy-preserving and efficient search over encrypted social graphs. IEEE Trans. Inf. Forensics Secur. **17**, 3179–3194 (2022)
16. Wang, Y., Su, Z., Pan, Y., Luan, T.H., Li, R., Yu, S.: Social-aware clustered federated learning with customized privacy preservation. IEEE/ACM Trans. Netw. (2024)
17. Xu, G., Chen, G., Cheng, Z., Hong, Y., Qi, H.: Consistency of stackelberg and nash equilibria in three-player leader-follower games. IEEE Trans. Inf. Forensics Secur. **19**, 5330–5344 (2024)
18. Xu, R., Gao, S., Li, C., Joshi, J., Li, J.: Dual defense: enhancing privacy and mitigating poisoning attacks in federated learning. Adv. Neural. Inf. Process. Syst. **37**, 70476–70498 (2024)
19. Xu, R., Li, B., Li, C., Joshi, J.B., Ma, S., Li, J.: Tapfed: threshold secure aggregation for privacy-preserving federated learning. IEEE Trans. Dependable Secure Comput. **21**(5), 4309–4323 (2024)
20. Yao, A.C.: Protocols for secure computations. In: 23rd Annual Symposium on Foundations of Computer Science (SFCS 1982), pp. 160–164. IEEE (1982)
21. Yazdinejad, A., Dehghantanha, A., Karimipour, H., Srivastava, G., Parizi, R.M.: A robust privacy-preserving federated learning model against model poisoning attacks. IEEE Trans. Inf. Forensics Secur. **19**, 6693–6708 (2024)
22. Yin, D., Chen, Y., Kannan, R., Bartlett, P.: Byzantine-robust distributed learning: towards optimal statistical rates. In: International Conference on Machine Learning, pp. 5650–5659. PMLR (2018)

23. Zhang, N., Ma, Q., Chen, X.: Enabling long-term cooperation in cross-silo federated learning: a repeated game perspective. IEEE Trans. Mob. Comput. **22**(7), 3910–3924 (2022)
24. Zhang, X., et al.: Fltracer: accurate poisoning attack provenance in federated learning. IEEE Trans. Inf. Forensics Secur. **19**, 9534–9549 (2024)
25. Zheng, J., Li, K., Yuan, X., Ni, W., Tovar, E.: Detecting poisoning attacks on federated learning using gradient-weighted class activation mapping. In: Companion Proceedings of the ACM Web Conference 2024, pp. 714–717 (2024)

Physical Layer Security via Movable Antenna in Near-Field

Yinghui Wang[1,2], Lei Zhang[1(✉)], and Hang Chen[1]

[1] Hubei Polytechnic University, Huangshi 435003, China
{zhanglei,chenhang}@hbpu.edu.cn
[2] Hubei Normal University, Huangshi 435002, China

Abstract. Research focuses on the physical layer security (PLS) of mobile antenna arrays (MA) in near-field (NF) scenarios. A base station (BS) with an MA array serves a user with a single antenna, while multiple eavesdroppers with single antennas listen in. In order to reduce the risk of eavesdropping, a near-field MA-assisted secure transmission framework is proposed. The aim of this framework is to maximize achievable secrecy rates by jointly optimizing the base station's beamforming vectors and mobile antenna positions. For this problem, high-quality suboptimal solutions are obtained through the Alternating Optimization (AO) algorithm and the Projected Gradient Ascent (PGA) method. Simulation results demonstrate that, compared to secure communication assisted by far-field MA and secure communication assisted by fixed antennas (FPA) in the near-field, this near-field MA secure transmission framework significantly enhances the security of information transmission. Specifically, when the base station transmission power is $10\,\mathrm{W}$, the secure transmission rate increases by approximately 15% and 18%, respectively.

Keywords: Movable antenna · Physical layer security · Transmit beamforming

1 Introduction

Over the past few decades, cryptographic encryption/decryption has been regarded as the most crucial technology for information security [1]. To avoid the heavy key management and computational costs associated with traditional encryption/decryption schemes, Physical Layer Security (PLS) technology has attracted widespread attention across various fields in recent years [2]. Specifically, the rapid advancement of multi-antenna technologies has facilitated the widespread application of secure beamforming /precoding techniques in PLS [3]. Extensive research has focused on secrecy rate maximisation (SRM) [4,5], demonstrating the effectiveness of beamforming in improving system security performance.

Traditional beamforming techniques rely on fixed-position antenna (FPA) arrays. The steering vectors of these arrays remain fixed, resulting in limited

L. Zhai et al. (Eds.): SocialSec 2025, LNCS 16327, pp. 117–128, 2026.
https://doi.org/10.1007/978-981-95-7027-0_7

beamforming gain [6]. In contrast, mobile antennas (MAs) connect to the radio frequency (RF) chain via flexible cables, enabling the antenna position to be adjusted and the channel to be reconstructed [7]. Research indicates that systems assisted by MA outperform those assisted by FPA in terms of enhanced signal power, interference mitigation, flexible beamforming and spatial multiplexing [8]. Research on MA technology has shown that integrating MA can enhance physical layer security. Using the additional spatial degrees of freedom (DOF) provided by MA can improve the secure transmission rate [9]. Explored the physical layer security of MA in far-field scenarios, with the objective of jointly optimizing MA position and transmit beamforming vector to minimize transmit power and maximize signal ratio (SR) [10] and [11]. Jointly designed beamforming vectors and MA position to maximize SR and minimize the probability of secure interruption, respectively.

Research on MA-enhanced PLS has focused on far-field conditions. With high-frequency bands and large-aperture antennas, near-field effects have become more significant [12]. How to enhance physical layer security in near-field conditions remains an open research question. Inspired by this, we investigate an MA-assisted physical layer secure communication system for near-field scenarios. The main contributions are summarized as follows: (1) A secure transmission framework for MA-assisted communication in near-field environments is established, enabling the base station to convey secure information to legitimate users despite the presence of potential eavesdroppers. This research aims to maximize the system's confidentiality performance under dual constraints of total base station power and mobile antenna positioning. This problem model constitutes a complex non-convex issue that cannot be solved directly. The paper employs the Alternating Optimization (AO) algorithm and Projected Gradient Ascent (PGA) method to transform the problem into a convex formulation, thereby seeking high-quality suboptimal solutions. (2) The numerical results show that the proposed MA-assisted scheme for near-field communication is more effective at mitigating security risks posed by eavesdroppers than MA-assisted wireless communication in far-field or FPA-assisted wireless communication in near-field. This provides new perspectives and solutions for secure physical-layer transmission in near-field communication.

2   System Model

As depicted in Fig. 1, this system considers a base station transmitting confidential information to a legitimate user while achieving maximum secrecy rate transmission in the presence of K eavesdroppers, denoted by $\{Eve\}_{i=1}^{K}$. The User and each of the M eavesdroppers are equipped with a single fixed-position antenna, while the transmitter is fitted with a linear MA array of size N. We assume the legitimate user and eavesdroppers reside within the near-field region, where λ denotes the wavelength of the narrowband systems, meaning their distances from the BS are less than the Rayleigh distance $2D^2/\lambda$. This system aims to maximize the communication quality for the legitimate user while minimizing

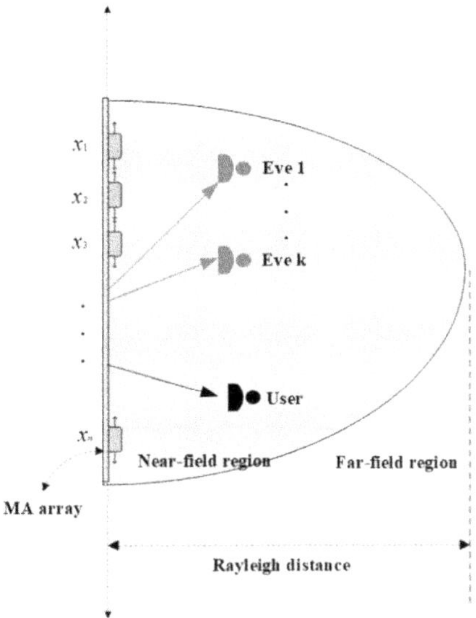

Fig. 1. Near-field mobile antenna system model.

the amount of information interceptable by eavesdroppers, thereby enhancing physical layer security.

As depicted in Fig. 2, establish a Cartesian coordinate system in the near-field region to analyze the moving antenna model. Consider a one-dimensional near-field wireless communication system with N movable antennas that estimate the user's angle and spatial parameters. These antennas can adjust their positions within a one-dimensional line segment of given length A. The position of the nth antenna at the transmitter is denoted by $s_n = [x_n, 0]^T$ and $1 \le n \le N$, the positions of the N antennas can be represented as $x = [x_1, x_2, ..., x_N]^T \in R^{N \times 1}$, where $(\cdot)^T$ denotes the transpose operation and $x_n \in [0, A]$. Without loss of generality, we assume that $0 \le x1 \le x2 \le \cdots \le x_N \le A$. Therefore, the effective aperture of the MA array can be represented as $D = x_N - x_1$. We assume that the User is located in the near-field region of the linear array but outside its reactive region, which means that the distance between the User and any position within the MA array is between the Fresnel distance and the Rayleigh distance, which are respectively given by $R_{FS} \triangleq \frac{A}{2}(\frac{A}{\lambda})^{\frac{1}{3}}$ [13] and $R_{RL} \triangleq \frac{2A^2}{\lambda}$ [14], where λ is the signal wavelength. The distance and angle from the User to the origin are denoted as r_u and θ_u respectively, thus the position coordinates at the User location can be expressed as $u = [r_u cos\theta_u, r_u sin\theta_u]^T$. The distance and angle from Eve to the origin are denoted as $r_e = [r_1, r_2, ..., r_k]$ and $\theta_e = [\theta_1, \theta_2, ..., \theta_k]$ respectively. Taking a legitimate User as an example, the distance $d_{n,u}$ between the User and the nth antenna x_n can be calculated.

$$d_{n,u} = |u - s_n| = \sqrt{r_u^2 - 2us_n + |s_n|^2} = \sqrt{r_u^2 - 2r_u x_n cos\theta_u + x_n^2}. \tag{1}$$

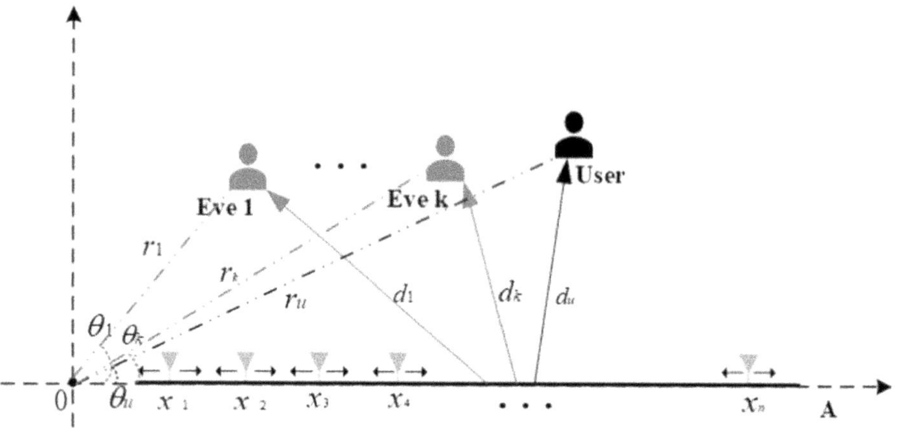

Fig. 2. Mobile Antenna System Model.

By invoking the Fresnel approximation of the near-field model [14,15], the distance d_n in (1) can be approximated as the second-order Taylor expansion of $\sqrt{1+x} \approx 1 + \frac{1}{2}x - \frac{1}{8}x^2$, where $x = \left(-2u \cdot s_n + |s_n|^2\right)/r_u^2$, that is,

$$d_{n,u} \approx r_u - x_n cos\theta_u + \frac{x_n^2(1 - cos^2\theta_u)}{2r_u}, 1 \leq n \leq N. \tag{2}$$

Therefore, the corresponding near-field steering vector for the MA array at the User location is given by:

$$\alpha(x, \theta_u) = \left[e^{j\frac{2\pi}{\lambda}d_{1,u}}, e^{j\frac{2\pi}{\lambda}d_{2,u}}, ..., e^{j\frac{2\pi}{\lambda}d_{N,u}}\right]^\top. \tag{3}$$

Then, assuming $\omega \in \mathbf{C}^{N\times1}$ represents the digital transmit beamforming of confidential information at the transmitter, the beam gain of the MA array at the User is derived as: where $(\cdot)^H$ denotes the conjugate transpose operation.

$$G_{x,\omega}(\theta_u) = |\alpha^H(x, \theta_u)\omega|^2, \theta_u \in [0, \pi). \tag{4}$$

Considering the worst-case scenario where K Eve attackers cooperatively process their received confidential information, the achievable secrecy rate in bits per second per hertz (bps/Hz) is given by:

$$R_{sec}(x, \omega) = \left[log_2(1 + \frac{|\alpha^H(x, \theta_u)\omega|^2}{\sigma^2}) - log_2(1 + \frac{\sum_{i=1}^k |\alpha^H(x, \theta_i)\omega|^2}{\sigma^2})\right]^+. \tag{5}$$

where $[r]^+ = \max(r, 0)$ and σ^2 denote the receiver noise power.

Our objective is to maximize the system secrecy rate by jointly optimizing the transmitter MA array position x and transmit beamforming ω. Therefore, the optimisation problem is formulated as follows:

$$P1 : \max_{\omega,x} R_{sec}(\omega, x) \tag{6}$$

$$s.t.\ tr(\omega^H \omega) \leq P_0 \tag{6a}$$

$$|x_z - x_q| \geq D_0, z, q \in \{1, 2, ..., N\}, z \neq q \tag{6b}$$

$$\{x_s\}_{s=1}^N \in [0, L]. \tag{6c}$$

3   Problem Description

As MA arrays permit flexible adjustment of all antenna positions, they can predictably achieve superior spatial diversity and multiplexing performance compared to conventional FPA arrays, thereby enabling higher confidentiality rates. However, objective (P1) is non-convex with respect to either x or ω. Furthermore, x and ω are coupled with each other in the objective function. These two aspects contribute to the high non-convexity of (P1). Consequently, an alternating minimisation algorithm is employed to iteratively solve for x or ω, which can be formulated as fixing one variable while optimize another.

3.1   Optimizing w Given x

We first define that

$$A = \frac{1}{\sigma^2}\alpha(x, \theta_u)\alpha^H(x, \theta_u), \tag{7}$$

$$B = \frac{1}{\sigma^2}\sum_{i=1}^k \alpha(x, \theta_i)\alpha^H(x, \theta_i), \tag{8}$$

Based on this, the problem of optimizing ω given x is expressed as P2,

$$P2 : \max_{\omega} \frac{1 + \omega^H A \omega}{1 + \omega^H A \omega} \tag{9}$$

$$s.t.\ \|\omega\|_2^2 = P_0. \tag{9a}$$

The optimal solution for (P2) is widely recognized as [4],

$$\omega = \sqrt{P_0}o_{max}. \tag{10}$$

where o_{max} denotes the normalized eigenvector corresponding to the largest eigenvalue of the matrix $\left(B + \frac{1}{P_0 I_N}\right)^{-1}\left(A + \frac{1}{P_0 I_N}\right)$, I_N denotes the identity matrix $N \times N$, and $(\cdot)^{-1}$ represents the inverse operation.

3.2 Optimizing x Given w

Express ω as $\omega = v + jz$, that is $C = vv^T + zz^T, D = vz^T - zv^T$. Then define

$$g_i = [g_{1,i}, g_{2,i}, ..., g_{N,i}]^\top, i = 1, ...K, \tag{11}$$

$$q_i = [q_{1,i}, q_{2,i}, ..., q_{N,i}]^\top, i = 1, ...K, \tag{12}$$

where

$$g_{n,i} = cos(\frac{2\pi}{\lambda} d_{n,i}), \tag{13}$$

$$q_{n,i} = sin(\frac{2\pi}{\lambda} d_{n,i}), \tag{14}$$

With these, $|a^H(x, \theta_i)\omega|^2, i = 1, ...K$ can be expressed as

$$|\alpha^H(x, \theta_i)\omega|^2 = g_i^\top C g_i + q_i^\top C q_i + 2 g_i^\top D q_i \triangle f(g_i, q_i). \tag{15}$$

Based on this, the problem of optimizing x given ω is denoted as P3.

$$P3 : \max_{x} log_2 \left(1 + \frac{f(g_u, q_u)}{\sigma^2}\right) - log_2 \left(1 + \frac{\sum_{i=1}^{K} f(g_i, q_i)}{\sigma^2}\right)$$

$$= \Psi \left(\{g_u, q_u\} + \{g_i, q_i\}_{i=1}^{K}\right) \tag{16}$$

$$s.t. \ |x_z - x_q| \geq D_0, z, q \in \{1, 2, ..., N\}, z \neq q \tag{16a}$$

$$\{x_s\}_{s=1}^{N} \in [0, L] \tag{16b}$$

Due to the complex objective, problem (P3) remains highly non-convex. To address this, the Projected Gradient Ascent (PGA) method is employed to find local optimal for (P3). Specifically, using PGA, the update rule for x is given by:

$$x^{t+1} = x^t + \delta \nabla_{x^t} \Psi \left(\{g_u, q_u\} + \{g_i, q_i\}_{i=1}^{K}\right). \tag{17}$$

$$x^{t+1} = \mathcal{B} \left(x^{t+1}, d_{min}, L\right). \tag{18}$$

In the above update rule, the first expression represents the conventional update of the variable x^{t+1}. The second equation expression employs the projection function $\mathcal{B}(\cdot)$ to restriction of the updated x^{t+1} within the set satisfying the constraints, thereby ensuring that the position of MA obtained at each iteration remains valid. Furthermore, $\nabla_{x^t} \Psi \left(\{g_u, q_u\} + \{g_i, q_i\}_{i=1}^{K}\right)$ denotes the gradient of $\Psi \left(\{g_u, q_u\} + \{g_i, q_i\}_{i=1}^{K}\right)$ with respect to x^t. δ represents the step size for gradient ascent. The expressions for updating x are obtained by solving $\nabla_{x^t} \Psi \left(\{g_u, q_u\} + \{g_i, q_i\}_{i=1}^{K}\right)$ and $\mathcal{B}(x^{t+1}, d_{min}, L)$ respectively.

Computing $\nabla_{x^t} \Psi \left(\{g_u, q_u\} + \{g_i, q_i\}_{i=1}^{K} \right)$

$$
\begin{aligned}
&\nabla_{x^t} \Psi \left(\{g_u, q_u\} + \{g_i, q_i\}_{i=1}^{K} \right) \\
&= ln2 \times \left(\frac{\nabla_{x^t} f(g_u, q_u)/\sigma^2}{1 + f(g_u, q_u)/\sigma^2} - \frac{\sum_{i=1}^{K} \nabla_{x^t} f(g_i, q_i)/\sigma^2}{1 + \sum_{i=1}^{K} \nabla_{x^t} f(g_i, q_i)/\sigma^2} \right).
\end{aligned}
\tag{19}
$$

$$
\nabla_{x^t} f(g_i, q_i) = \left[\frac{\partial f(g_i, q_i)}{\partial x_1^t}, \frac{\partial f(g_i, q_i)}{\partial x_2^t}, ..., \frac{\partial f(g_i, q_i)}{\partial x_N^t} \right]^{\top}.
\tag{20}
$$

For $\frac{\partial f(g_i, q_i)}{\partial x_n^t}$, this can be expressed as

$$
\begin{aligned}
\frac{\partial f(g_i, q_i)}{\partial x_n^t} &= \frac{\partial f(g_i, q_i)}{\partial g_{n,i}} \frac{\partial g_{n,i}}{\partial x_n^t} + \frac{\partial f(g_i, q_i)}{\partial q_{n,i}} \frac{q_{n,i}}{\partial x_n^t} \\
&= -sin\left(\frac{2\pi}{\lambda} d_{n,i}\right) \cdot \frac{2\pi}{\lambda} \left(\frac{2x_n(1 - cos^2\theta_i)}{2r_i} - cos\theta_i \right) \cdot \frac{\partial f(g_i, q_i)}{\partial g_{n,i}} \\
&\quad + cos\left(\frac{2\pi}{\lambda} d_{n,i}\right) \cdot \frac{2\pi}{\lambda} \left(\frac{2x_n(1 - cos^2\theta_i)}{2r_i} - cos\theta_i \right) \cdot \frac{\partial f(g_i, q_i)}{\partial q_{n,i}}.
\end{aligned}
\tag{21}
$$

Let $diag\,(\cdot)$ denotes the diagonal operation. W_i and S_i are expressed respectively as:

$$
W_i = diag \left(\left\{ \frac{2\pi}{\lambda} \left(\frac{2x_n(1 - cos^2\theta_i)}{2r_i} - cos\theta_i \right) \cdot sin(\frac{2\pi}{\lambda} d_{n,i}) \right\}_{n=1}^{N} \right).
\tag{22}
$$

$$
S_i = diag \left(\left\{ \frac{2\pi}{\lambda} \left(\frac{2x_n(1 - cos^2\theta_i)}{2r_i} - cos\theta_i \right) \cdot cos(\frac{2\pi}{\lambda} d_{n,i}) \right\}_{n=1}^{N} \right).
\tag{23}
$$

Thus, $\nabla x^t f(g_i, q_i)$ can be expressed as

$$
\nabla x^t f(g_i, q_i) = -W_i \frac{\partial f(g_i, q_i)}{\partial g_{n,i}} + S_i \frac{\partial f(g_i, q_i)}{\partial q_{n,i}}.
\tag{24}
$$

Based on the existing formula, the following expression can be derived:

$$
\begin{aligned}
&\left[\frac{\partial f(g_i, q_i)}{\partial g_{1,i}}, \frac{\partial f(g_i, q_i)}{\partial g_{2,i}}, ..., \frac{\partial f(g_i, q_i)}{\partial g_{N,i}} \right]^{\top} \\
&= \nabla_{g_i} f(g_i, q_i) = 2Cg_i + 2Dq_i,
\end{aligned}
\tag{25}
$$

$$
\begin{aligned}
&\left[\frac{\partial f(g_i, q_i)}{\partial q_{1,i}}, \frac{\partial f(g_i, q_i)}{\partial q_{2,i}}, ..., \frac{\partial f(g_i, q_i)}{\partial q_{N,i}} \right]^{\top} \\
&= \nabla_{q_i} f(g_i, q_i) = 2Cq_i - 2Dg_i.
\end{aligned}
\tag{26}
$$

Ultimately, $\nabla x^t f(g_i, q_i)$ can be expressed as:

$$
\nabla_{x^t} f(q_i, g_i) = -W_i(2Cg_i + 2Dq_i) + S_i(2Cq_i - 2Dg_i).
\tag{27}
$$

Based on the existing formulae, $\nabla_{x^t}\Psi\left(\{g_u, q_u\} + \{g_i, q_i\}_{i=1}^{K}\right)$ can be derived as follows:

$$\nabla_{x^t}\Psi\left(\{g_u, q_u\} + \{g_i, q_i\}_{i=1}^{K}\right)$$

$$= ln2\left(\frac{\frac{-W_u(2Cg_u+2Dq_u)+S_u(2Cq_u-2Dg_u)}{\sigma^2}}{1+f(g_u,q_u)/\sigma^2} - \frac{\sum_{i=1}^{K}\frac{-W_i(2Cg_i+2Dq_i)+S_i(2Cq_i-2Dg_i)}{\sigma^2}}{1+\sum_{i=1}^{K}f(g_i,q_i)/\sigma^2}\right)(28)$$

Determination $\mathcal{B}\left(x^{t+1}, d_{min}, L\right)$ Assuming x satisfies the condition $0 \leq x_1 \leq x_2 \leq ... \leq x_N \leq L$, then we can derive

$$x_2 - x_1 \geq d_{min}, ..., x_N - x_{N-1} \geq d_{min}$$
$$\Rightarrow x_N \geq x_{N-1} + d_{min} \geq ... \geq x_n + (N-n)d_{min} \geq ... \geq x_1 + (N-1)d_{min}$$
$$\Rightarrow x_n + (N-n)d_{min} \leq L, \forall n = 1, ..., N,$$
$$\Rightarrow x_n \in [x_{n-1} + d_{min}, L - (N-n)d_{min}], \forall n = 1, ..., N \quad (29)$$

In summary, the projection function $\mathcal{B}(x^{t+1}, d_{min}, L)$ can be derived as

$$\mathcal{B}(x^{t+1}, d_{min}, L)$$
$$x_1^{t+1} = max\left((0, min(L_(N-1)d_{min}, x_1^{t+1}))\right)$$
$$x_2^{t+1} = max\left((x_1^{t+1} + d_{min}, min(L_(N-2)d_{min}, x_2^{t+1}))\right)$$
$$...x_N^{t+1} = max\left((x_{N-1}^{t+1} + d_{min}, min(L, x_N^{t+1}))\right). \quad (30)$$

4   Numerical Results

This section presents numerical results to validate the effectiveness of the proposed physical layer security framework enhanced by mobile antennas in near-field scenarios. The minimum distance between any two MA is set to $d_{min} = \lambda/2$, with the MA array range defined as $[0, L] = [0, 10\lambda]$. The PGA method step size is set to $\delta = 0.01$. Noise power is set to $\sigma^2 = 1$ for normalising large-scale channel fading power. One communicating user and $M = 2$ potential eavesdroppers are present within the transmitter's near-field region. For comparison, this section simulates beamforming patterns for MA arrays with varying antenna sizes in the near-field environment. For confidentiality rate analysis, communication confidentiality rates of MA arrays in both near-field and far-field conditions are simulated, additionally, the confidentiality rates of MA and FPA arrays are analyzed and compared in the near-field environment under different numbers of antennas and transmit powers.

Figure 3 demonstrates the convergence performance of the proposed algorithm and its inner-loop optimization process. As shown in (a), the algorithm converges rapidly across different antenna configurations, with the secrecy rate stabilizing after 4–5 iterations. Performance improves by approximately 14% when $N = 4$ compared to $N = 3$. Simultaneously, Figure (b) reveals that the computational complexity of the inner-loop PGA method decreases significantly by over 70% during the initial iterations and remains at a low level thereafter.

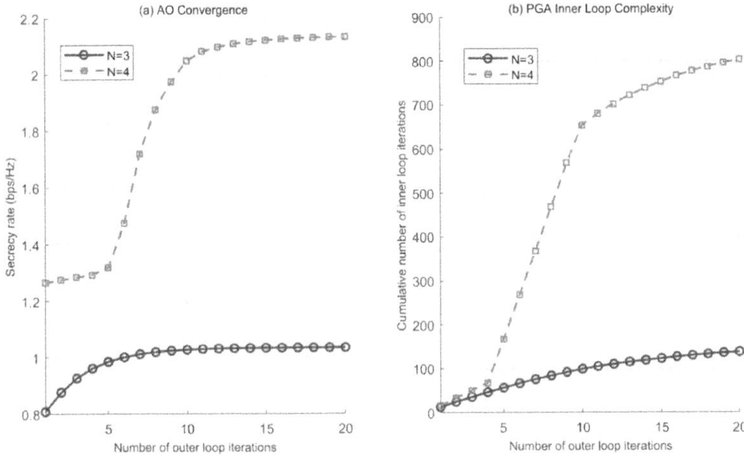

Fig. 3. (a) Convergence of the alternating optimization algorithm and (b) complexity of the PGA method.

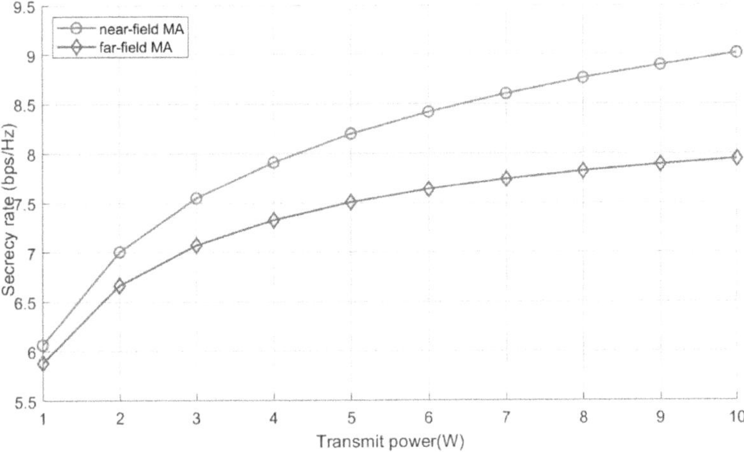

Fig. 4. Security rates achievable with MA arrays in near-field and far-field.

This validates that the proposed algorithm possesses the dual advantages of rapid convergence and high computational efficiency.

Figure 4 illustrates the achievable secure rates for MA arrays in both near-field and far-field environments when no transmit power is employed. Simulation results demonstrate that near-field Mobile Antenna (MA) arrays exhibit significant performance advantages over their far-field counterparts. With a fixed number of antennas $N = 64$, as transmission power P increases from 1 to 10, the secure rates of both systems rise with power. However, the near-field MA array consistently outperforms the far-field MA array, with the performance gap widening as transmission power increases. This phenomenon demonstrates that the near-field spherical wavefront effect significantly enhances channel diversity by introducing additional spatial degrees of freedom. Consequently, it more effectively leverages the beamforming capabilities of large-scale antenna arrays to improve physical layer security performance.

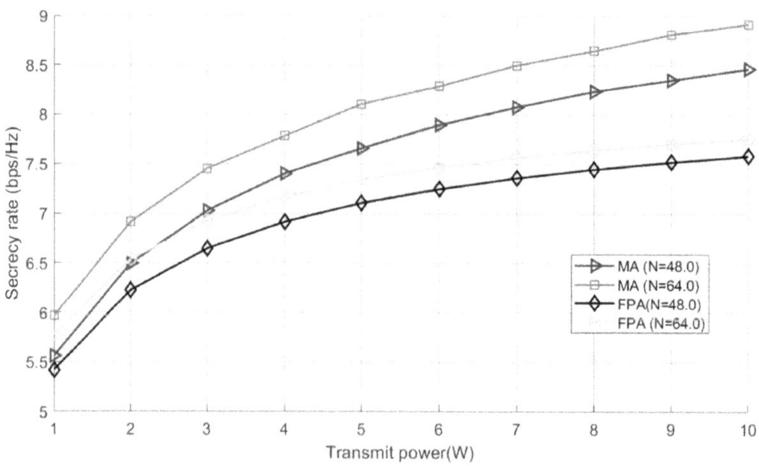

Fig. 5. Security rates achievable at different transmit powers for MA and FPA arrays.

Figure 5 illustrates the achievable security rates for MA and FPA arrays under varying transmit powers and antenna counts. Here, $M = 2$, with User and Eve angles respectively at $\theta_u = \frac{\pi}{2}, \theta_1 = \frac{\pi}{4}, \theta_2 = \frac{1.1\pi}{2}$. User and Eve distances from the origin are $10m$, $5m$, and $20m$. Analysis of simulation results reveals that the MA array demonstrates significant advantages over the conventional FPA array in physical layer security performance. Specifically, for the same number of antennas ($N = 48$ or $N = 68$), the MA array consistently achieves higher security rates than the FPA array, with this advantage increasing as power levels rise. Furthermore, an increase in both the number of antennas and transmission power exerts a positive effect on both types of systems, though the performance improvement is more pronounced for MA arrays, reaching its peak under the jointly optimized scenario of $N = 68$ and $10.0W$. These results validate the effectiveness of the MA array in enhancing channel diversity through dynamic antenna positioning, thereby improving the security performance of wireless communication systems.

Figure 6 illustrates the beam gain of the MA array at angles $\theta \in [0, \pi]$ for a given number of antennas. Under different antenna configurations ($N = 16, 32,$ and 64), the beam gain exhibits distinct performance trends. As the number of antennas N increases, the main lobe width of the beam gain gradually narrows, while the gain peak significantly rises, demonstrating improved directivity and energy concentration capabilities. Concurrently, the side lobe levels progressively decrease, indicating enhanced interference suppression. At the legitimate user's

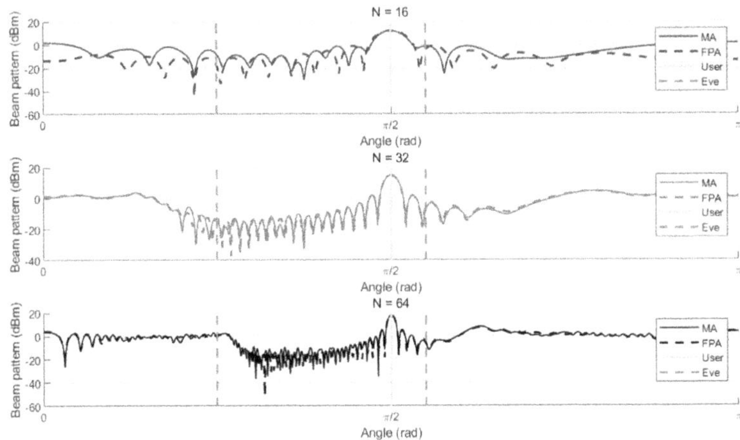

Fig. 6. Beam gain of MA array for given $N = 16, 32, 64$.

angle and Eve's position, the beam gain exhibits pronounced differences, particularly at N=64, the main lobe achieves maximum gain towards the target user while effectively suppressing gain towards Eve's direction. This demonstrates that the MA array enhances legitimate users' communication quality while maintaining robust security performance. It can be concluded that increasing the number of antennas significantly optimizes the beamforming performance of the MA array, thereby enhancing both transmission efficiency and system security.

5   Conclusion

This paper proposes a near-field beamforming design for MA arrays, aiming to optimize security performance in a near-field communication system. The proposed method uses the PGA and an AO algorithm to jointly optimize transmit beamforming and the positions of movable antennas at the transmitter, maximizing the secrecy rate. Simulations show that MA arrays enhance security compared to conventional FPA arrays through optimized antenna position. Future work will extend the proposed near-field MA system to multi-user environments, investigating how to optimize the dynamic positioning of MAs for multiple users to fulfill physical layer security requirements in wireless communications.

References

1. Stallings, W.: Network and Internetwork Security: Principles and Practice. Prentice-Hall Inc., Englewood Cliffs (1995)
2. Wang, D., Bai, B., Zhao, W., Han, Z.: A survey of optimization approaches for wireless physical layer security. IEEE Commun. Surv. Tutor. **21**(2), 1878–1911 (2019). https://doi.org/10.1109/COMST.2018.2883144

3. Hong, Y.W.P., Lan, P.C., Kuo, C.C.J.: Enhancing physical-layer secrecy in multi-antenna wireless systems: an overview of signal processing approaches. IEEE Signal Process. Mag. **30**(5), 29–40 (2013). https://doi.org/10.1109/MSP.2013.2256953

4. Khisti, A., Wornell, G.W.: Secure transmission with multiple antennas-Part II: the MIMOME wiretap channel. IEEE Trans. Inf. Theory **56**(11), 5515–5532 (2010). https://doi.org/10.1109/TIT.2010.2068852

5. Li, Q., Ma, W.K.: Optimal and robust transmit designs for MISO channel secrecy by semidefinite programming. IEEE Trans. Signal Process. **59**(8), 3799–3812 (2011). https://doi.org/10.1109/TSP.2011.2146775

6. Xiao, Z., Zhu, L., Bai, L., Xia, X.G.: Array Beamforming Enabled Wireless Communications. CRC Press, Boca Raton (2023)

7. Zhu, L., Ma, W., Zhang, R.: Modeling and performance analysis for movable antenna enabled wireless communications. IEEE Trans. Wirel. Commun. **23**(6), 6234–6250 (2023). https://doi.org/10.1109/TWC.2023.3330887

8. Zhu, L., Ma, W., Zhang, R.: Movable antennas for wireless communication: opportunities and challenges. IEEE Commun. Mag. **62**(6), 114–120 (2023). https://doi.org/10.1109/MCOM.001.2300212

9. Cheng, Z., Li, N., Zhu, J., She, X., Ouyang, C., Chen, P.: Enabling secure wireless communications via movable antennas. In: 2024 IEEE International Conference on Acoustics, Speech and Signal Processing, ICASSP 2024, pp. 9186–9190. IEEE Press, Seoul (2024). https://doi.org/10.1109/ICASSP48485.2024.10447471

10. Hu, G., Wu, Q., Xu, K., Si, J., Al-Dhahir, N.: Secure wireless communication via movable-antenna array. IEEE Signal Process. Lett. **31**, 516–520 (2024). https://doi.org/10.1109/LSP.2024.3359894

11. Hu, G., et al.: Movable antennas-assisted secure transmission without eavesdroppers' instantaneous CSI. IEEE Trans. Mob. Comput. **23**(12), 14263–14279 (2024). https://doi.org/10.1109/TMC.2024.3438795

12. Huang, T., Yu, Y., Yi, L.: Design of highly isolated compact antenna array for MIMO applications. Int. J. Antennas Propag. **2014**(1), 473063 (2014). https://doi.org/10.1155/2014/473063

13. Selvan, K.T., Janaswamy, R.: Fraunhofer and Fresnel distances: unified derivation for aperture antennas. IEEE Antennas Propag. Mag. **59**(4), 12–15 (2017). https://doi.org/10.1109/MAP.2017.2706648

14. Liu, Y., Wang, Z., Xu, J., Ouyang, C., Mu, X., Schober, R.: Near-field communications: a tutorial review. IEEE Open J. Commun. Soc. **4**, 1999–2049 (2023). https://doi.org/10.1109/OJCOMS.2023.3305583

15. Wang, Y., Mei, W., Wei, X., Ning, B., Chen, Z.: Antenna position optimization for movable antenna-empowered near-field sensing. In: 2025 IEEE International Conference on Communications Workshops, pp. 324–329. IEEE Press, Shanghai (2025). https://doi.org/10.1109/ICCWorkshops67674.2025.11162470

A Privacy-Preserving Data Aggregation Scheme with Inner-Product Encryption for Smart Grids

Zhe Xia[1,2], Sha Wu[1], Cheng Tan[1], and Yifei Wang[3(✉)]

[1] School of Computer Science and Artificial Intelligence, Wuhan University of Technology, Wuhan, China
{xiazhe,wusha,cheng_tan}@whut.edu.cn
[2] Hubei Key Laboratory of Transportation of Internet of Things, Wuhan University of Technology, Wuhan, China
[3] School of Information Science and Engineering, Wuhan University of Science and Technology, Wuhan, China
wangyifei@wust.edu.cn

Abstract. With rapid development of smart grids, how to efficiently aggregate and verify multi-source electricity consumption data while ensuring user privacy has become a key research problem, and a number of privacy-preserving data aggregation schemes have been introduced to alleviate this problem. However, most existing schemes only support simple additive homomorphic aggregation, lacking support for more complex functions. To address this challenge, this paper proposes an efficient and verifiable privacy-preserving data aggregation scheme that integrates functional encryption, DiffieHellman key exchange, and Schnorr signature to support linear function queries, resists collusion attacks, and ensures verifiability of aggregation results. Experimental results demonstrate that our proposed scheme achieves higher computational and communication efficiency compared with the existing schemes, e.g., Guard-Grid, while maintaining strong security and functional expressiveness. Therefore, it provides a feasible and effective approach for building efficient, scalable, and verifiable privacy-preserving systems in smart grids.

1 Introduction

With continuous growth of electricity demands, traditional power grid has gradually revealed numerous limitations in resource scheduling, real-time monitoring, and data management. To improve energy utilization efficiency and achieve intelligent regulation of power systems, the smart grid has been developed that enables real-time collection, remote transmission, and centralized processing of electricity consumption data.

However, while enhancing the intelligence level of the power system, smart grid also brings challenges to data privacy [8,10]. For example, the smart meters periodically upload high-frequency, fine-grained electricity consumption data, which can expose users' living habits if not properly protected. Existing studies

L. Zhai et al. (Eds.): SocialSec 2025, LNCS 16327, pp. 129–146, 2026.
https://doi.org/10.1007/978-981-95-7027-0_8

have shown that attackers can reconstruct users' behavioral patterns by analyzing electricity consumption data, and even exploit leaked data to carry out targeted burglary or sophisticated electricity-related fraud [6].

To address the above issues, a large number of works have focused on privacy-preserving technologies in smart grids [11,13,14] proposing various cryptographic solutions such as homomorphic encryption [2], secure multi-party computation [5], and differential privacy [3]. Among these approaches, functional encryption (FE) [7,12] has attracted increasing attentions due to its fine-grained access control mechanisms and flexible computational capabilities. Unlike traditional encryption methods, functional encryption allows authorized entities to obtain only the result of a specific function while preventing recovery of the original plaintext.

Within various instances of functional encryption, Inner-Product Encryption (IPE) [1] represents a typical and highly practical construction, whose goal is to enable encryption schemes that only reveal the inner product of input vectors. In smart grid, inner-product operations are widely used in several critical tasks, such as regional electricity consumption statistics (equal-weight inner products) and differentiated electricity pricing settlement (weighted inner products). Therefore, designing data aggregation schemes that support inner-product encryption can not only meet the demands in smart grid for flexible aggregation function computations but also effectively prevent attackers from inferring individual users' behavior from aggregate results.

Several studies have attempted to apply functional encryption to data aggregation and privacy protection in smart grids. For example, Liu et al. [9] proposed a privacy-preserving scheme for fog computing architectures that integrates functional encryption to achieve encrypted aggregation of users' electricity consumption data and flexible function queries. In [12], functional encryption was combined with verifiability mechanisms to build a data aggregation system that enables both function queries and result verification, demonstrating the broad adaptability and practical potential of functional encryption in smart grid applications.

Although the above studies have made certain progresses in utilizing functional encryption to protect privacy in smart grid, they still suffer from several limitations: low computational efficiency, inability to resist collusion attacks from internal entities, vulnerability to data mining attacks, and only support simple additive homomorphism without the ability to handle more complex functions. These shortcomings restrict their applications. Therefore, privacy-preserving data aggregation schemes based on functional encryption in smart grids still face several critical challenges. It is imperative to design more efficient, secure, and verifiable aggregation frameworks to meet the requirements in real-world deployment.

1.1 Our Contributions

To address the above challenges, this paper proposes a novel solution that is an efficient, verifiable, and privacy-preserving data aggregation scheme with inner-product encryption for smart grids. Specifically, the main contributions of this work are as follows:

- We design a scheme, called FES, which integrates functional encryption, DiffieHellman key exchange, and Schnorr signature, providing both strong security and practical applicability. By employing an improved inner-product encryption scheme based on the Bresson-Catalano-Pointcheval (BCP) structure [4], FES effectively defends against collusion and data mining attacks. It allows the control center (CC) to directly obtain the function computation result after decryption without solving discrete logarithm problems. In addition, batch verification of Schnorr signature is applied to significantly improve the efficiency of data verifiability, ensuring the integrity and trustworthiness of aggregation results during transmission.
- We conduct theoretical analysis and experimental evaluation of the proposed scheme in terms of data integrity, correctness, verifiability, flexible queries, and system efficiency. The results show that FES achieves the above security properties while enjoying higher computational and communication efficiency compared with the state-of-the-art scheme GuardGrid [12].

1.2 Organisation of the Paper

The rest of this paper is organised as follows. In Sect. 2, we outline some preliminaries. The models and definitions for our proposed scheme are described in Sect. 3. In Sect. 4, we present the proposed scheme and formally prove its security using our security model. Finally, we discuss and conclude in Sect. 5.

2 Preliminaries

2.1 Notations

The following table lists the symbols used in this paper and their corresponding meanings:

Notation	Description
λ	The security parameter
n	The number of users
$[n]$	The set of users with indices $\{1, 2, \ldots, n\}$
$\mathbf{x}$	A vector of users' electricity consumption
$\mathbf{y}$	The functional vector in inner-product decryption
k_i	The session key between smart meter and control center
c_i	The ciphertext generated by the smart meter SM_i
$sk_{\mathbf{y}}$	The functional decryption key of $\mathbf{y}$
σ_i	The signature generated by SM_i
C'	The aggregated ciphertext

2.2 Functional Encryption

Functional encryption is a fine-grained cryptographic technique that allows users to decrypt and obtain the result of a specific function on the ciphertext without accessing the original plaintext. Compared with traditional encryption, functional encryption offers significant advantages in privacy-preserving data processing and access control.

Among the various types of functional encryption, inner-product encryption (IPE) [1] is the most widely used technique. It enables the computation of inner products over encrypted vectors, allowing users holding only a function key to obtain the inner product value. It has been widely applied in scenarios such as encrypted aggregation and statistical analysis.

To better realize functional encryption, researchers have proposed Single-Input Functional Encryption (SIFE). Thanks to its lightweight structure, it is suitable for deployment on devices with limited computational resources. However, in traditional SIFE schemes, the decryption result takes the form of $y^{<x,y>}$, requiring the solution of a discrete logarithm problem to retrieve the actual inner product value, which leads to low efficiency.

To address this issue, we improve upon the BCP structure [4] to design an efficient SIFE scheme that directly outputs the plaintext inner product. This approach eliminates the decryption efficiency bottleneck and enhances the practicality of functional encryption in real-world scenarios such as smart grids.

2.3 Schnorr Signature

Schnorr signature is a digital signature scheme constructed based on the Discrete Logarithm problem. Due to its simple structure, short signature length, and high computational efficiency, the scheme plays an important role in both cryptographic theory and practical applications.

The Schnorr signature scheme consists of the following four algorithms:

- **Setup():** Let G be a cyclic group of prime order q with generator g, modulus p being a prime such that $q \mid (p-1)$. Let $H : \{0,1\}^* \rightarrow \mathbb{Z}_q$ be a collision-resistant hash function.
- **Keygen():** Randomly choose a private key $x \in \mathbb{Z}_q$. The public key is $y = g^x \bmod p$.
- **Sign():** Given a message $m \in \{0,1\}^*$, randomly choose $r \in \mathbb{Z}_q$, first compute the commitment value $t = g^r \bmod p$, and then compute the challenge value $c = H(m \parallel t)$. Finally, compute the response value $z = r + c \cdot x \bmod q$, and output the signature pair (c, z).
- **Verify():** The verifier, holding message m, signature (c, z), and public key y, computes $t' = g^z \cdot y^{-c} \bmod p$, and then $c' = H(m \parallel t')$. It accepts the signature if and only if $c = c'$; otherwise, rejects it.

2.4 Diffie-Hellman Key Exchange

The Diffie–Hellman (DH) key exchange protocol allows two parties to agree on a shared session key while communicating over an insecure channel, laying the theoretical foundation for modern cryptographic protocols. The protocol proceeds as follows:

- **Setup():** Select a large prime p and a generator $g \in \mathbb{Z}_p^*$, such that the order of g is a large prime factor of $(p-1)$. All parties perform exponentiation over the finite field $\mathbb{Z}_p^*$. The public parameters are (p, g).
- **Exchange():** The two communicating entities, $\mathcal{A}$ and $\mathcal{B}$, perform the protocol as follows:
  1. $\mathcal{A}$ randomly selects a private key $a \in \mathbb{Z}_p$, computes $A = g^a \bmod p$, and sends it to $\mathcal{B}$.
  2. $\mathcal{B}$ randomly selects a private key $b \in \mathbb{Z}_p$, computes $B = g^b \bmod p$, and sends it to $\mathcal{A}$.
  3. Now, $\mathcal{A}$ computes the shared key as $K = B^a \bmod p = g^{ab} \bmod p$.
  4. And $\mathcal{B}$ computes the shared key as $K = A^b \bmod p = g^{ab} \bmod p$.

Thus, both entities successfully agree on the same shared key K without disclosing their private keys.

3 Models and Definitions

3.1 System Model

The system model is illustrated in Fig. 1. It consists of four components: Smart Meter (SM), Aggregator (AG), Control Center (CC), and Trusted Third Party (TTP). In this model, users within a geographical area—such as a residential neighborhood—are organized into groups, each containing n users, and every user is equipped with a smart meter. The roles and responsibilities of these entities are summarized as follows:

- **Smart Meter (SM):** Each SM periodically collects power consumption data from the user's household appliances (e.g., refrigerator, air conditioner). It encrypts and signs the data separately, and then uploads the encrypted data and signature to the aggregator at short time intervals.
- **Aggregator (AG):** The AG is a lightweight edge server with both storage and computational capabilities. It receives encrypted data and signatures from the SMs, performs preliminary processing and aggregation, and then forwards the intermediate aggregated results and corresponding aggregated signatures to the control center.
- **Control Center (CC):** The CC supervises the entire smart grid, functioning similarly to a power system operator. With its abundant computational resources, it verifies the correctness of the aggregated results, decrypts them to obtain the actual aggregate data, performs analysis, and adjusts pricing strategies based on the findings.

- **Trusted Third Party (TTP):** The TTP is typically a trusted governmental entity responsible for initializing the system. It generates and distributes the necessary public and private parameters to all parties in the network. After the initialization phase, the TTP becomes inactive and does not participate in users' ongoing data uploads.

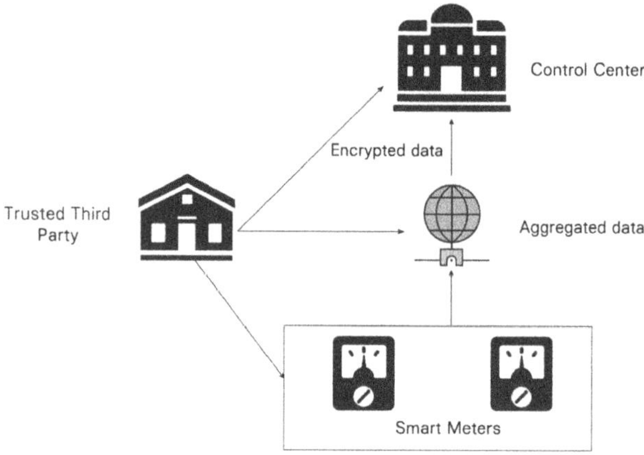

Fig. 1. The system model.

3.2 Adversary Model

In this study, the TTP is assumed to be fully trusted, while the SMs and CC are considered honest-but-curious. This means that they will follow the protocols but may attempt to infer private data. In contrast, the AG is regarded as a potentially misbehaving entity. The following security threats are considered:

- **Eavesdropping attack:** During data transmission, an attacker may eavesdrop on the communication channels, intercept sensitive information, and violate user privacy.
- **Tampering attack:** The AG may not honestly aggregate ciphertexts. For example, it might discard certain users' ciphertexts or provide random values to reduce computational load.
- **Data mining attack:** Attackers may employ data mining techniques to illegally obtain and analyze sensitive data within the system (such as user information or trade secrets).

3.3 Design Goals

- **Data confidentiality:** It ensures that users' electricity consumption data remain inaccessible to unauthorized parties during transmission and storage, thereby preventing plaintext disclosure and data exposure.

- **Data integrity:** It guarantees the accuracy and immutability of the aggregated computation results, ensuring that the final output faithfully reflects the statistical characteristics of users' original electricity consumption data.
- **Privacy preservation:** It allows aggregate analysis to be performed without revealing any individual user's plaintext data, ensuring that no entity can infer specific user information from the aggregated results.
- **Collusion resistance:** The system should be resilient against collusion among internal entities (such as users or aggregators), preventing them from jointly obtaining unauthorized data or reconstructing users' plaintext information.
- **Inference attack resistance:** It protects against passive eavesdropping and active interference by external adversaries, preventing them from reverse-engineering users' behavior patterns through the analysis of aggregated results and communication metadata.
- **Efficiency:** While maintaining the security features, the algorithm should be designed with low computational complexity and communication overhead, making it suitable for deployment in large-scale smart grid environments.

4 The Proposed Scheme

4.1 Modified SIFE Scheme

This paper proposes an improved SIFE scheme based on the BCP structure [4], aiming to address the low decryption efficiency of traditional SIFE schemes. In conventional SIFE, the decryption process can only obtain $g^{\langle x,y \rangle}$; to recover the actual inner product value $\langle x, y \rangle$, one must solve a discrete logarithm problem. However, this computation is extremely expensive and practically infeasible in large-parameter settings.

We utilize the BCP structure to overcome this limitation. As a result, the decryption phase can directly output the inner product value $\langle x, y \rangle$ without solving the discrete logarithm problem, while maintaining the same level of security. This improvement not only significantly simplifies the decryption process but also enhances the practicality and efficiency of the scheme in resource-constrained environments such as smart grids.

SIFE.Setup$(1^\lambda, 1^n)$: Let $N = pq$, where p and q are safe primes, i.e., $p = 2p' + 1$ and $q = 2q' + 1$. Let $G = QR_{N^2}$ be the group of quadratic residues modulo N^2, with order $\mathrm{ord}(G) = |\mathbb{Z}^*_{N^2}|/4 = N \cdot \lambda(N)$, where $\lambda(N) = p'q'$. Select a random element $a \in \mathbb{Z}^*_{N^2}$ and set $g = a^2 \bmod N^2$. Choose a random vector $s = (s_1, s_2, \ldots, s_n)$ where each $s_i \in [1, \mathrm{ord}(G)]$. The public key and secret key are defined as:

$$\mathrm{pk} = (g, \{h_i = g^{s_i} \bmod N^2\}_{i \in [n]}), \quad \mathrm{sk} = s.$$

SIFE.KeyDer(sk, y): Given the master secret key sk and vector y, compute and return the functional secret key as:

$$\text{sk}_y = \langle y, s \rangle \bmod N^2.$$

SIFE.Enc(pk, x): Given a message vector $x = (x_1, x_2, \ldots, x_n)$ where $x_i \in \mathbb{Z}_N$ represents the data of the i-th user, sample a random value $r \in \mathbb{Z}_{N^2}$ and compute the ciphertext:

$$c_i = (g^r,\ h_i^r (1 + N)^{x_i}) \bmod N^2.$$

SIFE.Dec$(\text{pk}, \{c_i\}, \text{sk}_y, y)$: Compute

$$D = \prod_{i \in [n]} \frac{[h_i^r (1 + N)^{x_i}]^{y_i}}{g^{r \cdot \text{sk}_y}} = (1 + N)^{\langle x, y \rangle} \bmod N^2 = (1 + \langle x, y \rangle N) \bmod N^2.$$

Finally, recover the inner product value:

$$\langle x, y \rangle = \frac{D - 1}{N} \bmod N^2.$$

4.2   Our Proposed Scheme

The detailed protocol works as follows:

- **FES.Setup**$(1^\lambda, 1^n)$: Run SIFE.Setup$(1^\lambda, 1^n)$, $pk = (g, h_i = g^{s_i} \bmod N^2)_{i \in [n]}$, $sk = s$; Each user and the CC execute the DiffieHellman key exchange protocol to establish a one-time session key k_i; Each user chooses a private key $u_i \in [1, N^2/4)$ and computes the public key $U_i = g^{u_i} \bmod N^2$; The Aggregator selects a private key $u_{ag} \in [1, N^2/4)$ and computes its public key $U_{ag} = g^{u_{ag}} \bmod N^2$; Finally, the algorithm returns (sk, pk, U_i, U_{ag}) and publish (pk, U_i, U_{ag}).
- **FES.Enc**(pk, k_i, x_i, u_i): Mask the plaintext: $x_i = x_i + k_i$; Run SIFE.Enc(pk, x_i) to obtain $c_i = (g^r, h_i^r (1 + N)^{x_i}) \bmod N^2$; Select a random $d_i \in [1, N^2/4)$ and compute $D_i = g^{d_i} \bmod N^2$; Compute the message digest $e_i = \mathsf{Hash}(D_i \| c_i)$; Compute the Schnorr signature $\sigma_i = d_i + e_i u_i$; Finally, the algorithm returns (c_i, D_i, σ_i).
- **FES.KeyDer**(sk, y): Run SIFE.KeyDer(sk, y) to obtain $sk_y = \langle y, s \rangle \bmod N^2$; Finally, the algorithm returns sk_y.
- **FES.Agg**$(pk, \{c_i\}_{i \in [n]}, sk_y, \{D_i\}_{i \in [n]}, \{\sigma_i\}_{i \in [n]})$:
  (Individual verification): For each $i \in [n]$, compute $e_i' = \mathsf{Hash}(D_i \| c_i)$ and verify whether $g^{\sigma_i} = D_i U_i^{e_i'}$ holds;
  (Batch verification): Randomly choose $\beta_i \in [1, N^2/4)$ for all $i \in [n]$, compute $e_i' = \mathsf{Hash}(D_i \| c_i)$, and verify:

$$\prod_{i=1}^{n} g^{\sigma_i \beta_i} = \prod_{i=1}^{n} (D_i U_i^{e_i'})^{\beta_i};$$

Aggregation: Run $\mathsf{SIFE.Dec}(pk, \{c_i\}_{i\in[n]}, sk_y, y) \to C' = \langle x, y \rangle$;
Signing: Select a random $d_{ag} \in [1, N^2/4)$ and compute $D_{ag} = g^{d_{ag}} \bmod N^2$;
Compute $e_{ag} = \mathsf{Hash}(D_{ag}\|C')$ and the signature $\sigma_{ag} = d_{ag} + e_{ag}u_{ag}$; Finally, it returns $(C', D_{ag}, \sigma_{ag})$.

– **FES.Dec$(\{k_i\}_{i\in[n]}, y, C', \sigma_{ag}, D_{ag})$:**
Verification: Compute $e'_{ag} = \mathsf{Hash}(D_{ag}\|C')$ and verify whether $g^{\sigma_{ag}} = D_{ag}U_{ag}^{e'_{ag}}$ holds;
Decryption: Compute the final result $\langle x, y \rangle = C' - \sum_{i=1}^{n} k_i y_i$.

4.3   Security Analysis

Correctness. The correctness of the aggregated result is shown as follows:

$$D = \prod_{i\in[n]} \frac{[h_i^r (1+N)^{x_i}]^{y_i}}{g^{r\cdot sk_y}}$$

$$= \frac{\prod g^{r\cdot s_i y_i}(1+N)^{x_i y_i}}{g^{r\cdot\langle y,s\rangle}}$$

$$= \frac{g^{r\cdot\sum s_i y_i}(1+N)^{\sum x_i y_i}}{g^{r\cdot\langle y,s\rangle}}$$

$$= \frac{g^{r\cdot\langle y,s\rangle}(1+N)^{\langle x,y\rangle}}{g^{r\cdot\langle y,s\rangle}}$$

$$= (1+N)^{\langle x,y\rangle} \bmod N^2$$

$$= (1+\langle x,y\rangle N) \bmod N^2.$$

Therefore, the functional decryption output is obtained as:

$$\langle x, y \rangle = \frac{D-1}{N} \bmod N^2.$$

Correctness of Batch Verification. The correctness of the batch verification process is as follows: if $e_i = e'_i$, the verification passes.

$$\prod_{i=1}^{n} g^{\sigma_i \beta_i} = \prod_{i=1}^{n} g^{(d_i+e_i u_i)\beta_i}$$

$$= \prod_{i=1}^{n} (D_i \cdot U_i^{e_i})^{\beta_i}$$

$$= \prod_{i=1}^{n} (D_i U_i^{e'_i})^{\beta_i}.$$

Hence, when $e_i = e'_i$, both sides of the equation are equal, which guarantees the correctness of the batch verification.

Data Privacy. An SIFE encryption scheme is said to be IND-CPA secure (Indistinguishability under Chosen Plaintext Attack) if, for any probabilistic polynomial-time (PPT) adversary $\mathcal{A}$, its advantage in the following game is negligible:

1. The challenger runs the setup algorithm to generate system parameters (pk, sk).
2. The adversary $\mathcal{A}$ submits two plaintext vectors of equal length (x_0, x_1).
3. The challenger randomly selects a bit $b \in \{0, 1\}$, encrypts x_b to obtain ciphertext c, and sends c to $\mathcal{A}$.
4. The adversary outputs a guess b'. If $b' = b$, $\mathcal{A}$ wins the game.

The adversary's advantage is defined as:

$$\mathrm{Adv}_{\mathcal{A}}^{\mathrm{IND\text{-}CPA}} = \left| \Pr[b' = b] - \frac{1}{2} \right|,$$

which must be negligible in the security parameter λ.

Theorem 1. *Under the Decisional Composite Residuosity (DCR) assumption, the SIFE encryption algorithm in the proposed FES scheme achieves IND-CPA security.*

Proof. The proof is given through a sequence of hybrid games: Game0, Game1, and Game2.

Game0

1. The challenger runs FES.Setup$(1^\lambda, 1^n)$ to generate system parameters (mpk, msk).
2. The adversary $\mathcal{A}$ submits two plaintext vectors of equal length $(x_0, x_1) \leftarrow \mathcal{A}(mpk)$.
3. The challenger randomly chooses $b \in \{0, 1\}$ and computes the ciphertext

$$c \leftarrow \mathsf{FES.Encrypt}(mpk, params, x_b, ID).$$

4. The adversary outputs a guess $b' \leftarrow \mathcal{A}(mpk, c)$. $\mathcal{A}$ wins if $b' = b$.

Game1

1. The challenger runs FES.Setup$(1^\lambda, 1^n)$ to generate system parameters (mpk, msk).
2. The adversary $\mathcal{A}$ submits two plaintext vectors of equal length (x_0, x_1).
3. The challenger randomly chooses $b \in \{0, 1\}$ and a random element $R \in \mathbb{Z}_{N^2}$. It then constructs the ciphertext

$$c = (R, \, h_i^r (1 + N)^{x_i}) \leftarrow \mathsf{FES.Encrypt}(mpk, params, x_b, ID).$$

4. The adversary outputs $b' \leftarrow \mathcal{A}(mpk, c)$ and wins if $b' = b$.

Game2

1. The challenger runs $\mathsf{FES.Setup}(1^\lambda, 1^n)$ to generate system parameters (mpk, msk).
2. The adversary $\mathcal{A}$ submits two plaintext vectors of equal length (x_0, x_1).
3. The challenger randomly chooses $b \in \{0, 1\}$ and two random elements $R, S \in \mathbb{Z}_{N^2}$. It then sets

$$c = (R, S) \leftarrow \mathsf{FES.Encrypt}(mpk, params, x_b, ID).$$

4. The adversary outputs $b' \leftarrow \mathcal{A}(mpk, c)$ and wins if $b' = b$.

Indistinguishability Argument. According to the DCR assumption:

$$\mathsf{Game0} \approx_c \mathsf{Game1} \quad \text{and} \quad \mathsf{Game1} \approx_c \mathsf{Game2},$$

where $\approx_c$ denotes computational indistinguishability.

Therefore, any PPT adversary $\mathcal{A}$ cannot distinguish $\mathsf{Game0}$ from $\mathsf{Game2}$ with non-negligible advantage. In $\mathsf{Game2}$, the ciphertext is completely independent of the plaintext. Thus, $\mathcal{A}$'s advantage in $\mathsf{Game0}$ is equivalent to random guessing, implying that

$$\mathrm{Adv}_{\mathcal{A}}^{\text{IND-CPA}} \le \mathrm{negl}(\lambda).$$

$\square$

Data Integrity (EU-CMA Security of Schnorr Signature)

A Schnorr signature scheme is said to be EU-CMA secure (Existential Unforgeability under Chosen Message Attack) if, for any probabilistic polynomial-time (PPT) adversary $\mathcal{A}$, its advantage in the following game is negligible:

1. The challenger generates a key pair (sk, pk).
2. The adversary $\mathcal{A}$ adaptively queries signatures for messages $(m_1, m_2, \ldots, m_q)$.
3. The challenger returns the corresponding signatures $(\sigma_1, \sigma_2, \ldots, \sigma_q)$.
4. Finally, $\mathcal{A}$ outputs a forged message-signature pair (m^*, σ^*), where m^* was not previously queried. If σ^* is a valid signature for m^* under pk, then $\mathcal{A}$ wins the game.

The adversary's advantage is defined as:

$$\mathrm{Adv}_{\mathcal{A}}^{\text{EU-CMA}} = \Pr[\mathsf{Verify}(pk, m^*, \sigma^*) = 1 \wedge m^* \notin \{m_1, \ldots, m_q\}],$$

which must be negligible in the security parameter λ.

Theorem 2. *Under the Discrete Logarithm Problem (DLP) assumption, the Schnorr signature algorithm in the proposed FES scheme achieves EU-CMA security.*

Proof. Assume that there exists a PPT adversary $\mathcal{A}$ that can win the above game with non-negligible advantage. We can then construct an algorithm $\mathcal{B}$ that uses $\mathcal{A}$ as a subroutine to solve the DLP instance.

Let $\mathcal{B}$ be given a DLP instance $(g, h = g^x)$ in group $\mathbb{G}$, where the goal is to compute $x = \log_g h$. Algorithm $\mathcal{B}$ interacts with $\mathcal{A}$ as follows:

1. When $\mathcal{A}$ requests a signature on message m_i, $\mathcal{B}$ simulates a valid Schnorr signature using the *forking lemma* to generate a consistent response indistinguishable from a real one.
2. When $\mathcal{A}$ outputs a forged message-signature pair (m^*, σ^*), $\mathcal{B}$ rewinds $\mathcal{A}$ and obtains two valid forgeries (m^*, σ_1^*) and (m^*, σ_2^*) corresponding to two different hash challenges.
3. Using these two forgeries, $\mathcal{B}$ computes the discrete logarithm:

$$x = \frac{\sigma_1^* - \sigma_2^*}{e_1 - e_2} \bmod q,$$

where e_1 and e_2 are the distinct hash values involved in the two signatures.

By the *forking lemma*, the probability that $\mathcal{B}$ succeeds in solving the DLP instance is non-negligibly related to the advantage of $\mathcal{A}$. This contradicts the DLP assumption, which states that computing $\log_g h$ is infeasible. Therefore, under the DLP assumption, the Schnorr signature in the FES scheme is secure against forgery and tampering, ensuring the integrity of transmitted data.

Privacy Preservation. An attacker cannot recover the original electricity consumption values from the ciphertexts generated by smart meters (SMs). If a malicious aggregator (AG) tampers with any ciphertext, the modification will be detected by the dual verification mechanism of the Schnorr signatures. Even if the ciphertexts are intercepted during transmission, the semantic security of the SIFE encryption prevents the adversary from learning any meaningful information about the plaintext data. A semi-honest control center (CC) can only decrypt and obtain the inner-product result, without being able to infer any individual user's data. Furthermore, even if some SMs collude with the AG, they cannot compromise the privacy of other users, since the Diffie–Hellman session keys are generated independently for each user. In summary, the proposed FES scheme ensures end-to-end privacy protection of users' electricity consumption data through a combination of encryption, signature verification, and key isolation mechanisms.

Collusion Resistance. In the proposed scheme, each user establishes a one-time session key k_i with the control center (CC) through the Diffie–Hellman key exchange protocol. The plaintext data x_i is masked using this session key k_i, which is independent of the user's long-term private key u_i. Even if a malicious aggregator (AG) colludes with a subset of smart meters (SMs) and obtains their private keys $\{u_i\}$, it cannot derive the session keys of other users, and thus cannot decrypt their encrypted data. Therefore, the proposed FES scheme is resistant to collusion attacks.

Resistance to Data-Mining Attacks. During the process of data aggregation in a smart grid, an attacker may attempt to infer individual users' consumption behaviors by repeatedly querying or analyzing the aggregation results, thereby launching a data-mining attack. To mitigate such privacy threats, the proposed FES scheme adopts an inner-product encryption design, in which the aggregation result reveals only the inner product of the encrypted vectors, without disclosing any user's raw data or individual contribution to the aggregation.

Moreover, since each user's data is preprocessed and mixed with a dynamically generated session key k_i before encryption, even an adaptive adversary performing multiple rounds of carefully constructed queries cannot isolate or reconstruct any single user's exact information. This effectively prevents any mapping between aggregated outcomes and individual data records.

Compared with traditional schemes that rely solely on homomorphic encryption, the FES framework exhibits a structurally stronger resistance to inference attacks, significantly reducing the risk of privacy leakage and enhancing the system's defense against behavior-analysis-based attacks. Such a property makes FES particularly suitable for smart-grid scenarios where user behavior patterns are highly sensitive and privacy protection is of critical importance.

4.4 Some Comparisons

To comprehensively evaluate the applicability and performance advantages of the proposed FES scheme in smart grid scenarios, we compare it with several representative existing schemes. The results are summarized in the following table. The comparison criteria cover key performance dimensions such as user data verifiability, aggregation result verifiability, computational efficiency, resistance to collusion attacks, and resistance to data-mining attacks. The analysis demonstrates that, through the joint design of lightweight cryptographic primitives and coordinated security mechanisms, the FES scheme achieves superior overall performance across multiple functional aspects. The detailed comparison is as follows:

User Data Verifiability. FES adopts a batch verification mechanism based on the Schnorr signature, enabling each smart meter (SM) to attach an unforgeable digital signature to its uploaded data. The aggregator (AG) can efficiently verify all n users' signatures through a single aggregated multiplication operation, significantly reducing computational overhead and improving verification efficiency.

Aggregation Result Verifiability. By generating and attaching an additional signature to the aggregated result, which is verified by the control center (CC), the FES scheme ensures the authenticity and integrity of the aggregation output, effectively preventing the AG from tampering with intermediate data.

Computational Efficiency. The encryption and decryption processes in FES involve only addition and exponentiation operations, maintaining polynomial-time computational complexity. During decryption, near-constant time performance of approximately $O(1)$ is achieved. In a test environment with 1,000 participating users, the decryption process completes within 10 ms. Compared with the *GuardGrid* scheme, FES exhibits a substantial improvement in overall efficiency, meeting the low-latency and high-concurrency requirements of real-time electricity pricing and grid control applications.

Resistance to Collusion Attacks. FES integrates the Diffie–Hellman key exchange mechanism to dynamically generate an independent one-time session key k_i for each user, masking the original data as $x_i + k_i$. Even if the AG colludes with a subset of users and obtains their private keys u_i, it remains unable to recover other users' actual data, thus ensuring key isolation and collusion resistance.

Resistance to Data-Mining Attacks. FES employs an inner-product encryption design that reveals only the overall aggregation result without exposing fine-grained information of individual users. This structure effectively prevents adversaries from inferring user behavior through multiple aggregation queries or data modeling, thereby preserving the privacy of power consumption patterns (Table 1).

Table 1. Functional Comparison of FES with Existing Schemes

Feature	[2]	[7]	[9]	[12]	FES
User Data Verifiability	✓	✓	✓	×	✓
Computational Efficiency	✓	×	×	×	✓
Collusion Resistance	✓	×	×	✓	✓
Data-Mining Resistance	✓	✓	×	✓	✓
Functional Query Support	×	×	✓	✓	✓

Summary. The comparative results clearly indicate that the proposed FES scheme achieves comprehensive functional advantages over existing approaches, providing enhanced verifiability, efficiency, and privacy protection suitable for large-scale smart grid deployments.

4.5 Efficiency Analysis

To evaluate the practical execution efficiency of the proposed scheme, we designed experiments to measure the time overhead of each phase in the FES scheme. Our implementation was developed using the open-source Python cryptographic library Charm-Crypto, and all experiments were conducted on a laptop running the Ubuntu 20.04 operating system, equipped with an AMD Ryzen 7 8845H CPU and 32 GB RAM. The security parameter was set to $\lambda = 512$ to ensure a high level of security. Since our cryptographic system operates on integer values, all experimental data were scaled by a factor of 1000 to convert floating-point values into integers. After aggregation, the results were divided by 1000 to restore the correct arithmetic values.

Both the FES scheme and the GuardGrid scheme adopt a *user-side independent encryption mechanism*, in which each user independently encrypts their local electricity consumption data. Consequently, the computational cost of the encryption phase exhibits parallel characteristics and does not scale linearly with the total number of smart meters. Experimental results show that the encryption overhead of the FES scheme is 0.4 ms, while that of the GuardGrid scheme is 0.3 ms.

To provide a more representative evaluation of practical deployment performance, we focus primarily on the computational costs during the *data aggregation* and *result decryption* phases.

We compared and analyzed the trend of aggregation overhead for both the FES and GuardGrid schemes under varying numbers of smart meters. As illustrated in Fig. 2, the overall aggregation overhead of the FES scheme is slightly higher than that of the GuardGrid scheme as the number of smart meters increases. This difference mainly stems from the introduction of the *Schnorr signature mechanism* in the FES scheme, which is employed to verify the integrity of user-reported data and to ensure that no tampering or forgery occurs during transmission.

Specifically, the aggregator in the FES scheme must perform signature verification operations for each user's data, thereby incurring additional computational overhead. In contrast, the GuardGrid scheme does not implement an explicit data-verification mechanism, resulting in lower computational burden during the aggregation phase.

Although the aggregation overhead of the FES scheme is slightly higher, the incorporation of Schnorr signatures significantly enhances the system's security and anti-tampering capabilities. We consider this additional overhead to be within an acceptable range, as the enhanced security guarantees are critical in smart grid scenarios with high security requirements. This demonstrates a well-balanced trade-off between performance and security.

We systematically compared the decryption overhead trends of the FES scheme and the GuardGrid scheme under varying numbers of smart meters. As shown in Fig. 3, with the increase in the number of smart meters, the performance disadvantage of GuardGrid during the decryption phase becomes increasingly evident. This is because GuardGrid relies on solving the discrete logarithm problem during decryption, whose computational complexity grows significantly with the user scale, leading to a rapid increase in total computation cost.

In contrast, the FES scheme requires only simple linear operations to recover the aggregated inner-product result during decryption, without involving high-complexity number-theoretic computations. Therefore, in terms of decryption

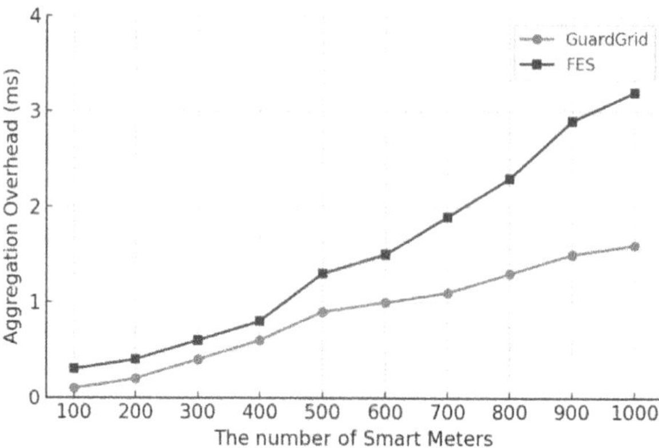

Fig. 2. Aggregation Efficiency.

efficiency, the FES scheme demonstrates a clear advantage over GuardGrid, exhibiting superior scalability and practical applicability in large-scale smart grid environments.

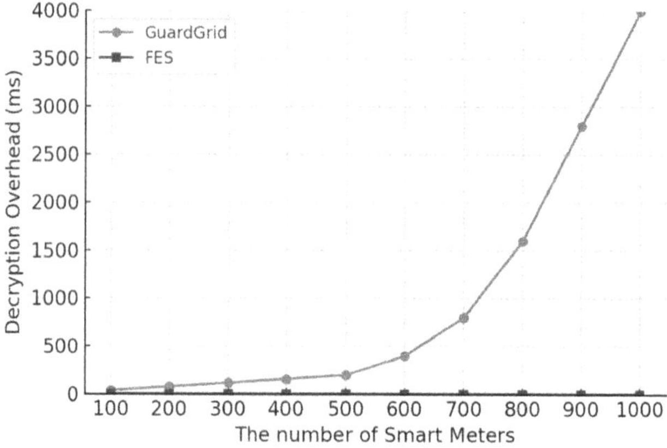

Fig. 3. Decryption Efficiency.

5   Conclusion

This paper proposes an efficient privacy-preserving scheme, FES, designed for real-time data aggregation scenarios in smart grids. The scheme integrates inner-product encryption with a one-time session key management mechanism, enabling verifiable data aggregation while effectively resisting collusion and data-mining attacks from malicious aggregators or users. It ensures both user privacy and data integrity throughout the aggregation process.

Compared with traditional schemes that rely on discrete logarithm computations, FES achieves significantly higher computational efficiency during the decryption phase, making it suitable for resource-constrained smart grid applications with stringent real-time requirements. Amid the growing demand for data processing and privacy protection in modern smart grids, FES offers a practical solution that balances security and performance.

Acknowledgement. This work was supported by Hubei Key Laboratory of Transportation Internet of Things Technology (Grant No. WHUT-IOT-006). We are very grateful to the anonymous reviewers for their valuable comments on the paper.

References

1. Abdalla, M., Bourse, F., De Caro, A., Pointcheval, D.: Simple functional encryption schemes for inner products. In: Katz, J. (ed.) PKC 2015. LNCS, vol. 9020, pp. 733–751. Springer, Heidelberg (2015). https://doi.org/10.1007/978-3-662-46447-2_33
2. Abdallah, A., Shen, X.S.: A lightweight lattice-based homomorphic privacy-preserving data aggregation scheme for smart grid. IEEE Trans. Smart Grid **9**(1), 396–405 (2016)
3. Almaleh, A., Lahiq, S., Al-Shehri, F.: Smart grid privacy via differential privacy of smart metering data. In: 2023 3rd International Conference on Computing and Information Technology (ICCIT), pp. 556–561. IEEE (2023)
4. Bresson, E., Catalano, D., Pointcheval, D.: A simple public-key cryptosystem with a double trapdoor decryption mechanism and its applications. In: Laih, C.-S. (ed.) ASIACRYPT 2003. LNCS, vol. 2894, pp. 37–54. Springer, Heidelberg (2003). https://doi.org/10.1007/978-3-540-40061-5_3
5. Guan, Z., Zhou, X., Liu, P., Longfei, W., Yang, W.: A blockchain-based dual-side privacy-preserving multiparty computation scheme for edge-enabled smart grid. IEEE Internet Things J. **9**(16), 14287–14299 (2021)
6. Chunqiang, H., Liu, Z., Li, R., Pengfei, H., Xiang, T., Han, M.: Smart contract assisted privacy-preserving data aggregation and management scheme for smart grid. IEEE Trans. Dependable Secure Comput. **21**(4), 2145–2161 (2023)
7. Jiang, Y., Zhao, B., Tang, S., Hao-Tian, W.: A verifiable and privacy-preserving multidimensional data aggregation scheme in mobile crowdsensing. Trans. Emerg. Telecommun. Technol. **32**(5), e4008 (2021)
8. Khurana, H., Hadley, M., Lu, N., Frincke, D.A.: Smart-grid security issues. IEEE Secur. Priv. **8**(1), 81–85 (2010)
9. Liu, J.-N., Weng, J., Yang, A., Chen, Y., Lin, X.: Enabling efficient and privacy-preserving aggregation communication and function query for fog computing-based smart grid. IEEE Trans. Smart Grid **11**(1), 247–257 (2019)
10. McDaniel, P., McLaughlin, S.: Security and privacy challenges in the smart grid. IEEE Secur. Priv. **7**(3), 75–77 (2009)
11. Mohammadali, A., Haghighi, M.S.: A privacy-preserving homomorphic scheme with multiple dimensions and fault tolerance for metering data aggregation in smart grid. IEEE Trans. Smart Grid **12**(6), 5212–5220 (2021)
12. Yu, P., Huang, W., Zhang, R., Qian, X., Li, H., Chen, H.: Guardgrid: a queriable and privacy-preserving aggregation scheme for smart grid via function encryption. IEEE Internet Things J. (2025)

13. Zhan, Y., Zhou, L., Wang, B., Duan, P., Zhang, B.: Efficient function queryable and privacy preserving data aggregation scheme in smart grid. IEEE Trans. Parallel Distrib. Syst. **33**(12), 3430–3441 (2022)
14. Zhang, W., Liu, S., Xia, Z.: A distributed privacy-preserving data aggregation scheme for smart grid with fine-grained access control. J. Inf. Secur. Appl. **66**, 103118 (2022)

A Privacy-Preserving Cross-Chain Access Control Scheme Based on Threshold Fully Homomorphic Encryption

Huan Zhang[1,2], Pei Li[1,2(✉)], and Yuanfang Chen[1,2]

[1] Central China Normal University, Wuhan 430079, China
`peili@ccnu.edu.cn`
[2] Hangzhou Dianzi University, Hangzhou 310018, China

Abstract. With the growing demand for cross-platform collaboration in blockchain systems, cross-chain interoperability mechanisms have attracted widespread attention. However, the lack of trust among cross-chain entities poses serious challenges to the privacy protection of inter-chain data. Attribute-based access control (ABAC) enables fine-grained and flexible permission management, but existing schemes often disclose policies and attributes in plaintext, making it easier for attackers to exploit public on-chain information to launch attacks. To address this issue, this paper proposes a cross-chain access control scheme that combines ABAC with threshold fully homomorphic encryption (ThFHE). The scheme utilizes Cheon–Kim–Kim–Song (CKKS), a widely-used fully homomorphic encryption (FHE) scheme, to encrypt access policies and user attributes. Benefiting from the properties of FHE, smart contracts can perform permission verification directly in the ciphertext domain without exposing any sensitive information. Furthermore, the scheme achieves decentralized collaborative decryption by aggregating the partial decryption results from multiple relay nodes. Experimental results demonstrate that the scheme achieves secure and efficient cross-chain data access control with reasonable computational overhead.

Keywords: Access control · Cross-chain · Threshold fully homomorphic encryption · ABAC

1 Introduction

As an immutable distributed ledger technology, blockchain is promoting digital transformation in various fields, such as finance, healthcare, agriculture, and supply chain management [6]. The continuous expansion of blockchain application scenarios has led to the emergence of an increasing number of blockchain systems with diverse functionalities. These systems exhibit significant differences in architecture, consensus mechanisms, and other core aspects. As a result, direct interaction between blockchains becomes difficult, leading to an ecosystem where multiple blockchains coexist but remain isolated from each other [17]. There is an

L. Zhai et al. (Eds.): SocialSec 2025, LNCS 16327, pp. 147–165, 2026.
https://doi.org/10.1007/978-981-95-7027-0_9

urgent need to enable data sharing and exchange across different blockchains [21]. In this context, research on cross-chain interoperability mechanisms has gained increasing attention. Cross-chain technology enables interoperability across multiple blockchains by breaking data silos. It supports use cases such as asset transfer, information sharing, and multi-party collaboration [17], and holds significant practical and commercial value. However, with the rapid growth of cross-chain business scenarios, data privacy protection and access control have gradually become key bottlenecks limiting its development. On the one hand, blockchain data is inherently public and transparent, and there exists a certain degree of mutual distrust among cross-chain participants. Without effective access control, sensitive information can be stolen or misused by malicious nodes during cross-chain processes. On the other hand, the cross-chain environment involves numerous participants with complex relationships. Their access requirements are dynamic and continuously evolving, making it difficult for traditional static or coarse-grained control mechanisms to meet these needs.

To address the challenges, this paper proposes an access control scheme for cross-chain application scenarios that integrates attribute-based access control (ABAC) and threshold fully homomorphic encryption (ThFHE). Compared with existing solutions, the proposed model does not require user attributes or access policies to be exposed on-chain. While enabling secure data sharing across blockchains, it effectively protects user privacy and enhances the system's auditability and robustness. The main contributions are as follows:

(1) We design a fine-grained access control model for multi-blockchain systems, utilizing the ABAC model to achieve dynamic and scalable permission management, which is particularly suitable for cross-chain scenarios involving multi-party collaboration.
(2) We employ the CKKS algorithm, a fully homomorphic encryption (FHE) scheme to encrypt both access policies and user attributes. FHE enables direct computation on ciphertexts, yielding results identical to those on plaintexts after decryption. This allows smart contracts to evaluate permissions directly in the ciphertext domain. As a result, sensitive data is protected from exposure at the source.
(3) We construct a relay chain–based authorization platform. The relay chain is responsible for uniformly processing access requests and recording logs, providing verifiable records for auditing. Additionally, the multiple relay nodes of the relay network collectively form the joint decryption group for the (t, n) threshold FHE scheme. Only when at least t nodes jointly participate in the joint decryption can the authorization result be decrypted.

The remainder of this paper is organized as follows. Section 2 reviews some related work. Section 3 introduces some key concepts. Section 4 provides a detailed description of the system model. Following this, Sect. 5 explains the scheme process. Sections 6 and 7 present the security and performance analyses, respectively. Finally, Sect. 8 concludes the paper.

2   Related Work

In recent years, many researchers have explored the integration of blockchain technology with access control mechanisms to eliminate reliance on centralized entities [8,12,15,20]. Cong et al. [5] proposed the IIACC model, which combines Ciphertext-Policy Attribute-Based Encryption (CP-ABE) and IPFS to achieve blockchain-based, user-initiated, and auditable access control for secure health data sharing. However, due to the tight binding between ciphertext and attribute policies in CP-ABE, the process of key redistribution and ciphertext update becomes highly inefficient when attributes change, making it difficult to support dynamic attribute management. Gao et al. [7] introduced the TrustAccess scheme, which adopts an optimized OHP-CP-ABE algorithm and integrates ElGamal homomorphic encryption to improve access efficiency while preserving attribute privacy. Nevertheless, this approach is designed for single-chain environments and does not consider access control requirements in cross-chain scenarios, limiting its applicability in practice.

Table 1. Functional comparison of access control schemes.

Schemes	Features				
	Policy hiding	Fine-grained	Dynamic permissions	Auditability	Cross-chain
[5]	✓	✓	✗	✗	✗
[7]	✓	✓	✗	✗	✗
[2]	✗	✗	✓	✗	✓
[14]	✗	✗	✗	✓	✓
[11]	✓	✗	✗	✗	✓
Ours	✓	✓	✓	✓	✓

Some studies have begun to focus on access control in cross-chain environments. Chang et al. [2] proposed SynergyChain, a multi-chain framework that aggregates data across blockchains and implements access control through smart contracts and hierarchical permission mechanisms. However, it only supports coarse-grained data-level control and fails to meet the dynamic and fine-grained access requirements of large organizations. Zhao et al. [27] designed a cross-chain medical data sharing model based on dynamic identity and role-based access control, enabling secure access across heterogeneous consortium blockchains using smart contracts. However, the scheme does not address privacy protection for attributes and policies, posing significant security risks. Li et al. [14] developed a two-layer blockchain-based access control model for IoT environments, incorporating linear secret sharing to achieve fine-grained control over resources. Yet, similar to other approaches, it stores attributes and policies in plaintext within smart contracts, which fails to adequately prevent information leakage. Jiang et al. [11] proposed a cross-chain framework that uses a consortium blockchain as the control hub and interacts with other blockchain platforms via off-chain channels. A notary mechanism is introduced to confirm cross-chain transactions. However, the framework heavily relies on the honest behavior of notaries, introducing centralization risks. Moreover, the lack of effective auditing mechanisms in off-chain channels makes it difficult to ensure the transparency and traceability of access operations.

Finally, we compare the proposed scheme with existing approaches in Table 1. Here is the following explanation of the table: policy hiding refers to protecting access control policies through encryption to prevent the leakage of sensitive information. Fine-grained access control enables precise and flexible permission management. Dynamic permission updates allow real-time adjustments to access rights. Auditability ensures that all access activities are traceable and verifiable. Cross-chain support allows the scheme to enforce access control across multiple blockchain platforms. The comparison results show that our scheme offers a more comprehensive set of features than the listed approaches.

3   Preliminaries

3.1   Attribute-Based Access Control

Attribute-based access control (ABAC) is a flexible access control model that allows permissions to be defined based on any security-related characteristics, referred to as attributes [25]. In the ABAC model, access policies are a set of execution criteria that specify the conditions a user must meet to be granted access. These access policies are formulated based on combinations of various attributes, including subject attributes, resource attributes, and environmental attributes. Through the multi-dimensional combination of these attributes, ABAC enables more precise and efficient access control decisions, thus effectively addressing the diverse challenges in modern security requirements.

3.2   Threshold FHE

The core idea of threshold cryptography is to distribute the functionality of a single key among a set of participants to avoid the centralization of power. The most typical application is Shamir's Secret Sharing (SSS) [22], a cryptographic technique based on polynomial interpolation theory. Applying this idea of threshold cryptography to FHE constitutes threshold FHE. The multi-party operational mode of threshold FHE avoids the single point of failure problem caused by the uniqueness of the private key in traditional public-key cryptography, and it significantly enhances the system's resistance to attacks and its robustness. CKKS [4] is a FHE scheme that supports approximate computations on floating-point numbers, proposed by Cheon et al. in 2017. The scheme is based on the Ring Learning with Errors (RLWE) problem [19] and is highly resistant to most attacks. Appendix A provides a detailed description of the standard CKKS scheme. We now introduce its threshold extension scheme, which primarily modifies the key generation and decryption steps. The homomorphic addition and multiplication operations are unaffected and follow the standard definitions in Appendix A.

- **Setup**. According to the CKKS initialization description mentioned in Appendix A, select the parameters (N, Δ, p, L, q_l) satisfying the security level. The secret key and error distributions χ_s and χ_e, are discrete Gaussian distributions. The threshold is t and the number of parties is n, where $1 < t \leq n$. The set of parties is $P = \{P_1, \ldots, P_n\}$.
- **KeyGen**. Sample a secret $s \leftarrow \chi_s$, $a \leftarrow R_{q_L}$, $e \leftarrow \chi_e$, and generate $pk_{ckks} = (b = -a \cdot s + e, a) \in R_{q_L}^2$. Let the threshold be t, and randomly choose coefficients $a_1, \ldots, a_{t-1} \in R_{q_L}$.
- **KeyShare**. Construct the polynomial: $F(x) = s + \sum_{k=1}^{t-1} a_k x^k$. Select the Shamir public points $\alpha_1, \ldots, \alpha_n \in R_{q_L}$ such that they form an exceptional sequence, i.e., $\alpha_i - \alpha_j$ is a unit in R_{q_L}, $\forall i \neq j$. For each participant P_i, compute the share: $s_i = F(\alpha_i) \in R_{q_L}$.
- **Encryption**. A message vector $z \in \mathbb{C}^{N/2}$ is encoded into a plaintext polynomial m. Sample $v \leftarrow \chi_s$, $e_0, e_1 \leftarrow \chi_e$. The encoding and encryption procedures follow the standard CKKS scheme. Use pk_{ckks} and output a ciphertext $c = (c_0, c_1) = (b \cdot v + e_0 + m, \, a \cdot v + e_1)$.
- **P.Decryption**. Let $c = (c_0, c_1)$ be a ciphertext at modulus level q_l. Each party P_i uses its private share s_i to compute a partial decryption share: $d_i = c_1 \cdot s_i \pmod{q_l}$.
- **Combine**. Select any subset $P' \subseteq P$ with $|P'| \geq t$, aggregating their partial decryptions d_i. Output the plaintext polynomial $m' = c_0 + c_1 s = c_0 + \sum_{i \in P'} \lambda_i(0) d_i$, where $\lambda_i(0) = \prod_{j \in P', j \neq i} \frac{-\alpha_j}{\alpha_i - \alpha_j} \pmod{q_l}$. Finally, decode the polynomial m' to recover the message vector z.

3.3 Relay Chain

Among current mainstream cross-chain technologies, the relay chain mechanism has been widely adopted for enabling interoperability among heterogeneous blockchain systems due to its unified structure, strong scalability, and high verification efficiency [16]. A relay chain can be regarded as a coordinating hub blockchain that serves as a unified verification layer, coordinating consensus and communication among multiple parallel chains. It operates an independent consensus protocol through its own validator set to verify and order cross-chain transactions from individual chains, thereby ensuring the security and consistency of the data between chains [3]. Currently, the main platforms available for implementing sidechains or relay chains include Cosmos [13] and Polkadot [23]. Cosmos employs the Tendermint consensus algorithm and supports cross-chain interactions among heterogeneous blockchains. Polkadot, on the other hand, is designed to enable a scalable heterogeneous cross-chain system and exhibits broader applicability across various use cases. Compared to hash-locking [18] and notary [9] schemes, the relay chain does not rely on bidirectional asset locking or centralized intermediaries, offering better compatibility and decentralization. As such, the relay chain is widely regarded as one of the most efficient and reliable solutions in the domain of cross-chain technologies.

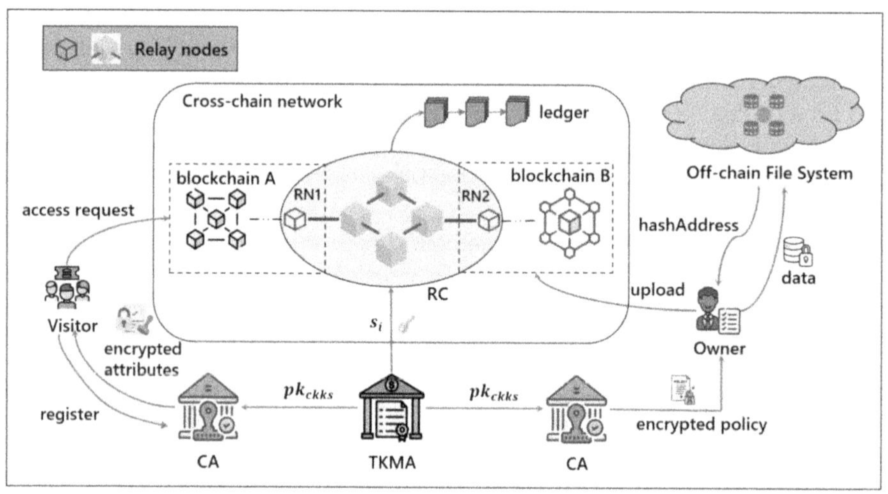

Fig. 1. System architecture.

4   System Architecture

As shown in Fig. 1, our solution involves the following entities: trusted key management authority (TKMA), Owner, Visitor, certificate authority (CA), and relay chain (RC). Their definitions and detailed descriptions are as follows.

CA: The CA is a trusted entity within each blockchain network. It verifies the legitimacy of new users and issues digital certificates and attributes. Attributes are specific characteristics that define a user's permissions, roles, or access levels. A digital certificate includes the user's identity, public key, validity period, encrypted attributes, and the CA's signature. These elements enable authentication and ensure data integrity. The CA also encrypts attributes and access control policies using the CKKS public key.

Owner: The Owner is an entity or organization that possesses private data and wants to share it in a cross-chain environment. When uploading data, the Owner specifies an access control policy, which defines the criteria for access. The policy is encrypted by the CA and uploaded to the blockchain along with the data.

Visitor: The Visitor is an entity or organization requesting access to specific private data. The CA assigns it an encrypted attribute set, which the Visitor provides when initiating a cross-chain data request.

TKMA: TKMA is a trusted authority across the cross-chain network. It generates a CKKS key pair, distributes the public key to all CAs, and splits the private key into shares, distributing them to joint decryption nodes in the relay network.

RC: The RC is the core component for cross-chain access control. Each application chain selects some of its nodes to form a relay chain, with these nodes called relay nodes (RNs). RNs handle cross-chain requests and collaboratively determine authorization results through joint decryption. All cross-chain access records are uploaded to the RC ledger to ensure immutable auditability and traceability.

5   Scheme Process

In this section, we will provide a detailed description of the proposed scheme, including the following stages: system initialization, data upload, access request, ciphertext computation, decryption and authorization. In our scheme, three types of smart contracts are defined: user contract, cross-chain contract, and access control contract (ACC). The user contract serves as the primary interaction interface between users and the blockchain system, performing operations such as data storage, query, and updates that involve ledger read and write processes. The cross-chain contract acts as a bridge connecting users, the blockchain, and relay chain nodes, and is responsible for verifying and forwarding cross-chain transactions while coordinating data exchange between the source and target chains. The ACC is used to match access policies and handles the business logic related to permission management and control. Figure 2 shows the process of the proposed scheme.

5.1   System Initialization

Initially, each application chain's administrator selects at least one node to form the relay network. These selected nodes are referred to as RNs. A cross-chain network is composed of multiple application chains and a relay chain. The TKMA is responsible for executing the key generation process. It creates the public key pk_{ckks} and private key s for the entire cross-chain system by strictly following the key generation protocol described in Sect. 3.2 and in accordance with the security parameters jointly negotiated by all CAs. The pk_{ckks} is transmitted to the CA of each application chain.

To achieve decentralized key management, the TKMA first sets a threshold t and designates n relay nodes to form a joint decryption group, which must include RNs from both the source and target chains. Subsequently, following KeyShare procedure of the threshold FHE scheme introduced in Sect. 3.2, the authority splits the private key s into n key shares s_i. These shares are then distributed to the corresponding relay nodes in the decryption group via a secure transmission protocol. The original private key s is immediately destroyed to ensure forward security, mandating that any decryption requires the collaboration of at least t RNs. Users register with a CA to receive a digital certificate containing their attributes. To ensure interoperability and prevent conflicts,

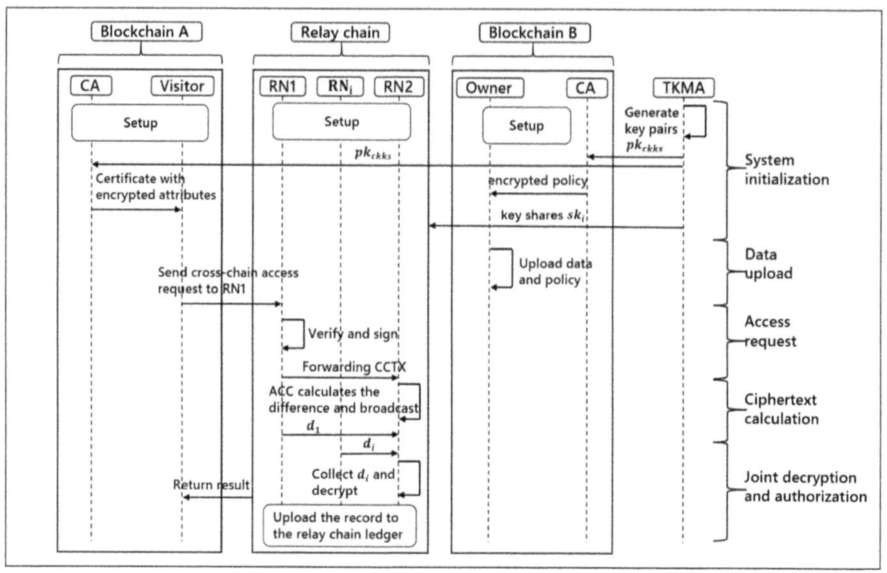

Fig. 2. Process of cross-chain access control scheme.

attribute standards are defined globally by the TKMA and applied consistently across the entire network. To protect privacy, the CA encrypts all attribute values using pk_{ckks} before they are assigned to a user. An attribute set consists of key-value pairs, for example:

$$S = \{(Att_1 : A), (Att_2 : B), (Att_3 : C)\} \tag{1}$$

$$E(S) = \{(Att_1 : E(A)), (Att_2 : E(B)), (Att_3 : E(C))\} \tag{2}$$

5.2 Data Upload

As previously discussed, implementing access control for data is an essential measure to ensure data security. Therefore, before the Owner uploads data to the blockchain ledger, it must specify the access control policy corresponding to the data. The CA is responsible for encrypting this policy. The encryption process for the policy is fundamentally the same as that for attributes. For example, a policy and its encrypted form could be represented as

$$P = (Att_1 : X \text{ OR } Att_2 : Y) \text{ AND } (Att_3 : Z) \tag{3}$$

$$E(P) = (Att_1 : E(X) \text{ OR } Att_2 : E(Y)) \text{ AND } (Att_3 : E(Z)) \tag{4}$$

To alleviate on-chain storage pressure, the Owner can store data in an off-chain file system and publish the corresponding off-chain address on the ledger.

The off-chain address is represented by the *hashAddress*. The Owner can initiate an upload transaction TX_{upload} by invoking the upload function of the user contract, which can be expressed as

$$TX_{upload} = \{dataID, metadata, E(P), hashAddress, signature\} \tag{5}$$

In this transaction, the *dataID* uniquely identifies the data. The *metadata* provides descriptive information related to the data. Its primary function is to assist other organizations or users in efficiently discovering and locating the data within a cross-chain environment, enabling them to decide whether to request access further. It is important to note that the metadata must not contain any sensitive information or directly expose the content of the data. The *signature* represents the digital signature of the Owner on the transaction, generated using the Owner's private key. It is used to verify the integrity and authenticity of the data source. Only the TX_{upload} that has been validated through blockchain consensus and verification can be added to the blockchain ledger.

5.3   Access Request

The Visitor will check the metadata in the network to determine whether to initiate a data access request. Specifically, the Visitor first calls the user contract, submits the encrypted attribute set and the *dataID*, and applies for access to the target data. Based on the *dataID*, the user contract checks whether the data exists in the current blockchain network's ledger. If the data is not on the current chain, user contract will further invoke the cross-chain contract to initiate a cross-chain transaction and generate a cross-chain access request. This request is then sent to the RN of the chain where the Visitor resides. The RN signs the request and encapsulates it into a cross-chain access transaction request (CCTX). Then forwards it to the corresponding RN of the target blockchain. CCTX can be represented as

$$\begin{aligned}CCTX =&\{CCTXID, srcChainID, destChainID, dataID, \\ &TXProof, timestamp, E(S), TX_{result}\}\end{aligned} \tag{6}$$

srcChainID and *destChainID* represent the IDs of the source chain and the destination chain, respectively. The *CCTXID* is generated by combining *srcChainID*, *destChainID*, and an incremental code, ensuring that each cross-chain transaction is uniquely identified. The TX_{result} indicates the authorization outcome of the cross-chain request. The *TXProof* field contains the Merkle root hash of the transaction, the hash value of the cross-chain transaction and the signature of the RN on the source chain, and other verification information, which can be used by the RN of the destination chain to verify the integrity and correctness of the transaction. The relay chain maintains the address information of all RNs participating in the cross-chain network, allowing the address of the RN on the destination chain to be queried.

Algorithm 1 Ciphertext calculation

Input: CCTX, TX_{upload}
Output: $Enc(TX_{result})$
  begin
1. // Verify the legitimacy of cross-chain requests
2. **If** ACC.Verify(CCTX.TXProof) == false **then**
3.   Verification failed
4.   **return**
5. **else**
6. $E(S)$, $dataID \leftarrow$ CCTX
7. $E(P) \leftarrow$ ACC.policyRetrieval(dataID)
8.   // Calculate difference between policy and attribute
9. $Enc(TX_{result}) \leftarrow E(S.Att_i)$ - $E(P.Att_i)$
10. **return** $Enc(TX_{result})$
  end

5.4 Ciphertext Calculation

When the RN of the target chain receives the CCTX, it first verifies the legality of the transaction. This includes checking the validation information in the *CCTXID, TXProof, timestamp*, and other key details. This process ensures that the transaction has not been tampered with and that the source is authentic. After the verification, the RN parses and extracts the Visitor's encrypted attribute set $E(S)$ and the data identifier *dataID*. The RN then invokes the policy retrieval function of the contract ACC, passing *dataID* as an argument to retrieve the corresponding encrypted policy $E(P)$. Subsequently, for each attribute name Att_i with the same name in $E(P)$ and $E(S)$, the ACC calculates the difference between their attribute values, denoted as $Enc(result)$, while preserving the boolean structure. For example, based on the previous example, $Enc(TX_{result})$ can be represented as

$$\begin{aligned} Enc(TX_{result}) = &(E(X) - E(A) \text{ OR} \\ &E(Y) - E(B)) \text{ AND} \\ &(E(Z) - E(C)). \end{aligned} \tag{7}$$

According to the characteristics of FHE, which enables computations on encrypted data without decryption, the result TX_{result} can be expressed as

$$TX_{result} = (X - A \text{ OR } Y - B) \text{ AND } (Z - C). \tag{8}$$

Through this process, the ACC can evaluate the difference between the Visitor's attributes and the policy defined by the Owner in their encrypted state. The RN on the target chain then automatically becomes the temporary aggregator for this decryption task and broadcasts the encrypted authorization result $Enc(TX_{result})$ to all other RNs in the joint decryption group. The ciphertext calculation process between the policy and attributes in their encrypted state is provided in Algorithm 1.

5.5   Joint Decryption And Authorization

Upon receiving the task, each participant in the joint decryption group computes a partial decryption result d_i, using their private key share s_i. This process follows the P.Decryption protocol defined in Sect. 3.2. The resulting share d_i, is then securely sent back to the aggregator. When the number of received partial decryption results reaches the threshold t, the aggregator can then perform the final combination computation. According to the combination formula $m' = c_0 + \sum_{i \in P'} \lambda_i(0) d_i$, the plaintext difference between the attributes and the policy TX_{result} can be directly obtained. The TX_{result} represents the authorization outcome. The final authorization is determined by the ACC, and the cross-chain transaction along with its result is recorded in the relay chain's ledger for future traceability and auditing. At this point, the complete access control process is concluded. Furthermore, cross-chain transactions and their authorization results are uniformly recorded on the distributed ledger of the relay chain. Algorithm 2 provides the details of the joint decryption process and the authorization process.

Algorithm 2 Joint decryption and authorization

Input: key shares s_i, Δ, $Enc(TX_{result})$, P(joint decryption group)

Output: TX_{result}

   begin

1. Let $(c_0, c_1) = Enc(TX_{result})$

2. RN in target chain broadcasts (c_0, c_1) to all RNs in P

3. Initialize an empty set of partial shares $D \leftarrow \emptyset$

4. **for** each (RN$_i$ in P) **do**

5. $d_i = s_i \cdot c_1$

6.   send d_i to RN in target chain

7. **end for**

8. Aggregator RN collects the received d_i into the set D

9. **If** the number of (shares in D) < t

10.   //Insufficient number of shares, decryption failed

11.   **return**

12.**else**

13. $TX'_{result} \leftarrow Combine(c_0, D)$

14. $TX_{result} \leftarrow CKKS.Decode(TX'_{result}, \Delta)$

15.   **If** $TX_{result} ==$ true

16.   Visitor.permission = true

17.   **else**

18.   Visitor.permission = false

19. **return** TX_{result}

   end

---

6   Security Analysis

To clearly evaluate the security of our proposed scheme, we first define its threat model and trust assumptions. In this model, the TKMA and CA are considered honest but curious, while the relay nodes are considered semi-honest. They will faithfully execute the protocol but may attempt to infer additional information from the data they can access. We primarily consider an external attacker whose objective is to compromise the system's access control. This attacker can control malicious visitors and collude with relay nodes also under its control to attempt to obtain unauthorized information. We assume the attacker knows all public parameters of the system and on-chain information. However, the attacker's core capabilities are limited by two constraints: first, they cannot compromise or control the threshold t or more relay nodes; second, they cannot tamper with or destroy the integrity of the blockchain ledger. This section will analyze the security of the scheme under this threat model.

6.1   Foundational Correctness

First, we will prove the foundational correctness of the cryptographic components on which the scheme relies.

Definition 1. If a sequence $(\alpha_1, \ldots, \alpha_n)$ satisfies the condition that for all $i \neq j$, $\alpha_i - \alpha_j$ is a unit in the ring R, then $(\alpha_1, \ldots, \alpha_n)$ is an exceptional sequence.

Correctness Analysis of Secret Sharing over the R. The standard Shamir's secret sharing scheme is instantiated over a field. This guarantees that all non-zero elements are units. Therefore, in the formula $\lambda_i(0) = \prod_{j \in P', j \neq i} \frac{-\alpha_j}{\alpha_i - \alpha_j}$, each term in the denominator has a multiplicative inverse, thus ensuring the existence of the Lagrange coefficients. In fact, a field is not a necessary condition for a secret sharing scheme. Our scheme ensures feasibility over a ring by explicitly requiring that the selected Shamir public points $(\alpha_1, \ldots, \alpha_n)$ must constitute an exceptional sequence. According to Definition 1, an exceptional sequence guarantees that each term $\alpha_i - \alpha_j$ is a unit (i.e., has a multiplicative inverse). Therefore, the denominator term of the interpolation formula $\prod_{j \neq i}(\alpha_i - \alpha_j)$ is guaranteed to be invertible. The correctness of our scheme is guaranteed by the following theorem: Let R be a commutative ring and $(\alpha_1, \ldots \alpha_n)$ be an exceptional sequence in R. Then, a Shamir secret sharing scheme instantiated in R with Shamir public-points $(\alpha_1, \ldots \alpha_n)$ is correct and secure [1].

Correctness Analysis of the Algorithm. According to the description in Sect. 3.2, the decryption formula is: $m' = c_0 + \sum_{i \in P'} \lambda_i(0)d_i = c_0 + c_1 \cdot \left(\sum_{i \in P'} \lambda_i(0)s_i\right) = c_0 + c_1 s$, where $c_0 = (-as + e) \cdot v + m + e_0$, $c_1 = a \cdot v + e_1$. Therefore, we have:

$$m' = [(-as + e) \cdot v + m + e_0] + [a \cdot v + e_1]s$$
$$= -as \cdot v + e \cdot v + m + e_0 + as \cdot v + e_1 s \qquad (9)$$
$$= m + (e \cdot v + e_0 + e_1 s)$$

m' is the sum of the plaintext polynomial m and a small noise term $(ev + e_0 + e_1 s)$. As long as the magnitude of this noise term is significantly smaller than the scaling factor, the subsequent decode step can eliminate this noise and accurately recover the original message vector. This proves the correctness of the algorithm.

6.2   Data Confidentiality

The proposed scheme aims to achieve the confidentiality of policies and attributes during the processes of on-chain storage, cross-chain transmission, and homomorphic computation. This security property can be formalized by the concept of Indistinguishability under Chosen Plaintext Attack (IND-CPA).

Definition 2. An access control scheme is IND-CPA secure if any probabilistic polynomial-time (PPT) attacker $\mathcal{A}$ cannot distinguish with a non-negligible advantage between the ciphertexts of two different plaintext policies (or attribute sets) of its choice.

Analysis. The data confidentiality of this scheme is directly based on the security of the adopted CKKS fully homomorphic encryption scheme. The security of CKKS is based on the hardness assumption of the Ring Learning with Errors (RLWE) problem. The RLWE problem is widely considered to be resistant to quantum attacks and can be proven to be IND-CPA secure in the standard model. Since all policy and attribute values always remain in an encrypted state during their publication to the chain, cross-chain transmission, and computation processes, any external attacker and on-chain participants can only observe ciphertexts that are consistent with IND-CPA security. Therefore, except for the data owner and the CA, no entity can obtain any specific content of the policies or attributes, thus ensuring the confidentiality of the data in a public environment.

6.3   Key Security

If the underlying (t, n) threshold secret sharing scheme is secure and correct, then our scheme can provide key security against single points of failure and $(t - 1)$-collusion attacks.

Analysis. Section 6.1 proves the correctness of the secret sharing mechanism we use over a ring, which is the technical prerequisite for achieving threshold key security. The decryption key is collectively maintained by multiple RNs in the form of shares. The original private key s is securely destroyed after the shares are generated and distributed. Crucially, it is extremely difficult for an attacker to compromise a sufficient number of nodes to obtain enough key shares to break the system. In the subsequent joint decryption process, the complete private key s is never reconstructed nor held by a single entity. The plaintext is computed directly by aggregating partial decryption results from a threshold number of relay nodes. This mechanism enables the threshold decryption of the authorization result without revealing the secret key.

7   Performance Analysis

To evaluate the performance and feasibility of our proposed scheme, we designed a series of simulation experiments. The detailed configuration of the experimental environment is presented in Table 2.

Table 2. Experimental deployment environment.

CPU	Intel(R) Core(TM) i5-11400F @ 2.60GHz
Memory	16GB RAM 2666MHz
Operation system	Ubuntu 20.04.1
Blockchain platform	Hyperledger Fabric 2.4.9
Development tools	go-1.23.2 docker-24.0.7 docker-compose-1.29.2 GoLand-2024.2.1
Other tools	Lattigo-v6 Caliper-0.5.0

7.1 Implementation Of The Scheme

We have built a system based on Hyperledger Fabric 2.4.9, consisting of three independent channels, where each channel represents a blockchain network. Each application chain includes two organizations and one orderer node, with each organization having one peer node. In the relay chain, we deployed two organizations with a total of four peer nodes and one orderer node. In terms of smart contract development, we implemented user contracts, cross-chain contracts, and access control contracts using Golang. Additionally, we developed a client application leveraging the Fabric SDK and gRPC framework to facilitate interaction with the blockchain network. We developed a program based on the Lattigo library to implement a fully homomorphic encryption module. In our experiments, we set $N = 2^{14}$ and $LogQ = [55, 45, 45, 45, 45, 45, 45, 45]$, where N represents the ring degree and Q represents the ciphertext modulus. Based on the homomorphic encryption standards, this configuration can provide a security level of 128 bits.

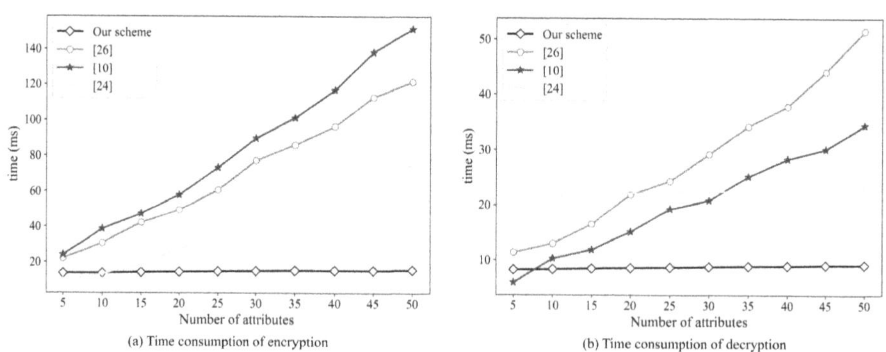

Fig. 3. Encryption and decryption time under different schemes.

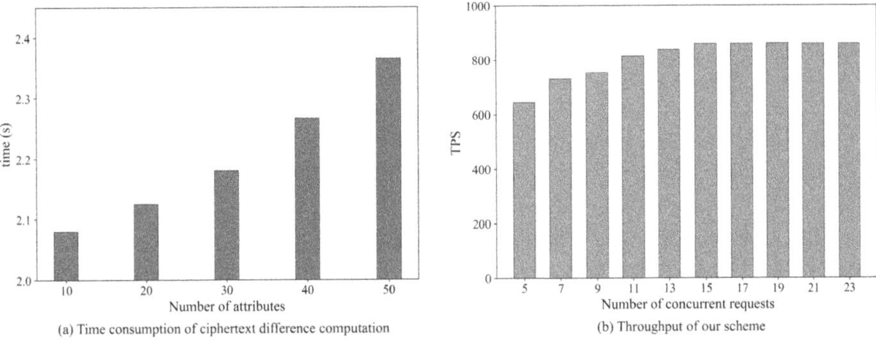

Fig. 4. Ciphertext computation time and throughput of our scheme.

7.2 Evaluation Of The Scheme

The performance of the proposed scheme is primarily influenced by the execution efficiency of FHE within the cross-chain network, the on-chain computation efficiency of ciphertext, and the inherent performance of the underlying blockchain platform. To evaluate the feasibility and performance of the scheme, we conducted simulation experiments focusing on the three aforementioned aspects. The experiment was repeated 100 times and the average values were used as evaluation criteria, as shown in Fig. 3 and Fig. 4.

(1) Figure 3 illustrates the encryption and decryption time trends of different schemes as the number of attributes increases from 5 to 50. Schemes [26] and [10] employ Attribute-Based Encryption (ABE) for access control in cloud and IoT scenarios, respectively, while [24] introduces outsourced computation and a pre-decryption mechanism to enhance performance. These three reference schemes all exhibit a clear linear increase in time overhead with the growing number of attributes. Among them, [10] incurs the highest encryption time, whereas [26] demonstrates the steepest increase in decryption time. In contrast, our scheme maintains nearly constant encryption and decryption times (approximately 15 ms and 9 ms), significantly outperforming the others. This performance stability benefits from the slot-based batching mechanism of the CKKS homomorphic encryption scheme, where the computational overhead depends primarily on the ring dimension and modulus chain depth, rather than the number of attributes. Therefore, our scheme exhibits strong scalability and efficiency in scenarios involving complex access policies.

(2) Given that the access control process proposed in this paper involves multiple parties, ciphertext computation is performed on-chain to ensure the transparency and verifiability of the entire process. Figure 4(a) illustrates the time overhead of executing ciphertext difference computation on-chain. It can be seen that as the number of attributes increases, the time cost in this phase also rises slightly, from 2.08 s to approximately 2.38 s. Although on-chain processing brings some performance loss, it provides essential transparency and veri-

fiability for the entire access control process, which meets the actual demands of cross-chain systems for secure and trustworthy execution.

(3) To verify the system's processing capability under high-concurrency cross-chain request scenarios, we used Caliper to evaluate the transactions per second (TPS), and the results are shown in Fig. 4(b). TPS is an important metric for measuring the processing capability of blockchain systems, reflecting the number of transactions that can be processed per unit time. In the experiment, we issued a total of 20,000 cross-chain requests, configured five workload units, and gradually increased the number of concurrent requests each unit could initiate. The results show that the TPS value steadily increases with the number of concurrent requests and reaches a peak of approximately 860 when the number of concurrent requests reaches 15 per unit. This demonstrates the stability of the proposed scheme in supporting high-concurrency access control requests within a reasonable load range, demonstrating good system throughput performance and the ability to meet the dual requirements of performance and efficiency in multiparty cross-chain interactions.

8   Conclusion

In this paper, we have designed a secure and efficient access control scheme based on the cross-chain data sharing requirements and privacy protection challenges. The scheme is based on the ABAC model, supporting fine-grained control and dynamic adjustment of data access permissions. By utilizing a threshold FHE cryptosystem, permission verification can be performed directly in the ciphertext domain without needing to decrypt any policies or attributes beforehand. The decryption process is distributed among multiple cross-chain participants for collaborative execution, ensuring the security of private data. Cross-chain access records and their authorization results can be stored on the relay chain's ledger. The immutability of blockchain guarantees the traceability and integrity of historical access records. As a result, our solution provides more comprehensive functionality. Experimental results show that the proposed scheme outperforms several existing solutions in terms of performance, and can efficiently handle large-scale cross-chain access requests in high-concurrency scenarios. To address the performance overhead of FHE, future work will explore adopting pre-computation techniques, hardware acceleration, and more lightweight cryptographic primitives for optimization. Concurrently, we plan to introduce Distributed Key Generation and Decentralized Identity technologies to build a fully decentralized trust model.

Acknowledgments. This research was funded by the Key Research and Development Program of Zhejiang Province No. 2023C01141, the Science and Technology Innovation Community Project of Yangtze River Delta No.23002410100. This work was also supported by the Open Research Fund of The State Key Laboratory of Blockchain and Data Security, Zhejiang University.

Appendix A CKKS Algorithm

As shown in Table 3, it provides definitions and explanations for some essential notations used in the CKKS scheme. The canonical embedding map σ is defined as: $\forall m \in \mathbb{R}, \sigma(m) = (m(\xi), m(\xi^3), \ldots, m(\xi^{2N-1})) \in \mathbb{C}^N$, where ξ^{2i-1} represents the N-th primitive roots of the polynomial $X^N + 1$. The detailed algorithmic process is provided below.

Table 3. Notations used in CKKS scheme

Notation	Description
λ	security parameter
p	base integer $(p > 0)$
q_0	modulus
L	number of levels
q_l	ciphertext modulus chain
χ_s	secret key distribution
χ_e	error distribution
R	polynomial ring $= \mathbb{Z}[x]/(x^N + 1)$
$\mathbb{H}$	a symmetric subring of $\mathbb{C}^N$, $\mathbb{H} = \{z \in \mathbb{C}^N : z_j = \overline{z_{N-j}}\}$
π	for $t \in \mathbb{H}$, $\pi(t) = (t_0, t_1, \ldots, t_{N/2}) \in \mathbb{C}^{N/2}$
σ	a canonical embedding map

- **_CKKS.Setup_**(1^λ): Select the modulus q_0, integers p, P(auxiliary modulus), L and K. Let $q_l = p^l \cdot q_0$ $(0 < l \leq L)$, $N = 2^K$, and ensure that they satisfy the required security .
- **_CKKS.KeyGen_**(1^λ): Sample $s \leftarrow \chi_s$, $a \leftarrow R_{q_L}$, and $e \leftarrow \chi_e$. Set secret key $sk \leftarrow (1, s)$ and public key $pk \leftarrow (b, a) \in R_{q_L}^2$, where $b \leftarrow -a \cdot s + e \pmod{q_L}$. Randomly sample $a' \leftarrow R_{P \cdot q_L}$ and $e' \leftarrow \chi_e$. Generate the evaluation key $evk \leftarrow (b', a') \in R_{P \cdot q_L}^2$, where $b' \leftarrow -a' \cdot s + e' \pmod{P \cdot q_L}$.
- **_CKKS.Encode_**(z, Δ): Given a vector $z \in \mathbb{C}^{N/2}$, compute the polynomial $m(X) = \sigma^{-1}([\Delta \cdot \pi^{-1}(z)]_{\sigma(R)}) \in R$.
- **_CKKS.Enc_**(m, pk): Sample $v \leftarrow \chi_s$ and $e_0, e_1 \leftarrow \chi_e$. Output the ciphertext $c = v \cdot pk + (m + e_0, e_1) \pmod{q_l}$.
- **_CKKS.Dec_**(c, sk): For $c = (c_0, c_1)$, output $m = c_0 + c_1 \cdot s \pmod{q_l}$.
- **_CKKS.Decode_**(m, Δ): Output the plaintext $z = \pi(\sigma(\Delta^{-1} \cdot m(X))) \in \mathbb{C}^{N/2}$.
- **_CKKS.Add_**(c_1, c_2): For two ciphertexts c_1, c_2, output $c_{Add} = c_1 + c_2 \pmod{q_l}$
- **_CKKS.Mul_**(c_1, c_2): For two ciphertexts $c_1 = (c_1^{(1)}, c_1^{(2)})$, $c_2 = (c_2^{(1)}, c_2^{(2)})$, compute $(d_0, d_1, d_2) = (c_1^{(1)} c_2^{(1)}, c_1^{(1)} c_2^{(2)} + c_1^{(2)} c_2^{(1)}, c_1^{(2)} c_2^{(2)}) \pmod{q_l}$. Output $c_{Mul} = (d_0, d_1) + \left[P^{-1} \cdot d_2 \cdot evk \right] \pmod{q_l}$.

- $\boldsymbol{CKKS.Rescale}_{l \to l'}(c)$: In each homomorphic operation, the noise within the ciphertext accumulates, and the rescale operation can control the growth of this noise. For a given ciphertext c, with $l' = l - 1$, and then get $c_{rescale} = \lfloor (q_{l'}/q_l) \cdot c \rceil \,(\mathrm{mod}\ q_{l'})$

References

1. Abspoel, M., Cramer, R., Damgård, I., Escudero, D., Yuan, C.: Efficient information-theoretic secure multiparty computation over $\mathbb{Z}/p^k\mathbb{Z}$ via galois rings. Cryptology ePrint Archive, Paper 2019/872 (2019). https://eprint.iacr.org/2019/872
2. Chang, J., Ni, J., Xiao, J., Dai, X., Jin, H.: Synergychain: a multichain-based data-sharing framework with hierarchical access control. IEEE Internet Things J. **9**(16), 14767–14778 (2022). https://doi.org/10.1109/JIOT.2021.3061687
3. Chen, B., et al.: A comprehensive survey of blockchain scalability: shaping inner-chain and inter-chain perspectives. arXiv preprint arXiv:2409.02968 (2024)
4. Cheon, J.H., Kim, A., Kim, M., Song, Y.: Homomorphic encryption for arithmetic of approximate numbers. In: Takagi, T., Peyrin, T. (eds.) ASIACRYPT 2017. LNCS, vol. 10624, pp. 409–437. Springer, Cham (2017). https://doi.org/10.1007/978-3-319-70694-8_15
5. Cong, R., Liu, Y., Tago, K., Li, R., Asaeda, H., Jin, Q.: Individual-initiated auditable access control for privacy-preserved IoT data sharing with blockchain. In: 2021 IEEE International Conference on Communications Workshops (ICC Workshops), pp. 1–6 (2021). https://doi.org/10.1109/ICCWorkshops50388.2021.9473508
6. Dutta, P., Choi, T.M., Somani, S., Butala, R.: Blockchain technology in supply chain operations: applications, challenges and research opportunities. Transp. Res. Part E: Logist. Transp. Rev. **142**, 102067 (2020)
7. Gao, S., Piao, G., Zhu, J., Ma, X., Ma, J.: Trustaccess: a trustworthy secure ciphertext-policy and attribute hiding access control scheme based on blockchain. IEEE Trans. Veh. Technol. **69**(6), 5784–5798 (2020). https://doi.org/10.1109/TVT.2020.2967099
8. Han, D., Zhu, Y., Li, D., Liang, W., Souri, A., Li, K.C.: A blockchain-based auditable access control system for private data in service-centric IoT environments. IEEE Trans. Industr. Inf. **18**(5), 3530–3540 (2022). https://doi.org/10.1109/TII.2021.3114621
9. Hope-Bailie, A., Thomas, S.: Interledger: creating a standard for payments. In: Proceedings of the 25th International Conference Companion on World Wide Web, pp. 281–282 (2016)
10. Huang, C., Wei, S., Fu, A.: An efficient privacy-preserving attribute-based encryption with hidden policy for cloud storage. J. Circuits Syst. Comput. **28**(11), 1950186 (2019)
11. Jiang, Y., Wang, C., Wang, Y., Gao, L.: A cross-chain solution to integrating multiple blockchains for IoT data management. Sensors **19**(9), 2042 (2019)
12. Kang, J., et al.: Blockchain for secure and efficient data sharing in vehicular edge computing and networks. IEEE Internet Things J. **6**(3), 4660–4670 (2019). https://doi.org/10.1109/JIOT.2018.2875542

13. Kwon, J., Buchman, E.: Cosmos: a network of distributed ledgers (2016). https://cosmos.network/whitepaper
14. Li, Z., Hao, J., Liu, J., Wang, H., Xian, M.: An IoT-applicable access control model under double-layer blockchain. IEEE Trans. Circuits Syst. II Express Briefs **68**(6), 2102–2106 (2020)
15. Liu, Y., Li, X., Ma, Y.: FGAC: a fine-grained access control framework for supply chain data sharing. Systems **10**(6), 208 (2022)
16. Mao, H., Nie, T., Sun, H., Shen, D., Yu, G.: A survey on cross-chain technology: challenges, development, and prospect. IEEE Access **11**, 45527–45546 (2022)
17. Ou, W., Huang, S., Zheng, J., Zhang, Q., Zeng, G., Han, W.: An overview on cross-chain: mechanism, platforms, challenges and advances. Comput. Netw. **218**, 109378 (2022)
18. Poon, J., Dryja, T.: The bitcoin lightning network: scalable off-chain instant payments (2016)
19. Rosca, M., Stehlé, D., Wallet, A.: On the ring-LWE and polynomial-LWE problems. In: Nielsen, J.B., Rijmen, V. (eds.) EUROCRYPT 2018. LNCS, vol. 10820, pp. 146–173. Springer, Cham (2018). https://doi.org/10.1007/978-3-319-78381-9_6
20. Rouhani, S., Belchior, R., Cruz, R.S., Deters, R.: Distributed attribute-based access control system using permissioned blockchain. World Wide Web **24**(5), 1617–1644 (2021). https://doi.org/10.1007/s11280-021-00874-7
21. Schulte, S., Sigwart, M., Frauenthaler, P., Borkowski, M.: Towards blockchain interoperability. In: Di Ciccio, C., et al. (eds.) BPM 2019. LNBIP, vol. 361, pp. 3–10. Springer, Cham (2019). https://doi.org/10.1007/978-3-030-30429-4_1
22. Shamir, A.: How to share a secret. Commun. ACM **22**(11), 612–613 (1979)
23. Wood, G.: Polkadot: vision for a heterogeneous multi-chain framework. White Pap. **21**(2327), 4662 (2016)
24. Yang, X., Chen, A., Wang, Z., Li, S.: Cloud storage data access control scheme based on blockchain and attribute-based encryption. Secur. Commun. Netw. **2022**(1), 2204832 (2022)
25. Yuan, E., Tong, J.: Attributed based access control (ABAC) for web services. In: IEEE International Conference on Web Services (ICWS 2005). IEEE (2005)
26. Zhang, Y., He, D., Choo, K.K.R.: Bads: blockchain-based architecture for data sharing with abs and CP-ABE in IoT. Wirel. Commun. Mob. Comput. **2018**(1), 2783658 (2018)
27. Zhao, F., Yu, J., Yan, B.: Towards cross-chain access control model for medical data sharing. Procedia Comput. Sci. **202**, 330–335 (2022)

FG-LAS: A Fault-Tolerant and Group Handover Lightweight Authentication Scheme for Dynamic and Heterogeneous STIN Environments

Yunxiang Zhang[1], Xuan Zhang[2], and Shixiong Yao[1(✉)]

[1] School of Computer Science, Central China Normal University,
Wuhan, Hubei, China
`zyx2023@mails.ccnu.edu.cn`, `yaosx@ccnu.edu.cn`
[2] Hunan Petrochemical Vocational and Technical College, Yueyang, Hunan, China

Abstract. Satellite-Terrestrial Integrated Networks (STIN) hold significant promise for future global communication, but robust authentication remains a primary challenge for their secure application. Current authentication schemes often exhibit deficiencies such as inadequate dynamic binding of device biometrics, insufficient lightweight computation for resource-constrained satellites, lack of truly decentralized trust, and inefficient group handover in high concurrency scenarios. To address these issues, this paper proposes FG-LAS, a lightweight, fault-tolerant, and group handover authentication scheme. FG-LAS innovatively: 1) Introduces a Device Biometric Binding Key (DBBK) to achieve dynamic, unique, and replay-resistant binding between user biometrics and device fingerprints; 2) Employs Threshold ECDSA to construct a decentralized trust architecture, enhancing key management robustness and mitigating single-point-of-failure risks; and 3) Leverages satellite orbit predictability to pre-generate authentication parameters and optimize handovers using group processing, thereby reducing latency and computational overhead. Security analysis and performance evaluations demonstrate the proposed scheme's feasibility, efficiency, and effectiveness for STIN environments.

Keywords: Satellite Terrestrial Integrated Networks (STIN) · Lightweight Authentication · Group Handover · Threshold ECDSA · Biometric-Device Binding

1 Introduction

Despite the rapid advancement of terrestrial communication networks, significant geographical and situational constraints leave a substantial portion of the global population without reliable broadband access. Vast and challenging terrains—such as deserts, oceans, and polar regions—remain communication "blind spots". Furthermore, terrestrial infrastructure is often ill-equipped to handle the massive, sudden surges in data traffic that occur during major events or crises. These inherent limitations necessitate a complementary communication architecture to achieve true global connectivity.

STIN have emerged to address these challenges by integrating Low Earth Orbit (LEO) satellite constellations with ground-based infrastructure. This architecture is designed to provide ubiquitous, high-throughput, and resilient connectivity on a global scale. Systems like SpaceX's Starlink exemplify this potential by delivering internet to previously underserved domains, leveraging inter-satellite links (ISLs) to establish low-latency communication pathways without requiring extensive new ground deployments.

However, the unique characteristics of STINs—including their open wireless links and highly dynamic network topology—introduce significant security vulnerabilities. The communication channels are susceptible to a range of attacks such as identity spoofing, session hijacking, and man-in-the-middle attacks. Furthermore, the high velocity of LEO satellites relative to ground users mandates frequent handovers. These must be performed efficiently to maintain session continuity, posing a major technical challenge for satellite platforms, which are typically constrained in computational power and energy resources.

This demanding operational environment reveals critical deficiencies in existing authentication protocols. A primary challenge lies in achieving robust identity management without imposing prohibitive computational burdens on the network. Many contemporary protocols struggle to establish a verifiably unique binding between a user's biometrics and their specific device, creating vulnerabilities to identity spoofing, especially if biometric templates are compromised [1]. Concurrently, the imperative for lightweight computation is acute for resource-constrained LEO satellites. However, numerous schemes employ computationally intensive operations, such as bilinear pairings, which scale poorly and are ill-suited for the real-time demands of STINs [2].

Furthermore, enhancing system robustness and managing high mobility present another set of significant hurdles. While decentralized mechanisms like threshold signatures are promising for eliminating single points of failure, their implementation can be computationally expensive [3] or may still depend on a fully trusted entity, negating some of the security benefits. Finally, the highly dynamic network topology necessitates frequent and efficient handovers to maintain session continuity. Existing protocols often incur substantial authentication overhead during this process, particularly in high concurrency scenarios, leading to service degradation and system bottlenecks [2]. These interconnected issues highlight the need for a holistic solution. However, merely combining existing techniques is insufficient to resolve the core security trilemma of STINs: achieving decentralized trust, strong identity binding, and high-performance mobility simultaneously. Our work's novelty lies in its synergistic design, which systematically resolves this trilemma by deeply integrating these elements into a unified framework, addressing not just individual challenges but the systemic vulnerabilities arising from their interplay.

The main contributions of this paper are as follows:

- We propose a novel ECC-based access and handover authentication protocol, FG-LAS, which not only supports lightweight secure access and subscription services in STIN but also effectively resists various attacks.

- We introduce DBBK, computed via hash functions to dynamically bind biometric traits with device physical fingerprints. By incorporating randomized nonces and runtime integrity checks, DBBK enhances resistance to replay and cloning attacks and ensures unique and reliable identity-to-device binding in high-latency, frequent-handover environments.
- We employ Threshold ECDSA to establish a decentralized trust architecture, effectively eliminating NCC single points of failure and thwarting private-key tampering attacks, thereby enhancing system robustness and security.
- Leveraging the predictability of satellite orbits, we pre-generate authentication parameters for each node and implement group-optimized handovers, reducing interaction rounds and computational overhead. This approach addresses the high-latency and resource-intensive bottlenecks in high-concurrency scenarios, improving authentication throughput, scalability, energy efficiency, and system latency to ensure stable access and service availability in dynamic environments.
- Formal security analysis, conducted within the Random Oracle Model (ROM) and an eCK-style security framework, together with informal analysis, collectively substantiates the robust security of the proposed scheme. Furthermore, performance evaluations demonstrate that FG-LAS achieves notable efficiency in terms of both computational and communication costs, highlighting its practicality for deployment in resource-constrained STIN environments.

The remainder of this paper is organized as follows. We review related work in Sect. 2. Section 3 covers preliminaries and Sect. 4 details the system model. The proposed FG-LAS scheme is presented in Sect. 5. We evaluate its performance in Sect. 6 and conclude in Sect. 7. A formal security analysis is provided in Appendix A.1.

2   Related Work

The unique operational demands of STINs have spurred diverse research efforts in authentication. These can be broadly categorized into three areas: lightweight cryptography for resource-constrained nodes, decentralized trust models to enhance robustness, and privacy-preserving mobility management for dynamic environments.

2.1   Lightweight Cryptography and ECC-Based Authentication in Satellite Networks

A significant body of research has leveraged Elliptic Curve Cryptography (ECC) to design lightweight authentication protocols suitable for resource-constrained satellite nodes. These schemes aim to reduce computational overhead by empowering LEO satellites with greater autonomy [4], enhance security with three-factor authentication incorporating biometrics [1,5], and minimize latency during frequent handovers through efficient key negotiation and simplified protocol flows [6,7]. Further adaptations have addressed specific contexts, such as cross-domain authentication in integrated maritime networks [8] and resilience against de-synchronization attacks using non-interactive identity mechanisms [9]. Foundational work has also analyzed how orbital dynamics influence handover strategies, which implicitly shapes the requirements for continuous authentication [10,11].

However, a prevalent limitation across many of these ECC-based protocols is their reliance on a centralized or semi-centralized trust architecture. This design choice often creates a single point of failure at the Network Control Center (NCC) and does not adequately provide distributed security or robustness against the compromise of a central authority, a critical vulnerability our work addresses with a decentralized model.

2.2   Blockchain-Based and Decentralized Trust Mechanisms for STIN Authentication

To address the shortcomings of centralized models, another line of research has explored blockchain and decentralized technologies to establish distributed trust. These approaches employ private or consortium blockchains with consensus mechanisms like PBFT for direct, NCC-independent authentication [12], or utilize zero-knowledge proofs and smart contracts for privacy-preserving, cross-provider billing [3]. Techniques such as certificateless cryptography combined with optimized Merkle Patricia Trees aim to reduce the inherent latency of blockchain queries during handovers [13]. Furthermore, distributed key management using threshold signatures has been proposed to secure telemetry, tracking, and command (TT&C) networks [14] and federated learning environments [15], demonstrating the viability of shared-key models.

While these methods significantly enhance system robustness and mitigate single points of failure, they often introduce substantial performance overhead. The latency associated with on-chain consensus, transaction finality, and computationally intensive primitives like bilinear pairings can be prohibitive for the real-time requirements of STIN operations, especially for satellite nodes with limited resources [3]. Our scheme, in contrast, leverages Threshold ECDSA to achieve decentralized trust without the high overhead of a full blockchain implementation.

2.3   Privacy-Preserving Mobility Management and Cross-Domain Authentication

A third critical research area focuses on managing user mobility and privacy during frequent handovers in the dynamic STIN environment. To ensure user anonymity and unlinkability, researchers have employed advanced cryptographic tools like Chameleon Hashes to generate dynamic, untraceable pseudonyms [16,17]. For handling simultaneous handovers efficiently, concepts from vehicular networking have been adapted, such as using Certificateless Aggregate Signatures (CL-AS) to consolidate multiple authentication requests into one [18] or pre-distributing group keys and identifiers to reduce signaling overhead [19–21].

In Although these protocols offer sophisticated solutions for mobility and privacy, they often address these aspects in isolation from a comprehensive trust model. Many handover optimization techniques do not fully integrate with a robust, decentralized security architecture or a strong biometric-to-device binding mechanism. Consequently, a holistic scheme that concurrently provides efficient group handover authentication, decentralized trust, and verifiable identity binding remains a significant research challenge—the very gap that FG-LAS is designed to fill.

3   Preliminaries

This section briefly reviews the cryptographic foundations and notations used throughout the paper.

3.1   Elliptic Curves and Hardness Assumptions

Let E be an elliptic curve defined over a finite field $\mathbb{F}_p$ by the equation $y^2 = x^3 + ax + b \pmod{p}$. The points on E, along with a point at infinity O, form an additive cyclic group G of prime order q. Scalar multiplication is denoted as kP for $k \in \mathbb{Z}_q^*$ and $P \in G$. The security of our protocol is predicated on the computational intractability of two well-established problems [22,23]:

- **Elliptic Curve Discrete Logarithm Problem (ECDLP):** Given $P, Q \in G$ where $Q = xP$, it is infeasible to compute x.
- **Decisional Diffie-Hellman Problem (DDHP):** Given $P, aP, bP \in G$, it is infeasible to distinguish abP from a random point $cP \in G$.

3.2   Biometric Fuzzy Extractor

To handle the inherent variability of biometric data (BIO_i), we employ a fuzzy extractor. It consists of two algorithms: a probabilistic generation algorithm, $\mathsf{Gen}(\text{BIO}_i) \rightarrow (\sigma_i, \nu_i)$, which extracts a uniformly random key σ_i and produces public helper data ν_i; and a deterministic reproduction algorithm, $\mathsf{Rep}(\text{BIO}_i', \nu_i) \rightarrow \sigma_i$, which recovers the original key σ_i from a noisy sample BIO_i' provided it is within a predefined tolerance of BIO_i.

3.3   Verifiable Secret Sharing (VSS)

Our protocol utilizes Feldman's Verifiable Secret Sharing (VSS) [24], an extension of Shamir's Secret Sharing [25]. A (t, N)-VSS scheme allows a dealer to distribute a secret $s \in \mathbb{Z}_q$ among N participants such that any group of t or more can reconstruct it, while any smaller group learns nothing about s. The scheme is defined by two primary functions:

- $\mathsf{SS.Share}(s, t, N)$: Generates and distributes N shares of the secret s.

- SS.Reconstruct($\{[s]_j\}_{j \in S}, t$): Recovers the secret s from a set S of at least t shares, typically via Lagrange interpolation.

VSS enhances this by requiring the dealer to publish cryptographic commitments $C_k = a_k \cdot G$ to the coefficients of the underlying secret-sharing polynomial $P(z) = \sum_{k=0}^{t-1} a_k z^k$. This allows each participant P_j with a public index idx_j to validate their received share $S_j = P(idx_j)$ by checking the following congruence:

$$S_j \cdot G \stackrel{?}{=} \sum_{k=0}^{t-1} (idx_j^k \cdot C_k)$$

This verification step ensures that all shares are consistent and correspond to a single, well-formed secret, preventing a malicious dealer from distributing invalid shares.

4   Model Design

4.1   System Model

The proposed STIN architecture, illustrated in Fig. 1, consists of the following main entities: the Network Control Center, Ground Stations, Satellite Nodes, Mobile Users, and a Blockchain Relay. Their respective roles and responsibilities are defined as follows:

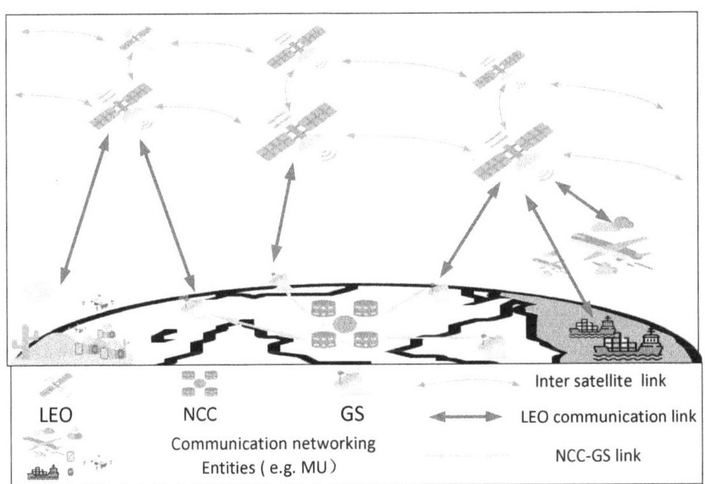

Fig. 1. System architecture

NCC: Operates as a fully trusted authority. During setup, it generates global system parameters and issues private credentials. Equipped with high-performance computing and storage, it handles registration for ground stations, satellites, and users, granting each legitimate access to the integrated network. The NCC also monitors network behavior, identifies malicious participants, and, if necessary, revokes their credentials to preserve system integrity.

Ground Station (GS): Deployed worldwide, ground stations interface with satellites via bidirectional links to deliver subscription services such as data relaying, remote monitoring, and multimedia broadcasting. Untrusted or compromised GS nodes may inject spurious or malicious content, posing disruption risks. Robust authentication and integrity checks are therefore essential to mitigate unauthorized interference.

Satellite Node: Registered satellites authenticate user access requests and, upon validation, provide a suite of subscription services—including positioning, navigation, communication, and broadband connectivity. LEO satellites serve as primary access and relay points due to their reduced latency. As a satellite's coverage moves beyond a user's locality, seamless handover to the next LEO satellite with stronger signal ensures uninterrupted service and maintains both performance and security guarantees.

User. Utilizes IoT-enabled devices (e.g. smartphones, connected vehicles, aircraft, vessels, UAVs) to request and consume network services. Remote users register via satellite links through the ground station infrastructure and then interact directly with satellite nodes for ongoing service.

Blockchain Relay (P_c)**.** Introduced as a semi-honest, non-colluding participant, P_c acts as a public broadcast channel and partial key manager. In threshold ECDSA protocols, P_c facilitates collective public-key and signature generation by storing and operating on secret shares. On-chain broadcasting via P_c obviates the need for direct peer-to-peer links, simplifying deployment and improving resilience to network delays. Publicly recorded state also supports auditability and protocol recovery when participants become unresponsive.

4.2   Threat Model

We adopt a threat model consistent with the Dolev Yao model [26], where a probabilistic polynomial time adversary has full control over all public communication channels. This adversary can intercept, modify, inject, or replay messages to compromise data integrity or impersonate legitimate entities. The model also considers attacks aimed at compromising user privacy by tracking user activities or linking pseudonyms to real identities. Furthermore, the security of long term credentials against physical device compromise or storage breaches is a key consideration, particularly concerning the protocol's ability to maintain forward and backward secrecy.

4.3   Security Requirements

A secure and reliable STIN protocol must satisfy the following fundamental security requirements.

Mutual Authentication: The user and the serving satellite must mutually verify each other's legitimacy before establishing a secure session.

Key Agreement: A shared and cryptographically strong session key must be negotiated between the user and the satellite after successful authentication.

Forward and Backward Secrecy: The compromise of a current session key must not affect the security of any past or future session keys.

User Anonymity and Unlinkability: An adversary should not be able to determine a user's real identity or link multiple distinct communication sessions to a single individual.

Distributed Security: The system's master private key must be distributed across multiple entities so that no single node possesses the complete key.

Robustness: The system must remain operational and continue to provide services even if a subset of network nodes fails or becomes unresponsive.

Attack Resistance: The protocol must be demonstrably resilient against a wide range of known cryptographic attacks, including replay, impersonation, and man in the middle attacks.

5   Proposed Scheme

This section provides a detailed description of the six stages of the FG-LAS protocol: system initialization, registration, user login, access authentication verification, satellite handover phase, and password and biometric updates. Table 1 lists the symbols used in the FG-LAS protocol and their corresponding descriptions.

5.1   System Initialization

The system's cryptographic foundation is established during the initialization phase, which is orchestrated by a designated Network Control Center, NCC_1. This entity is responsible for generating and disseminating the global parameters for the FG-LAS protocol. These parameters include a secure elliptic curve $E_p(a, b)$ over a prime field $\mathbb{F}_p$, a base point G of large prime order q, a suite of cryptographic hash functions $H(\cdot)$, and the biometric fuzzy extractor algorithms, Gen($\cdot$) and Rep($\cdot$).

Key Generation (Protocol 1). The security of the entire system relies on a global ECDSA key pair (X, x), which is generated in a distributed manner. To prevent a single point of failure and enhance robustness, the master private key x is never held by a single entity. Instead, it is created collaboratively by NCC_1 and the Blockchain Relay (P_c) leveraging Verifiable Secret Sharing (VSS), as detailed in Protocol 1. Each participating NCC and P_c instance holds only a share of the private key, $[x]_j$. The corresponding global public key, X, is reconstructed and broadcast system-wide after all shares are verified for consistency.

Table 1. Notations Used in the FG-LAS Protocol

Symbol	Description
Entities and Foundational Parameters	
MU_i, LEO_j	Mobile User i, LEO Satellite j
NCC, P_c	Network Control Center, Blockchain Relay
$H(\cdot)$	Cryptographically secure hash function
Gen/Rep	Fuzzy extractor generation/reproduction algorithms
SS.Share/Rec.	Shamir's Secret Sharing algorithms
Keys and Secret Values	
x, X	System master private/public key pair
$[x]_k$	Share of master private key x
sk, PK	A long-term private/public key pair
k, UPK	An ephemeral private/public key pair
SKey	Shared session key
a_c, A_c	P_c's secret scalar and public value
Identifiers and Protocol Data	
ID_i, PW_i, BIO_i	MU_i's identity, password, biometrics
$UDID, PID_i$	Unique device ID, Pseudonym identity of MU_i
TID_i	Temporary identity of MU_i
$DBBK_i$	Device Biometric Binding Key
DID_i, DR_i	Obfuscated credentials stored on-device
ver_i	Local parameter integrity verification token
T_n, T_{eff}	Timestamp, DBBK validity period
(s, r)	An ECDSA signature pair

Public Parameters and Signing Protocol Definition. Following the successful generation of the distributed key, the complete set of public parameters, $para = \{E_p(a, b), p, q, G, H(\cdot), \mathsf{Rep}(\cdot), \mathsf{Gen}(\cdot), X\}$, is published to all network entities.

PROTOCOL 1 (Key Generation: KeyGen)

1. **Share Generation by NCC_1:**
   a. Sample a secret $x_{\text{ncc1}} \leftarrow \mathbb{Z}_q^*$ and define a t-degree polynomial $P_1(z) = x_{\text{ncc1}} + \sum_{k=1}^{t} a_{1,k} z^k$.
   b. Compute and broadcast commitments $\mathcal{C}_1 = \{C_{1,k} = a_{1,k} \cdot G\}_{k=0}^{t}$, where $a_{1,0} = x_{\text{ncc1}}$.
   c. Securely send share $[x_{\text{ncc1}}]_i = P_1(i)$ to each participant (NCCs and P_c) with index $i \in [1, N]$.

2. **Share Generation by P_c:**

   a. Sample a secret $x_c \leftarrow \mathbb{Z}_q^*$ and define a t-degree polynomial $P_c(z) = x_c + \sum_{k=1}^{t} b_{c,k} z^k$.

   b. Compute and broadcast commitments $\mathcal{C}_c = \{C_{c,k} = b_{c,k} \cdot G\}_{k=0}^{t}$, where $b_{c,0} = x_c$.

   c. **Share Distribution:**
  - Securely send share $[x_c]_l = P_c(l)$ to each NCC_l for $l \in [1, n]$.
  - **Retain** shares $[x_c]_j = P_c(j)$ for its own managed indices $j \in [n + 1, N]$.

3. Compute and Verify Key Shares:

   a. **Each NCC_l ($l \in [1, n]$) performs:**
  i. Verify received shares $[x_{\text{ncc1}}]_l$ and $[x_c]_l$ against their respective public commitments. If any verification fails, abort.
  ii. Compute its final private key share: $[x]_l = ([x_{\text{ncc1}}]_l + [x_c]_l) \pmod{q}$.
  iii. Compute and send its public key share $X_l = [x]_l \cdot G$ to P_c.

   b. **P_c (for its managed indices $j \in [n + 1, N]$) performs:**
  i. Verify all received shares $\{[x_{\text{ncc1}}]_j\}$ from NCC_1. If any fails, abort.
  ii. For each index j, compute the final private key share: $[x]_j = ([x_{\text{ncc1}}]_j + [x_c]_j) \pmod{q}$.
  iii. For each index j, compute and hold the public key share $X_j = [x]_j \cdot G$.

4. Public Key Derivation and Validation (by $\mathbf{P}_c$):

   a. The global public key is computed from the dealers' public commitments: $X = C_{1,0} + C_{c,0}$.

   b. P_c collects all public key shares $\{X_l\}_{l=1}^{n}$ from the NCCs.

   c. For each available public key share X_i ($i \in [1, N]$), P_c validates its consistency against the combined commitment polynomials: $X_i \stackrel{?}{=} \sum_{k=0}^{t} (i^k \cdot (C_{1,k} + C_{c,k}))$.

   d. If all shares are consistent, P_c publishes the global public key X.

Public Parameters and Signing Protocol Definition. Following successful key generation, NCC_1 (or P_c) broadcasts the comprehensive set of public parameters, $para = \{E_p(a, b), p, q, G, H(\cdot), \mathsf{Rep}(\cdot), \mathsf{Gen}(\cdot), X\}$, to all entities within the STIN.

Furthermore, the system specifies a core threshold ECDSA signing routine, which will be instrumental for subsequent registration processes. This routine, detailed in Protocol **2**, is designed for non-interactive, on-chain-friendly execution. It allows a quorum of participants to collectively generate a valid signature without reconstructing the master private key, thus preserving the distributed trust model.

PROTOCOL 2 (Threshold ECDSA Signing)

- **Inputs:**
  1. Each participating $NCC_j, j \in [1, n]$ holds $([x]_j, X)$.
  2. Party P_c holds $([x]_j, X)$, for $j \in [n + 1, N]$.
  3. All parties hold message digest $m = H(M)$.
  4. A $(2t + 1, N)$ threshold scheme is used, where P_c manages $N - n$ shares (indices $k \in [n + 1, N]$) such that $t \leq N - n < 2t + 1$.
  5. Designated dealer is NCC_u.
  6. Public parameters include curve generator G (order q) and public key X.

- **Protocol:**

  1. **Share Generation (by Dealers $D \in \{NCC_u, P_c\}$):**
     a. **For each secret $\xi \in \{k_D, a_D\}$:** (where $k_D, a_D \leftarrow \mathbb{Z}_q^*$)
        i. D defines a t-degree polynomial $P_\xi(z) - \xi + \sum_{i=1}^t c_i z^i$.
        ii. D broadcasts commitments to coefficients $\{C_{\xi,i}\}_{i=0}^t$.
        iii. **Share Distribution:**
           - Each share $[\xi]_j$ for $j \in [1, n]$ is sent to the corresponding NCC_j.
           - For shares $\{[\xi]_j\}_{j=n+1}^N$:
             * If $D = NCC_u$, it sends them to P_c.
             * If $D = P_c$, it **retains** them for its own use.

     b. **For each mask $\zeta \in \{z_D, z_D'\}$ (where the mask ζ is 0):**
        i. D defines a $2t$-degree polynomial $P_\zeta(z) = \sum_{i=1}^{2t} d_i z^i$.
        ii. D broadcasts commitments $\{C_{\zeta,i}\}_{i=1}^{2t}$.
        iii. **Mask Share Distribution:** (handled identically to the secret share distribution above).

     NCC_u broadcasts $R_u = k_u G$. P_c broadcasts $R_c = k_c G$.

  2. **Verification (by all participants):**
     - For $\chi \in \{k_u, a_u, k_c, a_c\}$, check $[\chi]_j G = C_{\chi,0} + \sum_{i=1}^t j^i C_{\chi,i}$.
     - For $\psi \in \{z_u, z_u', z_c, z_c'\}$, check $[\psi]_j G = \sum_{i=1}^{2t} j^i C_{\psi,i}$.
     - If any check fails, the participant aborts.

  3. **Nonce Aggregation:** All participants compute $R = R_u + R_c$ and $r = R_x \bmod q$. If $r = 0$, they abort and restart.

  4. **Partial Signature Generation:**
     - Each participant combines shares: $[k]_j = [k_u]_j + [k_c]_j$, etc.
     - They compute partial signatures: $[s_1]_j = [a]_j(m + r[x]_j) - [z]_j$ and $[s_2]_j = [k]_j[a]_j - [z']_j$.
     - Each NCC_j sends its pair $([s_1]_j, [s_2]_j)$ to P_c.

> **5. Finalization (by P_c):**
>
>   a. Collect at least $t + 1$ valid pairs $([s_1]_j, [s_2]_j)$ from the set of NCCs, $\mathcal{L}$.
>
>   b. Select t of its own pairs, corresponding to indices in $\mathcal{K}_{Pc}$.
>
>   c. Reconstruct $s_1 \leftarrow \mathsf{SS.Reconstruct}(\{[s_1]_\ell\}_{\ell \in \mathcal{L} \cup \mathcal{K}_{Pc}})$ and $s_2 \leftarrow \mathsf{SS.Reconstruct}(\{[s_2]_\ell\}_{\ell \in \mathcal{L} \cup \mathcal{K}_{Pc}})$.
>
>   d. If $s_2 = 0$, abort. Else, compute final signature $s = s_1 \cdot s_2^{-1} \pmod{q}$.
>
>   e. Verify (r, s) and broadcast the result (signature or $\perp$).

5.2 Registration

The registration phase, crucial for onboarding entities into the STIN, involves distinct procedures for satellites and mobile users, both orchestrated with the involvement of the NCC and P_c. Figure 2 illustrates these processes.

Satellite Registration. A satellite, LEO_j, initiates registration by generating a key pair (sk_j, PK_j) and sending its identity ID_j and public key PK_j to user-side NCC (NCC_u). As depicted in Fig. 2, upon receiving the request, the NCC validates LEO_j's credentials and collaborates with P_c and other NCCs to generate a threshold ECDSA signature (s_j, r_j) over a digest containing LEO_j's information and a fresh public parameter A_c. This signature serves as a certificate of registration. LEO_j finalizes the process by verifying this signature using the global public key X. Successful verification confirms its legitimate status within the network, and it securely stores the necessary system parameters.

User Registration. A mobile user, MU_i, begins registration by providing its identity ID_i, unique device identifier $UDID$, password PW_i, and biometric data BIO_i. As shown in Fig. 2, the user's device processes these inputs locally to generate a secure password hash and an ephemeral key pair for the registration request.

Upon receiving the request, the NCC and P_c collaboratively compute the core security token for the user: DBBK. The $DBBK_i$ is a unique hash derived from user, device, and system parameters, designed to create a strong, dynamic link between the user's biometrics and their physical device. It is then published on-chain along with a pseudonym PID_i to ensure public verifiability and unlinkability.

Similar to satellite registration, the NCCs and P_c issue a threshold ECDSA signature (s_i, r_i) to certify the user's registration. After receiving and verifying this signature, the user's device performs a crucial final step: it obfuscates the user's credentials (e.g., ID_i and the registration nonce) and stores them locally. This privacy-preserving measure ensures that sensitive information is not stored in plaintext on the device, protecting it against physical compromise.

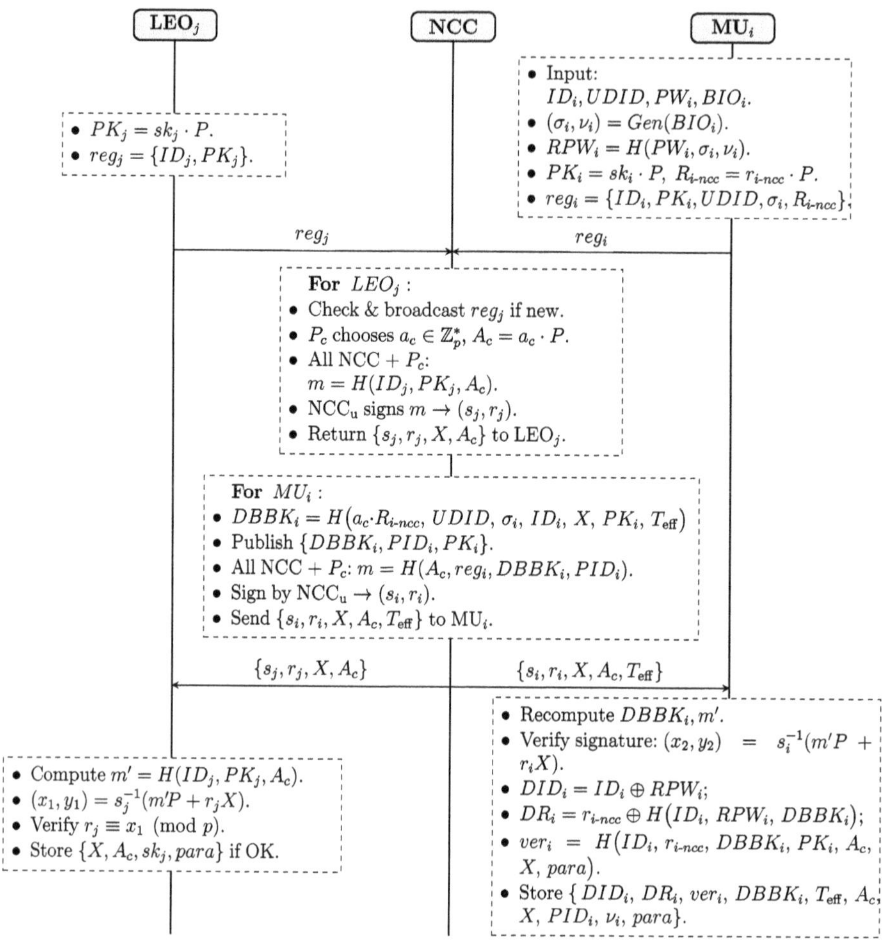

Fig. 2. Registration phase

5.3   User Login

The user login phase functions as a local authentication gateway to enable the device's STIN functionalities. Upon receiving the user's credentials, namely the password PW_i' and biometric data BIO_i', the device initiates a secure local verification sequence. It first employs the fuzzy extractor's reproduction algorithm to recover the sensitive biometric key from the fresh input, calculating $\sigma_i' = \mathsf{Rep}(BIO_i', \nu_i)$. This recovered key is then immediately used alongside the password to generate a temporary password hash, $RPW_i' = H(PW_i', \sigma_i')$. With this hash, the device de-obfuscates the credentials stored during registration by computing the user's identity as $ID_i' = DID_i \oplus RPW_i'$ and the ephemeral registration secret as $r_{i\text{-}ncc}' = DR_i \oplus H(ID_i', RPW_i', \sigma_i')$. Having successfully recovered these core components, the device proceeds to reconstruct the full Device

Biometric Binding Key, $DBBK_i' = H(r_{i\text{-}ncc}' \cdot A_c, \text{UDID}, \sigma_i', ID_i', X, PK_i, T_{\text{eff}})$. As a final integrity check, it computes a comprehensive verification token, $ver_i' = H(ID_i', r_{i\text{-}ncc}', DBBK_i', PK_i, A_c, X, para)$. A successful match of this recomputed token against the one stored during registration confirms both the user's authenticity and the integrity of all local parameters, thereby securely activating the device for STIN communication.

5.4   Access Authentication

The access authentication phase, depicted in Fig. 3, establishes a secure communication channel between a mobile user (MU_i) and a LEO satellite (LEO_j) through a two-round mutual authentication protocol.

First, MU_i initiates the connection by generating an ephemeral key pair and sending an authentication request, M_1. This message contains its temporary identity, its ephemeral public key, and a signature computed over the session's context, including a fresh timestamp T_1. This signature proves MU_i's possession of its long-term secret key and binds its identity to this specific session request.

Upon receiving M_1, LEO_j validates the timestamp and the signature. A successful verification authenticates MU_i. In response, LEO_j generates its own

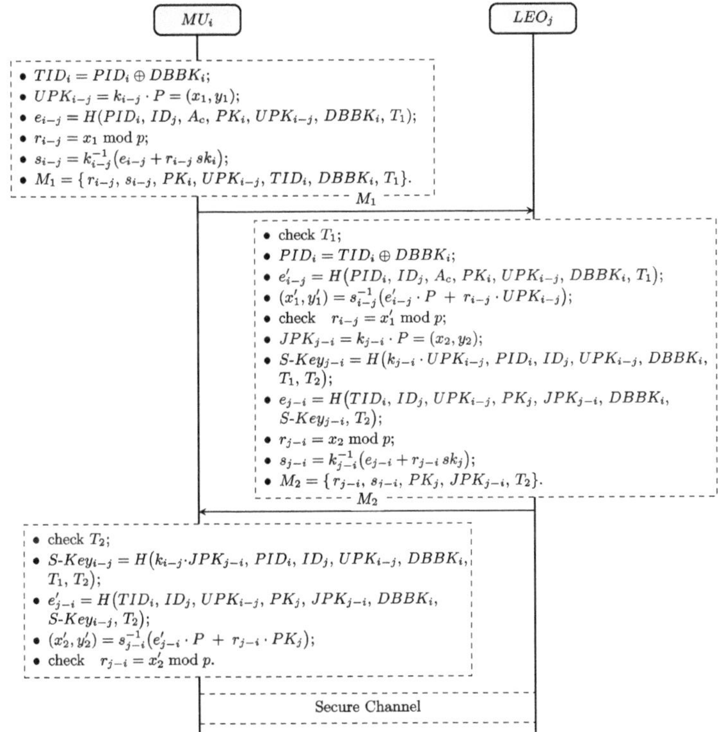

Fig. 3. Access authentication phase

ephemeral key pair and constructs the reply message, M_2. This reply includes its ephemeral public key and a corresponding signature, allowing MU_i to authenticate the satellite. Following this reciprocal verification, both parties derive the same shared session key, $S\text{-}Key$, from their respective private ephemeral keys and the received public ephemeral key, completing the secure key agreement process. The established $S\text{-}Key$ is then used to protect all subsequent communication.

5.5 Inter-satellite Handover Authentication

Due to the high mobility of LEO constellations, frequent handovers are essential to maintain service continuity for users. The proposed scheme implements an efficient group handover authentication protocol, as depicted in Fig. 4, to manage the simultaneous transfer of multiple mobile users (MU_i) from their current satellite (LEO_{now}) to the next one (LEO_{next}).

The process is initiated by LEO_{now}, which aggregates handover requests from a group of users. For each user, it computes a handover authentication token, $auth^i_{now\text{-}next}$, derived from the existing secure session context. LEO_{now} then securely forwards a batch of these tokens and corresponding user session

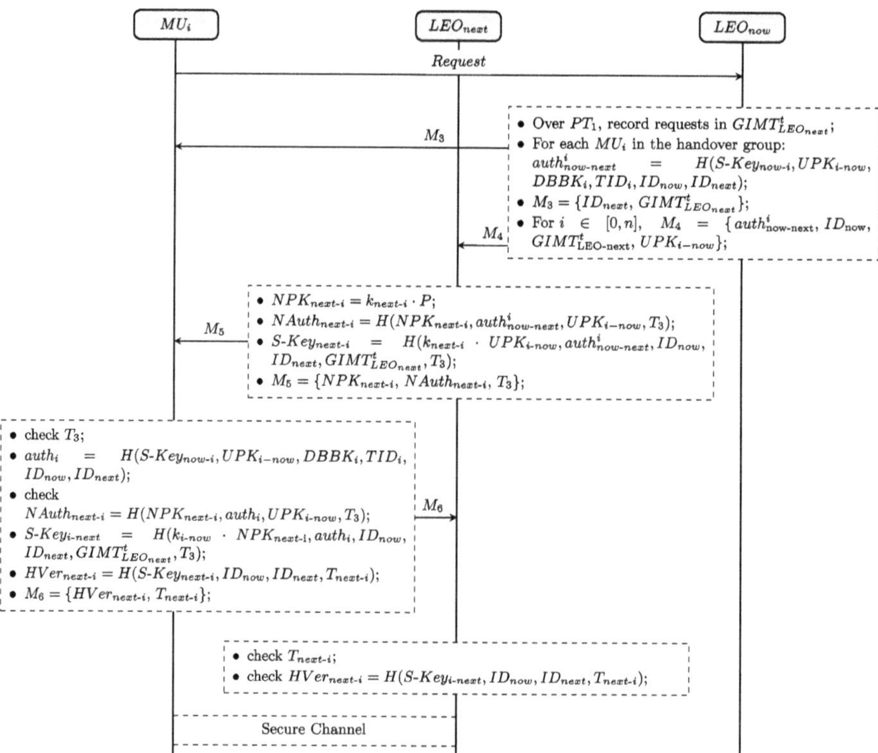

Fig. 4. Inter-satellite handover authentication phase

information to LEO_{next}, preparing it for the incoming group. Concurrently, it informs the users about the impending handover and the identity of LEO_{next}.

Upon receiving the batched information, LEO_{next} prepares a unique response for each user. This involves generating a new ephemeral key and creating a fresh authentication verifier, $NAuth_{next\text{-}i}$, which binds the old session context with the new one. After each user receives and validates the message from LEO_{next}, they compute a new session key, $S\text{-}Key_{i\text{-}next}$, and send a final confirmation message to LEO_{next}. The successful verification of this confirmation at LEO_{next} completes the mutual authentication and establishes a new secure channel for each user, ensuring a seamless and secure transition with minimal overhead.

5.6 DBBK Lifecycle Management and Revocation

The protocol incorporates robust mechanisms for managing the entire lifecycle of a user's credentials, from periodic renewal to conditional revocation.

Proactive DBBK Renewal. To maintain long-term security and prevent session linkability across extended periods, the FG-LAS protocol features a proactive renewal mechanism for the $DBBK_i$. As the predefined validity period T_{eff} nears expiration, the P_c initiates the update. P_c generates a fresh random scalar a'_c and its corresponding public value $A'_c = a'_c \cdot P$. Using this new nonce and a new validity timestamp T'_{eff}, it recomputes the binding key, $DBBK'_i$, based on the user's static registration parameters. The new credentials $(DBBK'_i, A'_c, T'_{\text{eff}})$ are then securely disseminated to both MU_i and the relevant NCCs, ensuring all parties maintain a synchronized and valid state for future authentications.

Conditional Identity Traceability and Revocation. The system provides a formal mechanism for conditional traceability in response to malicious activity. If an MU_i is detected engaging in protocol misuse—such as attempting to authenticate with an invalid $DBBK_i$ or a PID_i not registered on-chain—an identity disclosure procedure is triggered.

Leveraging the immutable on-chain records as evidence, P_c retrieves the user's public credentials and submits a formal disclosure request to the user's original registering authority, NCC_{near}. Upon verifying the evidence, NCC_{near} revokes the user's anonymity by publishing their real identity, ID_i, to the blockchain. This public disclosure serves as an authoritative revocation notice, prompting all LEO satellites to immediately terminate the user's service access and blacklist their credentials from the network.

6   Performance Evaluation

6.1 Comparison of Schemes

We summarize the security-attribute comparison of existing STIN authentication schemes alongside our proposed FG-LAS protocol in Table 2. The analysis reveals a clear progression in addressing the multifaceted security demands of STIN environments.

Early schemes from Li et al. [6] and Guo et al. [5, 27] established a strong baseline, providing core guarantees such as MA, KN, and FBS. However, they are built on centralized trust models, fundamentally lacking both DS and Rob, which makes them vulnerable to single-point failures. While robust in many areas, they exhibit specific gaps; for instance, the work by Li et al. and Yang et al. [2] does not mitigate DLA, and the N3PA protocol [27] omits resistance to PIMA.

In a different approach, the work by Liu et al. [3] successfully integrates DS and Rob via a decentralized architecture. This significant architectural improvement, however, involves trade-offs, notably the absence of FBS and LTA resistance. Crucially, none of these preceding schemes offer a mechanism for GHA, a critical feature for managing user mobility at scale.

FG-LAS is designed to be a holistic solution that synthesizes the strengths of prior work while addressing their collective shortcomings. As shown, it is the only protocol that satisfies all evaluated security and functionality attributes. It uniquely combines a robust, decentralized architecture (DS, Rob) with comprehensive threat mitigation (including against PIMA and DLA) and introduces native support for GHA. This synthesis of distributed trust, complete threat

Table 2. Comparison of Schemes with Respect to Security Attributes

Attribute	[2]	[3]	[5]	[6]	[27]	FG-LAS
MA	✓	✓	✓	✓	✓	✓
KN	✓	✓	✓	✓	✓	✓
FBS	✓	✗	✓	✓	✓	✓
CAU	✓	✓	✓	✓	✓	✓
DS	✗	✓	✗	✗	✗	✓
Rob	✗	✓	✗	✗	✗	✓
EA	✓	✓	✓	✓	✓	✓
RA	✓	✓	✓	✓	✓	✓
IA	✓	✓	✓	✓	✓	✓
TA	✓	✓	✓	✓	✓	✓
MITM	✓	✓	✓	✓	✓	✓
DLA	✗	✗	✓	✗	✓	✓
PIMA	✗	✓	✓	✗	✗	✓
LTA	✓	✗	✓	✓	✓	✓
AA	✓	✓	✓	✓	✓	✓
GHA	✗	✗	✗	✗	✗	✓
TRA	✓	✓	✓	✓	✓	✓

Legend: ✓ = Supported; ✗ = Not Supported.
Abbreviations: MA: mutual authentication; **KN:** key negotiation; **FBS:** forward/backward secrecy; **CAU:** users' anonymity and unlinkability; **DS:** distributed security; **Rob:** robustness; **EA:** eavesdropping attack; **RA:** replay attack; **IA:** impersonation attack; **TA:** tampering attack; **MITM:** man-in-the-middle attack; **DLA:** device loss attack; **PIMA:** privilege insider misuse attack; **LTA:** long-term authentication key leakage attack; **AA:** access authentication; **GHA:** group handover authentication; **TRA:** traceability.

resistance, and optimized mobility management makes FG-LAS a more suitable and forward-looking solution for dynamic STIN deployments.

6.2 Computation Cost

This section presents a comparative analysis of the computational overhead of FG-LAS against related works, considering both access authentication and inter-satellite handover scenarios. To ensure empirical accuracy, we benchmarked all cryptographic primitives using the MIRACL library [28] on a system with an AMD Ryzen 5 5600H CPU and 16.0 GB of RAM. The resulting execution times and parameter lengths, which form the basis for our performance evaluation, are detailed in Table 3.

Access Authentication Performance. In the access phase, FG-LAS demonstrates significant computational efficiency. The protocol imposes a total overhead of just 4.18 ms per session, a cost shared between the MU and LEO entities. As illustrated in Fig. 5a, this performance represents a substantial reduction compared to the schemes by Guo et al. (approx. 7.83 ms), Liu et al. (41.29 ms), and Yang et al. (31.37 ms). This efficiency is particularly noteworthy as it is achieved without a ground station's involvement and without compromising on foundational security properties like MA, KN, and FBS.

Table 3. Parameters for Performance Evaluation

Symbol	Description	Value
Cryptographic Operation Timings (ms)		
T_{sm}	Scalar multiplication on elliptic curve	0.5184
T_{sa}	Scalar addition on elliptic curve	0.0033
T_{sed}	Symmetric encryption/decryption time	0.0175
T_{mod}	Modular arithmetic operation time	0.0047
T_e	Modular exponentiation time in cyclic group $\mathbb{G}$	0.5261
T_{bp}	Bilinear pairing operation	16.4251
T_{sv}	Verification time of Schnorr digital signature	3.3911
T_H	Cryptographic hash function time	0.0011
Parameter Lengths (bits)		
l_k	Scalar on elliptic curve	256
l_p	Prime field size	256
l_G	Group element length	256
l_{sec}	Symmetric ciphertext length	256
l_{cred}	Credential ciphertext length	256
l_H	Hash function output length	256
l_{name}	Entity name length	64
l_{ts}	Timestamp length	32

Group Handover Performance. The efficiency of FG-LAS is even more pronounced in the group handover scenario, where costs scale linearly with the number of concurrent users (n). Our protocol incurs a total overhead of approximately $2.08n$ ms. As shown in Fig. 5b, this significantly outperforms most competing schemes, such as those by Li et al. ($4.69n$ ms) and Guo et al. ($3.13n$

ms). While the protocol by Liu et al. appears computationally cheaper on paper ($1.11n$ ms), this advantage is achieved by omitting critical security features, most notably GHA, FBS, and robust MA, all of which are natively supported by FG-LAS. Therefore, FG-LAS offers a superior balance of high-performance computation and comprehensive security, making it highly suitable for managing large-scale, concurrent handovers in dynamic STIN environments.

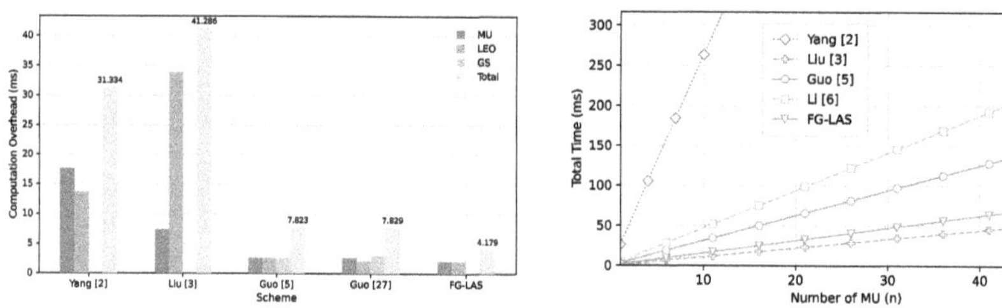

(a) Computational overhead of access phase entities

(b) Total computation overhead in handover phase

Fig. 5. Comparison of computational overheads.

6.3   Communication Cost

This section analyzes the communication overhead of FG-LAS against relevant schemes, with all calculations based on the parameter lengths for 128-bit security defined in Table 3. The results, visualized in Figs. 6a and 6b, highlight the protocol's efficiency in both access and handover phases.

Access Authentication Performance. In the initial access phase, FG-LAS demonstrates remarkable efficiency with a total communication cost of only 1920 bits per session. As shown in Fig. 6a, this lean profile is substantially lower than all evaluated peers, which range from 2560 bits to over 4400 bits. This reduction in data transmission is critical for minimizing latency and conserving bandwidth in resource-constrained STIN environments, especially as FG-LAS achieves this efficiency while providing a full suite of security guarantees.

Group Handover Performance. The protocol's optimized design is particularly evident in the more demanding group handover phase. As illustrated in Fig. 6b, the communication overhead of FG-LAS scales gracefully with the number of concurrent users (n) and remains highly competitive. While some alternative schemes, such as that by Li et al., may exhibit a marginally lower overhead, this comes at the explicit cost of omitting critical security features like DLA and PIMA resistance. Other protocols that appear efficient often lack essential functionalities like GHA altogether. Therefore, the communication footprint of FG-LAS represents a deliberate and effective engineering trade-off, balancing a lean data profile with the comprehensive security and unique group management capabilities required for practical, large-scale STIN deployments.

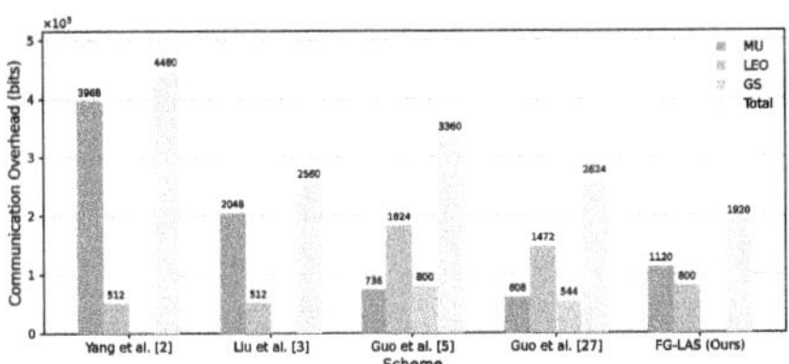

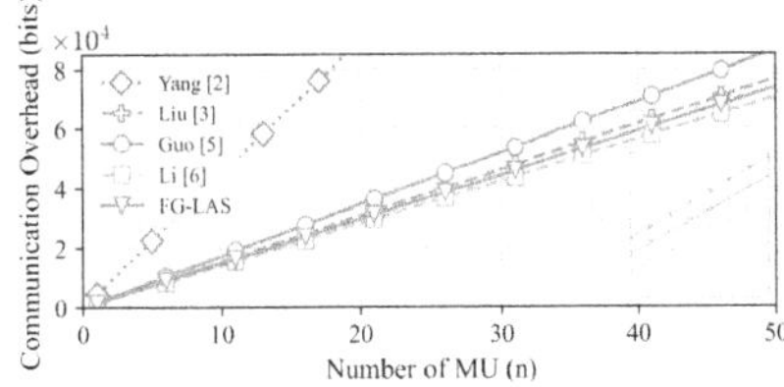

(a) Communication overhead of access phase entities

(b) Total communication overhead in handover phase

Fig. 6. Comparison of communication overheads.

7 Conclusion

This paper introduced FG-LAS, a comprehensive authentication scheme designed for the multifaceted demands of STINs. By uniquely integrating a DBBK for robust user-device binding (assuming secure initial enrollment), a Threshold ECDSA-based decentralized trust model to eliminate single points of failure, and an orbit-aware group handover mechanism to minimize latency (with robustness to minor prediction deviations), FG-LAS holistically resolves the critical trilemma of achieving robust security, decentralized trust, and high-performance mobility management. The presented security analysis and performance evaluations validate the scheme's efficacy, demonstrating that FG-LAS provides a practical and superior framework for securing next-generation dynamic STIN architectures. Future work could explore adaptive parameter tuning to further optimize the trade-off between efficiency and orbital prediction accuracy.

Acknowledgments. This work has been partly supported by the Natural Science Foundation of Hubei Province of China [grant number 2023AFB394], the Fundamental Research Funds for the Central Universities [Grant Number: CCNU24AI010, No. CCNU24JC004], and the National Natural Science Foundation of China [No. 62377019].

A Appendix

A.1 Security Analysis

This section rigorously evaluates the security posture of the proposed FG-LAS protocol. We undertake a two-pronged approach: first, a formal proof of security within a standard cryptographic model to establish strong theoretical guarantees, followed by an informal analysis assessing FG-LAS's resilience against various attacks and its fulfillment of key security properties pertinent to STIN environments.

Formal Security Analysis. We formally analyze the Authenticated Key Exchange (AKE) capabilities of FG-LAS within the ROM, employing a security model adapted from the extended Canetti-Krawczyk (eCK) framework. Our objective is to demonstrate that FG-LAS achieves session key indistinguishability against Probabilistic Polynomial-Time (PPT) adversaries, covering key establishment in both initial access and inter-satellite handovers. This considers the roles of Threshold ECDSA for registration and the $DBBK$ for user-device binding.

The security model defines protocol participants (Mobile Users MU_i, LEO Satellites LEO_j, Network Control Centers NCC_l, Blockchain Relay P_c) and their concurrent instances Π_U^s. Each instance maintains state including long-term and ephemeral keys, a session ID sid_U^s, and a transcript. An instance reaches an *accepted state* upon computing a session key $SKey_U^s$. Two instances Π_U^s, Π_V^t are *partners* if they mutually authenticate, share a sid_U^s, and compute identical session keys $SKey_U^s = SKey_V^t$. A key $SKey_U^s$ is *fresh* if not revealed by adversarial queries or corruption of its owner or partner.

The adversary $\mathcal{A}$ is a PPT algorithm with full network control, capable of standard Dolev-Yao actions. $\mathcal{A}$ interacts via oracles: NewInstance (creates instances), Send (sends messages, models active attacks), RevealSKey (reveals session keys), RevealState (reveals ephemeral keys), and Corrupt (compromises participants, revealing long-term keys or shares like sk_i for MU_i, $[x]_l$ for NCC_l, or x_c for P_c). The crucial TestKey(Π_U^s) query, on a fresh instance, returns either the true key $SKey_U^s$ or a random string, based on a hidden bit b; $\mathcal{A}$ wins by guessing b. Additional oracles include $H_k(M)$ (random oracle queries), FuzzyQuery (fuzzy extractor interactions), and ThreshSignQuery (threshold signature requests). The AKE security goal is that $\mathcal{A}$'s advantage, $\mathrm{Adv}_{\text{FG-LAS}}^{\text{AKE}}(\mathcal{A}) = |2 \cdot \Pr[\mathcal{A} \text{ wins TestKey game}] - 1|$, is negligible.

Cryptographic Assumptions. The security of FG-LAS relies on: (1) The **ROM**. (2) Hardness of the **Elliptic Curve Discrete Logarithm Problem (ECDLP)**. (3) Hardness of the **Computational Diffie-Hellman Problem (CDHP)**. (4) **Threshold ECDSA Security (EUF-CMA)** for registration. (5) **Individual Signature Security (EUF-CMA)** for access/handover signatures. (6) **Fuzzy Extractor Security**, ensuring σ_i is pseudorandom given ν_i, and ν_i hides BIO_i, σ_i. (7) DBBK **Security Properties**, encompassing unforgeability of $DBBK_i$ (requiring σ_i, $UDID_i$, $r_{i\text{-}ncc}$, or breaking CDHP/hash collision) and its binding integrity to user biometrics and device, verifiable via blockchain records.

Security Proof of FG-LAS

Theorem 1 (AKE Security of FG-LAS). *The FG-LAS protocol achieves AKE security in the ROM, under the ECDLP, CDHP, Existential Unforgeability under Chosen Message Attack(EUF-CMA) security of involved signature schemes, fuzzy extractor security, and* DBBK *security assumptions. For any PPT adversary $\mathcal{A}$, its advantage* $\mathrm{Adv}_{\text{FG-LAS}}^{\text{AKE}}(\mathcal{A})$ *is negligible, bounded by:*

$$\mathrm{Adv}^{AKE}_{FG\text{-}LAS}(\mathcal{A}) \leq \mathrm{negl}_H + q_S(\mathrm{Adv}^{EUF\text{-}CMA}_{ThreshSig} + \mathrm{Adv}^{EUF\text{-}CMA}_{IndivSig}$$
$$+ \epsilon_{fuzzy} + \epsilon_{\mathrm{DBBK}} + \mathrm{Adv}^{CDHP}_{\mathcal{G}}$$
$$+ \mathrm{Adv}^{ECDLP}_{\mathcal{G}}) + \mathrm{negl}_{other},$$

where negl_H *is from ROM simulation,* q_S *is session count,* $\mathrm{Adv}^{EUF\text{-}CMA}$ *terms are signature unforgeability advantages,* ϵ *terms are probabilities of breaking fuzzy extractor/DBBK properties,* $\mathrm{Adv}_{\mathcal{G}}$ *terms are for CDHP/ECDLP, and* negl_{other} *for minor terms.*

Proof (Proof Sketch via Game Hopping). The proof proceeds via a sequence of games $G_0, \ldots, G_F$. G_0 is the real AKE game. Let succ_k be $\mathcal{A}$'s success event in G_k. Then $\mathrm{Adv}^{AKE}_{FG\text{-}LAS}(\mathcal{A}) = |2 \cdot \Pr[\mathrm{succ}_0] - 1|$. Each transition from G_k to G_{k+1} introduces a change bounded by a cryptographic assumption, making $|\Pr[\mathrm{succ}_k] - \Pr[\mathrm{succ}_{k+1}]|$ negligible.

Game 1 (G_0 (Real Game)). *Standard AKE game.* $\mathrm{Adv}^{AKE}_{FG\text{-}LAS}(\mathcal{A}) = |2 \cdot \Pr[\mathrm{succ}_0] - 1|$.

Game 2 (G_1 (ROM Simulation)). *Hash functions* $H_k(\cdot)$ *are simulated by random oracles.* $|\Pr[\mathrm{succ}_0] - \Pr[\mathrm{succ}_1]| \leq \mathrm{negl}_H$.

Game 3 (G_2 (Threshold Signature Unforgeability)). *Aborts if* $\mathcal{A}$ *forges a threshold ECDSA signature for registration without corrupting* $\geq t$ *signers or valid replay.* $|\Pr[\mathrm{succ}_1] - \Pr[\mathrm{succ}_2]| \leq q_S \cdot \mathrm{Adv}^{EUF\text{-}CMA}_{ThreshSig}$.

Game 4 (G_3 (Individual Signature Unforgeability)). *Aborts if* $\mathcal{A}$ *forges an individual Schnorr-like signature (e.g.,* s_{i-j}*) for an uncorrupted entity on a new message without knowing the ephemeral secret.* $|\Pr[\mathrm{succ}_2] - \Pr[\mathrm{succ}_3]| \leq N_{sig} \cdot \mathrm{Adv}^{EUF\text{-}CMA}_{IndivSig}$.

Game 5 (G_4 (Fuzzy Extractor Security)). *Aborts if* $\mathcal{A}$ *distinguishes* σ_i *from random (given* ν_i*) or derives* σ_i *for an uncorrupted* MU_i *without a valid* BIO'_i *via* $\mathrm{FuzzyQuery}(Rep(\cdot))$. $|\Pr[\mathrm{succ}_3] - \Pr[\mathrm{succ}_4]| \leq q_S \cdot \epsilon_{fuzzy}$.

Game 6 (G_5 (DBBK Security)). *Aborts if* $\mathcal{A}$ *violates DBBK security for an uncorrupted* MU_i *and* P_c *(e.g., forges* DBBK_i*, uses inconsistent* DBBK_i *not caught by other checks, or derives* DBBK_i *components).* $|\Pr[\mathrm{succ}_4] - \Pr[\mathrm{succ}_5]| \leq q_S \cdot \epsilon_{\mathrm{DBBK}}$.

Game 7 (G_6 (Session Key Indistinguishability - CDHP)). *For a* $\mathrm{TestKey}$ *query on a fresh instance, the core Diffie-Hellman shared secret (e.g.,* $k_{i-j}k_{j-i}P$*) is replaced by a random group element* $R^* \in \mathcal{G}$. *This is undetectable if CDHP is hard and ephemeral secrets are unknown.* $|\Pr[\mathrm{succ}_5] - \Pr[\mathrm{succ}_6]| \leq q_S \cdot \mathrm{Adv}^{CDHP}_{\mathcal{G}}(\tau'')$.

Game 8 ($G_F = G_7$ (Final Game)). *The tested session key is* $H(R^*, transcript)$*, where* R^* *is random (from* G_6*) and* H *is a random oracle. The key is indistinguishable from random. Thus,* $\Pr[\mathrm{succ}_F] = 1/2 \implies \mathrm{Adv}_F(\mathcal{A}) = 0$. *The transition* $|\Pr[\mathrm{succ}_6] - \Pr[\mathrm{succ}_F]|$ *is negligible, bounded by ROM properties.*

Summing the advantages across games demonstrates that $\mathrm{Adv}^{AKE}_{FG\text{-}LAS}(\mathcal{A})$ is negligible, as per Theorem 1. The proof covers both access and handover AKE by ensuring reliance on secure ephemeral DH exchanges (G_6) and authentic preceding messages/identities ($G_2 - G_5$).

A.2   Informal Security Analysis

This section provides an informal assessment of FG-LAS's security posture, demonstrating its resilience against common attacks and its fulfillment of critical security requirements.

Mutual Authentication. FG-LAS achieves robust mutual authentication through a challenge-response mechanism embedded within its signature-based message exchanges. For instance, in the access phase, MU_i authenticates LEO_j by validating a signature that is computationally dependent on LEO_j's long-term private key (sk_j) and a fresh ephemeral secret (k_{j-i}). Conversely, LEO_j authenticates MU_i by verifying a signature contingent on MU_i's secrets (sk_i, k_{i-j}). As forging these signatures is infeasible under the ECDLP assumption, both parties can be assured of each other's legitimacy. This principle of signature-based verification extends directly to the handover phase, ensuring continuous trust as users transition between satellites.

Key Agreement and Secrecy. Session keys are established via an authenticated Elliptic Curve Diffie-Hellman (ECDH) exchange. Both parties compute a shared secret (e.g., $k_{i-j} \cdot JPK_{j-i} = k_{j-i} \cdot UPK_{i-j}$) derived from their private ephemeral keys. The final session key is then computed by hashing this shared secret along with the unique session context. The security of this key is predicated on the hardness of the CDHP.

Furthermore, the protocol guarantees perfect forward and backward secrecy. Since each session key is derived from newly generated ephemeral key pairs that are securely erased post-session, the compromise of long-term keys does not expose past session keys (forward secrecy), nor does the compromise of a current session key reveal information about future ones.

Anonymity, Unlinkability, and Traceability. User anonymity is preserved by using temporary identifiers (TID_i) that mask the user's real identity. An adversary cannot resolve TID_i to ID_i without knowledge of the $DBBK_i$, which is protected by device- and biometric-specific secrets. Unlinkability across different sessions is achieved through the periodic renewal of the $DBBK_i$ and the mandatory inclusion of fresh nonces and timestamps in every transaction.

While providing anonymity, the protocol supports conditional traceability. In cases of malicious behavior verified on-chain, the system provides a formal mechanism for P_c and the NCC to collaboratively and authoritatively disclose the real identity of the malicious user, enabling revocation.

Distributed Security and Robustness. The protocol's architecture achieves distributed security and fault tolerance by leveraging Threshold ECDSA. The master private key is shared among multiple NCCs and P_c, ensuring no single entity holds the entire key. This design mitigates single points of failure and protects against catastrophic key compromise from a single insider attack. The system remains operational as long as a sufficient threshold of participants is available to collectively generate signatures.

Attack Resistance. FG-LAS is engineered to thwart a comprehensive range of threats.

Passive Attacks Eavesdropping is rendered ineffective, as all sensitive information exchanged over public channels is protected by cryptographic primitives (hashing and scalar multiplication) whose security is rooted in well-established computational hardness problems.

Active Attacks Replay, impersonation, and Man-in-the-Middle (MITM) attacks are systematically prevented. The mandatory inclusion and verification of fresh timestamps defeat replay attempts, while the cryptographic signatures ensure message integrity and bind each message to its legitimate originator, preventing forgery and impersonation.

Credential Compromise The protocol is resilient to both device loss and long-term key leakage. Physical device compromise is insufficient for an attacker, as they would still need the user's live biometric input and password to reconstruct the necessary credentials and pass local integrity checks. Due to the use of ephemeral keys, the leakage of a long-term key does not compromise the confidentiality of any past or future communication sessions.

Acknowledgments. This work has been partly supported by the Natural Science Foundation of Hubei Province of China [grant number 2023AFB394].

Disclosure of Interests. The authors declare that they have no known competing financial interests or personal relationships that could have appeared to influence the work reported in this paper.

References

1. Guo, J., Du, Y.: A secure three-factor anonymous roaming authentication protocol using ECC for space information networks. Peer-to-Peer Netw. Appl. **14**(2), 898–916 (2021). https://doi.org/10.1007/S12083-020-01050-W
2. Yang, Y., et al.: PkT-SIN: a secure communication protocol for space information networks with periodic k-time anonymous authentication. IEEE Trans. Inf. Forensics Secur. **19**, 6097–6112 (2024). https://doi.org/10.1109/TIFS.2024.3409070
3. Liu, X., Yang, A., Huang, C., Li, Y., Li, T., Li, M.: Decentralized anonymous authentication with fair billing for space-ground integrated networks. IEEE Trans. Veh. Technol. **70**(8), 7764–7777 (2021). https://doi.org/10.1109/TVT.2021.3091775
4. Xue, K., Meng, W., Li, S., Wei, D.S.L., Zhou, H., Yu, N.: A secure and efficient access and handover authentication protocol for internet of things in space information networks. IEEE Internet Things J. **6**(3), 5485–5499 (2019). https://doi.org/10.1109/JIOT.2019.2902907
5. Guo, J., Du, Y., Zhang, Y., Li, M.: A provably secure ECC-based access and handover authentication protocol for space information networks. J. Netw. Comput. Appl. **193**, 103183 (2021). https://doi.org/10.1016/J.JNCA.2021.103183
6. Li, K., Cui, Q., Zhu, Z., Ni, W., Tao, X.: Lightweight, privacy-preserving handover authentication for integrated terrestrial-satellite networks. In: IEEE International Conference on Communications, ICC 2022, Seoul, Korea, 16–20 May 2022, pp. 25–31. IEEE (2022). https://doi.org/10.1109/ICC45855.2022.9838599

7. Liu, Y., Ni, L., Peng, M.: A secure and efficient authentication protocol for satellite-terrestrial networks. IEEE Internet Things J. **10**(7), 5810–5822 (2023). https://doi.org/10.1109/JIOT.2022.3152900

8. Khan, M.A., Alzahrani, B.A., Barnawi, A., Al-Barakati, A., Irshad, A., Chaudhry, S.A.: A resource friendly authentication scheme for space-air-ground-sea integrated maritime communication network. Ocean Eng. **250**, 110894 (2022)

9. Ibrahim, M.H., Kumari, S., Das, A.K., Odelu, V.: Jamming resistant non-interactive anonymous and unlinkable authentication scheme for mobile satellite networks. Secur. Commun. Netw. **9**(18), 5563–5580 (2016). https://doi.org/10.1002/SEC.1717

10. Voicu, A.M., Bhattacharya, A., Petrova, M.: Handover strategies for emerging LEO, MEO, and HEO satellite networks. IEEE Access **12**, 31523–31537 (2024). https://doi.org/10.1109/ACCESS.2024.3368503

11. Wu, J., Su, S., Wang, X., Zhang, J., Gao, Y.: Accelerating handover in mobile satellite network. In: IEEE INFOCOM 2024 - IEEE Conference on Computer Communications, Vancouver, BC, Canada, 20–23 May 2024, pp. 531–540. IEEE (2024). https://doi.org/10.1109/INFOCOM52122.2024.10621115

12. Arshad, M., Jianwei, L., Khalid, M., Khalid, W., Cao, Y., Khan, F.A.: Access authentication via blockchain in space information network. PLoS ONE **19**(3), e0291236 (2024)

13. Wang, B., Chang, Z., Li, S., Hämäläinen, T.: An efficient and privacy-preserving blockchain-based authentication scheme for low earth orbit satellite-assisted internet of things. IEEE Trans. Aerosp. Electron. Syst. **58**(6), 5153–5164 (2022). https://doi.org/10.1109/TAES.2022.3187389

14. Wang, C., Zhang, Y., Zhang, Q., Xu, X., Chen, W., Li, H.: SE-CAS: secure and efficient cross-domain authentication scheme based on blockchain for space tt&c networks. IEEE Internet Things J. **11**(16), 26806–26818 (2024). https://doi.org/10.1109/JIOT.2024.3401178

15. Chen, J., et al.: Industrial blockchain threshold signatures in federated learning for unified space-air-ground-sea model training. J. Ind. Inf. Integr. **39**, 100593 (2024). https://doi.org/10.1016/J.JII.2024.100593

16. Liu, G., Li, H., Wang, N., Chen, B., Le, J., Liu, Y., Xiang, T.: Pecha: privacy-preserving and efficient cross-domain handover authentication for heterogeneous networks. IEEE Trans. Dependable Secure Comput. (2024)

17. Zhang, Y., Deng, R.H., Bertino, E., Zheng, D.: Robust and universal seamless handover authentication in 5G hetnets. IEEE Trans. Dependable Secur. Comput. **18**(2), 858–874 (2021). https://doi.org/10.1109/TDSC.2019.2927664

18. Yan, X., Ma, M., Su, R.: Efficient group handover authentication for secure 5G-based communications in platoons. IEEE Trans. Intell. Transp. Syst. **24**(3), 3104–3116 (2023). https://doi.org/10.1109/TITS.2022.3221147

19. Wang, M., Zhao, D., Yan, Z., Wang, H., Li, T.: XAuth: secure and privacy-preserving cross-domain handover authentication for 5G hetnets. IEEE Internet Things J. **10**(7), 5962–5976 (2023). https://doi.org/10.1109/JIOT.2022.3223223

20. Yan, X., Ma, M.: A privacy-preserving handover authentication protocol for a group of MTC devices in 5G networks. Comput. Secur. **116**, 102601 (2022). https://doi.org/10.1016/J.COSE.2021.102601

21. Yao, S., Guan, J., Wu, Y., Xu, K., Xu, M.: Toward secure and lightweight access authentication in SAGINs. IEEE Wirel. Commun. **27**(6), 75–81 (2020). https://doi.org/10.1109/MWC.001.2000132

22. Williams, H.C. (ed.): Advances in Cryptology - CRYPTO '85, Santa Barbara, California, USA, August 18–22, 1985, Proceedings, Lecture Notes in Computer Science, vol. 218. Springer (1986). https://doi.org/10.1007/3-540-39799-X
23. Koblitz, N.: Elliptic curve cryptosystems. Math. Comput. **48**(177), 203–209 (1987)
24. Feldman, P.: A practical scheme for non-interactive verifiable secret sharing. In: 28th Annual Symposium on Foundations of Computer Science, Los Angeles, California, USA, 27–29 October 1987, pp. 427–437. IEEE Computer Society (1987). https://doi.org/10.1109/SFCS.1987.4
25. Shamir, A.: How to share a secret. Commun. ACM **22**(11), 612–613 (1979). https://doi.org/10.1145/359168.359176
26. Dolev, D., Yao, A.C.: On the security of public key protocols. IEEE Trans. Inf. Theory **29**(2), 198–207 (1983). https://doi.org/10.1109/TIT.1983.1056650
27. Guo, J., Yao, S., Song, Y., Han, X., Zheng, Z., Chang, L.: N3PA-STIN: a novel three-party authentication protocol for multiuser access in satellite terrestrial integrated networks. IEEE Internet Things J. **12**(10), 14952–14968 (2025). https://doi.org/10.1109/JIOT.2025.3527214
28. MIRACL Team: MIRACL cryptographic SDK: Multiprecision integer and rational arithmetic cryptographic library. https://github.com/miracl/MIRACL. Accessed 1 June 2025

Wavelet Residue Contrastive Learning for Deep Steganalysis

Zhihuai Zhao and Liming Zhai[✉]

School of Computer Science, Central China Normal University, Wuhan 430079, China
zhihuaizhao@mails.ccnu.edu.cn, limingzhai@ccnu.edu.cn

Abstract. Generative steganography embeds secret messages during the image synthesis process, producing artificial images that lack the distortion signatures exploited by classical steganalysis. This shift introduces substantial challenges for reliable detection, particularly when the detector encounters stego images generated by previously unseen models. To address these limitations, we propose WaReCo, a wavelet residue contrastive learning framework designed to improve both feature sensitivity and cross-model generalization in deep steganalysis. Our method employs multi-level discrete wavelet transform to decompose images into frequency subbands, capturing high-frequency residual anomalies introduced by embedding operations. Supervised contrastive learning enhances feature discriminability by maximizing intra-class similarity and inter-class separation without requiring traditional cover-stego pairs. Extensive experiments on typical generative steganography methods across multiple datasets demonstrate that WaReCo consistently outperforms existing steganalysis networks. In particular, it achieves substantial gains in cross-model detection accuracy, often improving performance by more than ten percentage points over prior methods when training and testing generative models are different, validating WaReCo's practical applicability for real-world generative steganalysis.

Keywords: Generative steganography · Steganalysis · Wavelet convolution · Supervised contrastive learning

1 Introduction

Steganography aims to conceal secret information within digital media such that the presence of the hidden content remains imperceptible to observers [13]. Traditional image steganography typically embeds messages by modifying pixel-level statistics of natural images, and its security has been extensively studied over the past two decades [14,15,45]. With the rapid advancement of modern generative models [23], however, steganography has undergone a significant shift. Generative steganography integrates message embedding directly into the image synthesis process, producing images that never existed in the wild. Because these images are synthesized conditioned on latent codes carrying hidden information,

L. Zhai et al. (Eds.): SocialSec 2025, LNCS 16327, pp. 192–208, 2026.
https://doi.org/10.1007/978-981-95-7027-0_11

they no longer exhibit the classical distortion patterns caused by pixel modifications, thereby rendering many conventional steganalysis techniques ineffective.

This paradigm shift introduces new security risks. First, the fusion of generation and embedding means that the hidden channel is intertwined with the generative distribution, leaving almost no explicit modification trace. Second, classical steganalysis pipelines rely on paired cover–stego samples to learn discriminative features, but generative steganography inherently lacks natural covers. Without access to such pairs, existing detectors struggle to learn reliable supervisory signals. These challenges highlight the urgent need for steganalysis methods tailored for generative steganography.

Despite its importance, research on detecting generative steganography remains extremely limited. To the best of our knowledge, only one prior work [8] has specifically addressed this detection problem. However, this approach suffers from poor generalization across different generative models. Specifically, a steganalyzer trained on clean images (acting as covers) and stego images produced by one generative model fails to effectively detect stego images created using different generative architectures. This lack of cross-model generalization severely limits the practical applicability of current detection methods, as real-world scenarios involve diverse generative models with varying architectures.

To address these issues, we propose a Wavelet Residue Contrastive (WaReCo) learning framework to enhance the cross-model generalization capability of steganalysis through two complementary strategies. First, we conduct feature learning in the wavelet domain to improve sensitivity to residual statistical anomalies. Since generative steganography primarily perturbs high-frequency components of images, and residual analysis is crucial for constructing effective steganalysis features, wavelet transform provides an ideal framework for decomposing and analyzing these residual patterns. Second, we employ supervised contrastive learning to enhance feature discriminability between clean and stego images, even in the absence of traditional cover-stego pairs. Our experimental results demonstrate significant improvements in detection accuracy, particularly in cross-model scenarios where the testing data originates from generative models different from those used during training. This enhanced generalization capability makes our approach more practical for real-world deployment.

The main contributions of this work are summarized as follows:

- **Wavelet-domain feature learning:** We introduce a multi-level wavelet decomposition to extract informative high-frequency residual cues that are particularly sensitive to generative hiding artifacts.
- **Supervised contrastive learning:** We leverage label-guided contrastive objectives to enhance intra-class compactness and inter-class separation, compensating for the absence of cover–stego pairs.
- **Cross-model generalization:** Our proposed method maintains stable detection performance across different generative architectures, demonstrating broad applicability to real-world generative steganography scenarios.

2   Related Work

2.1   Image-in-Image Steganography

Deep learning has substantially advanced traditional image-in-image hiding techniques by enabling high-capacity embedding and improved visual fidelity. Early work introduced adversarial learning to the hiding process, demonstrating that GAN-based generation can enhance the natural appearance of stego images [6,28]. Later extensions incorporated additional discriminator networks or auxiliary constraints to increase realism and reduce detectable artifacts [32].

A second line of research employs invertible neural networks (INNs) [3,12] to realize hiding and revealing as perfectly reversible mappings. Because INNs preserve information flow through symmetric transformations, they have been applied to high-capacity image steganography [13]. Several frameworks build on this idea by integrating wavelet losses or multi-branch designs to further improve visual quality or support multi-image embedding [5,10,16,17,39]. However, most INN-based architectures rely on stacks of affine coupling blocks, which significantly increase the model size and training difficulty as network depth grows.

Overall, although image-in-image techniques can achieve high payloads and strong fidelity, they remain fundamentally modification-based schemes operating on natural images. Their embedded distortions differ from the implicit generation-time encoding used in generative steganography, and thus their characteristics and detection challenges do not fully align with the focus of this work.

2.2   Generative Steganography

Generative steganography embeds secret information during or prior to the synthesis process rather than modifying an existing image. Because the resulting stego image is produced entirely by a generative model, the distinction between cover and stego becomes ambiguous. Consequently, for detection tasks, generative steganography is often treated as a coverless paradigm. Existing approaches can be broadly grouped according to how the secret information is injected into the generation pipeline.

Early methods directly mapped message bits into pixel values or specific pixel positions and then completed the remaining content through a generator [20,40]. These schemes are simple but extremely fragile because pixel-level perturbations can be easily disrupted during transmission. Other handcrafted procedures embed information into predefined textures or patterns, producing highly constrained outputs that may raise suspicion due to their limited diversity [19,38,46].

Label-guided approaches encode secret data as semantic attributes of the target image, which are then used to condition a generative network [2,21,26]. Although visually plausible, these methods usually have low embedding capacity and become impractical for transmitting larger payloads. More recent transformation-based techniques hide information within diffusion or style-transfer processes [9,24,42], or embed during style transfer using a reference image [33], but often require auxiliary reference images or strict reconstruction procedures, making them unsuitable for general coverless scenarios.

Latent-space mapping has emerged as the most promising strategy. These methods associate message bits with latent vectors of GAN- or Glow-based generators, enabling robust embedding and high-quality image synthesis [7,18]. Several frameworks extend this idea by injecting data into intermediate feature maps or using invertible generative models to ensure stable extraction [22,27,30,36,47]. With advancements in large-scale image generators, latent-mapping steganography now achieves high hiding capacity and strong realism, making it a primary target for modern steganalysis research.

2.3   Image Steganalysis

Steganalysis aims to determine whether an image contains concealed information, a task made challenging by the subtle nature of steganographic modifications. Traditional systems rely on hand-crafted residual features such as SRM [4] and GFR [29], followed by external classifiers. While effective for older steganographic schemes, these high-dimensional descriptors struggle against the increasingly complex hiding techniques enabled by deep generative models.

The introduction of CNN-based steganalysis marked a major shift. Early architectures demonstrated that learned features could outperform manually designed descriptors [25,31]. Subsequent networks, such as refined residual models [1,37], spatial pyramid pooling structures [44], and more recently siamese-based detectors [41], have continued to improve accuracy and robustness. These designs exploit high-pass residual preprocessing and deep hierarchical features to capture minute statistical anomalies introduced by embedding operations.

Color-image steganalysis has also progressed. Newer networks use channel-wise residual aggregation or unified architectures capable of operating in both spatial [43] and JPEG domains [35]. State-of-the-art models now handle arbitrary image sizes without retraining, significantly improving their practicality [34].

Despite these advances, existing steganalysis research is primarily tailored to modification-based natural-image hiding. These detectors rely on explicit pixel-level distortions and often require paired cover–stego samples for training, both of which are absent in generative steganography. This mismatch limits their effectiveness when applied directly to generative stego images. Our work addresses this gap by designing wavelet-residual features and supervised contrastive learning mechanisms that enhance generalization across diverse generative models.

3   Methodology

3.1   Motivation

Generative steganography embeds secret information during the image synthesis process, effectively merging embedding with generation. This integration conceals explicit modification patterns that are commonly observed in traditional steganography. However, the generative pipeline is not immune to subtle distortions introduced by the embedding operation. In latent-space–based methods, which currently represent the mainstream of generative steganography, message bits must be mapped to distributions consistent with the generator's latent space. To guarantee reliable extraction, this mapping inevitably perturbs the latent vectors. Such perturbations propagate through the generative network and may manifest as irregular textures, degraded local structures, or inconsistencies in fine-grained details. Although these deviations are often small and visually imperceptible, they leave behind statistical traces that can be exploited by a well-designed steganalysis model. These intrinsic residues motivate the need for representation learning that is sensitive to subtle generative inconsistencies.

Wavelet-domain analysis provides a natural tool for capturing such residual artifacts. Wavelet decomposition separates an image into multi-scale subbands, isolating low-frequency structural information from high-frequency texture and edge components. Generative steganography tends to disturb high-frequency patterns, and it either directly through latent perturbations or indirectly through generative inconsistencies. Therefore, the wavelet domain amplifies informative discrepancies that may be largely suppressed in the spatial domain. Moreover, multi-level decomposition enables the model to examine residuals at different scales, allowing it to detect abnormalities that occur in both coarse and fine-grained regions. These properties make wavelet-based feature learning well-suited for modeling the irregular residual signals characteristic of generative stego images. The detailed architecture implementing this wavelet-based feature extraction is presented in Sect. 3.2.

Despite these inherent traces, detecting generative steganography remains challenging. One fundamental difficulty is the absence of a true cover image. Traditional steganalysis relies heavily on paired cover–stego samples, using supervised learning to capture minimal pixel-level differences. Generative steganography, however, produces images without a corresponding natural cover, preventing direct use of such pairwise supervision. Compounding this issue, different generative steganography schemes introduce heterogeneous disturbance patterns. Methods based on latent mapping, diffusion processes, or structure–texture manipulation each produce distinct artifacts. As a result, a steganalyzer trained on a specific generative process often generalizes poorly to others, highlighting the need for features that remain discriminative across diverse generative pipelines.

To address these challenges, we adopt supervised contrastive learning to enhance feature separability. We categorize images into two classes: generative images without hidden messages and generative images containing embedded information. Under this framework, all samples within the same class serve as positives, while samples from the opposite class act as negatives. This formulation leverages label information more effectively than standard cross-entropy training, encouraging the model to cluster latent representations according to the presence or absence of hidden content. Importantly, the contrastive objective disregards the type of generative model, allowing the learned features to emphasize steganographic cues rather than generator-specific characteristics. Consequently, the network acquires representations that are more robust and more transferable across different generative steganography methods. The detailed implementation of this contrastive learning strategy is described in Sect. 3.3.

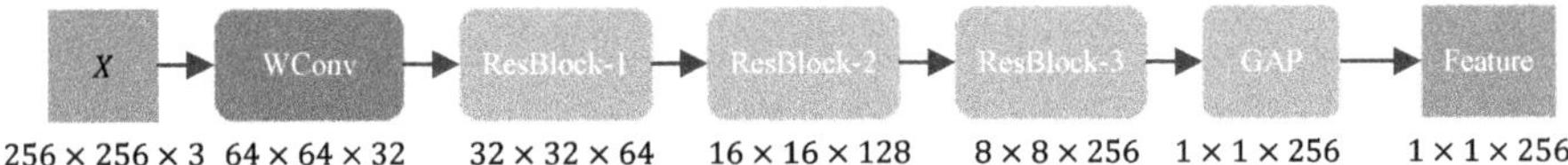

Fig. 1. Overall framework of wavelet residue network.

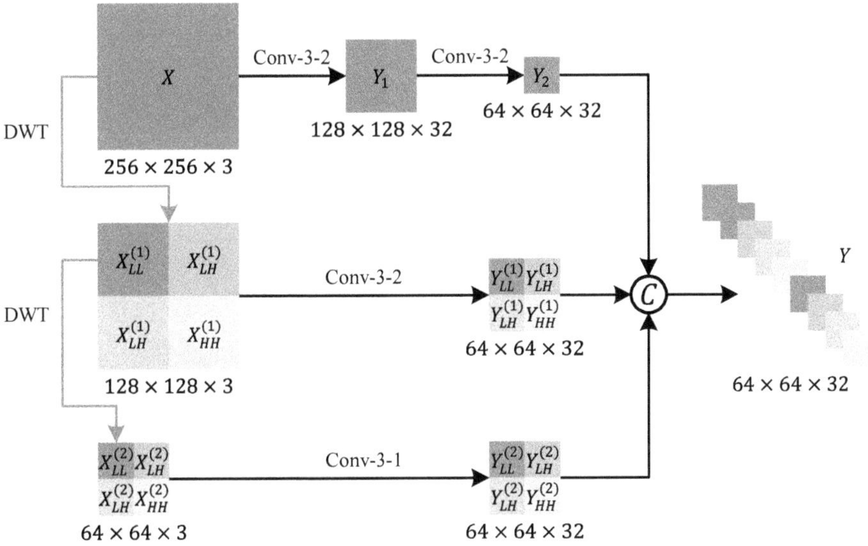

Fig. 2. Structure of wavelet convolution.

3.2 Wavelet Residue Network

We begin by clarifying the term "residue" as it appears in different contexts throughout this section. The first usage refers to residual signals associated with high-frequency image components and texture details, which capture the subtle artifacts introduced by steganographic embedding. The second usage pertains to residual representations in deep residual networks, where skip connections enable identity mappings to facilitate gradient flow during training.

We denote our steganalysis architecture as the Wavelet Residue Network. The central idea is that residual high-frequency signals contain the most informative steganographic artifacts, so these signals must be extracted explicitly at the earliest stage of feature learning. We therefore apply a multi-level discrete wavelet transform (DWT) to decompose the input image and isolate its residual components. Subsequent layers then rely on residual convolution modules, following the design principles of deep residual networks, to learn increasingly discriminative representations.

The final residual module produces a feature map that is aggregated using global average pooling (GAP) to obtain the final feature vector. Figure 1 illustrates the overall pipeline, where the numbers beneath each block indicate the spatial resolution and channel dimensionality (*e.g.*, $64 \times 64 \times 32$ denotes resolution 64×64 with 32 channels). Wavelet decomposition is applied only at the beginning of the network. Once appropriate residual signals are extracted in the first stage, deeper layers can focus on representation learning without repeatedly invoking wavelet transforms.

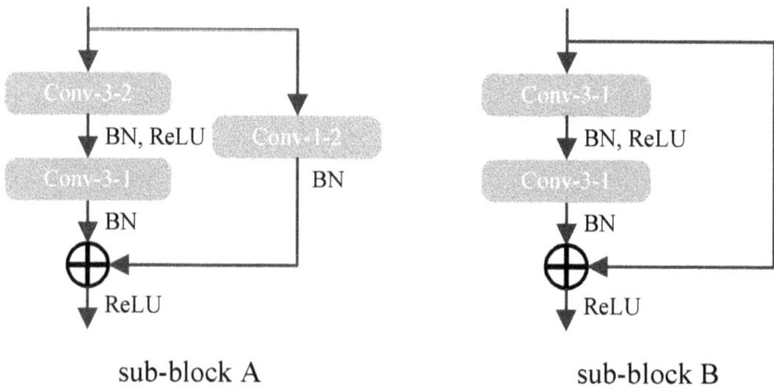

Fig. 3. Illustration of two sub-blocks in a residual block.

The first module of our Wavelet Residue Network is the wavelet convolution (WConv) module, designed for multi-scale wavelet decomposition as shown in Fig. 2. The input image $X \in \mathbb{R}^{H \times W \times 3}$ undergoes first-level wavelet decomposition, producing four subbands:

$$X_{LL}^{(1)}, X_{LH}^{(1)}, X_{HL}^{(1)}, X_{HH}^{(1)} \in \mathbb{R}^{H/2 \times W/2 \times 3} \tag{1}$$

where $X_{LL}^{(1)}$ represents the low-frequency approximation, while $X_{LH}^{(1)}$, $X_{HL}^{(1)}$, and $X_{HH}^{(1)}$ capture horizontal, vertical, and diagonal high-frequency details, respectively. Each subband is processed through a convolutional layer with 32 filters of size 3×3 and stride 2 to extract preliminary residual features. Since different subbands represent distinct residual signals, we apply independent convolution operations to prevent inter-subband interference and learn discriminative features. This is implemented by concatenating the four subbands along the channel dimension and applying group convolution based on the number of channels per subband.

We further decompose the low-frequency subband $X_{LL}^{(1)}$ to obtain finer-scale information:

$$X_{LL}^{(2)}, X_{LH}^{(2)}, X_{HL}^{(2)}, X_{HH}^{(2)} \in \mathbb{R}^{H/4 \times W/4 \times 3}, \tag{2}$$

Similar to the first level, these second-level subbands are processed using group convolution to extract refined residual features. However, we employ 3×3 convolutional filters with stride 1 and 32 filters per group. The stride-1 configuration ensures that the resulting feature maps maintain the same spatial resolution as those from the first-level subbands, enabling effective feature integration in subsequent stages.

While wavelet decomposition extracts frequency-domain residual signals, we simultaneously extract features from the spatial domain to capture complementary information. The input image X is directly processed through two consecutive convolutional layers, each containing 32 filters of size 3×3 with stride 2. This spatial pathway provides context that complements the wavelet-based residual analysis, allowing the network to learn both frequency-specific and spatially-coherent representations.

After processing the original image and the two levels of wavelet sub-bands, we concatenate all resulting feature maps along the channel dimension. This yields nine feature groups, each containing 32 channels: four groups from the first-level subbands, four from the second-level subbands, and one from the spatial domain processing. This concatenated representation Y integrates multi-scale residual information across different frequency bands and spatial characteristics.

The concatenated features Y are fed into three residual modules (ResBlock-1/2/3 in Fig. 1) for hierarchical feature learning. Each residual module comprises two sub-blocks connected sequentially, as depicted in Fig. 3, where the first convolutional layer in the initial sub-block performs downsampling using a stride-2 convolution. Since the wavelet convolution outputs independently learned residual features, each residual module remain employs group convolution to maintain independent processing of different residual feature types, enhancing their discriminability. This design both preserves the diversity of residual cues and reduces model parameters, improving training efficiency.

After passing through the three residual blocks, the network outputs a feature representation with dimension 256×9. This serves as the final input to contrastive learning and classification components described in later sections.

3.3   Supervised Contrastive Learning

Our approach incorporates supervised contrastive learning, inspired by [11], adapting it specifically for steganalysis tasks. Unlike self-supervised contrastive learning methods that rely solely on data augmentation to define positive pairs, supervised contrastive learning leverages label information to construct more effective training objectives. The core principle involves pulling together feature representations of samples belonging to the same class while pushing apart representations of samples from different classes in the embedding space. This supervised formulation enables the network to learn more discriminative features by explicitly encoding class relationships into the learned representations. By maximizing agreement among same-class samples and disagreement among different-class samples, the learned features exhibit enhanced class separability, which is particularly valuable for the subtle distinction between clean and stego images in generative steganalysis.

To enhance the generalization capability of our steganalyzer across diverse generative steganography methods, we adopt a model-agnostic classification framework. Rather than distinguishing images based on their originating generative models, we categorize all images into two fundamental classes: clean generated images without embedded secret information (covers) and stego images containing hidden data (stegos). Critically, both the cover and stego classes encompass images produced by multiple generative architectures, including GANs, autoencoders, and flow-based models. This deliberate design choice encourages the network to learn universal steganographic signatures that transcend specific model characteristics. By training on heterogeneous samples within each class, the learned features capture the essential statistical properties that distinguish steganographic content from clean generation, regardless of the underlying generative mechanism. This approach directly addresses the cross-model generalization challenge, enabling the steganalyzer to detect previously unseen generative steganography methods.

During training, we construct mini-batches with careful consideration of sample diversity to maximize the effectiveness of supervised contrastive learning. Each mini-batch contains both cover and stego images sampled from multiple generative models to ensure balanced representation across different architectures. This uniform sampling strategy prevents the network from learning model-specific biases while promoting robust feature extraction. For a given mini-batch, let $\mathcal{B}$ denote the set of N samples, where each sample is associated with a binary label $y \in \{0, 1\}$ indicating cover ($y = 0$) or stego ($y = 1$) class. The diversity within each class encourages the network to identify invariant steganographic patterns rather than artifacts specific to particular generative models.

The supervised contrastive loss is computed for each sample in the mini-batch by contrasting it against all other samples. For a given anchor sample i with label y_i, we first obtain its normalized feature representation $\mathbf{z}_i = f(\mathbf{x}_i)/\|f(\mathbf{x}_i)\|$ from the Wavelet Residue Network, where $f(\cdot)$ denotes the feature extraction function. The set of positive samples for anchor i is defined as

$$\mathcal{P}(i) = \{p \in \mathcal{B} : y_p = y_i, p \neq i\}, \tag{3}$$

which includes all samples in the batch sharing the same label as the anchor, excluding the anchor itself. The supervised contrastive loss for sample i is then formulated as:

$$\mathcal{L}_{\text{SC}}^{(i)} = -\frac{1}{|\mathcal{P}(i)|} \sum_{p \in \mathcal{P}(i)} \log \frac{\exp(\mathbf{z}_i \cdot \mathbf{z}_p / \tau)}{\sum_{a \in \mathcal{B} \setminus \{i\}} \exp(\mathbf{z}_i \cdot \mathbf{z}_a / \tau)}, \tag{4}$$

where τ is a temperature parameter controlling the concentration of the distribution, and $\mathbf{z}_i \cdot \mathbf{z}_p$ denotes the cosine similarity between normalized feature vectors.

The numerator encourages high similarity between the anchor and positive samples, while the denominator normalizes over all samples except the anchor itself, effectively pushing negative samples away.

3.4 Overall Loss Function

The total training loss combines the supervised contrastive loss with standard cross-entropy classification loss

$$\mathcal{L}_{\text{total}} = \lambda\mathcal{L}_{\text{SC}} + (1 - \lambda)\mathcal{L}_{\text{CE}} \tag{5}$$

where $\mathcal{L}_{\text{SC}} = \frac{1}{N}\sum_{i=1}^{N}\mathcal{L}_{\text{SC}}^{(i)}$ is the averaged contrastive loss over the mini-batch, $\mathcal{L}_{\text{CE}}$ is the cross-entropy loss obtained by a fully-connected layer and a 2-way softmax layer, and $\lambda \in [0, 1]$ is a weighting factor balancing the two objectives. The cross-entropy loss provides direct supervision for classification, while the contrastive loss enhances feature discriminability in the embedding space. This joint optimization encourages the network to learn features that are both separable and aligned with classification boundaries. During training, the feature vectors output by the Wavelet Residue Network are used for both contrastive learning and classification through separate projection heads, enabling end-to-end optimization of the entire architecture.

4 Experiments

4.1 Experimental Setup

Detection Targets. We evaluate the proposed method on three representative generative steganography techniques: GSN, IDEAS, and S2IRT. These methods cover a broad spectrum of generative architectures: GAN-based generation (GSN), autoencoder-based generation (IDEAS), and flow-based generation (S2IRT). This diversity ensures that our experiments reflect realistic and heterogeneous generative pipelines. The embedding payload differs across methods: GSN and S2IRT embed 1 bit per pixel (1 bpp), while IDEAS embeds a fixed 256-bit message.

Datasets. We conduct experiments on three widely used image datasets: LSUN-bedroom, LSUN-church, and CelebA. For each dataset, we randomly sample 30,000, 1,000, and 5,000 images as the training, validation, and test sets, respectively. All images are resized to 256 × 256. Each generative steganography method is applied to all three datasets to produce corresponding cover and stego samples, ensuring consistent data coverage across methods.

Baselines. We compare our steganalysis model WaReCo against two categories of baseline steganalysis approaches. The first is conventional deep steganalysis networks including ZhuNet and SiaStegNet. The second is generative-steganography-oriented detectors, represented by FMISNet, which incorporates explicit modeling of generative artifacts and serves as a strong baseline for detecting content manipulated by generative models.

Evaluation Metric. We adopt average detection accuracy, computed as the mean of the true positive rate (TPR) and true negative rate (TNR), as the main evaluation metric. To reduce variance and obtain stable estimates, results are averaged over three independently trained models for each method.

Implementation Details. All experiments are implemented in PyTorch and conducted on an NVIDIA L40 GPU server. We use the Adam optimizer with a batch size of 32. The initial learning rate is set to 0.0005, and is reduced by a factor of 0.2 every 50 epochs. The total training schedule is 200 epochs. The weighting factor in the overall loss function is set as $\lambda = 0.65$.

4.2   Single-Model Detection

We evaluate four steganalysis models (ZhuNet, SiaStegNet, FMISNet, and our WaReCo) on the detection of three generative steganography methods across the LSUN-bedroom, LSUN-church, and CelebA datasets. The results are reported in Table 1, where the best accuracy in each setting is highlighted in bold.

Traditional deep steganalysis networks achieve solid performance on all datasets, but their detection accuracy rates are lower that those of FMIS-Net. This limitation is expected, as ZhuNet and SiaStegNet were primarily designed for spatial-domain steganalysis and lack mechanisms to explicitly capture the structured distortions introduced by generative steganography. FMIS-Net, designed specifically for generative stego detection, consistently outperforms ZhuNet and SiaStegNet. Its strength lies in its mutual information estimation design, which enhances sensitivity to distortions of different regions in generated images.

In contrast, our WaReCo model achieves the highest accuracy across nearly all settings. The consistent high performance demonstrates that our wavelet-domain feature learning effectively captures multi-scale residual anomalies across different generative architectures, while supervised contrastive learning enhances feature discriminability.

4.3   Cross-Model Detection

To evaluate the generalization ability of our framework in cross-model scenarios, we conduct experiments where a steganalyzer trained on samples generated by one synthesis model is used to detect stego images produced by other models. This setting reflects the practical challenge that steganalysis systems often face: the distribution shift introduced by heterogeneous generative pipelines. The experimental setup employs the same four steganalysis and steganography methods as in single-model detection. Experiments are conducted on both the LSUN-bedroom and CelebA datasets, where each dataset includes cover–stego pairs synthesized by GSN, IDEAS, and S2IRT. The cross-model detection results are summarized in Table 2 and Table 3.

Table 1. Detection accuracy of steganalysis for three generative steganography methods on three datasets.

Dataset	Steganography	ZhuNet	SiaStegNet	FMISNet	WaReCo
LSUN-bedroom	GSN	0.9745	0.9812	0.9953	**0.9970**
	IDEAS	0.9802	0.9789	0.9922	**0.9949**
	S2IRT	0.9766	0.9758	0.9960	**0.9978**
LSUN-church	GSN	0.9632	0.9691	0.9757	**0.9815**
	IDEAS	0.9688	0.9706	0.9818	**0.9892**
	S2IRT	0.9573	0.9632	0.9824	**0.9906**
CelebA	GSN	0.9660	0.9642	0.9868	**0.9937**
	IDEAS	0.9736	0.9739	**0.9925**	0.9920
	S2IRT	0.9712	0.9685	0.9837	**0.9881**

The results demonstrate a consistent trend across datasets and models. ZhuNet and SiaStegNet exhibit a noticeable drop in detection accuracy once the training and testing generative models differ. This suggests limited robustness to distribution shifts in their learned feature representations. FMISNet achieves better transferability and reduces this accuracy degradation, reflecting its stronger capability in capturing high-level steganographic cues. In contrast, our WaReCo model delivers the most stable and highest cross-model detection performance across nearly all settings. Compared with the strongest baseline in each configuration, WaReCo often improves detection accuracy by several to over ten percentage points, showing substantial gains even in the most challenging transfer directions. These results confirm that the wavelet-residue contrastive learning strategy effectively promotes invariance to differences among generative models, enabling WaReCo to retain discriminative power when the testing data deviate significantly from the training distribution.

Table 2. Cross-model detection accuracy of steganalysis on LSUN-bedroom dataset.

Training	Testing	ZhuNet	SiaStegNet	FMISNet	WaReCo
GSN	IDEAS	0.7135	0.6952	0.8693	**0.9266**
	S2IRT	0.6558	0.6804	0.8758	**0.9421**
IDEAS	GSN	0.5537	0.5624	0.7687	**0.8922**
	S2IRT	0.5360	0.5289	0.7534	**0.8625**
S2IRT	IDEAS	0.5728	0.5483	0.7026	**0.8557**
	S2IRT	0.5560	0.5598	0.7241	**0.8803**

Table 3. Cross-model detection accuracy of steganalysis on CelebA dataset

Training	Testing	ZhuNet	SiaStegNet	FMISNet	WaReCo
GSN	IDEAS	0.6826	0.6329	0.8336	**0.9045**
	S2IRT	0.6495	0.6540	0.8219	**0.8862**
IDEAS	GSN	0.5279	0.5386	0.7478	**0.8753**
	S2IRT	0.5266	0.5435	0.7652	**0.8790**
S2IRT	IDEAS	0.5416	0.5396	0.7158	**0.8269**
	S2IRT	0.5542	0.5733	0.7402	**0.8442**

4.4 Ablation Study

Table 4. Ablation experiment results of our WaReCo. WConv and SC denote wavelet convolution and supervised contrastive loss, respectively.

WConv	SC	IDEAS → IDEAS	S2IRT → S2IRT	GSN → IDEAS	GSN → S2IRT
✓	✗	0.8651	0.8910	0.7028	0.6933
✗	✓	0.8279	0.8455	0.7859	0.7632
✓	✓	**0.9920**	**0.9881**	**0.9045**	**0.8862**

To assess the individual contributions of the wavelet convolution module and the supervised contrastive (SC) loss, we conduct an ablation study by selectively removing these components from WaReCo and re-evaluating its steganalysis performance. We examine both single-model detection and cross-model detection settings to provide a comprehensive understanding of how each component influences generalization. In the single-model case, the steganalyzer is trained and tested on samples synthesized by the same generative model (IDEAS or S2IRT). In the cross-model case, the detector is trained on GSN-generated images and tested on stego samples produced by IDEAS or S2IRT. The results are summarized in Table 4.

The ablation results reveal distinct and complementary roles played by the two components. Wavelet convolution yields the most substantial improvement in single-model detection, where removing this module reduces accuracy by a noticeable margin. This behavior is expected because wavelet decomposition enhances sensitivity to fine-grained, model-specific embedding traces, which directly benefits within-distribution detection. In contrast, the supervised contrastive loss shows a stronger influence in cross-model scenarios. Without SC loss, the performance under distribution shift drops considerably, whereas including it provides gains of several percentage points. These improvements indicate that supervised contrastive learning encourages feature representations that remain discriminative even when the generative model changes. When both components are incorporated, WaReCo achieves the highest performance in all settings, demonstrating that wavelet-guided residual features and contrastive supervision jointly enhance robustness and transferability.

5   Conclusion

This work presents WaReCo, a steganalysis framework designed for the unique challenges posed by generative steganography. By combining wavelet-domain residual learning with supervised contrastive objectives, the method produces feature representations that are both sensitive to embedding artifacts and robust to variations across generative architectures. Our experiments show that WaReCo achieves competitive or superior performance in single-model detection while delivering notable improvements in cross-model generalization, a key requirement for real-world applications where the underlying generative model is often unknown.

Although further exploration is needed to extend detection to broader generative families and more diverse datasets, the proposed approach provides a principled and effective solution for analyzing synthetic images carrying hidden information. WaReCo demonstrates that integrating frequency-domain decomposition with contrastive representation learning is a promising direction for advancing deep steganalysis against modern generative threats.

Acknowledgments. This work was supported by the Hubei Provincial Natural Science Foundation of China under Grant 2024AFB932.

References

1. Boroumand, M., Chen, M., Fridrich, J.: Deep residual network for steganalysis of digital images. IEEE Trans. Inf. Forensics Secur. **14**(5), 1181–1193 (2018)
2. Cao, Y., Zhou, Z., Wu, Q.M.J., Yuan, C., Sun, X.: Coverless information hiding based on the generation of anime characters. EURASIP J. Image Video Process. **2020**(1), 1–15 (2020). https://doi.org/10.1186/s13640-020-00524-4
3. Dinh, L., Sohl-Dickstein, J., Bengio, S.: Density estimation using real NVP. In: International Conference on Learning Representations (2017)
4. Fridrich, J., Kodovsky, J.: Rich models for steganalysis of digital images. IEEE Trans. Inf. Forensics Secur. **7**(3), 868–882 (2012)
5. Guan, Z., et al.: DeepMIH: deep invertible network for multiple image hiding. IEEE Trans. Pattern Anal. Mach. Intell. **45**(1), 372–390 (2022)
6. Hayes, J., Danezis, G.: Generating steganographic images via adversarial training. Adv. Neural Inf. Process. Syst. **30** (2017)
7. Hu, D., Wang, L., Jiang, W., Zheng, S., Li, B.: A novel image steganography method via deep convolutional generative adversarial networks. IEEE Access **6**, 38303–38314 (2018)
8. Hu, M., Wang, H.: Mutual information-optimized steganalysis for generative steganography. IEEE Trans. Inf. Forensics Secur. (2025)
9. Hu, X., Li, S., Ying, Q., Peng, W., Zhang, X., Qian, Z.: Establishing robust generative image steganography via popular stable diffusion. IEEE Trans. Inf. Forensics Secur. (2024)
10. Jing, J., Deng, X., Xu, M., Wang, J., Guan, Z.: HiNet: deep image hiding by invertible network. In: Proceedings of the IEEE/CVF International Conference on Computer Vision, pp. 4733–4742 (2021)

11. Khosla, P., et al.: Supervised contrastive learning. Adv. Neural. Inf. Process. Syst. **33**, 18661–18673 (2020)
12. Kingma, D.P., Dhariwal, P.: GLOW: generative flow with invertible 1×1 convolutions. Adv. Neural. Inf. Process. Syst. **31** (2018)
13. Kombrink, M.H., Geradts, Z.J.M.H., Worring, M.: Image steganography approaches and their detection strategies: a survey. ACM Comput. Surv. **57**(2), 1–40 (2024)
14. Li, B., Wang, M., Huang, J., Li, X.: A new cost function for spatial image steganography. In: 2014 IEEE International Conference on Image Processing (ICIP), pp. 4206–4210. IEEE (2014)
15. Li, B., Wang, M., Li, X., Tan, S., Huang, J.: A strategy of clustering modification directions in spatial image steganography. IEEE Trans. Inf. Forensics Secur. **10**(9), 1905–1917 (2015)
16. Li, F., Sheng, Y., Wu, K., Qin, C., Zhang, X.: LiDiNet: a lightweight deep invertible network for image-in-image steganography. IEEE Trans. Inf. Forensics Secur. (2024)
17. Li, F., Sheng, Y., Zhang, X., Qin, C.: iSCMIS: spatial-channel attention based deep invertible network for multi-image steganography. IEEE Trans. Multimedia **26**, 3137–3152 (2023)
18. Li, J., et al.: A generative steganography method based on WGAN-GP. In: Sun, X., Wang, J., Bertino, E. (eds.) ICAIS 2020. CCIS, vol. 1252, pp. 386–397. Springer, Singapore (2020). https://doi.org/10.1007/978-981-15-8083-3_34
19. Li, S., Zhang, X.: Toward construction-based data hiding: from secrets to fingerprint images. IEEE Trans. Image Process. **28**(3), 1482–1497 (2018)
20. Liu, J., Zhou, T., Zhang, Z., Ke, Y., Lei, Y., Zhang, M.: Digital cardan grille: a modern approach for information hiding. In: Proceedings of the 2018 2nd International Conference on Computer Science and Artificial Intelligence, pp. 441–446 (2018)
21. Liu, M.M., Zhang, M.Q., Liu, J., Zhang, Y.N., Ke, Y.: Coverless information hiding based on generative adversarial networks. arXiv preprint arXiv:1712.06951 (2017)
22. Liu, X., Ma, Z., Ma, J., Zhang, J., Schaefer, G., Fang, H.: Image disentanglement autoencoder for steganography without embedding. In: Proceedings of the IEEE/CVF Conference on Computer Vision and Pattern Recognition, pp. 2303–2312 (2022)
23. Manduchi, L., et al.: On the challenges and opportunities in generative AI. arXiv preprint arXiv:2403.00025 (2024)
24. Peng, Y., Hu, D., Wang, Y., Chen, K., Pei, G., Zhang, W.: StegaDDPM: generative image steganography based on denoising diffusion probabilistic model. In: Proceedings of the 31st ACM International Conference on Multimedia, pp. 7143–7151 (2023)
25. Qian, Y., Dong, J., Wang, W., Tan, T.: Deep learning for steganalysis via convolutional neural networks. In: Media Watermarking, Security, and Forensics 2015, vol. 9409, pp. 171–180. SPIE (2015)
26. Rehman, H.A., Bajwa, U.I., Raza, R.H., Alfarhood, S., Safran, M., Zhang, F.: Leveraging coverless image steganography to hide secret information by generating anime characters using gan. Expert Syst. Appl. **248**, 123420 (2024)
27. Ren, Y., Liu, T., Zhai, L., Wang, L.: Hiding data in colors: secure and lossless deep image steganography via conditional invertible neural networks. arXiv preprint arXiv:2201.07444 (2022)

28. Shi, H., Dong, J., Wang, W., Qian, Y., Zhang, X.: SSGAN: secure steganography based on generative adversarial networks. In: Zeng, B., Huang, Q., El Saddik, A., Li, H., Jiang, S., Fan, X. (eds.) PCM 2017. LNCS, vol. 10735, pp. 534–544. Springer, Cham (2018). https://doi.org/10.1007/978-3-319-77380-3_51
29. Song, X., Liu, F., Yang, C., Luo, X., Zhang, Y.: Steganalysis of adaptive JPEG steganography using 2D gabor filters. In: Proceedings of the 3rd ACM Workshop on Information Hiding and Multimedia Security, pp. 15–23 (2015)
30. Su, W., Ni, J., Sun, Y.: StegaStyleGAN: towards generic and practical generative image steganography. In: Proceedings of the AAAI Conference on Artificial Intelligence, vol. 38, pp. 240–248 (2024)
31. Tan, S., Li, B.: Stacked convolutional auto-encoders for steganalysis of digital images. In: Signal and Information Processing Association Annual Summit and Conference (APSIPA), 2014 Asia-Pacific, pp. 1–4. IEEE (2014)
32. Volkhonskiy, D., Nazarov, I., Burnaev, E.: Steganographic generative adversarial networks. In: Twelfth International Conference on Machine Vision (ICMV 2019), vol. 11433, pp. 991–1005. SPIE (2020)
33. Wang, Z., Gao, N., Wang, X., Xiang, J., Liu, G.: STNet: a style transformation network for deep image steganography. In: Gedeon, T., Wong, K.W., Lee, M. (eds.) ICONIP 2019. LNCS, vol. 11954, pp. 3–14. Springer, Cham (2019). https://doi.org/10.1007/978-3-030-36711-4_1
34. Wei, K., Luo, W., Huang, J.: Color image steganalysis based on pixel difference convolution and enhanced transformer with selective pooling. IEEE Trans. Inf. Forensics Secur. (2024)
35. Wei, K., Luo, W., Tan, S., Huang, J.: Universal deep network for steganalysis of color image based on channel representation. IEEE Trans. Inf. Forensics Secur. **17**, 3022–3036 (2022)
36. Wei, P., Li, S., Zhang, X., Luo, G., Qian, Z., Zhou, Q.: Generative steganography network. In: Proceedings of the 30th ACM International Conference on Multimedia, pp. 1621–1629 (2022)
37. Xu, G., Wu, H.Z., Shi, Y.Q.: Structural design of convolutional neural networks for steganalysis. IEEE Signal Process. Lett. **23**(5), 708–712 (2016)
38. Xu, J., et al.: Hidden message in a deformation-based texture. Vis. Comput. **31**(12), 1653–1669 (2015)
39. Xu, Y., Mou, C., Hu, Y., Xie, J., Zhang, J.: Robust invertible image steganography. In: Proceedings of the IEEE/CVF Conference on Computer Vision and Pattern Recognition, pp. 7875–7884 (2022)
40. Yang, K., Chen, K., Zhang, W., Yu, N.: Provably secure generative steganography based on autoregressive model. In: Yoo, C.D., Shi, Y.-Q., Kim, H.J., Piva, A., Kim, G. (eds.) IWDW 2018. LNCS, vol. 11378, pp. 55–68. Springer, Cham (2019). https://doi.org/10.1007/978-3-030-11389-6_5
41. You, W., Zhang, H., Zhao, X.: A Siamese CNN for image steganalysis. IEEE Trans. Inf. Forensics Secur. **16**, 291–306 (2020)
42. Yu, J., Zhang, X., Xu, Y., Zhang, J.: CRoSS: diffusion model makes controllable, robust and secure image steganography. Adv. Neural. Inf. Process. Syst. **36**, 80730–80743 (2023)
43. Zeng, J., Tan, S., Liu, G., Li, B., Huang, J.: WISERNet: wider separate-then-reunion network for steganalysis of color images. IEEE Trans. Inf. Forensics Secur. **14**(10), 2735–2748 (2019)
44. Zhang, R., Zhu, F., Liu, J., Liu, G.: Depth-wise separable convolutions and multi-level pooling for an efficient spatial CNN-based steganalysis. IEEE Trans. Inf. Forensics Secur. **15**, 1138–1150 (2019)

45. Zhou, W., Zhang, W., Yu, N.: A new rule for cost reassignment in adaptive steganography. IEEE Trans. Inf. Forensics Secur. **12**(11), 2654–2667 (2017)
46. Zhou, Z., et al.: Generative steganography via auto-generation of semantic object contours. IEEE Trans. Inf. Forensics Secur. **18**, 2751–2765 (2023)
47. Zhou, Z., et al.: Secret-to-image reversible transformation for generative steganography. IEEE Trans. Dependable Secure Comput. **20**(5), 4118–4134 (2022)

A Privacy-Preserving Semi-supervised Algorithm for Non-Gaussian Noise Environments

Ling Zuo[1], Heng Xiao[2], and Chi Cheng[3]

[1] School of Science, Hubei University of Technology, Wuhan, China
[2] Maxvision Technology Co., Ltd., Wuhan, China
[3] Central China Normal University, Wuhan, China
chengchi@ccnu.edu.cn

Abstract. In real-world applications where massive datasets are often stored across distributed computing units, traditional centralized semi-supervised learning (SSL) methods face significant challenges. These limitations include potential privacy risks and sensitivity to non-Gaussian noise. To address these issues, this paper proposes a novel distributed SSL approach that enhances privacy protection by processing data locally and eliminating the need for raw data exchange between units. Unlike conventional SSL algorithms rooted in the minimum mean squared error criterion, our method adopts the maximum correntropy criterion, substantially improving predictive accuracy in the presence of non-Gaussian noise frequently encountered in real-world data. Experiments on both synthetic and real-world datasets confirm that the proposed method outperforms existing approaches in terms of both prediction accuracy under non-Gaussian noise and privacy preservation.

Keywords: Semi-supervised learning · non-Gaussian noise robustness · correntropy · distributed learning · privacy preserving

1 Introduction

In many machine learning domains, obtaining labeled data can be challenging or expensive, while unlabeled data is often easily accessible in large quantities. This poses the question of how to train a learner effectively when there are relatively few labeled examples and a significant proportion of unlabeled data. Semi-supervised learning (SSL) addresses this problem that involves a combination of labeled and unlabeled data [20]. To leverage the large amount of unlabeled data, it is common to make certain assumptions about the dataset. Two prevalent assumptions are the cluster assumption and the manifold assumption [22]. Under the manifold assumption, various graph-based methods have emerged, such as those proposed in [18]. These methods aim to learn from the data's underlying manifold structure, assuming that the data points lie on a low-dimensional manifold. By constructing and utilizing graphs to represent the relationships between

L. Zhai et al. (Eds.): SocialSec 2025, LNCS 16327, pp. 209–224, 2026.
https://doi.org/10.1007/978-981-95-7027-0_12

data points, these methods have demonstrated good performance in capturing the data's underlying patterns.

Traditional SSL formulations are commonly built upon the mean square error criterion (MSEC), and they exhibit strong performance when dealing with data containing Gaussian noise, as demonstrated by algorithms like regularized least squares (RLS) in [2], LapRLS in [2], and GraphL1 in [26]. However, real-world datasets often contain outliers [19]. Unfortunately, methods relying on MSEC are highly susceptible to the presence of outliers, leading to a substantial degradation in learning performance [25]. Consequently, there is a need to explore alternative approaches that can improve the robustness of SSL algorithms and mitigate the negative impact of outliers in the learning process. By devising techniques that can better handle noisy and outlier-laden data, researchers aim to enhance the applicability and performance of SSL in practical scenarios.

Meanwhile, most existing semi-supervised approaches adopt a centralized manner [9,10,17], where data collected from all sub-nodes are aggregated to a central node for comprehensive processing. However, this learning approach has several drawbacks [7,16] . Firstly, the processing of all data by the central node leads to a substantial increase in its storage and computing pressure, potentially causing scalability issues. Secondly, transmitting large amounts of raw data to the central node elevates the risk of privacy leakage, especially when dealing with sensitive information. Thirdly, if the central node experiences a failure or is subject to an attack, the entire network becomes paralyzed, impacting the overall system's functionality.

Under the maximum correntropy criterion (MCC), this paper introduces a semi-supervised algorithm with privacy preservation and non-Gaussian noise robustness, named LapMCCL1. The key advantages of our approach are twofold:

- Robustness to Non-Gaussian Noise: The use of the correntropy-induced criterion equips the algorithm with superior robustness against outliers and non-Gaussian noise.
- Inherent Privacy Protection: A distributed learning framework is employed to enhance data privacy. The dataset is randomly divided into disjoint subsets, and the optimal predictor is derived by aggregating knowledge from these local models without sharing the raw data itself.

Empirical evaluations on both synthetic and real-world benchmarks demonstrate that LapMCCL1 achieves higher predictive accuracy in the presence of non-Gaussian noise and provides stronger privacy guarantees compared to related methods.

The paper is organized as follows: In Sect. 2, we introduce relevant preliminaries, including the semi-supervised regression problem, the MCC, and common privacy preserving techniques. Section 3 presents the proposed semi-supervised method with privacy preservation and non-Gaussian noise robustness. In Sect. 4, we conduct extensive experiments to evaluate the algorithm's performance. Finally, the conclusions are provided in Sect. 5.

2 Preliminaries

2.1 Semi-supervised Regression Problem

In this subsection, we introduce the semi-supervised regression (SSR) problem [8]. Given an input space X and an output space Y, let $X \subset \mathbb{R}^d$ be a compact metric space, $Y = [-M, M]$ be a bounded closed interval, and M is a positive constant. Let ρ be the underlying probability distribution on $Z := X \times Y$. We assume that the data are generated by the following model

$$y = f_\rho(x) + \xi, \tag{1}$$

where $x \in X$ is the input variable, ξ is the noise process and the output variable $y \in Y$ is the label of x. $f_\rho(x)$ is the regression function given by $\int_X y d\rho(y|x)$, where $\rho(y|x)$ is the conditional distribution of ρ. In the SSL, the data set consists of a small proportion of labeled examples $D_L = \{(x_i, y_i)\}_{i=1}^{l}$ and a large number of unlabeled samples $D_U = \{x_j\}_{j=l+1}^{l+u}$. The SSR problem aims at searching the best approximation of $f_\rho(x)$ based on D_L and D_U.

The Tikhonov regularization scheme is usually employed to solve the SSR problem [3]. When the squared function is used as the empirical risk, we recognize it as MSEC. For examples, RLS method in [2] is based on the MSEC, which is given by

$$\min_{f \in \mathcal{H}_K} \frac{1}{l} \sum_{i=1}^{l} \left(y_i - f(x_i)\right)^2 + \lambda \|f\|_K^2, \tag{2}$$

where the first term is the empirical risk of $f(x)$ on the labeled samples and λ is the non-negative regularization parameter. $\|f\|_K$ is the norm restricted in the reproducing kernel Hilbert space, which is used to control the complexity of the model and prevent overfitting. Note that Eq. (2) is a supervised algorithm.

For the semi-supervised setting, in [2] Belkin introduced LapRLS, which is formulated as

$$\min_{f \in \mathcal{H}_K} \frac{1}{l} \sum_{i=1}^{l} \left(y_i - f(x_i)\right)^2 + \gamma_1 \|f\|_K^2 + \frac{\gamma_2}{(l+u)^2} \hat{f}^T L \hat{f}, \tag{3}$$

where γ_1 and γ_2 are nonnegative regularization parameters and $\hat{f} = (f(x_1), f(x_2), ..., f(x_{l+u}))^T$. The third term in (3) is the manifold regularizer, which is equal to

$$\frac{\gamma_2}{2(l+u)^2} \sum_{i,j=1}^{l+u} \left(f(x_i) - f(x_j)\right)^2 W_{ij}.$$

Here W_{ij} is the weight of x_i and x_j, which is given by the Gaussian kernel function $K_\sigma(x_i, x_j) = \exp\{-\frac{(x_i - x_j)^2}{\sigma^2}\}$. The more similar x_i and x_j, the larger W_{ij} will be. Denote W be the weighted matrix with weight W_{ij} between the samples x_i and x_j. $L = D - W$ is the unnormalized graph Laplacian, where D is a diagonal matrix with diagonal entries $D_{ii} = \sum_{j=1}^{l+u} W_{ij}$. Existing results have demonstrated that when data is embedded into a low-dimensional manifold, the manifold regularizer can exploit the intrinsic data distribution information. This can help enhance the learning performance of the algorithms [2].

Both (2) and (3) are based on the MSEC, which relies heavily on the Gaussian assumptions. However, when the samples contain outliers, the quadratic function will amplify the contribution of the data far from the mean value, which will greatly reduce the performance of the approaches. Therefore, MSEC is optimal for data involving Gaussian noise while it is very sensitive to non-Gaussian noise and outliers.

2.2   Maximum Correntropy Criterion

In this section, we introduce the MCC, which can effectively deal with learning problems involving non-Gaussian distribution samples. Correntropy is an information-theoretic metric, which measures the similarity between two arbitrary random variables. It has been proved to be robust to non-Gaussian distributed noise and outliers [14]. Given two random variables X and Y, the correntropy is defined as

$$V(X,Y) = E_{XY}[K(X,Y)] = \int K(x,y)dF_{XY}(x,y), \tag{4}$$

where $E[\cdot]$ is expectation operator, $K(\cdot,\cdot)$ is any continuous positive definite kernel, and $F_{XY}(x,y)$ denotes the joint distribution function of (X,Y). However, in real-world problems, the joint distribution function is usually unknown and only a finite number of samples $\{(x_i,y_i)\}_{i=1}^{N}$ can be obtained. So the samples estimator of correntropy can be defined as

$$\hat{V}(X,Y) = \frac{1}{N}\sum_{i=1}^{N} K(x_i,y_i). \tag{5}$$

In this paper, we choose the Gaussian kernel as the kernel of the correntropy, which is given by

$$K(x,y) = K_\sigma(e) = \exp\{-\frac{e^2}{\sigma^2}\}, \tag{6}$$

where e is the error denoted by $x - y$ and σ is the non-negative bandwidth parameter. We can see from (6) that the correntropy is positive, smooth and bounded. And the maximum value is reached as $e = 0$, that is, $x = y$. To decrease the bias of x from y, one has to maximize the value of the correntropy. This is referred to be the MCC.

Property 1. Correntropy $V_\sigma(X,Y)$ involves all the even moments of the random variable $(X-Y)$:

$$V_\sigma(X,Y) = \sum_{n=0}^{\infty} \frac{(-1)^n}{n!}\mathbf{E}_{XY}[\frac{(X-Y)^{2n}}{\sigma^{2n}}].$$

Property 1 demonstrates that the MCC considers higher moments of the error e while the MSEC only concerns its second-order statistics. Therefore, the methods based on the MCC can effectively handle the data with outliers in the learning procedure.

2.3   Privacy Preserving Techniques

Recall that in SSR problems, usually a massive amount of samples are available. So the protection against the disclosure of confidential information in data mining is an important issue [13]. The existing privacy preserving works mainly fall into two categories [24]. One is the perturbation and randomization in sample surveys [1]. Methods in this category protect the sensitive information by adding random noise to the data. But this may lead to the loss of the important information [21]. So approaches of this kind may only provide a relatively limited privacy preserving effect. Moreover, it needs to consider the balance between data privacy preservation and utility.

The other category is the distributed learning (DL) [11,23,28]. Under DL each computing node learns local data independently without sharing any raw data information with each other. Through this way approaches can effectively reduce the leakage of the sensitive information. Moreover, in DL, each node performs local calculations on the data stored by itself, which can greatly relieve the pressure of the computational in that of the centralized way.

3   The Proposed Privacy-Preserving Semi-supervised Algorithm for Non-Gaussian Noise Environments

In this section, we propose the privacy-preserving SSL algorithm with non-Gaussian noise robustness, for the regression problem. Recall that in the SSR, the purpose is to learn the best approximation for the regression function.

We denote $\mathbf{z}$ as the dataset, which is generated from (1). It consists of l labeled samples $\{(x_i, y_i)\}_{i=1}^{l}$ and u unlabeled samples $\{x_j\}_{j=l+1}^{l+u}$. Concerning the privacy preserving problem, we propose the SSL algorithm under a distributed way. Specifically, the learning set $\mathbf{z}$ is randomly divided into m subsets, and the kth subset with $1 \leq k \leq m$. Let $|\mathbf{z}_k|$ be the cardinality of the subset $\mathbf{z}_k$. The number of the labeled and unlabeled samples in $\mathbf{z}_k$ are given by $|\mathbf{z}_k^l|$ and $|\mathbf{z}_k^u|$ respectively.

Our local LapMCCL1 is formulated as below

$$f_{\mathbf{z}_k,\lambda} = \arg \min_{f \in \mathcal{H}_K} \left\{ \mathcal{E}_{\mathbf{z}_k}^{\sigma}(f) + \lambda_1 \Omega_{\mathbf{z}_k}(f) + \lambda_2 \mathcal{I}_{\mathbf{z}_k}^{\sigma}(f) \right\}, \tag{7}$$

where λ_1 and λ_2 are the non-negative regularization parameters.

The first term on the right side of (7) is

$$\mathcal{E}_{\mathbf{z}_k}^{\sigma}(f) = \frac{1}{|\mathbf{z}_k^l|} \sum_{i=1}^{|\mathbf{z}_k^l|} \ell_\sigma \left(y_i, f(x_i) \right), \tag{8}$$

where $\ell_\sigma\Big(y_i, f(x_i)\Big)$ is the correntropy-induced loss function [27] given by

$$\ell_\sigma\big(y_i, f(x_i)\big) = \sigma^2\Big(1 - K_\sigma(e_i)\Big), \tag{9}$$

where $f(x_i)$ is the prediction of label y_i, and the corresponding error is denoted as $e_i = y_i - f(x_i)$. The discussions in Sect. 2.2 demonstrates that the smaller the error e_i, the higher the value $K_\sigma(e_i)$. To find the best predictor, we aim to minimize the empirical loss (9).

By the Representer Theorem in [2], we know that the solution of (7) can be written as

$$f_{\mathbf{z}_k}(x) = \sum_{i=1}^{|\mathbf{z}_k|} \alpha_i K_\sigma(x, x_i), \tag{10}$$

which is an expansion of kernel functions over the subset $\mathbf{z}_k$ and α_i is the coefficient of the predictor. In (7), the second term is the L1 regularizer given by

$$\Omega_{\mathbf{z}_k}(f) = \sum_{i=1}^{|\mathbf{z}_k|} |\alpha_i|. \tag{11}$$

And the last term in (7) is the correntropy-based manifold regularizer, which is defined as

$$\mathcal{I}_{\mathbf{z}_k}^\sigma(f) = \frac{1}{2|\mathbf{z}_k|^2} \sum_{i,j=1}^{|\mathbf{z}_k|} \ell_\sigma\Big(f(x_i), f(x_j)\Big) W_{ij}. \tag{12}$$

Here, W_{ij} is the weight of x_i and x_j, which is given by the Gaussian kernel function $K_\sigma(x, y)$. Denote W be the weighted matrix with entries W_{ij}. Note that this term is approximately equivalent to $\frac{1}{|\mathbf{z}_k|^2}\hat{f}^T L \hat{f}$, where $\hat{f} = (f(x_1), f(x_2), ..., f(x_{|\mathbf{z}_k|}))^T$, $L = D - W$ is the unnormalized graph Laplacian, and D is a diagonal matrix with diagonal entries $D_{ii} = \sum_{j=1}^{|\mathbf{z}_k|} W_{ij}$.

According to the definition of $f_\rho(x)$, we know that $|f_\rho(x)| \le M$ for any $x \in X$. So we use the following operator to restrict the approximation functions to $[-M, M]$.

Definition 1. *The projection operator $\pi = \pi_M$ is defined on the space of the measurable functions $f : X \to \mathbb{R}$ as*

$$\pi(f)(x) = \begin{cases} M, & f(x) > M; \\ -M, & f(x) < -M; \\ f(x), & otherwise. \end{cases}$$

The final sparse and privacy preserving SSL algorithm is given by

$$\bar{f}_{\mathbf{z},\lambda} = \sum_{k=1}^{m} \frac{|\mathbf{z}_k|}{|\mathbf{z}|} \pi(f_{\mathbf{z}_k,\lambda}). \tag{13}$$

Compared with the traditional semi-supervised algorithm, (13) learns the data set in a distributed way, which can effectively reduce the risk of sensitive information leakage during the learning process. And based on the MCC, the proposed approach (13) can deal with problems with non-Gaussian distributed noise and outliers.

By substituting Eq. (10) into Eq. (7), we have to solve the following optimization problem

$$\alpha = \arg \min_{\alpha \in \mathbb{R}^{|\mathbf{z}_k|}} \frac{1}{|\mathbf{z}_k^l|} \sum_{i=1}^{|\mathbf{z}_k^l|} \ell_\sigma\left(y_i, \alpha K_\sigma(x, x_i)\right) + \lambda_1 \|\alpha\|_1 + \frac{\lambda_2}{|\mathbf{z}_k|^2} \alpha^T K L K \alpha. \quad (14)$$

Since (14) is non-convex and non-differentiable, some optimization techniques are applied. Firstly, through the adoption of the half-quadratic optimization technique, the complex correntropy-based optimization problem is transformed into a weighted quadratic optimization problem. Additionally, the alternating direction method of multipliers is employed to update the parameters for the non-differentiable problem with L1 regularization. Finally, the optimal predictor is derived based on the Representer Theorem.

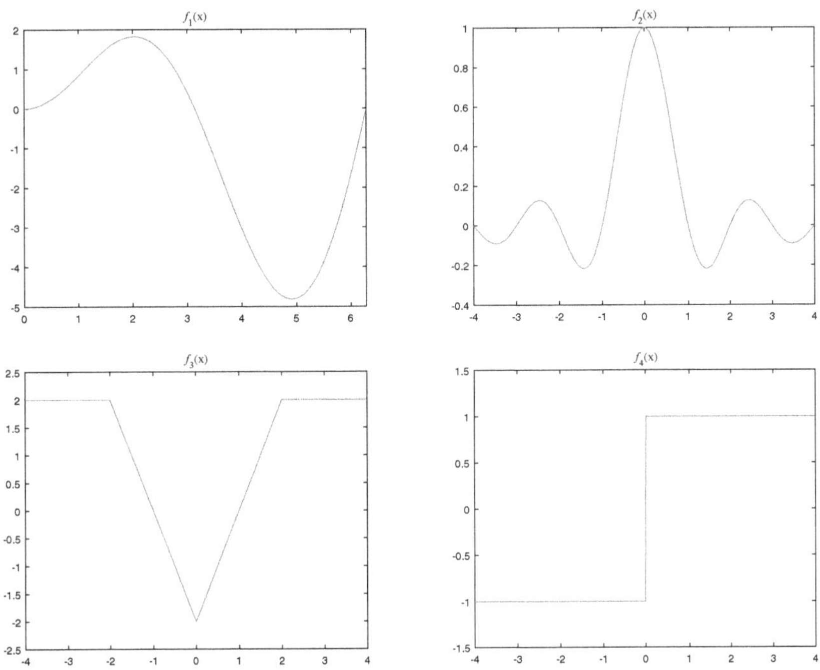

Fig. 1. Graphs of the regression functions.

4   Numerical Experiments

In this section, to demonstrate the performance of the proposed LapMCCL1, we compare it with five other algorithms. They are the LapMCC introduced by Eq. (5) [27], GraphL1 introduced by Eq. (2) [26], LapRLS given by (3), RLS defined by (2), and SMCC introduced by Eq. (2) [6]. Here the RLS and SMCC are the supervised methods, while the LapMCC, GraphL1 and LapRLS are the semi-supervised algorithms. The experiments are conducted over the synthetic datasets and the real-world datasets in terms of the predictive correctness under the non Gaussian noise and privacy preservation. For the real-world datasets, Table 1 displays their detailed characteristics including the names, the numbers of instances and attributes. The eight real-world datasets are derived from the UCI Machine Learning Repository (http://archive.ics.uci.edu/ml/), which is commonly used for evaluating various algorithms.

$$f_1(x) = x\sin(x), \quad x \in [0, 2\pi]$$

$$f_2(x) = \frac{\sin(\pi x)}{\pi x}, \quad x \in [-4, 4]$$

$$f_3(x) = 2\min(|x| - 1, 1), \quad x \in [-4, 4]$$

$$f_4(x) = \text{sign}(x), \quad x \in [-4, 4].$$

The graphs of the four functions are shown in Fig. 1, which implies that $f_1(x)$ and $f_2(x)$ are smooth, $f_3(x)$ is continuous but not smooth, and $f_4(x)$ is not continuous. In order to demonstrate the robustness of our algorithm against outliers, we add non-Gaussian distributed noise to the samples. In this paper, we consider four typical noises, which follow the exponential distribution with mean $\mu = 2$, the chi-square distribution with one degree of freedom, the standard Cauchy distribution and the standard Laplace distribution.

Table 1. Eight real-world datasets description.

Datasets	Instances	Attributes
airfoil_self_noise	1503	6
concrete_data	1030	9
qsar_aquatic_toxicity	546	9
qsar_fish_toxicity	908	7
winequality_red	1599	12
winequality_white	4898	12
abalone	4177	9
yacht_hydrodynamics	308	7

In order to investigate the performances of the algorithms, we use the following two error evaluation criterias, which are defined as the mean square error

(MSE) and the relative sum of the squared errors (RSSE)

$$\text{MSE} = \frac{1}{n}\sum_{i=1}^{n}(y_i - \hat{y}_i)^2,$$

$$\text{RSSE} = \frac{\sum_{i=1}^{n}(y_i - \hat{y}_i)^2}{\sum_{i=1}^{n}(y_i - \bar{y})^2},$$

where y_i is the real label, $\hat{y}_i$ is the corresponding predicted value, n is the number of testing samples and $\bar{y}$ is the average value of sample labels on the testing set. These two regression evaluation indicators are commonly used as the deviation measurement between the real values and predicted values. The smaller the MSE and RSSE, the higher the prediction accuracy.

Experiments are conducted under two different learning ways, which aims to compare the effects through distributed learning and centralized learning. For distributed learning, the training datasets are randomly divided into two subsets with the same number of samples. And the optimal predictor is derived by averaging the local solutions of the two subsets.

4.1 Predictive Correctness Under the Non Gaussian Noise

In this subsection, we do experiments to compare the regression errors of our algorithm LapMCCL1 with GraphL1, LapRLS, RLS and SMCC under both the centralized and the distributed learning ways. We aim to verify: (1) the robustness of our algorithm in dealing with data sets involving non-Gaussian distributed noise; (2) the effectiveness of the manifold regularizer which can mine the distribution structure of data; (3) some of the regression error under the distributed learning is comparable to those of centralized learning.

Specifically, in each experiment, we use the regression functions f to generate 200 labeled data, and non-Gaussian noise is added to the corresponding label values. In addition, 200 random numbers following the uniform distribution are generated as unlabeled data for SSL. Then the model is trained based on the labeled data and unlabeled data to derive the optimal predictor. For each regression function, 1000 samples are randomly generated to make up the testing set. For the real-world datasets, in order to eliminate the influence caused by the different feature dimensions and value ranges, we need to standardize the data. In this paper, we employ the Z-score Normalization, which is the most widely used method of standardization. In each test, the Gaussian kernel function

$$K_\sigma(x_i, x_j) = \exp\{-\frac{\|x_i - x_j\|_2^2}{\sigma^2}\}$$

is applied with the bandwidth parameter $\sigma = 1$, and regularization parameters λ_1, λ_2 and ρ are searched in the discrete set $\{10^{-5}, 10^{-4}, 10^{-3}, 10^{-2}, 10^{-1}, 1, 5, 10\}$. In order to avoid the accidental errors during the experiments and make the results more convincing, each test is repeated 100 times, and the average MSE and RSSE are calculated.

218　　L. Zuo et al.

Table 2 and Table 3 show the average regression errors of the proposed algorithm and four other methods on both synthetic and real-world datasets. Firstly, by horizontal comparison, it demonstrates that our algorithm LapMCCL1 has the lowest MSE and RSSE on almost all datasets compared with other formulations. Recall that the GraphL1 and LapRLS are semi-supervised algorithms while RLS is a supervised method. All of them are formulations based on the MSEC. We see from Table 2 and Table 3 that comparing with the MSEC, the MCC is robust for dealing with non-Gaussian distribution noise. When comparing with SMCC, the LapMCCL1 also has a superior performance. Although both of them learn the data sets under the MCC, our LapMCCL1 involves the manifold regularizer, which can mine the intrinsic manifold structures of the data through the unlabeled samples. Thus our approach can obtain a better prediction effect when comparing with the SMCC. Next, we analyse the regression errors vertically, that is to compare all the five algorithms under both the centralized and the distributed learning manners. We can find that, in most cases, the regression errors of the integral learning are smaller than those of the combined ways. The reason is that under the integral learning the number of training sample is twice of that in the combined way. It is worth noting that our distributed learning algorithm can outperform centralized learning in some cases, especially as data involving with exponentially distributed noise.

Table 2. Average MSE and RSSE of five algorithms on the synthetic data. The best results are marked bold.

			Cauchy					Chi-square				
			LapMCCL1	GraphL1	LapRLS	RLS	SMCC	LapMCCL1	GraphL1	LapRLS	RLS	SMCC
$f_1(x)$	MSE	Integral	**0.5181**	57.5331	51.3414	66.2806	0.8809	**0.1816**	1.0997	1.1009	1.1239	0.4604
		Combined	**1.2393**	448.3591	28.3458	328.9133	2.1844	**1.4432**	3.2300	2.9976	1.7197	1.6240
	RSSE	Integral	**0.0974**	10.8155	9.6515	12.4599	0.1657	**0.0340**	0.2061	0.2063	0.2106	0.0863
		Combined	**0.2329**	84.3501	5.3288	61.8541	0.4106	**0.2703**	0.6051	0.5615	0.3222	0.3042
$f_2(x)$	MSE	Integral	**0.0273**	1.2835	1.3512	1.7630	0.1169	**0.1604**	1.0114	1.0141	1.0344	0.3070
		Combined	**0.0389**	3.1294	0.4607	2.0511	0.0960	**0.2345**	0.7723	0.5689	2.2234	0.2380
	RSSE	Integral	**0.2555**	11.9989	12.6310	16.4811	1.0922	**1.4962**	9.4282	9.4534	9.6430	2.8628
		Combined	**0.3715**	29.2434	4.3038	19.1670	0.8952	**2.1880**	7.1973	5.3012	20.7394	2.2193
$f_3(x)$	MSE	Integral	**0.1830**	6.0402	5.6002	7.8208	0.8757	**0.1632**	1.1005	1.1109	1.1731	0.3735
		Combined	**2.4150**	339.9294	14.5320	186.1113	2.6878	0.5473	1.2682	**0.3970**	2.9747	1.0525
	RSSE	Integral	**0.1104**	3.6419	3.3760	4.7128	0.5285	**0.0984**	0.6638	0.6700	0.7077	0.2254
		Combined	**1.4583**	205.3837	8.7734	112.4098	1.6234	0.3303	0.7657	**0.2396**	1.7962	0.6353
$f_4(x)$	MSE	Integral	**0.1247**	0.9822	1.0751	1.9516	0.1786	**0.2839**	1.0094	1.0043	1.0336	0.4770
		Combined	**0.1889**	28.4211	2.1443	6.7241	0.3265	**0.4884**	0.7653	0.5713	1.5717	0.6015
	RSSE	Integral	**0.1248**	0.9833	1.0763	1.9536	0.1788	**0.2842**	1.0104	1.0054	1.0347	0.4775
		Combined	**0.1891**	28.4415	2.1466	6.7310	0.3268	**0.4889**	0.7661	0.5719	1.5731	0.6021

			Exponential					Laplace				
			LapMCCL1	GraphL1	LapRLS	RLS	SMCC	LapMCCL1	GraphL1	LapRLS	RLS	SMCC
$f_1(x)$	MSE	Integral	**1.0174**	4.0257	4.0565	4.1387	1.9140	**0.0956**	0.1042	0.1202	0.2151	0.2040
		Combined	**2.4500**	3.6399	4.3463	6.4037	3.6718	1.8045	**1.5708**	1.6152	1.6544	1.7711
	RSSE	Integral	**0.1913**	0.7570	0.7628	0.7782	0.3599	**0.0180**	0.0196	0.0227	0.0405	0.0384
		Combined	**0.4604**	0.6842	0.8169	1.2036	0.6901	0.3396	**0.2957**	0.3040	0.3114	0.3334
$f_2(x)$	MSE	Integral	**1.1181**	3.5201	3.5151	3.5703	2.0234	**0.0674**	0.1632	0.1978	0.2826	0.2187
		Combined	**0.5757**	2.5964	1.8422	3.4306	1.1980	**0.0478**	0.0716	0.0759	0.0976	0.0902
	RSSE	Integral	**10.4951**	33.0298	32.9809	33.4983	18.9864	**0.6240**	1.5114	1.8334	2.6202	2.0273
		Combined	**5.4019**	24.3507	17.2744	32.1870	11.2361	**0.4418**	0.6616	0.7017	0.9029	0.8351
$f_3(x)$	MSE	Integral	**1.5891**	3.8509	3.8203	3.9198	2.2827	**0.0234**	0.0457	0.0487	0.0750	0.0274
		Combined	**0.2099**	2.7935	1.3026	7.4978	0.3377	**0.8314**	1.0575	0.9305	2.1030	1.0773
	RSSE	Integral	**0.9622**	2.3310	2.3124	2.3726	1.3821	**0.0139**	0.0272	0.0291	0.0447	0.0163
		Combined	**0.1270**	1.6904	0.7877	4.5383	0.2043	**0.4962**	0.6310	0.5553	1.2549	0.6428
$f_4(x)$	MSE	Integral	**1.0934**	3.5301	3.5111	3.5373	1.7426	**0.1099**	0.1697	0.1837	0.2308	0.1400
		Combined	**0.6605**	2.5659	2.1784	3.6194	0.9055	0.2845	0.3010	0.3057	0.3697	**0.2696**
	RSSE	Integral	**1.0942**	3.5330	3.5140	3.5401	1.7440	**0.1100**	0.1699	0.1839	0.2310	0.1402
		Combined	**0.6610**	2.5680	2.1802	3.6224	0.9062	0.2848	0.3013	0.3060	0.3700	**0.2699**

Table 3. Average MSE and RSSE of five algorithms under real-world datasets. The best results are marked bold.

		airfoil_self_noise					concrete_data					qsar_aquatic_toxicity					qsar_fish_toxitity				
		LapMCCL1	GraphL1	LapRLS	RLS	SMCC	LapMCCL1	GraphL1	LapRLS	RLS	SMCC	LapMCCL1	GraphL1	LapRLS	RLS	SMCC	LapMCCL1	GraphL1	LapRLS	RLS	SMCC
MSE	Integral	**0.3395**	0.4489	0.4655	0.4156	0.5040	**0.3670**	0.4439	0.4246	0.3943	0.4496	**0.5758**	0.6033	0.5942	0.5802	0.6675	0.4891	0.4806	**0.4694**	0.6057	0.4997
	Combined	**0.5380**	0.6208	0.6281	0.6622	0.6743	**0.5435**	0.6222	0.6196	0.6306	0.6472	**0.7298**	0.7857	0.8009	0.7861	0.8343	**0.6468**	0.6761	0.6929	0.6850	0.6510
RSSE	Integral	**0.3474**	0.4586	0.4758	0.4240	0.5147	**0.3752**	0.4543	0.4348	0.4030	0.4600	**0.5393**	0.5639	0.5554	0.5424	0.6242	0.4928	0.4813	**0.4696**	0.6144	0.5030
	Combined	**0.5492**	0.6341	0.6417	0.6764	0.6884	**0.5559**	0.6364	0.6339	0.6450	0.6620	**0.6829**	0.7354	0.7499	0.7360	0.7812	**0.6496**	0.6794	0.6964	0.6913	0.6540

		winequality_red					winequality_white					abalone					yacht_hydrodynamics				
		LapMCCL1	GraphL1	LapRLS	RLS	SMCC	LapMCCL1	GraphL1	LapRLS	RLS	SMCC	LapMCCL1	GraphL1	LapRLS	RLS	SMCC	LapMCCL1	GraphL1	LapRLS	RLS	SMCC
MSE	Integral	**0.7167**	0.7791	0.7254	0.7376	0.7559	0.7547	0.7807	**0.7398**	0.8451	0.9469	**0.5334**	0.5781	0.5566	0.5534	0.6354	**0.5308**	0.7570	0.7442	0.5968	0.7286
	Combined	**0.7832**	0.8297	0.8122	0.8268	0.8377	**0.9626**	1.0283	0.9655	1.0998	1.1603	**0.7409**	0.7773	0.7704	0.7635	0.8054	**0.6536**	0.7974	0.7835	0.7642	0.8436
RSSE	Integral	**0.7634**	0.8214	0.7718	0.7849	0.8037	0.8867	0.9169	**0.8699**	0.9948	1.1139	**0.5253**	0.5687	0.5475	0.5444	0.6253	**0.5186**	0.7429	0.7282	0.5838	0.7121
	Combined	**0.8339**	0.8827	0.8640	0.8797	0.8908	**1.1296**	1.2076	1.1350	1.2933	1.3641	**0.7289**	0.7642	0.7576	0.7508	0.7921	**0.6395**	0.7823	0.7677	0.7492	0.8279

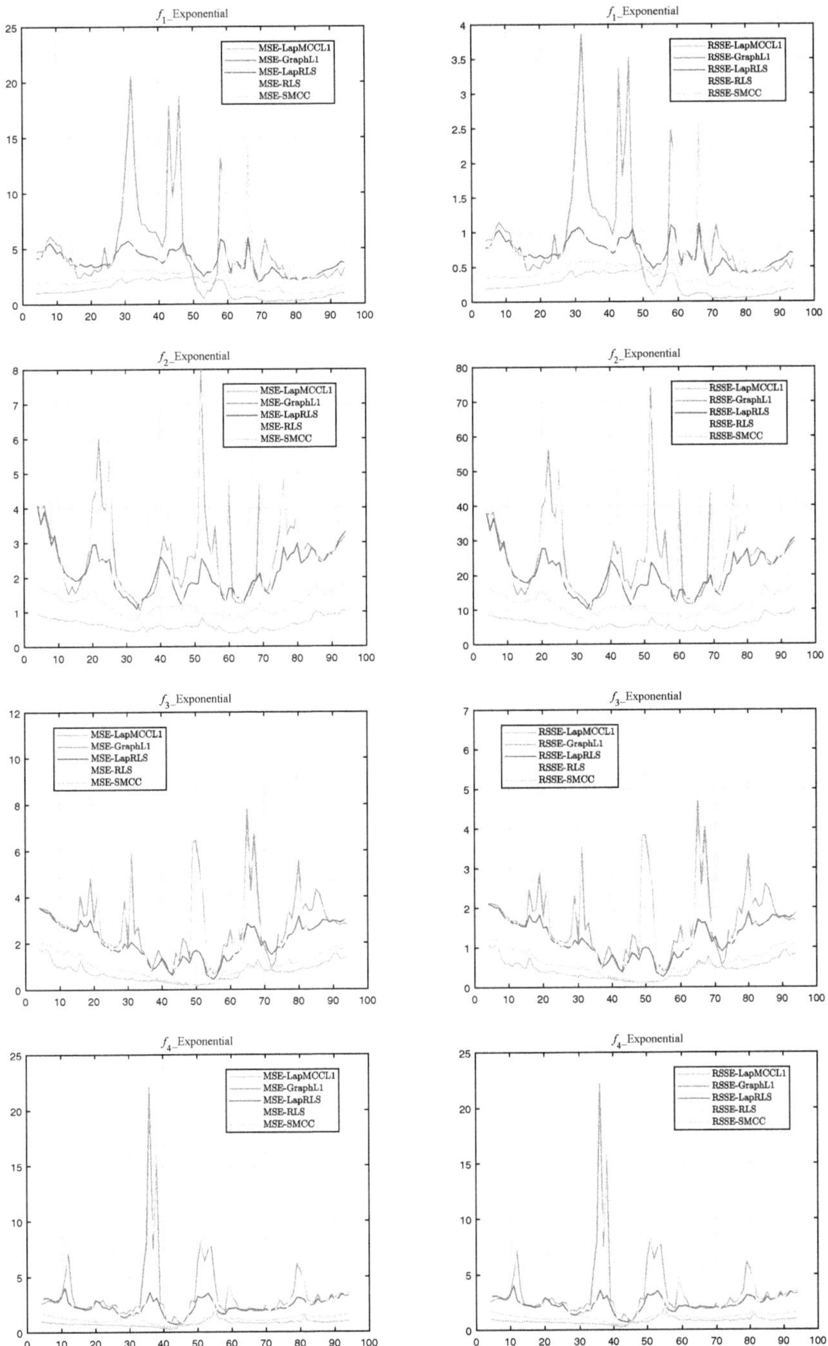

Fig. 2. Average MSE and RSSE of five algorithms on synthetic datasets with different proportions under the Exponential distributed noise.

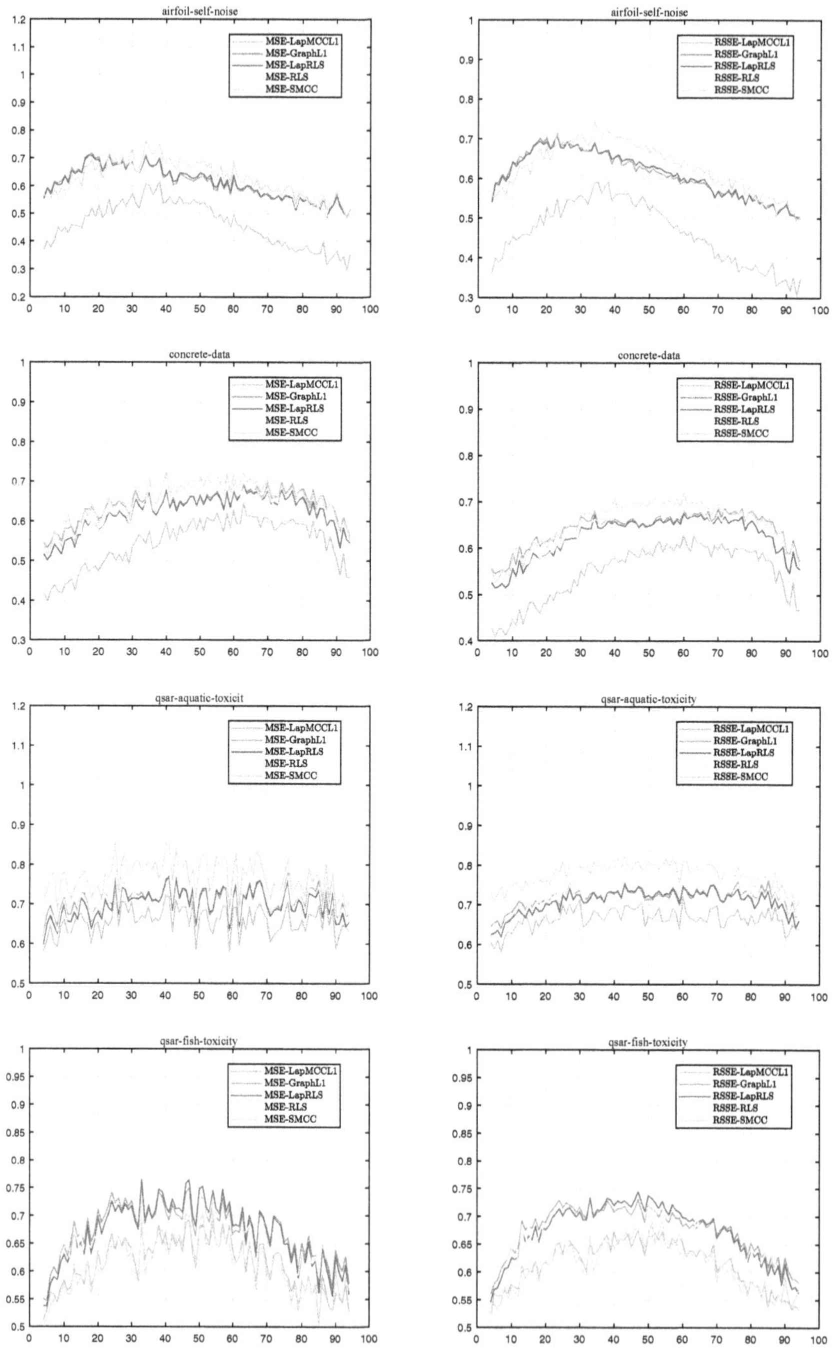

Fig. 3. Average MSE and RSSE of five algorithm on real-world datasets with different proportions.

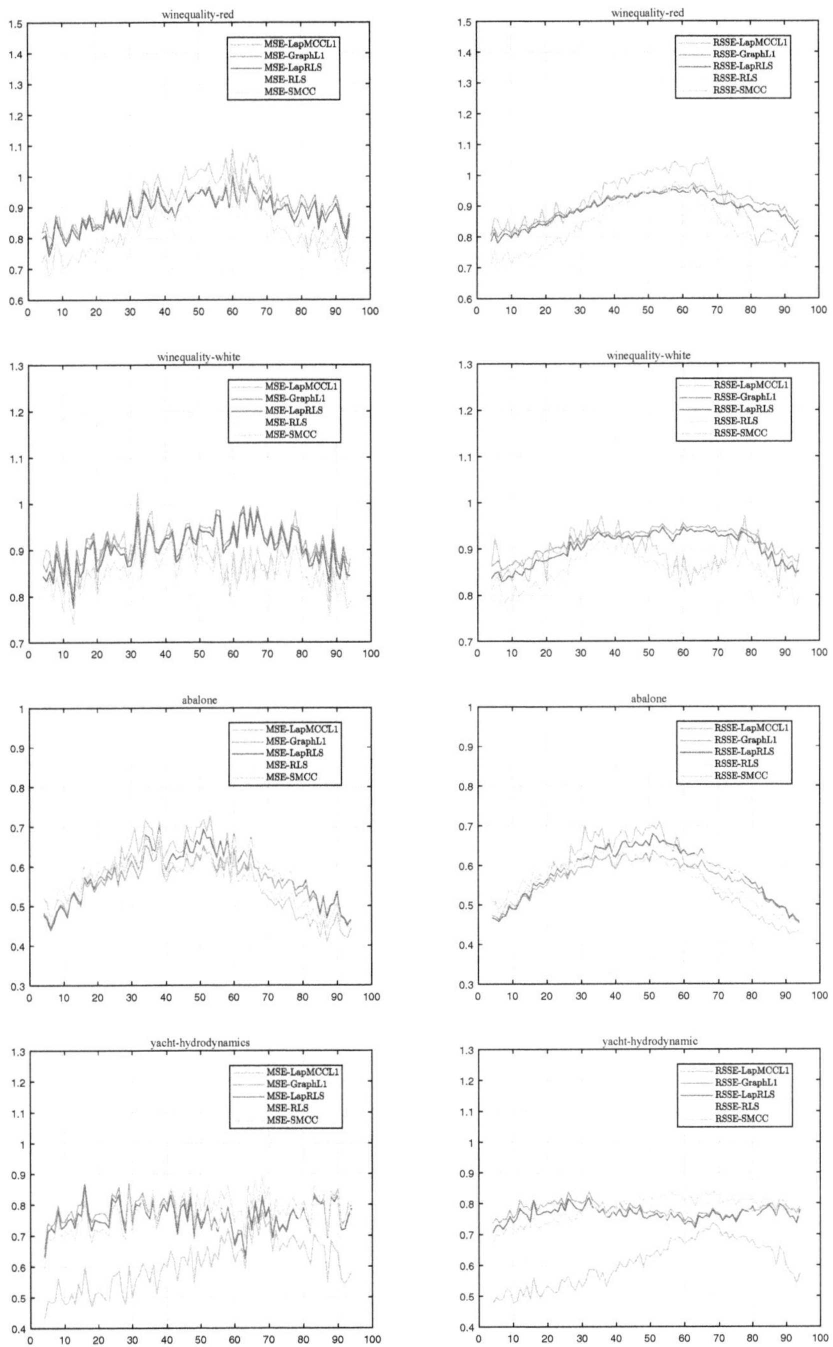

Fig. 4. Average MSE and RSSE of five algorithm on real-world datasets with different proportions.

4.2 Privacy Preservation

Privacy considerations have attracted more attention in machine learning research [12,15]. When the data is trained in the centralized way, it increases the risk of privacy leakage of sensitive information. To deal with this drawback, we propose a privacy preserving algorithm under the distributed way. The experiments have been conducted to investigate the privacy preserving performance of our algorithm on both the synthetic datasets and the real-world datasets. Specifically, the training data is randomly divided into two subsets, which can protect the sensitive information through learning the examples separately. The synthetic datasets are generated by four regression functions with the Exponential distributed noise. The sample ratio of the two subsets is changed, which may has impacts on the regression errors of the method. To evaluate this effect, we vary the sample ratio from 0.05 to 0.95 and observe regression error as well as the stability of the algorithm. The experimental results are given by Fig. 2, 3 and 4. The figures show that compared with GraphL1, LapRLS, RLS and SMCC, our algorithm LapMCCL1 is the most stable method. Meanwhile, it has the smallest regression error as the sample ratio changes.

Meanwhile, we utilize the differential privacy technique to investigate the privacy preservation performance of our method. It is well known that the differential privacy is a widely used privacy protection technology, which belongs to a method of data distortion [5]. This method protects privacy by adding random noise to the data. Generally, the random noise drawn from Laplace distribution is added to the data to protect privacy [4]. So we evaluate the prediction performance under the Laplace noise, and the results are given by Table 2. It demonstrates that under the differential privacy preservation technique, our approach has the best prediction performance compared with other methods. In addition, it also shows that the differential privacy protection technology has little impact on the performance of our algorithm.

5 Conclusion

This paper introduces a privacy preserving semi supervised method for non-Gaussian noise environments. The proposed LapMCCL1 algorithm offers two principal advantages. First, by leveraging the correntropy-induced loss, it effectively handles non-Gaussian noise in the data. Second, it enhances privacy by adopting a distributed learning scheme: the dataset is partitioned into random subsets, and the final predictor is aggregated from models trained locally on these subsets, thereby preventing the exposure of raw data. Extensive experiments on synthetic and real-world datasets confirm that our method surpasses existing alternatives in predictive accuracy under non-Gaussian noise while ensuring robust privacy preservation.

References

1. Agrawal, R., Srikant, R.: Privacy-preserving data mining. Sigmod Rec. **29**(2), 439–450 (2000)
2. Belkin, M., Niyogi, P., Sindhwani, V.: Manifold regularization: a geometric framework for learning from labeled and unlabeled examples. J. Mach. Learn. Res. **7**(1), 2399–2434 (2006)
3. Cucker, F., Zhou, D.X.: Learning Theory: An Approximation Theory Viewpoint (Cambridge Monographs on Applied and Computational Mathematics). Cambridge University Press, USA (2007)
4. Du, M., Wang, K., Xia, Z., Zhang, Y.: Differential privacy preserving of training model in wireless big data with edge computing. IEEE Trans. Big Data **6**(2), 283–295 (2020)
5. Dwork, C.: Differential privacy. In: ICALP (2006)
6. Feng, Y., Huang, X., Shi, L., Yang, Y., Suykens, J.A.: Learning with the maximum correntropy criterion induced losses for regression. J. Mach. Learn. Res. **16**(30), 993–1034 (2015)
7. Gao, Y., Liu, L., Zheng, X., Zhang, C., Ma, H.: Federated sensing: edge-cloud elastic collaborative learning for intelligent sensing. IEEE Internet Things J. **8**(14), 11100–11111 (2021)
8. Georgios, K., Stamatis, K., Sotiris, K., Omiros, R.: Semi-supervised regression: a recent review. J. Intell. Fuzzy Syst. **35**(2), 1483–1500 (2018)
9. He, H., Han, D., Dezert, J.: Disagreement based semi-supervised learning approaches with belief functions. Knowl.-Based Syst. **193** (2020)
10. Huang, W., Shi, Y., Xiong, Z., Wang, Q., Zhu, X.X.: Semi-supervised bidirectional alignment for remote sensing cross-domain scene classification. ISPRS J. Photogramm. Remote. Sens. **195**, 192–203 (2023)
11. Jia, Q., Guo, L., Fang, Y., Wang, G.: Efficient privacy-preserving machine learning in hierarchical distributed system. IEEE Trans. Netw. Sci. Eng. **6**(4), 599–612 (2019)
12. Ku, H., Susilo, W., Zhang, Y., Liu, W., Zhang, M.: Privacy-preserving federated learning in medical diagnosis with homomorphic re-encryption. Comput. Stand. Interfaces **80**, 103583 (2022)
13. Liu, B., Ding, M., Shaham, S., Rahayu, W., Farokhi, F., Lin, Z.: When machine learning meets privacy: a survey and outlook. ACM Comput. Surv. **54**(2) (2021)
14. Liu, W., Pokharel, P.P., Principe, J.C.: Correntropy: properties and applications in non-gaussian signal processing. IEEE Trans. Signal Process. **55**(11), 5286–5298 (2007)
15. Ma, X., Zhou, Y., Wang, L., Miao, M.: Privacy-preserving byzantine-robust federated learning. Comput. Stand. Interfaces **80**, 103561 (2022)
16. Ren, J., Yu, G., Ding, G.: Accelerating DNN training in wireless federated edge learning systems. IEEE J. Sel. Areas Commun. **39**(1), 219–232 (2021)
17. Sang, W., Yuan, S.: Porosity prediction using semi-supervised learning with biased well log data for improving estimation accuracy and reducing prediction uncertainty. Geophys. J. Int. **232**, 940–957 (2022)
18. Sawant, S.S., Prabukumar, M.: A review on graph-based semi-supervised learning methods for hyperspectral image classification. Egypt. J. Remote Sens. Space Sci. **23**(2), 243–248 (2020)
19. Tang, K., Su, Z., Liu, Y., Jiang, W., Zhang, J., Sun, X.: Subspace segmentation with a large number of subspaces using infinity norm minimization. Pattern Recogn. **89**, 45–54 (2018)

20. Van Engelen, J.E., Hoos, H.H.: A survey on semi-supervised learning. Mach. Learn. **109**(2), 373–440 (2020)
21. Virupaksha, S., Dondeti, V.: Subspace based noise addition for privacy preserved data mining on high dimensional continuous data. J. Ambient Intell. Humaniz. Comput. (2020)
22. Wang, Y., Han, J., Shen, Y., Xue, H.: Pointwise manifold regularization for semi-supervised learning. Front. Comput. Sci. **15**(1) (2021)
23. Yang, J., Liu, J., Han, R., Wu, J.: Transferable face image privacy protection based on federated learning and ensemble models. Complex Intell. Syst. **7**(5), 2299–2315 (2021). https://doi.org/10.1007/s40747-021-00399-6
24. Zhang, L., Zhu, T., Zhang, H., Xiong, P., Zhou, W.: FedRecovery: differentially private machine unlearning for federated learning frameworks. Trans. Info. For. Sec. **18**, 4732–4746 (2023)
25. Zhang, T., Huang, X., Wang, S.: Minimum kernel risk sensitive mean p-power loss algorithms and their performance analysis. Digit. Signal Process. **104**, 102797 (2020)
26. Zuo, L., Li, L., Chen, C.: The graph based semi-supervised algorithm with ℓ^1-regularizer. Neurocomputing **149**, 966–974 (2015)
27. Zuo, L., Xu, Y., Cheng, C., Choo, K.K.R.: A privacy-preserving semisupervised algorithm under maximum correntropy criterion. IEEE Trans. Neural Netw. Learn. Syst. **33**(11), 6817–6830 (2021)
28. Zuo, X., Wang, M., Zhu, T., Zhang, L., Yu, S., Zhou, W.: Federated learning with blockchain-enhanced machine unlearning: a trustworthy approach. IEEE Trans. Serv. Comput. **18**(03), 1428–1444 (2025)

Author Index

GPSR Compliance
The European Union's (EU) General Product Safety Regulation (GPSR) is a set
of rules that requires consumer products to be safe and our obligations to
ensure this.

If you have any concerns about our products, you can contact us on

ProductSafety@springernature.com

In case Publisher is established outside the EU, the EU authorized
representative is:

Springer Nature Customer Service Center GmbH
Europaplatz 3
69115 Heidelberg, Germany